Clinical Studies
of Personality

Volume I

Clinical Studies
of Personality

Volume I

Personality Disorders in Adults

Edited by
Arthur Burton & Robert E. Harris

*Preface to the Torchbook edition by
Arthur Burton*

HARPER TORCHBOOKS ❦ *The University Library*
Harper & Row, Publishers, New York

CLINICAL STUDIES OF PERSONALITY: Volume I

CONTENTS

Volume I

Preface to the Torchbook Edition

More than ten years have passed since *Clinical Studies of Personality*, Volume II of a series, was first published; it followed its earlier prototype, *Case Histories in Clinical and Abnormal Psychology*, by eight years. This work thus spans two decades of intensive and productive growth in clinical psychology which could hardly have been predicted when, in 1946, Volume I was merely a gleam in our congregate eye. At that time I felt rather strongly that the life history method was being slighted for more quantitative/mechanistic procedures and that training in clinical psychology suffered for it. We had not yet attained what the law schools had found in the case method, and what economics and cognate social sciences were soon to discover. That these were not idle or fanciful ratiocinations can be seen by the more or less continuous publication of case books in clinical psychology since these were first published.

The intervening twenty years have not by any means seen a diminution in the need for the student to correlate his raw behavioral or observational data with some anchoring theory of the personality. Of analysis and analytics he has had much; but in learning how to synthesize the standard deviation or a low FM score with the symptom, the fixation, and the symbol, he is on less safe ground. The putting-of-things-together in the study of the personality has always been the great mysterium—and possibly the distinguishing clinical skill of the practitioner. I cannot think of any way by which it can still be taught efficiently—by self or other—without the observed life and its noted considerations.

The case history importunes one to be synthesizing, unifying, and global in place of partial, categorical, and factorial, and it remains to this day the supreme method for describing the actualized or non-actualized life. Today, more than ever, we question the normative and not so normative "rubrics," and psychological tests have, to my way of thinking, fallen far short of their promise as the royal road to the personality. There is today, *mirabile dictu,* even some question whether or not there is such a phenomenon as mental illness and, at any rate, we have become a profession of healers of something, rather than diagnosticians, and seem more content in our role because of it. We are less certain in today's world just who is abnormal, for we often have difficulty defining the pathology, and the identified patient more than frequently turns out to be merely a surrogate for someone else. It would seem that every hallmark upon which our identity and function as clinical psychologists was then based is now passing into one limbo or other.

The genotypical is again yielding to phenotypical—the molecular to the molar—the life *in situ* to the life *in vivo,* if the phenomenologists are correct. Whatever modern-day critics may say of the contemporary novel, the novelist flourishes, as did Dostoevski, Stendahl, Proust, and Joyce, because the novelist describes his hero and the hero's vicissitudes in a minute, depthful, insightful, and universal way which immediately leads the reader to closure. The existential essence is not drained by the need to find general laws. The best of these are, to my way of thinking, better than the best of the case histories. Thus we must learn to become better novelists if we are to become better clinicians and this means a proper appreciation of the psychological and philo- sophical forces which constitute existence. It is necessary to see the client in his world design, his style of life, or his mode-of-being-in-the- world, before his symptoms or personality can be ordered scientifically to some practical rehabilitative end. This requires, of course, the exquisite but highly nebulous blending of both art and science by which the supreme practitioner is identified. In the absence of a com- prehensive personality theory, or detailed instruction for its analysis and reconstruction, the case history, while often missing the mark in its more pedestrian aspects, does attain such representation of a life in that more than rare occasion when a master clinical psychologist is at work.

Clinical Studies of Personality, in many of its aspects, remains yet the ideal for which the clinical psychologist strives. In the section entitled *Studies of Normal Persons* we see that mastery applied to special groups of non-diseased personalities in a most transporting way. These studies are the prototypes of the newer investigations into the personality in which clinical methodology is at the service of under- standing rather than cure. The goal of improving the general constructs of personality, and the deepening of our insights into the core of that personality, is what makes these studies profound. In this they have been successful, as the years have evidenced.

But this is not to slight pathology. The many and varied descriptions of symptom-full people, the multifold conceptual and technical methods for delineating their phenomenology and, in a few instances, the outline of treatment approach, apply today as they did yesterday. These cases given on a blind basis to another and equally gifted set of clinicians would return similar findings. They thus warrant reading and study today.

As long as personality and its manipulation remains an intimate, individual rather than group affair, the study of a life, or an important fraction of it, will remain one necessary vehicle for its scientific rendering; in this I am pleased to have participated in a small way.

April 1, 1966

ARTHUR BURTON

Preface

In the first volume of this series, some forty case studies represented what we thought were the best efforts of clinical psychologists to come to an understanding of the persons, usually patients, with whom they work professionally. Some effort was made to cover the range of personality and behavior disturbances: the psychoses, neuroses, psychosomatic disorders, mental deficiencies, disorders associated with organic brain damage, and other problems. To some extent, the aims of the present volume are similar, but for a number of reasons we have attempted to sample diagnostic categories less widely.

Most importantly, we feel that in the intervening years clinical psychodiagnostic methods have become widely known and their merits and limitations for the study of various diagnostic categories pretty well outlined. At this point it seems that the kinds of inferences which can reasonably be extracted from projective test protocols, personality inventories, and tests of intellectual functioning can be more fruitfully studied by methods other than reports of individual cases. Systematic research in this area is reported in the journals and in the *Annual Reviews of Psychology*. Therefore we have selected cases, not because they were representative or typical of any presumably homogeneous group of patients, but because of their intrinsic interest.

Another reason: The interests of many clinical psychologists have turned away from psychodiagnostic methods, at least where their findings are used simply to supplement a clinical psychiatric study and are filed in the patient's folder along with his blood counts, EEG, the social worker's account of her interviews with the relatives, and the institution's official diagnostic label. Many psychologists have turned to therapy, either as a routine activity or as an appropriate research topic. And in therapy the past has receded. Under the influence of Rogerian, Sullivanian, and other post-Freudian points of view, genetic reconstructions and overall conceptualizations of a life history are less often attempted. What is happening in the "here-now," between patient and therapist and between the patient and other important figures in his everyday living, is the focus of interest. A militantly modern therapist is likely to attach little significance to the fact that a patient had a twin who died in childhood, if, indeed, he is aware of the incident at all. Diagnostic tests can be utilized to illuminate a patient's behavior in the present, his defenses, motives, and social techniques, but this is a more difficult task and seems to come less naturally than an effort to integrate Rorschach findings with a Kraepelinian diagnosis or TAT themas with actually occurring events and real persons in the patient's past.

A consequence of this trend is that the psychoses are receiving scant attention from clinical psychologists, and only a few case studies of schizophrenics and none of depressives are included in the present volume. In their place the reader will find studies of neurotic and psychosomatic patients who are thought to be more accessible with psychotherapeutic techniques. Unfortunately, space does not permit detailed accounts of treatment procedures, but the reader may note a more "therapeutic" attitude toward patients than was evident in the first volume.

A new section has been added: studies of persons who came to the attention of clinical psychologists not because they had problems but because they had been selected as members of special groups for intensive psychological investigation—normal children, research scientists, college students, displaced persons, etc. The processes underlying normality and superior functioning are elusive, just as in embryology the conditions for producing an anatomical monster become understandable while the processes which guide normal development remain obscure. It is hoped that studies of the kind reported here will lead to an understanding of the synthesizing functions of the personality, that is, those characteristics of an organism which permit survival and productive achievement in spite of what we call—in the histories of persons with less fortunate outcomes—pathogenic events.

A word about the authors of these reports: Most of them appear here because they have made distinguished contributions to the psychological literature. They are identified with a clinical method or have done systematic research in clinical psychology. A few are not well known and have come to the attention of the editors or other people from whom we made inquiries because of the high quality of their clinical skills. We wish there were more of them. Case studies provide an opportunity for professionally trained people to exhibit their clinical skills, and represent the present stage of development of clinical psychology, perhaps even better than many reports of research on selected aspects of large numbers of cases. Without the constraints of conventional methods and the ubiquitous null hypothesis, case studies permit a boldness of conception which often leads to the invention of useful hypotheses, later integrated into the existing body of psychological theory. Unfortunately, the publishing climate is not favorable to this inductive stage of scientific endeavor, nor is the impulse to publish highly correlated with the ability quietly to reflect on one's experiences with patients. It is from this latter kind of activity that many of our useful concepts in personality theory have come. If the editors may be allowed a bit of exhortation: let every clinical psychologist spend a month of every year working up a single case!

And a last editorial note: As in the previous volume, names, dates, places, and other information which might identify the persons described have been modified. It is possible that someone may find himself described in this book. If he does, he will learn little that is new to him, and we are confident that he will not be recognized by others.

July, 1955

ARTHUR BURTON
ROBERT E. HARRIS

CHAPTER ONE

Introduction

BY HENRY A. MURRAY

The Introduction to the first volume of *Case Histories in Clinical and Abnormal Psychology* consisted largely of an inquiry into the roots of man's developed interest in his self and in other selves as objects of contemplation, his increased devotion to the office of representing the careers of personalities in words, vivid or abstract. Though that inquiry was little more than a hurried hop, skip, and jump down the centuries from the rare autobiographers, King Sargon and St. Augustine, and the rare biographers, Xenophon and Plutarch, to the present plenty of composers of lives and case reports, it was long enough, I would surmise, to try the patience of many readers, not to speak of the book's forbearing editors, Burton and Harris. In any event, no repetition, summary, or extension of that initial survey would be fitting at this point.[1] History is prelude. Let us look at what is being done today.

A comparison of this second collection of case studies with those comprising Volume I indicates that in the intervening seven years the roles, orientations, or opportunities of clinical psychologists have been, to a heartening degree, expanded. In 1947 most of the members of our profession seemed to have chosen or been assigned positions peripheral to the vital center of psychic happenings. They were on the outside looking in—and, for the most part, looking in no farther than is possible with the responses to a little battery of tests. The crucial data, the validating facts and diagnoses, had to be obtained from the psychiatrist in charge, whether that gentleman was concerned or not con-

[1] See Chapter Two, this volume.

1

cerned, seriously and competently, with the advance of knowledge. Consequently, with some exceptions the chapters of Volume I were not so much case histories, not so much accounts of retarded or deviant developments, of the genesis and intrusion of disturbing complexes, as they were reports of the diagnostic efficacy of this or that conventional test or method. As such they were, and still are, most valuable, indeed invaluable, to clinical psychologists in the making. They proved, among other things, that testing—psychodynamic as well as psychometric—had come of age and been accepted as an integral and indispensable part of every first-rate psychiatric hospital, clinic, or guidance center. More specifically, Volume I demonstrated in some detail how much such familiar instruments as the Wechsler-Bellevue, the Rorschach, and the Minnesota Multiphasic could contribute to the task of discriminating nicely between this and that type of abnormality.

In the present volume one finds these selfsame virtues and, in addition, others. Like its predecessor, it provides numerous and varied illustrations of the utility of our better standardized procedures and thus comes forth as an instructive adjunct to today's array of technical manuals. But, in larger measure than before, it also offers vistas of new domains to be explored with a multiplicity of tests, some of which were not published, not designed, or not even adumbrated in 1947. Equally notable, it seems to me, are certain other papers in which the psychological effects, common and rare, of a specified brain lesion are systematically detailed.

More striking perhaps are the case histories written by psychologists who have succeeded in arriving at the vital core, or very close to the vital core, of personality. One sign of this advance is that pertinent psychoanalytic theory is handled by these authors with more expertness than it was in 1947. The reader hungering for basic stuff is no longer disregarded. He is periodically appeased with first-hand histories attentive to depth dynamics, such as those composed by Doctors Karen and Solomon Machover and by several others. Not enough of these, of course, because enough would be unsuitable to the broad framework of this book. The editors' intention was to exhibit, by means of representative specimens, several kinds of psychopathology—as well as a few relatively normal types. Long detailed reports were therefore not admissible. The next best substitute are short, concisely formulated histories highlighting certain extraordinary dispositions or developments.

The scarcity of these testifies to the generally acknowledged fact that a comprehensive scheme for the analysis and theoretical reconstruction of personalities has yet to be created. But the reader will find here several approximations to this ideal, such as Dr. Waldfogel's interesting report, in which effective principles of therapy are related to restorations of progressive functioning in the patient.

There are here, to be sure, rewards of other sorts. But these have been left perforce unheralded. Say what I might, each reader will pick and garner according to his own wants and tastes. By chance, love, or logic the chapter which at this point of time contributed to my mill the most needed kind of grain is peculiarly entitled: "Hemerography of Mary Ennis."

CHAPTER TWO

Introduction to Volume I[1]

BY HENRY A. MURRAY

This book is an emergent, the first of its kind; but it is not so much an emergent as a foreseen event, resultant of the inevitable combination of converging forces. It comes, in fact, as a belated response to a long-standing need, or, since the desire for an instrumental book of this sort is not old in consciousness, we had better call it the first response to a belatedly acknowledged need.

Since the authors of the better textbooks in abnormal psychology and psychiatry have in recent years been allotting more and more space to illustrative case histories, and since the histories that lie before you differ, by intent, from these only in respect to one significant dimension, that of length, there is sufficient reason to regard this volume as the necessary next step in the extension of an already accepted trend in the field of psychopathology, and as such to welcome it.

Forerunners in the field could be mentioned: several books that are constituted almost wholly, as this book is, of case reports, but confined, as this book is not, to a special topic. Krafft-Ebing's collection of studies in sex pathology would be one example familiar to most psychiatrists and psychologists and, indeed, to many a layman, curious about this walled-off, sphinx-guarded district of hectic tensions. But Krafft-Ebing's notorious work was designedly limited in scope and today

[1] NOTE: This chapter appeared as the introductory chapter to Volume I, *Case Histories in Clinical and Abnormal Psychology*. Because we believe that Dr. Murray's essay on the development of the case method is a milestone in the history of clinical psychology, it is reprinted here with minor omissions.

stands behind us, a memorable mark on the hotly contested path of unseemly and unflattering truth.

Turning now to other, neighboring regions of professional concern, we find an inviting array of books of this class. In criminology, for instance, the publication of abstracted life histories has been lively and, most of us would judge, definitely contributive to the progress of this specialty. An American is apt to think first of *The Individual Delinquent* (1915) by Healy and of the later *Judge Baker Foundation Case Studies* (1923) by Healy and Bronner, and then of the succession of works which came thick and fast upon the heels of these pioneering studies, such books as Burt's *The Young Delinquent* (1925), *500 Criminal Careers* (1930) by S. S. and E. T. Glueck, and *Roots of Crime* (1935) by Healy and Alexander.

A parallel development has occurred in sociology since, say, 1920, when Thomas and Znaniecki, persuasive in practice as in exhortation, confronted their scholarly colleagues—many of whom were given to traveling by way of the stratosphere of abstractions—with five volumes of *The Polish Peasant*. After this huge stimulus the conviction that records of individual lives merited the scrutiny of trained scientists advanced, through cross fires of criticism, at such a pace that by 1935 Dollard's precise sense of timeliness informed him that the moment for strategic planning had arrived. His *Criteria for the Life History* proved a powerful incentive to other sociologists and, happily, to himself: Dollard followed the admirable policy of demonstrating his own principles by applying them, with Davis, in *Children of Bondage* (1940).

Still more striking as exhibits of the person-conscious ideology of our time are the single-case books which have been hospitably received of late by social scientists. Americans might be tempted to date this particular trend from the published story of Prince's Mrs. Beauchamp (1906), whose experiences became better known to psychiatrists the world over, thirty years ago, than were the experiences of most of their own patients. The question of whether this document should be celebrated as the most influential of the first generation of intensive psychiatric case studies is of no great moment. It deserves a prominent place, certainly, in the succession of books—books as dissimilar as *Edgar Poe* by Bonaparte and *Black Legend* by Wertham—which has led to the shared opinion that several years spent in dissecting the in-

tricate plexus of motivational forces at the core of a single personality
can be scientifically rewarding. The record of such an investigation
may prompt advances on the theoretical level even when the scientist
confines his function to that of a recording instrument or to that of a
commentator, the subject being permitted to recount his experiences
in his own words. At this point three books come to mind: Radin's
Crashing Thunder (1926), Shaw's *The Jack-Roller* (1930), and
Dyk's *Son of Old Man Hat* (1938).

Let these few scattered titles suffice, because this is not the place,
you will acknowledge, for a comprehensive review of the expanding
literature of case studies in the social sciences. Much of the ground
has been surveyed recently in two highly recommendable publications:
The Use of Personal Documents in Psychological Science (1942) by
G. W. Allport and *The Use of Personal Documents in History, Anthropology and Sociology* (1945) by Gottschalk, Kluckhohn, and Angell,
both under grants from the Social Science Research Council. An examination of their contents should convince most readers that nowadays a respectable number of scientists would unreluctantly agree with
Redfield's mature judgment that: "To understand man in society it is
apparent that we must come to know the mental states of particular
men in particular societies."

Considered in conjunction with these developments in other
branches of social science, this book falls into line simply as one more
manifestation of a progressing trend. Its advent, therefore, could properly be taken as an occasion to raise the provocative question: What
are the determinants of this trend, this mounting appreciation of the
scientific value of case histories, of detailed chronological accounts of
selected episodes in the lives of individuals?

In essaying a comprehensive answer to this question a man might be
inclined, if his energies were coming in like a full-moon tide and space
were unrestricted, to look beyond the boundaries of social science and,
setting no limits to the prospect, glance down the courses of history
with an eye to evidences of a similar concern, of a refined, if not professional, preoccupation with the proceedings of single personalities.

Were a psychologist seriously to commit himself to this ambitious
undertaking, he could scarcely do better at the outset than to settle on
biographies and autobiographies as the most direct and unequivocal
manifestations of the preoccupation in question, and then, passing the

world's literature under review, estimate roughly the relative number of these person-centered books in each era, from Xenophon and Plutarch to Strachey and Sandburg, from King Sargon and St. Augustine to Havelock Ellis and H. G. Wells. It would require months of methodical application on the part of a large staff of experts to obtain figures of decisive accuracy; but we can safely predict, I trust, on the basis of general information, that the graph would show a rise in the rate of production of biographies and autobiographies over the course of the last three centuries, with a notable degree of acceleration during the last three decades.

If our hypothetical psychologist, playing in his own amateurish way the part of a historian, were then to reach out and, in his sweep down the centuries, include realistic novels (especially those which, like *Wilhelm Meister, Le Rouge et le Noir, Pierre,* and *Look Homeward, Angel,* portray, with some autobiographical fidelity, stages in the development of the hero's character), and if, after this, he were to extend the scope of his researches still further so as to embrace other, lowly as well as lofty forms of literature—calculating, say, the proportion of space devoted to detailed accounts of living persons in typical newspapers and magazines from 1800 down to the present era of boundless voyeur-exhibitionism—if the psychologist, with an army of assistants, were to do all this, he would probably assemble an impressive array of facts which would corroborate the afore-stated tentative conclusion: namely, that in the Occident the publication rate of literature indicative of a concentrated and expert regard for the dispositions and actions of unique individuals (the self and other selves) has been increasing for two hundred years or more, and with marked rapidity since World War I.

Compared to this huge wave of personalistic enthusiasm in the world at large, the interest in case histories within the domain of social science looks like a little ripple, late in its appearance. In all likelihood, the huge wave and the little ripple are dynamically related.[2]

---

[2] A future historian of social science may be surprised to find that, in writing case histories such as are published here, the psychologists of our time show no signs of having been influenced in any way by the twenty-five centuries of literature which have preceded them. The lines of derivation are quite different. Perhaps there is no enlightenment for a clinician in Aristotle, Lucian, Plutarch, Montaigne, Shakespeare, Bayle, Stendhal, Balzac, Dostoevski, Tolstoy, Nietzsche, Proust, and others of their stature; but my suspicion persists that the science of man would be carried forward more surely if those of us who undertook to unravel, interpret, and

More support for the huge-wave theory could surely be obtained through a careful analysis of representative samples of person-centered books from successive eras. It is probable, for example, that such a study would specifically confirm certain widely accepted conclusions which are in agreement with our hypothesis: the conclusion that the concept of personality (individuality), in our sense, was not born until the Renaissance; the conclusion that biography, defined as "the faithful portrait of a soul in its adventures through life," did not unmistakably appear until the seventeenth century, and so forth. But even if these particular judgments were not sustained, the investigation, we can safely predict, would reveal a number of tendencies pertinent to the present inquiry. Although the history of literature exhibits no uniform and steady current in any single direction, but rather a multiplicity of tastes, some advancing, some receding, long-term trends are not unknown. Rousseau started something which is still alive. The Romantic movement made a difference. Anyhow, I would suspect that if sporadic exceptions—works prophetic of a distant future, such as Montaigne's *Essays*—were disregarded, a historical study of person-centered books would show that they had become increasingly personalistic, more concentratedly devoted to precise realistic portrayals of the most distinguishing and telling intimate particularities of an individual's behavior. Certainly many of the most typical biographies, novels, and short stories of the last thirty years are marked—if general impressions are at all dependable—by a relative increase in the number of observations which serve to set forth the subject as a unique person, distinct from others: less vagueness, more sharply perceived detail, fewer references to abstract traits, more precise descriptions of concrete acts, attention to idiosyncratic qualities; less concern with public or official conduct, more emphasis upon home life, interpersonal relations, love affairs, private matters; more space devoted to subjective processes at the center of personality—feelings, sentiments, beliefs, aims, and expectations—and to situations and undertakings in which these processes are strongly involved; a larger part of the life history devoted to the conditions and events of childhood, depicted with some realization of their effect upon the developing structure of

---

formulate the life histories of normal or abnormal personalities were familiar with the works of the great masters who, assuming that the understanding and portrayal of human motives belonged to their special province, directed their acute intelligences to this office.

personality; more adroit attempts to penetrate the surface of behavior, greater depth and insight in analyzing the subject's motives; closer adherence to the facts of life, more accurate observations, especially of highly revealing, though seemingly trivial, episodes; greater impartiality and objectivity, less praise or condemnation, and less reluctance to admit the defects of heroes and the virtues of villains.

In these trends we may discern evidences of the differentiation of the art of literary portrayal as well as evidences of the adoption of the scientific attitude. But besides these, I submit, one must take account of something quite different, namely, the intensification and spread of individuation and self-centeredness. Self-centeredness, I would say, is rudimentary; person-centeredness is its projection. Thus biography is not infrequently the externalization of a suppressed, latent, or impotent need to write some form of autobiography.

Conclusions of great interest to psychologists and sociologists might come out of a penetrating study of the history of self-centeredness, its forms and determinants, with some attention to two related phenomena: an intense (sometimes desolate) awareness of the incommunicable uniqueness (or emotional isolation) of the self, and a heightened evaluation of the self (often combined with feelings of inferiority). In seeking for determinants of the introverted stream of self-centeredness one would have to consider the effects of monastic seclusion, of prolonged preoccupation with subjective life, with questions of guilt, damnation, and redemption, and the effects of the Protestant's estrangement from the fellowship and infallible authority of the Catholic Church, his conception of the individual soul engaged in an islanded interpersonal relationship with God, and, then, the effects of atheism. The extroverted stream of self-centeredness would be easier to follow in its manifold expressions and assertions from the Renaissance down to the age of rugged individualism and self-reliance to the meeting place of introversion and extroversion, the doctrine of transcendentalism, by which every person becomes his own prophet, a superman in embryo. These developments from superordinate homogeneity to heterogeneity would then have to be correlated with changes in the social structure, with different systems of sovereignty, with the gradual waning of ecclesiastical totalitarianism and the rise of democracy. Reversals of the trend in countries recently given over to political totalitarianism would call for careful analysis, the hypothesis being that in ideologically homogeneous societies the necessary object of interest is not the self or the other self, but God, or the Leader, or the State.

Since self-centeredness cannot long flourish in a vacuum, we would expect to find the parallel extension of a complementary tendency; and this is just what we do find in the growth of the Hebraic-Christian tradition, in Christ's affirmation of the worth of the meekest person, in the democratic concept of the dignity and equality of man, in the last hundred years' tide of humanitarianism. There is pity in the world for self-pity, for the apostles of affliction. The influence of humanitarianism in the applied social sciences is very clear: the objects of scientific study are not commonly the strong, the powerful, and the rich, but the sick, the weak, the poor, the underprivileged. Once upon a time authors were almost solely interested in mythological figures, in gods and demigods; and after that in kings and princes and resplendent heroes; but nowadays they are very likely to spend themselves on miserable failures and castaways, criminals, and lunatics. This brings us to one more determinant of person-focused research coming from outside the domain of the social sciences.

For thirty years or more the human situation has excited the profound concern of socially oriented thinkers, and since the summer of 1945 their apprehensions have been shared by the majority. It all comes down to a widespread distrust in the determination and ability of man to organize a world which can prevent the catastrophe that is looming just ahead of us—the mutual destruction of nations. This distrust is based on a realistic appraisal of man's hereditary constitution, his ungovernable drives, his innate depravity. Is reformation possible? In their perplexity, some of our leaders have turned hopefully to the social sciences as offering a possible path to salvation, and have turned to the young generations and at commencements each spring repeated the old dictum: The proper study of mankind is man. The urgency of the appeal increases as the gravity of man's strait becomes more obvious, as evidences accumulate of his incurable discontent, his insatiable ambition, his ferocity and greed. Now those who enter the social sciences in response to such considerations are in no mood to be drawn to the brass instruments. They go for the quick; and the chances are that in a few years they will be writing up histories of real people.

Once more we conclude that science does not pursue an entirely insulated and autonomous career, but is responsive to social forces.

Indeed there is some justification for the surmise that the recent surge of interest in the basic social sciences—dynamic psychology, psychoanalytic psychiatry, anthropology, and sociology—is, to no small extent, a product of a mounting intensification of concern with the plight of the individual in a disordered world.

Among the forces within the realm of science that have led to the systematic study of individual lives is the doctrine of positivism, which is neither more nor less than an affirmation of the basic scientific faith in facts—critical facts observed under controlled conditions. As this hereditary conviction gains ground, as the science of man becomes more truly scientific, more psychologists will devote more time, as have the authors of this book, to the careful analysis of critical events in the lives of the objects whose behavior it is their function to interpret and predict; that is, in Comte's language, they will pass from *l'état métaphysique ou abstrait* to *l'état scientifique ou positif*. This does not mean, of course, that the goal of our science is a huge aggregate of data; the goal is a theoretical system that has been verified by accurate observations of significant proceedings in the course of personality development. Up to now a great many psychologists have been positivistic on the physiological level or on the biological level, but metaphysical on the psychological level in so far as they have acted and speculated on the assumption that measurements of insignificant events occurring in an artificial laboratory situation or measurements of the behavior of lower organisms could provide sufficient validation for comprehensive theories of human behavior.

According to operationism, a derivative of positivism, a man's understanding of a concept goes no further than his ability to define it by the recital of precise observations made in a specified manner under specified conditions. And so, one might affirm, extending this principle a little further, that the most usable definition of a nosological entity, such as involutional melancholia, is an apperceptive cluster of clear images (differentiated and integrated) portraying scores of closely studied patients suffering from this ailment. As an aid in constructing apperceptive clusters of this sort, in adding vital substance to the skeleton of each entity as described in the textbooks, this collection of case studies should prove invaluable.

Two important determinants of the trend with which we are now concerned—the trend toward a person-focused strategy of research—

have arisen within the domain of psychology itself. One of these is the great principle of organismic and gestalt psychology, stressed for our benefit by Lewin, which states that action is a product of the structure of the whole field, or total situation, at the moment. The psychologist must learn a lot—everything that is operating in the subject and in the environment—to understand a little. This excellent theory calls for actions which no field theorist, as far as I know, has ever taken, namely, exhaustive studies of each subject shortly before, during, and after the event which requires formulation. It calls, in fact, for a good deal more than this, since some of the variables influencing the course of action are apparent neither to the psychologist nor to the subject. They are unconscious mental processes which can be discovered only by indirect methods, one of which is to obtain from the subject or from others, or from both, valid reports of relevant incidents in his past. This brings us to the second important determinant of the trend we have been considering. It is the conviction—derived from a long series of animal experiments initiated along one line by Pavlov and along another by Thorndike, and a compelling array of evidence brought forth by Freud and his followers—that every satisfying or dissatisfying experience from birth onwards has its fateful irreversible effect upon the development of the personality. Consequently, a painstaking survey of the past history of every subject must be undertaken, not only to discover the more consistent components of his character and the current directions of its growth, but to reveal the chief determinants of these components, many of which are still represented by active unconscious traces. Thus two great modern theories (field theory, learning theory) combine to persuade us that one very promising path of advance into the unknown is by means of extremely detailed studies of critical occurrences in the lives of individuals. Case studies such as these, therefore, are in accord with modern research strategy.

If now, instead of thinking of the multifarious manifestations of the personalistic trend throughout the social sciences, we concentrate on this book here, as one specific manifestation of the trend, a little reflection will persuade us that none of the determinants so far mentioned played much part in its production. The following forces have been far more compelling: (1) a national situation (press) consisting of an increased awareness of an increasing incidence of mental illness; (2) in response to this, the invasion of the field of mental illness by humanitarians (need to relieve suffering), by social reformers (need to correct societal defects), and by scientists (need for knowledge and understanding), and as a result of these forces, the construction of new and enlarged hospitals and clinics with facilities for research under the direction of psychiatrists; (3) technical developments within the field of psychology—the perfection of intelligence tests, word association tests, projective tests, etc., also the accomplishments of applied psychologists in World Wars I and II; (4) in recognition of their technical abilities, the creation of jobs in hospitals and clinics affording livelihood to clinical psychologists; (5) the acquisition by psychologists of certain medical principles and practices, especially the case method.

Thus, the prime influence in the shaping of this book has been the ancient and honorable discipline of medicine. First there was the impact of medical psychology, of Janet, Prince, Freud, Jung, Adler, and all the company of analysts, upon academic psychology, evidenced by the steady, though reluctant, admission into the curriculum of courses in abnormal psychology. And second, there has been the more direct and obvious influence of the psychiatric institutions to which clinical psychologists have been expected to adjust. Hippocrates the Great, we know, was master of the case history method; and ever since his day, though for two thousand years no physician surpassed him in the use of it, this method has been the medical man's preferred way of accumulating knowledge. The adoption of the traditional procedure by the psychologist is simply the result of bringing him within the sphere of the psychiatric branch of medicine.

Since this book is designed primarily for teaching purposes, one last determinant should be listed. As a teaching device which forces the student into an active role by making him apply the theories he has gained from lectures and books to the solution of a diversified series of concrete problems, the case system, as employed first in medicine and then in law, is being adopted more and more by other disciplines. Recently, in fact, Dorham, in his *Education for Responsible Living* (1945), has urged experiments with the case system in substantial parts of the curriculum in general education. Thus this book here conforms to a theory of education that is clearly gaining ground.

So much for the main tendencies which have resulted in the person-centered trend of which this book is one outgrowth. Weighing these forces—the artist's long endeavor to hold the mirror up to nature, the growing individuation and self-centeredness of man, the spread of humanitarianism, the tradition of medicine, the developments in psychoanalytic psychiatry, the evolution of theories and techniques within the discipline of psychology itself, the seriousness of man's present strait, the urgent need for knowledge and understanding—reflecting on these forces, the publication of the present series of case histories appears as so inevitable an outcome of their combined action that a new question leaps to mind, and with much more insistence than the one with which I have just dealt. It is this: What conditions have, for so long, been standing in the way of the writing and publication of a book of this sort?

How is it that up to now no psychologist has assembled a comparable collection of normal cases—short life histories with formulations of personality? One would suppose that psychologists would have commenced, as other scientists have commenced, with careful observations of the objects whose behavior they would eventually be expected to understand, predict, and control within limits. And one would suppose that today, after half a century of industry, the members of the profession would have for their enlightenment a five-foot shelf, if not, as lawyers have, a vast library, of case records. But no. For reasons which need not be examined here, academic psychology was not begun at the beginning. Born from an aristocratic marriage of philosophy and physics, the child was started on its eccentric career as an exclusive laboratory specialty, and it is only recently that its character has been attacked, invaded, and expanded by men with broader views of its possibilities and obligations. For years the specialist has sat in the seat of the generalist, a part has suppressed the whole, a highly trained tail has wagged an undernourished dog.

(As I see it, he who confines his attention to one functional segment of an organism—such as the process of perception—or to one temporal segment—such as a single experimental procedure—is more or less of a specialist, whereas he who attempts to formulate the whole life of a whole man is a generalist, a psychologist in the widest sense. Perhaps a clinical psychologist—one who studies the life histories of patients in a clinic or hospital—is today the nearest thing we have to a general practitioner of psychology, or psychologist proper.)

Whether or not the retardation of psychology is best explained, as I have suggested, by reference to the constitution it inherited from its parents and to the overshielded shut-in nursery in which it was reared, the truth is that until very recently the study of lives—the only possible way of obtaining the granite blocks of data on which to build a science of human nature—has generally been depreciated in academic circles as an undertaking to which no true scientist would commit himself; it has attracted very few psychologists and only rarely has it been granted a place in the prescribed curriculum. Happily we can point to G. W. Allport as one outstanding member of our profession who has ceaselessly and unashamedly emphasized the value of life histories (the *Locomotive God* for one) as data for psychology. But a few conspicuous exceptions do not nullify the general statement that students of psychology have not been educated to construct adequate case histories; they have been fully trained neither in the various skills necessary for requiring all the relevant information nor in the use of the principal concepts available today for ordering and interpreting the findings. This is the chief reason why we had to wait until 1947 for a book of case studies written by psychologists.

Other factors which have interfered with the building of a library of case histories, normal and abnormal, are not far to seek. Many of them are unchangeable. Consider, first of all, the conditions which make it difficult to obtain the data necessary for an understanding of any personality: (1) Every life, swift to the self as it may be, is long and complicated to the psychologist, and many hours are required for the exploration of a few portions of it. (2) Man's power to recall his past is, at best, deficient, and, at worst, radically subverted by the devious devices of his vanity. (3) Man is a reputation-guarding animal who bristles with defenses when the cool eye of scientific scrutiny is cast on a crucial area of his secret life. (4) The psychologist's conscience, acknowledging that every man is entitled to his privacy, forbids unscrupulous intrusions. To be added to these are the difficulties commonly encountered in trying to make dependable observations under clinical or experimental conditions—in controlling or distinguishing the main components of an environmental situation (chief among which is the psychologist himself), in administering different kinds of tests in a standard fashion and inviting participation, in obtaining precise records of the subject's behavior, physical and verbal, et cetera. And finally, of course, the greatest of difficulties—those experienced in making correct interpretations. Our multiple areas of ignorance, the inadequacies of our conceptual schemes, and the end-less failures of our imaginations, on the one hand, and of our critical faculties, on the other—these are among the impediments to the certain recognition of genetic relationships, the identification of determinants, the representation of the current personality, the diagnosis of the present condition, the assessment of energy resources and abilities.

Beyond these hindering deficiencies, however, there is a still more forbidding barrier to a book of this sort: the network of forces, in the psychologist, in his subject, and in society, which prohibit the publication of a truly revealing, recognizable portrait of a still living fellow creature. In order to reach and then to transmit a satisfactory conception of a man's personality it is usually necessary to invade and then to describe certain private regions of his mind. But the only way to do this without opening the subject to anybody's scorn is to change the record so that no one can recognize the hero. Now, tampering with the facts to this extent is a ticklish affair which calls for a steady conscience that is at home in science and not embarrassed by neurotic scrupulousness. Anyhow, many nice decisions are involved, and the task devours time, and at the end of it one may be forced to conclude that the case is not publishable, that it is impossible to conceal the identity of the subject without falsifying significant items.

Finally, after all these obstacles have been surmounted, there is the problem of finding a publisher and an audience. So far no one has responded to G. W. Allport's exhortation in favor of "a truly clinical journal of individual psychological cases and discussions of method." Case writing and case reading are habits which are yet to be acquired by psychologists. To tell the truth, most of us have not learned how to write case histories that may be read with great profit and enjoyment; and so, when we come on one in a scientific journal, we are inclined to skip it, confident that we are not missing a great deal. One trouble is that we are not masters of a generally accepted scheme of concepts in terms of which the multiplicity of facts constituting a life history can be condensed, ordered, and interpreted. Lacking that great shorthand, scientific terminology, everything must be spelled out in plain English and this means a lot of type.

These interferences are negligible when it comes to writing a medical case history. A physical examination can be performed more easily, more quickly, and more surely than a psychological examination; a patient is much less defensive about his bodily symptoms than he is about his mental deviations; the developmental history of a physical ailment is usually shorter and simpler; the physician has a great many more instruments of precision at his disposal than the psychologist has; our knowledge of physical ailments is extensive and well organized; medical diagnosis is, therefore, more dependable; only at the frontiers do we find doctors disputing terms; with a conceptual scheme that is accepted the world over and a more or less standardized form for writing case histories, doctors are able to compress a mass of data into a relatively small space. An accredited physician in Amsterdam, Holland, for example, will examine patients and write histories in very much the same style as will a physician in Amsterdam, New York; but within a single city block one would not be surprised to find two clinical psychologists measuring entirely different variables with entirely different tests and concluding with reports which are poles apart in form and content. Finally, the medical case writer enjoys two further advantages: It is no trick for him to conceal the identity of his patient, and, when he is through his work, he can rely on a multitude of hospitable editors, publishers, and readers. These are some of the reasons why there are thousands of physical case histories available today, but very few psychological case histories. I have little doubt that this book here will serve as an incentive to other members of our profession and in a few years a library of life studies will be in the making. . . .

Personality Disorders in Adults

CHAPTER THREE

A Compulsive Personality with Psychosomatic Reactions

BY SOLOMON MACHOVER

Presenting Complaint

Ezra K. was accompanied by his wife when he came for psychological consultation. It was her insistence and her appeal to his deeply moral sense of fairness that finally prevailed over his reluctance and his thoroughly honest feeling of injured innocence, and so persuaded him to come. As he saw it, the conflict was between them, and the fault was hers. Since their marriage, fifteen years before, he had been a devoted husband, giving way to the least of her whims and treading with careful restraint lest he offend her. True, a week before, he had exploded violently and without warning with the aid of a desperate tumblerful of whiskey, the first that had ever passed his lips. And it was true that, before falling into a drunken stupor, he had frightened them all with his raving, ranting, unhappy protest against the years of silently endured exploitation. But in his view he had richly earned the right to his outburst. Any normal man would have done the same in his place.

He had passed the years in single-minded dedication to the welfare of his wife and 7-year-old son and in building, brick by careful brick, the sturdy structure of their economic security. His two modest business enterprises took almost all his time and imposed on him a tense preoccupation which contaminated the rare opportunities for social and recreational activity. His evenings at home he was driven to spend in

going over accounts and figuring and refiguring his present and anticipated economic status. His wife, on the other hand, far from appreci-
ating the bitter realities of life which made a virtue of his selfless,
well-ordered, and responsible conduct, actually dared to complain that
its humdrum dullness threatened to stifle her labile emotional needs
and her intellectual and cultural strivings. He regarded her as a self-
centered, impulsive, rather shallow person, deeply frustrated, and restless in pursuit of nameless goals. He was 45 and she 33. He had no
illusions about his own charm, and he was convinced that she was
incapable of deep or lasting affection for anyone. He was nothing if
not a realist. He would have been content to maintain the slightly sad
tenor of his way if only his wife had taken half a step toward meeting
his need for grateful appreciation of his generous paternal tolerance.

The process of alienation between husband and wife had been
moving with slow sureness over the years, he dutifully absorbed in the
affairs of the workaday world, she in zealous flight from her discon-
tents. It was an accident that brought matters to a head. Some three
months before, Ezra had smashed up his car. He had escaped unhurt,
but he could have been killed. The accident was a forceful reminder
of his mortality. He was too humble a man to admit it, but he had
lived a life of self-abnegation and the time for reward was suddenly
in danger of running out. Almost at once, he discovered the resentment that had tensed his body almost beyond endurance and pushed
the beat of his heart till it boomed in his ears. Anger spurred his courage. His secret prayer for love turned into a frank cry for attention,
his begrudging submissiveness into a desperate demand to dominate.
He protested his wife's cold inconsiderateness and was determined no
longer to tolerate the self-centered pattern of her ways. In search of
fulfillment of a self that had never formed, Mrs. K. had developed a
passion for amateur theatricals and for square dancing. Hers was a
need for the safe and impersonal release of feelings and urges that
rapidly became intolerably pent up. She needed roles and settings
which, making no demands on her for enduring commitments, gave
her variety and the illusion of freedom, while ingratiating her narcissism. Her activities took most of her evenings, often till the small hours
of the morning, while Ezra, home alone with the child, paced the
floor conjuring up fearsome images of horrible foul play to which she
fell victim. If only, for her own good, he could spank her as a mother

spanks a child that, in a heedless dash across the road, has just barely escaped being run down.

Staidly correct and stoically controlled, long-suffering Ezra was doubtlessly flattered to appear the possessor, the ostensible conqueror of his wife's rebellious spirit. But he was also deeply offended by its implicit negation of his values, his way of life, the anchoring core of his personality. He charged no offense. He demanded simply that she go nowhere without him, that she give up her theatricals and her dancing, and that she stay home to minister to his needs. How, he hardly knew. She could hold his hand, share a little in his cares, scratch his back, at least be present. All he knew was that he needed her. He had given everything, and the time for reckoning had come, the time for some little recompense.

Mrs. K. took no responsibility for the alienation. Ezra had failed to recognize her needs, and his absorption in matters of minor concern to her had forced her to seek outlets in which, because of the atrophy of his interest and skill, he could not participate. Unable to move her with a rational exposition of the situation, Ezra resorted to the desperate measure of the masochistic alcoholic tantrum. She would see the poignancy of his need for her. In the unaccustomed intemperateness of his behavior, she would see her culpability and, out of the pangs of insufferable remorse, would reform herself and make amends. Actually, Mrs. K. was frightened by the sudden turn in Ezra's conduct. A major base of her own neurotic operations seemed in danger of crumbling. She thought him ill and feared that more serious illness lay ahead. He resisted her urging that he go for psychological treatment. Partly, he was content to have her think him ill so that he might enjoy the fruits of her expiation. Partly, he could not risk undermining the outer righteousness of his position. Mostly, he feared the exposure of his inner doubts. But the assumed confidence in his outer righteousness demanded that he stand up and meet the test. Besides, for Ezra, the other person's position inevitably has enough merit to sway his acts if not his beliefs. And, too, he was not unaware of warming up to the intriguing possibilities of laying bare the dramatic, extraordinary facets of his soul.

Ezra weathered the psychological consultation extremely well. Never before had he had a forum for the communication of his position, his complaints, his inner experiences. It was a thrilling relief to discover that he could reveal his intimate thoughts, the bad ones together with the good ones, and yet survive. He was too defensive at first to acknowledge the need for therapeutic intervention, and later he remained too cautious and too resigned to anticipate any substantial change. But he welcomed eagerly the prospect of regularly scheduled opportunities for cathartic release. He was impelled to boast that it would take forever to disentangle the intricate web of his life.

Present Personality

It was difficult for Ezra to realize that the crisis in his marriage came as a virtually inevitable emergent out of the interplay of two neurotic personalities, each fashioning the relationship between them as an externalization of his own deep-seated problems. He came seeking corroboration of his stand and condemnation of his wife's. But he remained to gain insight into his own personality and its part in creating the situations which pained and saddened him. Out of the subsequent interviews and out of the psychological tests there gradually emerged an enormously complex, yet singularly self-consistent picture of dynamically interrelated ambivalences. There emerged a picture of great strength and brittle weakness, of tender compassion and bitter contempt, of grandiose fantasy and apologetic humility, of love and hate, of masochistic self-sacrifice and unconscious sadism, of courage and fear, of heedless rebellion and abject, penitent conformity.

Ezra did not think of himself as a neurotic. He knew he was a heavily burdened man, and he was proud that he carried his burden so well. He remarked he had two weights to carry, his own and the stone around his neck. All the promise of his youth had gone into the stone. The stone was his tension and his fear. Waking and sleeping, he rarely knew a moment of relaxation. He would waken fatigued and weighted with the feeling of having slept rigid as a board. When he used his personal car to carry materials for commercial purposes the dread of being detected was such that a half-hour's ride sufficed to send him to bed because of the insufferable ache in the tensed muscles of his back and his legs. At all times, his jaws were set against each other with a pressure that traumatized his teeth.

The somatic toll exacted by Ezra's intense emotional stress was not limited to the constant fatigue and the severe headaches resulting from his extreme tenseness. He complained of frequent palpitation, tachycardia, and precordial pain, although no cardiac pathology was ever noted. In fact, he was proud of his strong heart. Respiratory symptoms included severe hay fever, a tendency to frequent catarrh, and a susceptibility to attacks of asthma. Heartburn was an almost daily reminder of his hypersensitive alimentary tract. At times it proved to be an unpleasant precursor of a more dreaded attack of peptic ulcers. Occasional abdominal pain put him in fear of cancer. Despite the distress these symptoms and fears caused him, Ezra confided in few, and he would seek medical help only with reluctance. His love of life has never waned for a moment, and often he takes occasion to rue the mortality which must finally deprive him of the opportunity to witness the confidently anticipated wonders of the developing world. Yet, as much as possible, he avoided doctors. If ill, he would hate to be told; if well, he might be regarded a hypochondriac.

It was some time before Ezra could bring himself to appreciate that these physical symptoms had anything to do with his psychological problems, with his wishes, witting and unwitting, the anxieties they provoked, and the coping mechanisms through which he strove to achieve a relative, if costly, equilibrium. It was consistent with his sado-masochistic defense system that Ezra should suffer his ailments in stoical and fatalistic silence. Evading recognition of his present implicit motivations, he was content to refer his somatic defects and his adaptational inefficiencies to external forces or circumstances for which he had served as passive victim. He had a ready explanation for his heart symptoms. He recalled an incident during World War I. Enemy soldiers were occupying the town and had herded all residents into a number of cellars. But Ezra, then 9 years old, was stubborn. He ran defiantly out into the street only to be shocked into a trembling paralysis of fear when a grenade exploded a block away. On another occasion, once more in defiance of strict injunction, he slipped out of a concentration area to go to his own home. He was huddled on the floor in the darkness in fear of reprisal when the distant sound of Cossack hoofbeats bore in upon him with a rising crescendo that paced the frantic beat of his heart. These and similar incidents were for him the sufficient cause of his present cardiac symptoms. He was unaware that implicit grandiose aspirations and hostile impulses had anything to do with the matter. He was, in fact, unaware that he had not given up the strivings of his childhood, and he was quite certain that his own hostile impulses were amply justified by offenses against him. Besides, they were transient and quickly controlled by his better judgment.

Ezra attributed his asthmatic attacks to inherited allergic disposition and to adventitious circumstance. His mother had been asthmatic since the age of 3 and had died of heart failure in the midst of an asthmatic attack. The precipitating circumstance in Ezra's case occurred when, at 32, he lay down in the damp grass after an exerting tennis match and suppressed urges to sneeze and cough. He had heard that psychological factors were sometimes considered of importance in asthma. But he had never isolated the image of himself as a dependent person masochistically demanding succorance from potentially rejecting parental figures.

The tendency to heartburn and to peptic ulcers was explained and assimilated in quite as impersonal a way. It was a matter simply of physiology and diet. He had heard that worrisome people who assumed heavy responsibilities were somewhat more susceptible than others to peptic ulcer. Nevertheless, he could not see how this applied to his case, even though he had to acknowledge that his sense of responsibility was overdeveloped and that he was a mass of anticipations which, on the positive side, guaranteed the perfection of his planning and, on the negative side, filled him with anxiety and compelled him to erect in advance a hundred defenses for each humble assertion.

If he failed consciously to recognize the hostile core of his drives and to realize that the resulting ambivalence between hostility and dependence was in some way connected with his susceptibility to peptic ulcer, his rigid prophylactic diet seemed a symbolic expression of implicit recognition. His breakfast is invariably limited to milk warmed by the addition of an equal quantity of hot water. Lunch consists of a chocolate malted milk, while dinner is restricted to broiled steak, followed by milk an hour later for his health's sake. In his diet, Ezra thus knows no gradations between virtually passive ingestion and active oral destruction. The separation between these two extremes in diet takes on a ritualistic significance abetted by a deep religious compulsion. Ezra is intellectually emancipated. He believes that many religious proscriptions were amply justified by hygienic considerations at their inception but that under modern conditions they are no more than vestigial symbols. Nevertheless, there are certain proscriptions from which he cannot free himself. He does not hesitate to ride on the Sabbath and to handle money, and he may even tolerate nonkosher food in the home of a Gentile business associate. But the very thought of non-kosher food at home, or of mixing meat with milk excites him to violent nausea. He acknowledges that in this he is the helpless victim of a compulsion. Against all his reason, the orthodox injunction "Do not mix meat with the mother's milk" carries for him the threat of the righteous God's vengeance. The problem of how to regard the cow's udder through which the milk passes in contact with the flesh has always fascinated him.[1] The intensity of Ezra's feeling over the milk-meat injunction testifies to its deep personal significance for him. There is evidence that in some way it expresses a core aspect of his self-concept. On Plate VI of the Rorschach he saw an animal that looked like a tiger in front and a goat in back. The tiger, he said, is a ferocious, voracious meat eater, while the goat gives milk, is stubborn yet harmless, and "better than a tiger." He is far more ready to acknowledge identification with the goat than with the tiger. Yet he cannot gainsay the fact that the beautiful, vivacious young girl who later became his wife had been attracted by his precocious appearance of masterfulness and of promising ambitiousness when, at 25, he was placed in charge of a department of over 100 people in a large merchandising concern.

Ezra's emphasis on *mother's* milk with which meat is not to be mixed if he is to escape a painful retribution calls attention to the role his relationship to his mother has occupied in the dichotomous organization of his personality and in the apparently contradictory quality of many of his attitudes and acts. Ezra's drawing of a female (see Fig. 1) leaves little to the imagination as a codified representation of his by now unconscious perception of his mother. He had great difficulty in drawing a female altogether. He described the unflattering image that finally emerged as having the appearance of "an executioner of 400 or 500 years ago; a warrior like Napoleon; a person who seems to wear a religious shield on his chest, like the high priest in the temple: Holy! Do not touch."

A brief historical digression is necessary at this point if the astonishingly literal, yet completely unconscious significance of Ezra's con-

---

[1] Reference is made to the *Kitzur Schulchan Aruch,* the Code of Jewish Law (1), in which detailed instructions are given for rendering kosher the udder of the cow.

fession in the drawing is to be appreciated. Ezra's mother was a pillar of determined strength during the most difficult years of his childhood. The family suffered great hardship and privation during the First World War, and it was her dauntless, disciplined courage and unfailing ingenuity that carried them through. As a child, Ezra had little knowledge of his father, who was something of an irresponsible rake and whose work as an itinerant tinker excused his long absences from home. His father had migrated to this country well before the outbreak of the war. His mother, as a result, he now remembers, "over-exercised the authority of both father and mother." She had been a protective mother, but also one who demanded discipline and obedience. She had been devoutly religious and she required strict observance in her children. Ezra's younger brother had been her favorite, while his handicapped older brother elicited her special protectiveness. As a result, it was to Ezra that the heaviest responsibility fell for sharing with his mother the care of the family. His mother's confidence in him and her praise for his precocity were precious food for his narcissism. They helped to deprive him of his childhood and they abetted realistic circumstance in encouraging his father-replacement fantasies and in restraining the expression of growing rebellious resentments.

Rebellious resentments there were in plenty and these were most vigorous in connection with the religious observances his mother enforced. From 6 years of age Ezra was required to recite daily hourlong prayers before taking nourishment in the morning. The urge to revolt was there long before it broke into the open. The break which occurred when he was 9 constitutes one of Ezra's most vivid childhood recollections. He recalls running barefoot out of the house into the snow while his mother shouted after him, "Pray before you eat," and he countered, "Eat before praying."

It is perhaps now understandable, yet somehow nevertheless astonishing, that at 45 his hampered, awkward effort to draw a woman should produce a man, an executioner of 400 or 500 years ago, a temple priest whose shield where would be the woman's breast, the source of the infant's nourishment, warns, "Do not touch!" It is perhaps now a little clearer, too, why for Ezra the meat of rebellion, the flesh of masculine assertion, must not be mixed with the milk of the mother.

Ezra has long since quelled his rebellion against religious authority, but, because he had not worked through its roots in his relationship to his mother, it continued to find expression in the form of compulsive symptoms and in detached impersonal fantasies. He is chagrined to find on going to the synagogue that, while the bearded zealots casually perform the ritual washing of their begrimed, encrusted hands, he is compelled to do a thorough job lest he be guilty of entering the House of the Lord with a heretical speck on his hands. Here no concealment could suffice, for his image of God, the heritage of his fear-filled childhood, is as a universe of eyes against which no barrier can prevail. On entering the pew and taking up the prayer book, he is invariably seized with an urge to defecate, a besmirching affront which drives him down to another scrupulous, penitent hand-washing.

The *Kitzur Schulchan Aruch* advises that only the purest of thoughts are permissible in the Lord's House. It advises, too, that when defecating all thought of God must be pushed out of mind and concern with accounts substituted. In this Ezra has been an apt pupil. He has effected an outward conquest of his self-indulgent and sadistic urges in a passionate, dutiful, and defensive interest in figuring accounts. It is no accident of circumstance that Ezra numbers among his accomplishments a degree in accountancy! The temptation to defy religious coercion, however, still persists. From time to time he wonders what it must be like to have the courage to depart to the most distant extreme from one's religion. He recalls that, in a neighboring town of his childhood, there was a towering basilica on whose façade the word "Jehovah" in giant Hebrew letters stood out boldly, dominating the town. The basilica had been built by an apostate Jew. Ezra wondered if the giant Hebrew-lettered Jehovah had been deliberately intended as a mockery of the faith of the town's predominantly Jewish population.

By all ordinary counts Ezra is a good man. He reveres his elders to the point of ancestor worship. In a drawer of his private desk he keeps photographs of his deceased mother and father-in-law. Daily he is drawn to take out the pictures and to kiss them. He neither smokes nor drinks, and yet he is no intolerant bluenose. His very occasional hypermoralistic cynicism over the drinking, swearing, whoring masses is chastened by sadness at the spectacle. If he thought them deserving of punishment, it was only that they might be taught to mend their waywardness. Besides, his cynicism is more than compensated by his generosity, his active sympathy for the disinherited. Though a minor capitalist, he is all for legislation in the interests of the working class. The personal problems of his employees are his problems. He would make any sacrifice for his wife and child, and for his siblings and their families. His most earnest wish is for peace on earth and good will to all men. He is an earnest believer in the emancipation of women, although wryly fearful that too many women, notably his wife, seek the privileges while shunning the responsibilities of men. He is not aware of having ever taken advantage of anyone and is, if anything, rather easily exploited.

Among his recollections, recent and remote, are numerous instances in which, accidentally failing to pay a bill, or having been undercharged, he trudged back like Lincoln to make restitution. On the other hand, if he is overcharged he makes no protest. He simply takes his patronage elsewhere. If he catches himself watching the scale as his order is weighed, he blushes and casts his eyes down lest it be erroneously thought that he questioned the honesty of the clerk. He bears no one any malice and deplores only that he cannot bring himself to the level of noisy, crass bravado he feels all but necessary for the successful conduct of his manufacturing business in a primitively principled, dog-eat-dog field. His reputation in business is of scrupulous honesty, utmost responsibility, and reliability. He is opposed to capital punishment with a crusading fervor, has a profound faith in the reality and the value of penance, and is whole-heartedly committed to reformist rather than punitive measures. His credo is "Understand and forgive; we don't know what gets into youngsters to make them misbehave. We ought not to be like 300 years ago, when a criminal was considered responsible and guilty, and that God wanted him punished."

Fantasies

No, one cannot doubt that Ezra is a good man, an honest, responsible, genuinely contributing citizen. His is a rigorously coercive superego, and his capitulation is so complete, at least on the surface, that he is simply not aware of the slightest inclination on his part to protest. Yet, for one so good, Ezra owned to curious quirks and fantasies, which he accepted as incidental oddities when they did not bewilder him. For all his generosity toward others he feels unaccountably annoyed when his brother speaks of having met a brilliant physicist, a brilliant mathematician, a brilliant linguist. Ezra depreciates his own intelligence, yet somehow finds it hard to acknowledge that any mere mortal with whom he has had personal contact can be brilliant. Ezra declares, a little defiantly, that he has met no geniuses. His complaint has the ring of a frustrated man's ungenerous envy. Somewhere along the line of his development he pushed into the limbo of his repressions a childish grandiose self-concept leaving an unaccepted resentful sense of his mediocrity. In a half-wail of self-pity he has wondered aloud, "Where is the genius of my childhood?"

Ezra is often drawn to the obituary columns of the daily paper. His interest is in keeping check on the necrology of the great and the near-great. He knows only that he deplores the premature passing of people whose continued social contribution our sorely racked world direly needs. He is not quite aware that the pain of his own aspiration's disappointment is abated by the leveling mortality of those whose promise was realized in manifest performance. Ezra has sour-graped his fantasied goals lest his safety and his self-esteem suffer from failure of an effort honestly committed to their attainment. He vividly recalls a panicky fear of death that suddenly beset him when he fell into a concealed crevice on his way up a Carpathian mountain on a forage for food during the war. He was 11 at the time, but the memory still sears. When he reached the top of the mountain his spirits fell again. He had nurtured a vision of great glory. What he found was just a mountaintop.

Allusion has already been made to Ezra's compulsive interest in figuring and in keeping accounts. He thinks of this as an innocuous habit sufficient to account for the fact that, on reading that a single imaginary atom bomb in a civilian defense drill produced 250,000 imaginary deaths, he found himself automatically calculating that it would take 25 bombs properly placed to kill everyone in New York and to wipe out the city besides.

A favored fantasy finds the world riven by a gigantic earthquake. All the people of the world are sucked into the yawning chasm—all but Ezra, who in a graceful, effortless leap magically wafts himself to safety across the vast breach.

It has already been intimated that Ezra can be quite calamitous in anticipation of dreadful eventualities that never materialize. The victims of his calamitous fantasies are particularly those whom he admires and loves. A neighbor's child, a pretty, vivacious, popular little girl, narrowly escaped being run down by a car. When Ezra heard an account of the incident, his mind, in an automatic, almost dissociated way, took off on an elaboration of the event. He saw her actually struck down, and an image of her broken, bleeding body came before him with a vividness that left him shuddering in a cold sweat. So, too, his own son has suffered a hundred deaths in his tortured fantasy. Ezra sees in all these fantasies merely an unfortunately exaggerated expression of legitimate concern on the part of a sensitive man rendered not pessimistic, but prudent and planful, by the chastening experiences of a harsh life which would have made any ordinary man deeply cynical.

Ezra has been remarkably successful in avoiding recognition of the hostile feelings which seem so dramatically implicit in his fantasies. He has been equally successful in avoiding recognition of the guilt feelings which hostility may be expected to generate in so moral and masochistic a man. Here, again, his fantasies, as well as the selective character of his vivid identifications, supply the evidence. When he passes a chicken market the frantic clucking of the chickens slated for slaughter makes him faint with nausea for his is the neck being severed. He imagines himself lying wounded on the battlefield while huge impersonal tanks, on his own side, making no distinction between the living and the dead, roll on indiscriminately crushing all obstacles in their path. A brutal beating in a boxing match is absorbed as much by him as by the actual victim. The most painful of his identifications occurs when the hour of a scheduled execution for a capital crime approaches. The identity of the criminal, the nature of his crime are irrelevant. It is Ezra's doom the clock ticks out. And just as Ezra himself feels no guilt, so too the criminal must be innocent. Perhaps he has been falsely accused, misidentified, at least innocently involved. Surely new evidence will come in time to stay the execution. The current that kills the criminal passes through Ezra's body. Ezra pulls back exhausted from the ordeal. This is a fantasy which underscores the richly personal significance of the female figure drawing which he identified as "an executioner of 400 or 500 years ago." And if the reader, keeping in mind the "Holy! Do not touch" chest shield of the temple priest and the "Pray before you eat" incident of Ezra's childhood, will accept the symbolic equation of the transition of historical time from one era

to another with the passage of ontogenetic time through one generation, little doubt should remain as to Ezra's unconscious identification
of the executioner with the still effective if completely unwitting childhood image of his mother.

In calmer moments Ezra meets such situations better. He seats himself with calm dignity in the electric chair. The switch is thrown once.
Ezra smiles undaunted. He has concealed on his person wires which
ground the current. The voltage is increased and the switch is thrown
a second and a third time and Ezra marches off serenely a free man,
for is there not some unwritten law that confers innocence on anyone
who can withstand three trials by fire? In speaking of the concealed
wires, Ezra was moved to recall the myth that when Jesus left the
temple he took with him, illicitly hidden on his body, the secrets of
ethereal purity which enabled him to enact in the world the godly role
which, for all others, must be confined to the temple. In his fantasies,
Ezra moves from guilt to exoneration, to the grandiose magic of god-
liness.

For one so ridden with implicit guilt, the projected fantasy that the
victim of capital punishment is innocent and has been falsely accused,
and the fantasy of last-minute, miraculous escape seem curiously discrepant. Perhaps they testify to a futile wish that his own real "crimes"
of childhood had never really occurred. Perhaps they are a tacit acknowledgment that the crimes never really happened, never really
broke through the bonds that restrained his wishes.

The less dramatic events of daily life are scarcely less suggestive of
the implicit guilt which pervades Ezra's being. Almost every assertion
is tagged with unwitting hostility and penitently undone in some expiatory act or thought. The figure of Authority stands over him and
menacingly weighs his every thought and act. In his business he counts
carefully the items of a shipment, often giving more than the order
called for, lest he be accused of deliberately shipping short. He cannot
raid the icebox at midnight, if his self-conscious appropriation of a
prudent bit of milk can be called a raid, without wondering whether
his wife will think he has taken more than his proper share. He is im-
peded in writing to the point of paralysis lest his words be misunderstood by his correspondent. There looms over him, besides, Gottesman,
literally Man of God, the benevolent, yet austere, father figure and
mentor of his early adolescence. He recalls overhearing Gottesman

recount the story of poor, illiterate Private Ivan Ivanovitch, who failed
to answer roll call when the sergeant called out the unfamiliar Ivanovitch, Ivan. Gottesman's ridiculing laughter rings out whenever Ezra
now dares the pretense of literacy in writing a letter.

It has been noted that Ezra's preferences for compromise and peace,
his considerateness, and his generosity make him an easy target for
exploitation. He knows that people somehow take for granted that
they can look to him for a submissive reception of arbitrary, discrim-
inatory practices it simply never occurs to them to try on others. There
seems implicit in this aspect of Ezra's self-preoccupation a tacit self-
perception of guilt. Not to compromise, not to submit is to be hostile
and aggressive. Yet each submission to an unreasonable demand is
tensely stored in his gut. The explosion comes when the tension becomes unbearable and when his indignation comes to awareness with
a guilt-dissolving access of self-righteousness. Even then, the explosion
is experienced as an unseemly weakness for which the exploiter must
take the responsibility and so take to treating him with penitent care.
The question may well be raised as to whether Ezra's anticipatory
placation may not be in the service of a sadistic invidiousness unconsciously calculated to justify his scorn for the unprincipled portions of
humanity, and to pay in advance for the luxury of the ultimate explosion. Each concession at least adds an arrogant spire to the private
castle of his serenity.

What, then, is the quality of Ezra's goodness? Much of it is obviously a reaction formation in defense against drives and aspirations
perceived as dangerous. Yet his values accord with the best liberal
and democratic traditions. They are oriented toward reality and toward the social good and, seemingly, they make not too much demand
on others. It is their defensive function that traps others into exploiting
him and that leads him to an ultimate explosion. Does its defensive
origin, then, contaminate the quality of his goodness? Is another origin
for goodness conceivable? Perhaps these are questions which will be
thought out of place in a clinical description of personality. But Ezra
himself will need to find an answer to these questions. It seems intrinsic
to the psychologist's function to help the client identify his values, alter
them, or make his peace with them. The reader is left to ponder these
questions of value for himself.

Childhood Influences and Foreshadowings

Often in the course of subsequent interviews, as Ezra's present motivations and coping mechanisms came into focus, he would refer to childhood incidents, offering them as sufficient cause and justification for his present behavior and for his stoical acceptance of the present reality. A number of such incidents have already been described. There was his defiance, during the war, of the invader's order restricting the movements of the town's inhabitants. The exploding grenade and the beat of the Cossacks' hoofs on the cobbles first called attention to his heart and "explain" for Ezra his present cardiac over-reactivity. His fall into the crevice on his way up the mountain offered the still effective warning that the acting out of inner grandiose yearnings can be dangerous and, when successful, yield hollow attainments. His awe-struck image, when he was 6, of God as a ubiquitous eye was a precursor of his present dread of detection, although he remains completely unaware today, as at 6, of harboring any guilt meriting detection. The reappearance, in transparent symbolic disguise in his female figure drawing, of his association, in the identity of his mother, of the demand for religious observance with the threat of the refusal of nourishment and of execution is the most startling example of the all-but-literal transposition of the childhood past onto the adult present.

Ezra has been able to recover many incidents of his childhood which if, contrary to his belief, they did not serve as more than minor influences on the present certainly gave expression to already crystallized attitudes and thus foreshadowed aspects of his present personality pattern. It has been suggested that Ezra's helpless identification with those who are hurt or killed testifies to feelings of guilt, to the conviction that he may be deserving of a like fate. If this is true now, it was true when Ezra was much younger. When he was 10, standing in a queue before a butcher shop, he overheard a gossiper's excited report that a young man had just shot himself and his sweetheart. Ezra promptly went into a dead faint which, on his revival, earned him first place in line. He was as profoundly affected by the death of members of collateral branches of his family with whom he had had scant contact.

As a child Ezra was, as he is now, shy and self-conscious in social contacts. Economic factors, Ezra feels, had much to do with the development of these traits. His mother had been one of five sisters, four of whom had married well while the family fortunes were still intact. The marriage of Ezra's mother came after the collapse of the family fortunes. The unavailability of a dowry ordained a marriage to a man of equally gloomy economic prospects. The economic poverty of the family became economic distress during the war. Ezra remembers his hunger during the period, the meanness of his dress, his distrust of his manners, the tense feeling of marginality in his relation to the main currents of social activity around him. When he was 10, a rich cousin got him a job as a delivery boy for an apothecary. The job lasted a day. Later he overheard his cousin's explanation. The apothecary had been contemptuous of Ezra's awkward comportment, his appearance as a cross between a ragged street gamin and a country bumpkin. It is little wonder that about this time Ezra woke from his sleep shouting, "I can do it a million times better than you."

It is to be expected that one so ridden as Ezra with sadistic fantasies and with surges of implicit rebellion against authority should have a special history with regard to the development of attitudes toward anal function. Ezra's behavior in synagogue has already been described and his compulsive cleanliness, punctuality, and orderliness hinted at. Three childhood incidents bear on this matter. About his earliest recollection of shame occurred when he was 5 or 6 years old. A teacher, in making fun of Ezra's older, handicapped brother, called him a *Knobelfaertzer,* a garlic farter. This was a matter of deep personal humiliation for Ezra. When Ezra was 11 Gottesman, his revered mentor, took him to visit a friend, a teacher in a neighboring town. Tea was served, but Ezra refused stubbornly despite insistent efforts to penetrate what was thought to be his shyness. Ezra asserts he refused because he was secretly reluctant to deprive his hosts of their precious war-rationed sugar. It is of interest that in relating this incident, Ezra emphasized that he had been astonished and chagrined to find that there was an inside toilet, the first he had ever heard of such a thing. To make matters worse, the toilet opened off the kitchen. It is at least likely that an association in Ezra's mind between eating and excreting had much to do with the emergence of a magnanimous reason for refusing the tea. Ezra recalls that it was about at this period that he had used a public outhouse for defecation and had emerged to find Gottesman waiting to go in. Gottesman's comment to a companion still burns: "Ezra sits as long as a Rabbi." Ezra had not been aware that anyone was waiting, nor had he been unduly long. But Ezra is to this day extremely uncomfortable when defecating. He fears he may be keeping someone waiting.

It is unfortunate that no history of training for bowel control is available. We should expect Ezra to have been subjected to coercive measures. We do know that Ezra's mother was a dominating figure. She was a decisive, determined, ambitious, bright and competent, religiously devout woman. We know, too, that her temperament and the difficulty of raising five children under extremely straitened and unstable, threatening circumstances, with scarcely any help from her ne'er-do-well husband, drove her to exercise a rigorous discipline over her children.

It is important to emphasize that because of his precocity it was Ezra whom she chose to carry such responsibility for the children as she would delegate. It is one of Ezra's fondest recollections that once during the war, when his mother went for two weeks on a bartering trip for food, she chose him to take charge of the family. Clearly, Ezra had not been unappreciated. The recognition he received for his accomplishments as a child, and these included remarkable progress in school, fluency in five languages by the time he was 12, besides all the good works of an outwardly dutiful child, has undoubtedly contributed to the remarkable strength he now demonstrates in surviving the pressures of his inner conflicts and the very heavy demands of living which his conflicts magnify tenfold. What must be inferred, however, is that Ezra's portion of maternal love was paid out in the form of praise and delegated responsibility. His older brother earned the special protection of the handicapped, while his younger brother, as the brilliant and beautiful baby of the family, monopolized his mother's admiring love. Ezra is only vaguely aware of having experienced any jealousy for his brothers. Mostly he recalls his sympathy for his older brother and his pride over his younger brother's accomplishments, particularly in areas in which Ezra had coached and guided him.

Ezra's father's absence from the home, and his virtual dereliction of his marital and paternal responsibilities, did much to create a setting conducive to Ezra's precocious assumption of an adult, pseudo-paternal role. As Ezra's father traveled about on his tinker's route, stories would filter in from the mountain villages. His tall, red-headed, red-bearded figure had been seen carousing at the taverns. He was a

jolly and frolicsome man who never ignored an opportunity for a flir-
tation. Particularly galling to Ezra's mother were the tales of his gaily
abandoned dancing with the prettiest of the peasant *shicksas*. Ezra
was his mother's confidant as she railed bitterly against her husband.
Men in general were irresponsible, and her husband, Ezra's father,
was the worst offender of all. He was the cause of the family's desti-
tution and of her emotional suffering. When, shortly after the father's
departure for America during Ezra's seventh year, Ezra tearfully reported to his mother that he had dreamt his father was dead, she bitterly rebuked him, "Don't waste your tears. He was never a father to
you."

It was inevitable under the circumstances that there should grow
deep in Ezra's breast the firm resolve to make up for his father's dereliction. His need for self-esteem in his identity as a male conferred on
him the obligation to vindicate all fathers, all husbands, all men. He
would be the perfect husband, the perfect father. The difficulty is that
this was a child's resolution, a child craving for love, for understanding
and acceptance for himself alone. The difficulty is that his determination to be a perfect husband and father was part of his conception of
the good son, and the rewards he anticipated were those of maternal
love and support. Ezra is today a patient, provident, self-sacrificing
husband and father, and he still plainly, if unconsciously, seeks the reward of maternal love, only now, though she is so much younger than
he, from his wife. If, in selecting a mate, his wife sought a stalwart
father figure, she found one in Ezra. What she had not bargained for
was that she was to find in him also a son. She sought a tiger but
found a half-tiger, half-goat.

The picture of the dutiful son enacting the role of the perfect husband and father is only a half-picture. The guilt of his childhood was
more than a foreshadowing of the guilt of his adulthood. It was
symptomatic of currents in conflict with the major role Ezra had
adopted. The early usurpation of his father's place in the family, however much it may have been imposed on him by external forces, must
have generated guilt feelings and the threat of a castrative reprisal. It
is unfortunate that explicit evidence on this score is thus far lacking,
although Ezra's lifelong intimidation before authority and his ration-
alized retreat from grandiose goals would be consistent with an early
fear of castration in some form. There was also a lurking resentment,

which now and again burst out in open rebellion, over the cost his precocious adult role exacted. The strivings of revolt against his mother and against the religious authority she represented come to a head under the influence of Gottesman. This "man of God" was scornful of organized religion and emphasized instead the greater virtue of inner morality and spiritual feeling. When he was 13, Ezra joined the *Shumrin,* a group of agnostics who were philosophical stoics, renouncing all worldly pleasure, vowing never to smoke or drink, and dedicating themselves to a life of the purest morality. This was indeed a curious rebellion which demanded an even greater self-denial for the privilege of casting out the God of his mother.

Early Manhood

The open rebellion against his mother lasted for three years. When he was 16 Ezra came with his family to this country. His mother's attitude toward him changed abruptly. She no longer coercively directed his forced precocious maturity. She allowed him freedom and, for the first time, she gave him tenderness. The change in her attitude toward him, and the great need for her tenderness which the bewildering impact of the new world aggravated in him, made him her abject slave. The rebellion was over and the period of the great expiation was begun. Ezra became closely attached to his mother, tried to spare her the least pain, and rediscovered his religious orthodoxy. Curiously, yet understandably enough in light of this reactivation of an oedipal relationship, Ezra was the only one of his siblings who had no rancor toward the father, who had resumed his philandering activities in this country.

Up to the time of his marriage when he was 30, virtually all his social and recreational activities were confined to the parlor of his mother's home. His dates were all group dates with minor exceptions. His reverence for his elders became a passion which served him in good stead as a rationalization for the restrictions of his love life imposed by the castration threats implicit in his oedipal involvement. One incident should suffice to illustrate. A classmate of his at the school of accounting, a girl who admired his brilliance and deplored her own lack of it, asked him to help with her studies. When he arrived at her home he found her dressed in a kimono and not at all disposed to study. Ezra had no difficulty in interpreting the none-too-subtle hints of her intention. But how could he act on them? The girl had spoken ill of her parents. Surely one could not rely on a girl who had no respect for her elders. Ezra remained virginal until his marriage.

It is significant that the only girls who ever figured in Ezra's fantasies were, like his wife, much younger than he, decisive, demanding, self-centered. Youthfulness in the fantasied mate serves the fantasied tiger in him, fosters the paternal role, and attenuates the oedipal element. Dominating egocentricity in the fantasied mate guarantees that the tiger in him will give way to the goat in him and that the paternal role will have its filial setting.

If Ezra's childhood was spent in rebellion, his adulthood has been spent in penance. The period of expiation which began on his arrival in this country has continued to the present. This statement requires qualification. The expiation is in constant need of renewal for the rebellion remains latent within him. It remains a constant threat and does, indeed, find frequent symbolic expression which disturbs and bewilders him. It is this pattern of rebellion and expiation which projects itself in many ways and into many levels of expression. It is reflected in the association of defecation urges with ritual hand-washing in the synagogue. It is reflected in the tiger-goat self-image and in the related meat-milk diet. He believes in labor unions, but not the aggressive, rambunctious American kind—rather the settled, conservative German or English kind. His hatred for capital punishment is quickened by the distress that no opportunity for reformation is given. He was intensely disturbed when a man, convicted of a sex-killing in his youth, was refused parole despite some thirty years of exemplary conduct in prison. "Why," cries Ezra, "should the sins of the child be visited upon the penitent adult?" Thus, a self-image, a diet, a philosophy of labor organization, attitudes toward religion, defecation urges and ritual hand-washing, a penal philosophy, the ebb and flow of aggression and of dependent need all attain an inner coherence as expressions of a central pattern of motivation and adjustment. What seems particularly interesting about the coherence of the patterns of self-expression is that it embraces a wide range from concrete to highly abstract forms. Just as it is impossible to distinguish a point in his emergent behavior where reaction formations and defense leave off and desirably creative reality adjustment begins, so it seems idle to try to distinguish a point where the process of literal, concrete, physiognomic generalization merges with the processes of logical, abstract, integrative thinking.

Psychological Tests

It is logical to expect that the consistencies in Ezra's patterns of phenomenal experience and expressive and adaptive behavior should be reflected as well in the patterns of his adjustment to the psychological tests. An example of such consistency has already been given in connection with the female figure drawing. Attention has been directed to Ezra's difficulty in drawing a female altogether, and the associations to the drawing which express an implicit fear of castration at the hands of his mother, who is symbolically identified as the object of Ezra's rebellion-dependency, religious coercion-nourishment conflicts. The squat, stout, forbidding mien of the female figure, which contrasts markedly with the pathetic aspect of the male figure, is entirely consistent with the concept of castration threat. The large empty eye socket of the figure expresses a feeling of rejection, a perception of the mother as one who never allowed him to enter into her intimate experiences. By extension, this treatment of the eye expresses his feeling that no woman he has ever known has had eyes for him. There is a possibility that it may express as well voyeuristic interests in the maternal figure. This is a possibility that is psychologically consistent with what we know of Ezra's personality although no positive confirmatory information is available on this point.

Ezra represents himself quite as literally in his male figure drawing (Fig. 2). He describes the figure as a ". . . person [who] is about fifty years old, is very conservative, thoughtful, not too strong, is a very likable person; someone who lives on the Bowery and needs helps, but would not ask for any." This seems a clear statement of Ezra's psychological finances at the time his psychotherapy was begun. Ezra was asked what animal would best symbolize the personality of the man he drew. He said, "A lamb in the field, separated from its mother. Pitiful. Also a nervous little dog, a Pomeranian." More than a pleading, self-pitying self-representation is here involved. Ezra has an emotional block against eating lamb. Many years ago his mother had forbidden it, presumably on the grounds of health. Identification with the lamb has infused the injunction with the force of law. It is as though in eating lamb Ezra would be taking on the role of the castrator. In the

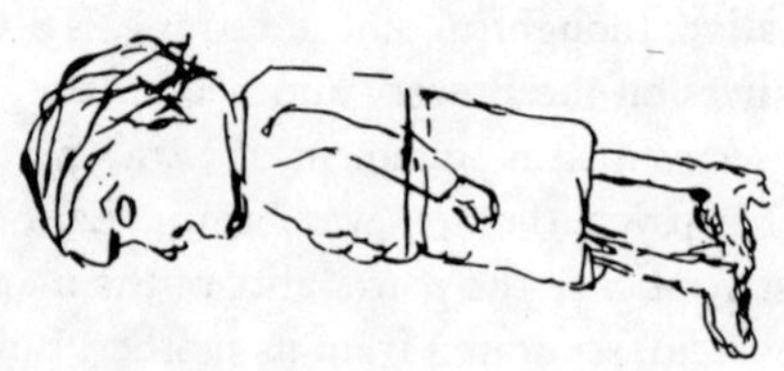

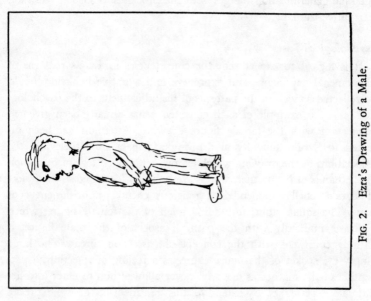

FIG. 1. Ezra's Drawing of a Female.

FIG. 2. Ezra's Drawing of a Male.

42

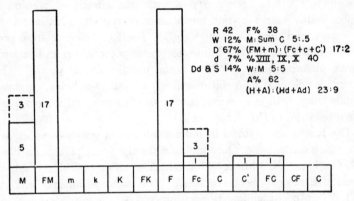

course of therapy, Ezra has come to acknowledge that this in fact is what he has been doing. "Instead of asserting myself, instead of expressing my anger, I have been eating myself up inside." For all the self-depreciation implicit in his identification with the lamb, the treatment of the chin in the male drawing testifies to the great determination that has been noted clinically. The bulging nose in the drawing, which seems to have attracted an excess of graphite, is fairly typical of the self-conscious fantasied phallic restitutions of the involutional. The treatment of the mouth identifies this area as a focus of conflict. The mouth is drawn inward as though it were toothless, yet a sharply

R 42   F% 38
W 12%   M:Sum C 5:.5
D 67%   (FM+m):(Fc+c+C') 17:2
d 7%   %VIII, IX, X 40
Dd & S 14%   W:M 5:5
        A% 62
        (H+A):(Hd+Ad) 23:9

FIG. 3.   Rorschach Profile and Summary.

pointed object protrudes outward from it. Oral aggression and passive oral dependence appear here in ambivalent conjunction.

Both drawings are noteworthy for their bulging, oversize heads and their disparaged, poorly differentiated bodies. This is a cathectic contrast which graphically expresses the effort to repress and isolate impulse and affect, while emphasizing the defensive values of intellectualization. The lines of the drawings are hesitant, tentative, light, broken, and in many places retraced. The expressive movement reflected in the lines would seem to stem from attitudes of insecurity and timidity in self-presentation.

The Rorschach response summary (Fig. 3), too, presents a recognizable picture of Ezra. Much has been made of Ezra's abandoned ambition. In the Rorschach this retreat from the child's promise of greatness is shown in the small number (five) of W responses particularly in relation to the large number of human-movement responses. The five, and three additional, M's and the seventeen animal-movement responses point to Ezra's very great potential capacity and the rich hyperactivity of his fantasy life. All the drive and all the capacity clinically noted are there in the Rorschach protocol and so too is their restriction to fantasy and to modest practical objectives (D = 67%, P = 5). A tremendous residue of immaturely developed drive remains from his childhood. Accomplishment is clearly restricted by anxiety's contamination of drives and affects (W:M = 5:5 + 3, and Fc = 1 + 3). Spontaneity of socialized affective expression is conspicuously absent despite much inherent capacity (M:Sum C = 5 + 3:.5, and Sum 8, 9, 10 = 40%). The Rorschach protocol presents a picture of marked failure to realize potentialities in line with Ezra's plaintive query, "Where is the promise of my youth?" The record is distinctly an introversive one, affect-isolating, fantasy-emphasizing, with evidence of fearful anticipations and some oppositional tendencies (Dd + S = 14%).

The Rorschach protocol includes a number of responses which are interesting contentwise. Outstanding is the tiger-goat percept on Plate VI. On Plate IX, "Mickey Mouse leading an orchestra" reminds us again of Ezra's childhood fantasies of great accomplishment. On Plate VII, "Two heads smiling to each other. I was going to say making faces at each other" expresses Ezra's ambivalence in interpersonal relationships. Ezra's percepts of a number of seals, described by him as capable of extraordinary feats of balance, are reminiscent of the difficult, narrow path Ezra feels he has always walked. Expressing the same self-concept is the woman on Plate V ". . . bending over backwards, like doing a ballet dance . . . an almost impossible position." In light of his attitude toward his wife's dancing, this percept would seem overdetermined, the more so since Ezra added on inquiry, "I thought these might be breasts . . . but no." Again, Ezra looks in vain to the wife-mother for gratification of his dependency needs.

The Word Association Test was significant in eliciting an excess of contrast responses which earned a 98th-percentile score. The implication here is of defensive, unemotional impersonality in relation to objects. The associative sequences *KISS . . . kick, SEX . . . not thinking of anything; I could say male and female,* and *DICK . . .*

what do you mean by that? suggest something of his discomfort in
sexual matters and of his typical effort to deny emotional involvement.
MOTHER . . . er, I was gonna say father, and *BREAST . . . er,
I'm thinking of head, er, chest,* raise again the familiar conflicts regarding his mother and his oral dependency.

The Vocabulary subtest of the Shipley-Hartford Scale produced an
I.Q. of 122, a superior rating particularly in light of the fact that
Ezra's major schooling had not been in English. The Abstraction subtest of the Shipley-Hartford Scale produced a headache and a panic.
He was simply unable to handle it. He gave up in four minutes with
only seven of the twenty items completed. All Ezra's conflicts over
aspiration and ambition, all the self-consciousness that ever attended
his hesitant, ambivalent wish to exhibit the superior intelligence of his
fantasy rushed out to bewilder him. Once again, the discrepancy between potentiality and accomplishment arose to mock him.

Ezra projected into his TAT fantasies his characteristic ambivalence,
his tendency to muted assertion and vigorous denial, to guilty doing
and penitent undoing. He shows in his stories a capacity for observation and an interest in human motivation which in the course of his
search for normative corroboration of his own tangled feelings have
grown less astute than eager and refined. His response to Plate 2, the
farm scene, is perhaps the most revealing. "Offhand," he said, getting
himself off the hook before he was fairly on, "the girl does not appear
part of the family. The family would not work so hard and dress the
girl so and send her to school. They couldn't afford it. They wouldn't
have the tendency. There is a fence between them." Most respondents
identify the girl as part of the family. In his overdetermined failure to
do so, Ezra accomplishes three things. Identifying with the girl, he
projects a bitter echo of his childhood's bewildered resentment over
the affectional neglect he suffered. In the same role of a girl young
enough to be the couple's daughter, yet artfully preserved for a more
interesting fate, he prepares the ground for a triangular entanglement
safely reminiscent of earlier oedipal fantasies. Identifying with the
hard-working man, he foreshadows the development of an amorous
affair in which, as in his own marriage and his continuing real-life
fantasies, the older man is the all-but-passive recipient of the advances
of the all-but-brazen younger girl. Ezra continued, "The girl, a neighbor, came close to ask something. The man is working hard, the

woman is leaning, haughty." Here, again, is the aggressive, accusatory assertion, but followed now by a hasty undoing. "Actually the girl makes these people haughty. The inferiority of farm people resolves itself in a resentful superiority and haughtiness." Identifying in this with "the farm people," Ezra, with a tacit confession of self-insight, thus chides all those in his past whose real and fancied unfeeling derision of the self-conscious gaucherie of his childhood filled him with a secret fierce pride. Hostility is now deflected onto the girl. "The girl is sad and disappointed. She hasn't come for the man. He can't be the woman's son." The oedipal plot has been conceived and rejected, only to be reinstated in the very next sentence. "The woman shows a twinge of jealousy that the girl has an interest in her husband. The girl will leave disappointed." In the next sentence Ezra's courage wanes under the impact of his guilt and all aggression and all evil intent are denied, at the same time that he forgives his tormentors. "Maybe the girl really feels for these people. She has a mutual sympathy and this has been misunderstood by the woman." Only the mother figure continues to earn his rancor. But his ambivalence is not yet done. "Considering women, though, maybe the girl was drawn to this man. Perhaps the man made some remark to indicate his interest in the girl."

Ezra's fantasy in response to 3BM also expresses feelings of rejection ambivalently handled, with the final undoing of despair aiding the repression of any urge to retaliation. He said, "I don't know if this boy has been reprimanded about something, or if he just fell asleep in this position. He cried himself to sleep. Perhaps he was playing with other boys and they said something he didn't like. When he wakes up, as I did under such circumstances, he'll feel much better."

The fantasy for Plate 5 finds Ezra in his usual manner timidly asserting and vigorously denying a covert interest in sexual adventure. "It looks like a study. It's late. The person working in the study may have fallen asleep. She came to check, and found him asleep. She didn't see anything unusual. Maybe she expected to find the man with a woman. But no, she didn't expect it and she didn't find it."

In his fantasy for 6BM Ezra projects a scene involving a mother and son. The son informs the mother that a fatal accident has befallen her husband.

The oedipal wish is more dramatically expressed in the fantasy for 8BM. The man being operated on is the father of the boy in the foreground. The man has been shot by his son. Spontaneously, Ezra remarked that he would place the scene "in the days of celluloid collars, about 1910." In 1910 Ezra was 6 years of age, and his mother was fanning his father-replacement fantasies with her constant railing against her irresponsible husband. As though to insure the efficacy of the patricidal "accident," Ezra remarked, "They didn't have the medical supplies or the know-how they have today."

The characters change and the plots vary in the remaining TAT fantasies. But the needs projected and the ambivalent mode of dealing with them remain consistent throughout. No additional technical point would be gained by reporting any more of the TAT stories here.

ADDENDUM

Ezra came for psychological consultation on account of a smoldering marital discord that burst suddenly into flame. The flare-up followed an accident which, heightening his awareness of involutional problems, reminded him that his mortality might overtake him before he had been compensated for his lifetime of self-abnegation. His dependence was too great to permit a forthright protest, and his coping mechanisms were too neurotic to allow an efficient reorganization of adaptive pattern. His demand for recompense, buttressed by a self-righteousness built up by years of self-imposed exploitation, was a masochistic one designed to punish his wife and elicit her pity.

The personality that emerged in psychotherapy and in psychological tests is clearly a compulsive one marked by extreme ambivalences. In manifest behavior, and in every wish and thought acceptable to his ego-ideal, Ezra is a thoroughly humble and virtuous man. But his virtue is subtly colored by its function as reaction formation against the hostility, the egocentric ambition, and the grandiosity which unwittingly find expression in fantasy. The reality and the vigor of the impulses held in repression are attested by his repudiation of high aspirations, and by the guilt implicit in his dramatic fantasies of identification with those being punished for capital crimes. His passionate plea that the efficacy and the moral value of penance and reform be recognized and credited underscores the severity of the guilt he wishes thus to expiate. Despite the earnestness of his expiatory motive, he has not been able to dismiss the resentment and the rebelliousness which, present in the beginning, his self-imposed, self-frustrating propitiations tend to aggravate.

There has emerged out of this welter of cross-purposes a self-image whose ambivalence is epitomized by the tiger-goat percept. The self-image of contradictory hostility and dependence, of sadism and masochism, reaches a kind of epitome in a pattern of somatic difficulties whose very variety must call in question any specificity of relationship between psychological constitution and psychosomatic symptomatology. The complaints of heartburn, of tendency to peptic ulcer, of asthma, and of precordial pain and frequent tachycardia and palpitation point to quite different psychological dispositions, yet each is appropriately expressive of the dynamics of Ezra's contradictory motivations, the asthma of his cry in desperation for the help of his rejecting mother, the gastric symptoms of his ambition's denial of his dependency, and the cardiac symptoms of his dependency's denial of his hostility. Perhaps it is the availability of alternate modes of suffering which prevents any one of them from becoming too serious.

Tiger and goat, meat and milk, defecation urge and hand-washing compulsion, pray-eat and eat-pray, mountain peak and dangerous crevice, rebellious crime and frantic penance, sadism and masochism, tenderness and tension, marriage to youth and reverence for elders—these are the ambivalences Ezra is challenged to reconcile. They are understandable in one who was praised more than loved, who was seduced into sacrificing his childhood, who was encouraged in oedipal fantasies and threatened with castration, who has carried into adulthood the conception, learned early in childhood, that the good son is the circumspect providing husband.

REFERENCES

1. Gansfried, Rabbi Solomon. *Code of Jewish Law: A compilation of Jewish laws and customs.* (Translated by H. E. Golden.) New York: Star Hebrew Book Co., 1927.

CHAPTER FOUR

To Be or Not to Be: A Schizophrenic Personality

BY MARIA A. RICKERS-OVSIANKINA and MARGARET M. RIGGS[1]

This is an account of the personality of a boy once hospitalized who is now going about the world freely making his own decisions and managing his own affairs. How is he doing it? We have considerable test and psychotherapy data to help us understand his inner dynamics in their conscious and unconscious aspects. We have his past history, as seen through his eyes, to account for his personality development. However, this material is not included here with the purpose of adding one more case history of a schizophrenic. It is not intended as a contribution to the field of psychodiagnosis. It will not demonstrate the effects of psychotherapy on an ambulatory patient. We present this young man in detail because the combined interview and diagnostic data put into vivid focus the way in which a one-time full-fledged psychotic can function in the outside world, given a particular native endowment together with a particular set of inner needs, interacting in a particular environmental setting. The resulting adjustment makes such good psychological sense that the old puzzle of the unhospitalized schizophrenic takes on fresh meaning.

[1] We wish to acknowledge the assistance of J. A. Davis and F. X. Schupper in collecting the material on which this study is based.

Brief History and Current Adjustment

The subject is a 22-year-old single male, oldest of seven children, of lower-middle-class family in a small New England town. He describes his parents as lacking affection, the father strict, the mother less defined. He went through public grammar and high schools uneventfully, working part time in a war factory during his junior and senior years. Though never a leader, he fitted in well with peer groups, except that he was always shy with girls. During high school he daydreamed much and did almost no formal studying. He had always liked books and enjoyed thinking for himself. He was fascinated by Nietzsche's philosophy, and this developed into an abiding influence. Although he graduated in the lowest quarter of his high-school class, he was among the ten highest on a comprehensive examination given at that time. Shortly thereafter he was drafted into the Army. After five months of service he was admitted into an Army psychiatric hospital, the presenting symptoms being grandiose ideas of literary genius, mutism, confusion, and fear of being poisoned. He spent approximately a year in the hospital, receiving EST but no psychotherapy. His discharge note reads: "Schizophrenic reaction, paranoid type." Two months after release from the service he enrolled as a freshman at a large university where he spent three semesters, barely making the necessary grades and finally dropping out for academic reasons. During this time he was successful, however, in launching a drama program on campus. When he entered the university, the Health Department suggested that he receive psychotherapy at the Psychological Clinic. He willingly kept up regular sessions while registered as a student and has coöperated in the follow-up interviews since that time.

After his disenrollment he remained in the university town, retaining a certain amount of contact by using the library and music-room facilities and attending the local student coffee shops talking with former friends. He shared living quarters with a graduate student from the English Department and supported himself by working in a restaurant as a dishwasher. He has been seen reading philosophy books at odd moments during working hours. He sleeps a good deal. At the coffee shop he "observes human nature," as he puts it. He met a girl and they spent time "discussing each other's psychoses." He has worked fairly regularly except for taking extra days off. He rather expects to be fired for this eventually, but he will not be sorry as he has been feeling out of touch with things.

While he was enrolled he revealed a genuine gift for creative writing. Primarily because the university recognized his promise and realized the stress imposed on him by his personality problems he has been readmitted for the summer on probation. He is taking English courses. If he does well he will be allowed to continue in the fall. The subject took the initiative in obtaining this compromise. He also arranged to continue the drama program he produced before. Thus he is on the verge of taking up again that pattern of academic life which has constituted adjustment for him since release from the hospital.

The present study is based on a summary from the Army hospital, therapeutic notes, autobiographical information from the interviews, three poetic essays, informal observations of his campus activities, a Bender Visual Motor Gestalt Test, Rorschach, and Draw-A-Person tests, all of which were repeated after nineteen months.

The Psychological Environment

Behind the behavioral picture emerges the psychological picture of a person who in a very few years has spanned clear autism (psychosis), on the one hand, and, in polar contrast, effective reality testing. He has seemed like a person going back and forth between two worlds: one, the inner reality, is personally meaningful, fluid, readily controllable, full of felt gratifications, but dangerous in its engulfing temptation; the other, outer perceived reality, is harsh, only superficially meaningful, more or less closed to penetration or participation, a world to which he had not quite found the key. In his clinic contacts he hovered over the entire continuum, consciously facing the problem of reconciling the poles again and again. How does each of these two worlds look to him and what attempts has he made to fuse them?

The outer reality, as seen through his eyes, seems to have the quality of a mysterious puzzle box with an impersonal set of push-button contingencies. One lives within the mechanistic universe as both controller and controllee. "I know I'm part of this, yet I'm a part of it removed. I can't grow away from the universe . . . I owe it awareness that it exists. It's like my finger. It doesn't know it exists . . . I know it does . . . I'm a dualist, too. It's a great big rat-race. I know I'm not breaking out of it, but at least I'm running faster than the rest in the treadmill." And at this point he recognizes objective reality as coercive. "All the while I have to get along of course. I have to make my way in the world; it can't be turned on and off, the one that is reality."

If the world's contingencies are met with accuracy, he seems to feel that roughly three levels of satisfaction are available. Most immediately obtainable would be sheer freedom from stress, so that he could "get along better, being more comfortable." As a prerequisite he must "learn to control" the environment and himself in relation to it; the learning process involves docility to the law of effect rather than an active domination of events. "Flexibility of itself is desirable. I could take one stand today and if I get rapped I can take the other stand tomorrow. If I get rapped on that, I'll keep looking." However, time itself shoves him along continuously in the objective world, forcing him into a series of uncomfortable and wholly realistic situations within which decision is inescapable, since inaction itself becomes a decision. He has trouble organizing his work; things will not stand still while he learns to deal with them, and stress continues.

At a somewhat higher hedonic level, he seems to feel that if one managed to be at the right place at the right time with the right equipment, especially money, one might encounter aesthetic pleasure as a passive by-product. For a time he considered joining a fraternity because "You can be beautiful only when you are surrounded by some beauty." He reflected on the lack of beauty in his past. "When you live from hand to mouth you certainly don't go to museums or to concerts. The next 22 years will have to be better." In his more pessimistic moments, however, he says that he doesn't expect to get real pleasure from anything, that he hopes to get the most out of life by putting the least physical or mental effort into it, in effect renouncing pleasure as a goal.

Finally, it is remotely possible to change some part of the environment so as to reduce its harsher characteristics and make it a more desirable abiding place. This would be the highest reward for learning the rules of reality, but also the least obtainable. "Actually on this earth I don't suppose I'll make very much of a scratch." Nevertheless, his only active striving takes this direction; e.g., in his drama program he is trying to impose something "better" on none-too-well-cultured university students in spite of the active needling he incurs.

People have a place in objective reality as fellow occupants and operators of the mechanistic world, seeking roughly the same levels of satisfaction, but with more success. They are also elements of his contingency system, satisfiers if used rightly and deprivers if handled wrongly. Therefore he wants to learn from the therapist, "what you know about handling people," to improve in the social amenities in order to get on more easily. With society, as with reality in general, "You have to join it, you can't buck it."

Every once in a while he finds himself disorganized by sudden unearned benefits thrown his way. For example, a girl inquired when he was sick and "It came as quite a surprise—I didn't think she cared if I lived or died." Such sudden personal experiences overstimulate him and he feels he does not respond normally. "I always hang myself at least seven times while I'm talking."

Meanwhile, quite apart from the difficult objective world, and in sharp contrast to it, he has a live inner world, plastic and vital rather than mechanistic, full of pleasures over which he is direct master without the rigid boundaries, barriers, and unknown push-button contingencies of outer reality. "In my own mind, in my imagination, I can live whatever I can create; whether it's colorful or real or unreal, it has its own reality." "I don't make mistakes in fantasy—I sometimes do in reality." "Deep inside me where things are important, where I make my adjustments I have my own political, religious ideologies. Whether it's taking over a sub-continent like Australia or the heart of Africa, when you're young you do have dreams, and that's what I have, wilder dreams than most of the rest. I know most of my dreams are in technicolor. . . ." This rich inner world even has its system of punishment for overindulgence. The sexual experiences he creates are filled with poetic pain, in which he hears "the raucous and rhapsodical liturgical cacophony of lust."

Meanwhile, miserably conscious of the discrepancy between this rich inner world and the sterile outer one, completely unable to fuse the two, the ego, the aware-self, clothed in a shifting self-concept, shuttles back and forth. As "Rex" (pen name for his writings) he is prince potentate of the inner world, but "Willy Lohman" from *Death of a Salesman* is consciously identified as his daily role. The two self-concepts are an unending humiliation to each other. Rex feels powerful beyond all imagining: "I have never seen a black so black; I must be about to create light, for it was never blacker; surely I am about to create God!" This proud prince cannot stand the docility of Lohman or the rejection he receives. When the drama program is criticized, the subject says, "The hell with people if they don't want to listen." After receiving a series of low grades, he declares that, not only does the university not have the answers he craves, "So far as I'm concerned, it doesn't even have the questions." Moreover, the sycophantic self is an inept servant, who cannot in fact procure the worldly gratifications the prince desires, especially wealth and women. If he were to write an index of his life, he says, besides ". . . a few pages of Nietzsche and a few of Plato . . ." there would be ". . . page after page of sex and the mishandling of it," and if any statement came out of ". . . the black years when I just lived hand to mouth . . . it would be that I needed money."

But if Lohman frustrates Rex, Rex actively threatens Lohman. The subject remarked to the therapist that he tries to keep things impersonal, but finds he injects too much of his inner self into many situations, distorting their meanings even for him. He still pushes certain thoughts from his mind because ". . . they are too dangerous." Instead of acting out his inner impulses he may slip back into the old feeling of not caring or trying—the possibility, he says, is always with him. If he yields to either side of the doubly vivid temptation, translating the inner world into reality or slipping back into irreality, he knows he will reap real worldly pain, i.e., rehospitalization, shock treatment, or at the very least deprivation of the little satisfactions he receives from intellectual self-expression. But if he stays normal, he will be punished in another way, for the existence of Rex shows up the loss of integrity in Lohman. He has thrown "smuttiness" into the poetic essays of Rex "to make them popular." He pays by loss of self. The more he conforms the less he finds Rex has to say. At one point he thought he had even given up being interested in poetry; he had lost sensitivity; things did not affect him so emotionally; he was no longer "pierced by adversity." In terms of normalcy he said he was improving, but "Every day that passes is one more day that I'm the way I don't want to be."

Thus he is at an impasse, his rich integral self sickened and betrayed by his attempt to comply with the real world as he sees it, yet too imperious to permit efficient subservience to convention. His behavior is epitomized by an episode in a chorus during high school. ". . . I never sang the part I was supposed to sing; I always sang the melody in the range that I could sing it. This was very disconcerting, I suppose, to people in the group."

He has made certain tentative efforts toward resolving his duplicity of roles. The simplest is to wear his outer self as a mere mask. At one point he was thinking of growing a goatee to hide behind. He knows his speech is often incomprehensible, and though this disturbs him occasionally, he deliberately "changes code" to keep from being understood. He feels he pushes people away to prevent close scrutiny. This attempt carries its own penalty. He confesses to recurring feelings of reference, though he rejects their reality; ". . . who the hell else thinks about you except yourself?"

At a more complicated and enduring level, the philosophy of Nietzsche seems to have appealed to him precisely because it seemed to offer a solution. He epitomized the mechanism as "The strong take from the weak and the clever from the strong." He knew himself to be clever, but he could not in fact master reality, i.e., the mechanics of making the strong give him what Rex and Lohman both want, namely, recognition, intellectual appreciation, and emotional acceptance. When he declared his genius he was hospitalized as a psychotic. Now he feels that Nietzsche himself became psychotic because of his own philosophy. He has relegated him to the inner world where real power limits don't exist. Though he still finds him irresistibly logical, as he says, "He can't do me as much damage now."

He has another solution which would be adequate if only he were a different personality. This consists of an idealized state of supernormalcy projected into the future—because he has decided that his real interests are human and not scientific he would like to teach in a high school in a small town. He would be married, in order to have children, and to have someone calm him emotionally so that he could work better, i.e., more productively in a literary sense. In a small community he feels he would have to join a church. This ideal of rural integration forms the foundation for whatever realistic vocational plan he follows. There is only one difficulty: as soon as he moves toward it he finds himself tempted to act out Rex.

Finally, the university itself offers him, at least in certain intellectual channels, a limited but real fusion of inner and outer reality, in his writing, in his drama program, in some of his long intellectual conversations. Even here he runs risks in both directions as well as deriving benefit in both. One of his programs became too esoteric and he was asked to produce it in a more conventional fashion; thus in revealing his inner world he bared himself to the charge of nonconformity even while he compromised some of his integrity to be allowed such revelation. Nevertheless his need for a social role is partially met. He has friends on a plane he can tolerate, and "You can't live without friends. . . ." He found a girl who was willing to listen to the Rex vs. Lohman idea, though he wondered why she should; he talked to a girl one night from 7 P.M. to 8 A.M. He was invited to an instructor's house for supper and showed him one of his poetic essays. "It was rather awkward because I'm not a social animal . . .," but he felt he had done relatively well in the situation. Yet, despite everything, "All in all I'm still not integrated into a society, religious or otherwise. . . . I spend a lot of time in the coffee shop and talk with many but I don't identify with any." Above all, though the university fusion works at least haltingly in the abstract realm, he feels the sexual problem still looms enormous (which indeed it does since he has channeled many other needs into it, as seen below). The university setting is no help to him here, because, he says, he cannot deal with females abstractly, even in a discussion. Thus, finally, he feels doomed to his uneasy shuttling unless and until he can solve this problem that shifts along with him, from one world to the other, tied to his self-concept in each.

Dynamics of the Personality Structure

So far we have presented the subject's own view of himself and his environment. Now, taking stock of Rex Lohman, what assessment can the clinical psychologist make?

In the first place, he is distinguished by living in thought and imagination much more than the average person. Problems he encounters in adjusting to his surroundings or satisfying his inner urges are readily handled and completely solved at this vicarious level, which in fact he prefers. His inclination is aided by his having at his disposal a fine endowment of intellect and imagination. A distinction should be made, however, between potential and functional intelligence. When alert to his surroundings, he can be very observant, capable of taking in a good many of the less obvious aspects of a situation, and retaining that to which he has been exposed. He has read widely in a variety of cultural areas, e.g., history, mythology, art, literature. In these topics he can show superior discerning judgment, originality, and creativity. He is able to think along abstract lines and has a nice feeling for theoretical reasoning.

Only under especially favorable circumstances, however, does he apply these superior intellectual qualities in a socially meaningful direction, as, for example, in producing a dramatic program acceptable to the public. Most of the time pressing personal problems are in the foreground of his mind so that he is unable to think realistically about such everyday matters as his relationships with other people, or else he makes half-hearted attempts in this direction without keeping to an objective framework for any length of time. This impairs his long-range goal-directedness. He entered college because of an adequate realization of the necessity of a college education for the life he had planned, but soon lost interest in his classes and either did not attend them or pursued his studies in accord with his interests rather than with an eye to academic requirements. He spends most of his time seeking, and to a certain extent finding, satisfaction in dreams about the world in which he would like to live.

This relative paralysis of his native ability very probably reflects the high state of tension under which he is laboring. Within the dynamics of his strivings lie acute unresolved conflicts between goals, both conscious and unconscious. At rock bottom he has a strong hunger for motherly love and care, for the secure and protected existence of a dependent child, for letting others cater to his wants. These needs, unsatisfied earlier in life, continue to occupy him though their real nature is by now so disguised that he does not recognize them. The disguise is necessary since his adult and conscious mind rejects such infantile urges as humiliating to his self-esteem. "The tyranny of having to depend on someone else for things is bad," he explains. As a reaction formation against these bothersome manifestations of childishness he has cultivated through the years an ego-ideal of personal autonomy, independence, and superiority. According to the projective material, he sees himself brilliant as Voltaire, powerful as Washington, strong as a football player, fearless as a soldier of the Roman Empire.

Fortunately, in one area of his life it is possible for him to express autonomy successfully and for real rather than fantasied rewards, namely, in the drama program mentioned before. Though he has chosen to include unrelieved dysphoric music and verse of a type not usually appealing to the college undergraduate, the high caliber of his contributions has managed to keep the program alive. Expression of his autonomy spreads more pervasively, however. Even though it threatened his educational security he rejected guidance from the Veterans Administration because it would have involved reporting himself, or otherwise submitting to supervision, and "If they're going to force me, no Lohman!"

Except for this limited intellectual outlet his contradictory strivings defeat each other; their compelling urgency on the other hand makes it impossible for him to banish them permanently, or even make them wait their turn. Because they are so deadlocked, a more or less permanent state of tension would be predicted, and it is not surprising that we find evidences of it in the test material. Life must be very uncomfortable under such constant emotional stress, as he points out. In fact he has had very little opportunity to experience the feelings of joy, anticipation, sympathy which usually accompany the manifestation of desires acceptable to the self and to one's fellow men. Instead he is driven by destructive wishes, by unrealistically high ambitions, by a hunger for nurturance, and most of all by anxiety and despair.

It might seem that the pattern described would lead to overt impulsiveness and aggressive acting out. Here again his great potential for vicarious imaginative thinking saves him by providing day-to-day release for many of his tensions. As he himself knows, in his inner world his emotions are free-flowing; here he has a right to feelings of satisfaction and attainment. When his efforts to translate needs into action are thwarted, and when his primary defense of sublimation in fantasy will not work, he can shift to a secondary set of mechanisms: first intellectualization, then suppression or evasion, and finally, as a last resort, increased repression. In using these, however, in relation to real-life situations, affect is dulled as the strivings to which it is related are covered over. Loss of emotion, though he regrets it intrinsically, is necessary to his secondary defensive system and therefore continuously reinforced by his conscious mind. For emotions expressed are dangerous; they lead to trouble with the world, and they may evoke the chaos and confusion of insanity, which he has experienced and fears more than anything.

His superego in particular is appeased by intellectualization of his feelings toward women, money, and religion. He spoke once of an ideational system concerned with problems of the finite-infinite, and the hereafter. In rejecting the latter, he feels he can reject the Christian ethic without guilt. He would feel no remorse he thinks over an unemotional sexual affair intended to allay his intellectual curiosity, and gain what he believes to be essential knowledge.

If he feels himself threatened with incipient emotional involvement, he employs conscious suppression. "I have found that if I cut off the things that trouble me I can concentrate." He could remember only two instances in several months in which he experienced real anger. Suppression seems to be the precondition for a variety of pseudo compliances, on which he bases his belief that he can adapt, that he is "a reasonable sort of duck," that he has been able to ". . . fit into whatever niche I had to, and it was usually what I want." To this he frankly adds, "and in the end I could always go my own way anyway." This happy evasive solution was manifested in near-continuous cutting of classes while he was enrolled, and was neatly underlined when he agreed to attend the Veterans Administration clinic but remarked to his therapist that "You know, and I know that I won't go." Thus his alleged adaptability seems only a very thin cover for the essential autonomy previously discussed, while evasion serves as autonomy's true primary defense.

His deeper defense of repression, supplemented by rationalization, identification, and projection, seems to operate primarily in relation to the threat of punishment. In his conscious philosophy as well as in his unconscious need system he manifests worship of raw power. He too would like to stand above the masses, as statesman, artist, philosopher, in control of himself and others. He has not told us that he hopes thereby to compensate for his own felt inferiorities, or that his true ego-ideal is Nietzsche's superman, but this seems virtually self-evident. However, it would not be necessary to have such a fantastically powerful inner self as Rex if there were not a very real and basic fear of psychological annihilation, repressed though it may be. While he retains reality testing toward the objective world, he cannot help seeing himself as a helpless, inferior creature, a pygmy before fate. He rationalizes this as a conscious fatalism, one of his favorite phrases being "That's the way the ball bounces." But his basic anxiety about himself is revealed clearly in an unstable and vague body image with symbolic overtones; he said at one time that he believed his eyes were hostile, though he didn't feel that way, and again that he had a feeling of expansion in his head plus a tic behind his ear. He worries about his health, his ideal of strength again belied by the nagging realization of weakness.

In all this, what seems to have been repressed is a conviction that to be weak is to be bad, in a superego sense. Though this seems implicit in Nietzsche's philosophy, our subject does not verbalize that aspect. He complains of the tyranny of being dependent; he does not express guilt over his dependency needs, obviously because they too are repressed. Probably they are kept so precisely because they are at the root of his weakness and hence his badness. Seemingly as a means to self-castigation, and as a way of borrowing strength against his own bad weakness, he identifies with authority, the punisher. As an extension of this, both consciously and unconsciously, he subscribes to the precept, "If you can't lick 'em, join 'em." He said he buckled under to the Army routine because he couldn't beat it. Earlier he had been attracted by various forms of militarism; "I always have been for it; I've become more liberal lately, because there's no sense fighting it." His Lohman personality seems to have had its foundation, in part at least, in this mechanism.

If the foregoing analysis of the subject's motivational and emotional make-up is correct, it becomes clear why all his relations with people must necessarily be precarious. In his essential dependency, he will want social support but will be incapable of admitting it, hence unable to share a give-and-take relationship. He himself stated at one point that he was unable to accept affection. We have said above that unearned social warmth disrupts him. He suppresses what warmth may be evoked in response. Because of his abiding resentment over his unfilled childhood hunger for mothering, and his own superego condemnation of that need, his problem of emotional warmth is particularly acute with women. In the first place, he has an intense inner hostility toward the female sex, probably aggravated by the four younger sisters who successively robbed him of the mother he so craved. In the second place, as this hostility grows he interprets his inability to handle sexual adjustment as his central frustration, which reinforces it again. The projective material abounds with attitudes toward women of frank aggression, unrestrained contempt, but also of unmistakable fear. If he is to avoid being flooded with such destructive affect, all his defenses must be used again and again. As mentioned before, he speculates about heterosexual matters in a bland, rational fashion, consciously compartmentalizing intellectually evaluative and emotionally modulated attitudes. He plays with the idea of "coldly approaching" a woman "to find out what sex is like. . . ." He thinks he may go and have an affair "to get this information first-hand. . . ." He usually admits that he does not expect to experience any emotion should he engage in such "explorations." Yet he says with real despair, "I can't continue to lead an incomplete sex life, as I have done." He does not want affective flatness. "I think there are too many things that are compartmentalized, that sex is something we put off in a corner; if we can spirit it out next Tuesday, all well and good; well, that's no good . . . certainly I think I'll lead a freer life if I take care of this business of me put away for Tuesday. . . ." Actually the three other needs which, in our culture, give ego control the most trouble, namely, aggression, domination, and possession, all seem to have been channeled into the sexual realm. His "curly head" gives him trouble because he cannot master her. He cannot get married because he lacks money. He says that he feels that if he could learn how to handle women it might solve his whole problem; symbolically he seems to be saying that if he knew the mechanics of sexual normality, somehow the conflict between dependency and autonomy, submission and power, weakness and strength could be resolved by the same formula. In actuality he has the cart before the horse. Precisely because of these problems, sexuality as a part of social relations in general is caught in the same dynamic deadlock.

Though his relation to men is somewhat less emotionally laden, it is by no means easy or spontaneous. Men represent authority to him, the authority he can neither cease to strive for nor attain. The ideal man is strong, fascinating, awe-inspiring, but distant and depersonalized. Repressed along with dependency needs, and probably bound up with them, he seems to have a strong feminine trend expressed in part by his passive-receptive attitude toward obtaining gratification. More specifically there is evidence suggesting an unconscious desire for and fear of homosexual attack. He told of a repetitive dream that "someone was chasing me—someone frightening me, and I turned around and told him that if he didn't stop I would wake up, and he didn't, and I did wake up." Consciously he specifically denies, and attempts to avoid, any such desire or identification; he says, "I may give up writing in poetic form since rightly or wrongly it's considered sissy. . . ." He was speculating at one point as to whether he should give up enjoying the works of people like Oscar Wilde and Tschaikovsky. Very probably his destructive wishes toward women are aimed as much at rooting out the weak bad woman in himself as at the significant female figures in his life.

It is no wonder, then, being forced to resist relationships with both men and women, that the subject finds himself socially isolated, suspicious, in need of a mask, plagued by feelings of reference, unable alike to compete or to experience social warmth, at times satisfied with his aloofness, and at times near despair.

Formative Factors in the History

How did the subject come to be what he is, Rex Lohman, with his own peculiar personality structure, psychological environment, and set of difficulties? Because he is currently functioning as a legally competent and self-directing adult, within the setting of a university clinic we could not seek a social history from the family without betraying the confidential relationship on which all self-referrals are predicated. However, a formal autobiographical interview at the end of the therapeutic session gave us many clues. Naturally all the information was selectively colored by his current felt needs and by his perceptions of the environment. From our point of view, many relevant influences are left out. Nevertheless, since memory itself is dynamically determined, what he gave may actually be the more directly related to his present personality.

Superficially, the family was quite normal, consisting of father, mother, a brother two years younger, four sisters following in quick succession, and then a wide gap ending with a brother. He does not tell us of any severe family discord; grandparents helped during family crises by taking the children, e.g., when the father was recovering from an automobile accident, when an uncle was injured, etc. The socioeconomic setting was also usual. They lived in a small town of about 2000, in which both agriculture and industry were prevalent, about 25 miles from a large New England city. There were no families above middle-middle class, and the subject's family moved with rising salaries after the war from upper-lower- to lower-middle-class standing. No external social stress thus complicates the dynamic picture. Rather, there were all the pressures toward normal conformity inherent in small-town structure. However, that was precisely the difficulty; the town simply did not suit the family's psychological needs, and therefore neither family nor town suited Rex Lohman's needs.

The subject gives us only a single, simple picture of the mother: she was too busy. Completely absorbed by work, she was "almost a recluse, just takes care of the house, goes out shopping, but that's all." She achieved no social integration; she did not attend church, and ". . . the old maids who ran the church [were] about the only social group . . .," thus leaving her isolated. Within the family he saw her as an ineffective force; she ". . . did what disciplining she could and then she'd always wait until the old man came home . . . she'd complain about this, she'd complain about that. After a while you couldn't stand the sound of it, all that nagging. You wondered how the old man stood it."

This father was the all-important factor in the family; the subject identified with him consciously and closely. At one and the same time he was the loved parent, the consistent parent, the feared parent, the distant parent, and the helper. Rightly or wrongly, the subject has endowed him with values, beliefs, and defenses which his own personality merely echoes.

Socially the father committed the worst sin in a small town—he was an individualist. He would "do a lot of working around the house . . . some of this was done on Sundays because it was the only day he had off, and he'd be hammering away and naturally the neighbors didn't like it but of course they were overawed by the old man's individuality anyway, and they never did complain about it. He never joined any of the local organizations, men's club, fire department, or anything like that. He figured, well, I don't think he had any strong ties to any of them, the people in the community; he must have gotten along with the people he worked with. He didn't have a lot of friends, he didn't need a lot of friends."

The father worked steadily, supporting the family through the depression and making high wages during the war as a factory foreman, but the subject says, "I know he's dissatisfied with it. I don't imagine it's very difficult." He was always ". . . trying to educate himself or prepare himself for a better job. He'd take part-time jobs in a book company to learn as much as he could . . . and after two or three years he saw he couldn't do much with it and he dumped that. Later on it was . . . a special printing outfit. He still has, I suppose, ideas about doing something with that. He still gets trade journals. . . . But it's after all as the old man said, a good many times, 'It's hell to be poor' and it certainly is . . . the only pictures you saw were on calendars." Thus the need for money was tied to cultural deprivation; there was a strong theme of upward mobility, but only in intellectual channels.

Given this general setting the patient's life probably took its basic twist when he was about 2. Unfortunately, we do not know the exact chronology, but within a year his strong father was suddenly rendered helpless by severe injuries from an automobile accident. The family lived with the grandparents while he convalesced. The mother's attentions were occupied by the birth of his first sibling, and he himself had diphtheria. Thus he was suddenly dislocated in all his infantile autism, relatively deprived of father, mother, familiar surroundings, and physical well-being. The twin themes of isolation and thwarting of dependent needs very probably had their origin during this year. Later, in the same setting, the subject was teased by being rendered helpless, and then abandoned. "I can remember the stairs, they were precarious . . . somebody had hung me up on a nail about halfway up and then came down and turned around and went out. I think I can remember someone hanging me up on a nail by the back of the neck." The sole gift he mentions was also in a sense symbolic of thwarted oral needs; his grandmother gave him a cookie tin. The only protective nurturance he recalls was when "I was very young . . . sitting on the running board of the grocery man's truck and the dog my grandmother had was barking and standing in front of the truck so it wouldn't go away. Of course the dog always barked at trucks, I don't know whether it was just because I was on the running board or not." By the time he was of school age, childish weakness seems to have been proudly but wistfully thrust behind him. "The first day of school, when I went in, there was some kid that bawled all during the day."

The family atmosphere was cool and conducive to independence. "I remember playing with the kids in the neighborhood and about two o'clock they all went off to take a nap and I was left alone because I never took a nap. I always stayed up till about midnight, too. I was always surprised that they had to go off and sleep in the middle of the day for a couple of hours. This may have been the beginning of being somewhat alone.

"I guess with six kids . . . they didn't spend much time wondering how any of them were turning out. . . . I don't think there was any particular affection there, at least not since my escape from early childhood, at least not as far back as I can remember. When the old man takes a stand, it's every man for himself anyway." As the eldest son he had responsibilities that brought him into contact with his father. "We helped around the place as much as we could . . . the rules were rather loose anyway, because after all they had enough to do to keep busy. I suppose my own individuality was able to develop by my helping the old man."

When he was asked which parent he preferred, the subject said, "I suppose I might've my father more because he was a stronger type. If he said he was going to hit you, he hit you." Punishment, which was "rather interesting when it began," involved "a rubber hose that was connected to the washing machine and it was connected with my backside a good many times, till it wore out, till the old man wore out. I don't think that with my youngest brother he's been as harsh and the result has been almost anarchy: the kid's pretty wild. I'm a firm believer in corporal punishment." On the other hand, when he was young he thought the siblings were punished more than he and he resented it because ". . . when I heard them wailing I imagined it was worse than it was." It seems fairly clear that his identification with authority as the punisher had its inception in his masochistic response to the hard emotional bargain he was forced to accept: some attention given to him, some consistency given to the world, but no warmth and no room for dependency, and this in return for worship, submission, acceptance, and identification. Thus the foundation for the passionate espousal of Nietzsche was ready made; he had lived with and loved one of the supermen; he had already agreed to forego dependency for the security of identifying with and being accepted by him.

Slowly, however, the subject has come to the realization that the father in reality does not live up to the child's giant image. He too was verbalized as a Willy Lohman. "He's always been at odds with society except for this recent capitulation to the Masons, which is perhaps understandable. I don't know; he told me to fight as long as you can and then give in." He has softened toward a younger sibling as quoted above, and ". . . he doesn't have as much energy as he had when he was younger."

Yet this distant father gave, and still gives, intellectual stimulation and support. He helped the subject plan one of his drama programs recently. He was probably responsible for the subject's early introduction to the world of literature. Though the subject played with other children, "When I was alone I thought, because it was just about the only thing I had to do. I suppose I stopped and thought more than the average; certainly I was introduced to books that were thought provoking . . . at a time when most children would be reading other types." He considered himself a quiet child.

He had a paper route and knew nearly everyone in town at one point. When he was about 12 he thought he became a hell-raiser like most children. During high school he had a small group of friends and went to the nearby town with them occasionally. "I got along with all kinds; when it came to the wits, I wasn't the funniest, and when it came to the hell-raisers I wasn't the worst offender. And yet I managed to remain in the front ranks of all the groups. . . . The only group I was shy with was women. I didn't get along with them—that's the only place I was subdued I suppose, with girls." All in all, apart from this one area, the high-school period seems the one time in the subject's life when he was socially comfortable, playing the Lohman role in the real world. Yet one wonders. The intellectual realm of Rex must have been becoming increasingly important to him judging from his interest in Nietzsche during the last year of high school. The Army hospital summary reports the patient as stating himself that he became more withdrawn after graduation, introverted, nomadic, and felt himself to be a "nervous wreck." Perhaps his high-school adjustment depended on a particular constellation of accepting people; when that dissolved, the deprivation may have been too much. We can only speculate.

There are other areas where the subject has been markedly silent. In particular we know nothing about his relations with his sisters, and about his attitude toward the brother who must have been his chief rival. Yet, on the whole, the main tendencies in his personality seem to have been accounted for. One central question remains unanswered, and probably must remain so: Why did he finally find it necessary to break with reality and what impelled him to return?

ADDENDUM

To be or not to be—this is the question our subject asks himself many times throughout this paper. The level of reality, the emotional intensity, the depth of involvement may vary, but it is still the same crucial question: Shall I be normal, i.e., play the game, accept the rules, and consequently be reduced to a sterile humdrum existence, or shall I defy this kind of world, retreat to my own ever-so-much more gratifying and richer inner kingdom, and then be called psychotic because of it?

Nietzsche likened man to a rope stretched over an abyss, and so is our admirer of Nietzsche suspended in midair, between being and not being, between health, conventionality, and tranquillity on the one side, isolation, power, and excitement on the other.

During the years in which he has struggled with this dilemma he has swung all the way to an autistic and regressive solution with consequent forced separation from society and legal "stamping" as psychotic. Subsequently he swung far enough in the reverse direction so that the hospital let him go, a university accepted him, and most recently a magazine published one of his poetic essays. He swung back a little and in the third semester had to drop out of school; however, his own initiative won him a second chance.

He has covered a wide range of possibilities and has alternated rapidly; yet these modes of adjustment should not be viewed as haphazard, but rather as genuine attempts at solution of his life problem (1, 3). In our presentation we have juxtaposed material obtained in the last month with that dating back two years, because we have not felt that there has been a real evolution of personality; he has simply been hovering over a repertory of behaviors in which chronological sequence has little meaning, trying again and again to find some fusion of existing trends. The predominance in these adjustive experiments of realistic, objectively effective solutions may be ascribed to the lucky circumstance of being in an environment that has use for sublimation and permits intellectual testing. It would seem that a schizophrenic endowed with rich and superior intelligence, a marked gift for mental creativity and for verbal facility, finds in a university setting room to work over his dilemma: in which world to be, and in which to give up being.

We have not worried ourselves and our readers throughout this paper with diagnostic speculations. Rex Lohman is a person and not a label; if we have described him accurately we believe that it becomes psychologically unimportant under what psychiatric category one might classify him. He was psychotic and now he is not. Whether he was once schizophrenic and now is normal, now schizophrenic and never normal, normal as a child and now schizoid, schizoid as a child with a temporary schizophrenic reaction, a process schizophrenic throughout his life, a simple schizophrenic on the basis of an immaturity reaction, a paranoid personality with schizoid trends—all this is somewhat tangential to the sociopsychological relationships epitomized so vividly by this case. There is continuity between his childhood and his present pattern of personality tendencies. This pattern makes psychological sense. His vacillations in adjustment are dynamically meaningful in the light of his particular personality structure.

In Rex Lohman's dilemma we see a prevalent problem of our civilization, as it were, in caricature. As F. Wickes tells us in *The Inner World of Man*, "The children had learned to conceal their phantasies from older people, but the older people had learned to conceal them from themselves. And so this inner world was a more and more deeply hidden world until to most it became almost unknown" (4, p. 4).

Similarly, Erich Fromm demonstrates aptly in *Man for Himself* how our culture encourages the "marketing orientation" in men, which puts a price on becoming "salable," on placing conformity to the accepted code above inner values and thus sacrificing one's individuality. "Our moral problem is man's indifference to himself. It lies in the fact that we have lost the sense of the significance and uniqueness of the individual, that we have made ourselves into instruments for purposes outside ourselves, that we experience and treat ourselves as commodities; the result is that we feel powerless and despise ourselves for our impotence. Since we do not trust our own power, we have no faith in man, no faith in ourselves or in what our own powers can create" (2, p. 248).

REFERENCES

1. Angyal, A. The psychodynamic process of illness and recovery in a case of catatonic schizophrenia. *Psychiatry,* 1950, *13,* 149–165.
2. Fromm, E. *Man for himself.* New York: Rhinehart & Co., 1947.
3. Jenkins, R. L. The schizophrenic sequence: withdrawal, disorganization, psychotic reorganization. *Amer. J. Orthopsychiat.,* 1952, *22,* 738–748.
4. Wickes, F. G. *The inner world of man.* New York: Henry Holt & Co., 1938.

CHAPTER FIVE

A Case with Low Back Pain

BY STARKE R. HATHAWAY

Ella Stein was born at the turn of the century into a German immigrant farm family. She had two older brothers and came to have three younger sisters. These children came at regular intervals and there was nothing unusual to report about the rest of the children. When Ella first was seen in the outpatient department of the hospital, her complaints were of the indefinite pattern that is often unofficially referred to as a sciatic or low back pain syndrome. At that time she was 35 years old. She had had one hospitalization, which seemed relatively routine and not related to the presenting problem. Aside from this there were no known previous illnesses or maladjustments of pertinent import. Ella had a few reflex inequalities and shifting hypesthesias in addition to her pain. There was a slight leukocytosis. On this symptom complex she was first admitted to the hospital and in the course of the next ten years gained a hospital chart that weighed well over five and a half pounds and was better than three inches thick in spite of the fact that there were no bulky extras included. In the course of the acquisition of this hospital record, which does not include the records of social agencies involved in her welfare, the direct and indirect monetary investment in Ella from state and county resources amounted to at least fifteen and perhaps as much as thirty thousand dollars.

Ella's more specific admission complaint featured pain that seemed to originate in the right hip and followed down the leg and upwards into the right side of the lumbar back. This complaint first developed about seven weeks before her appearance in the outpatient department.

At that time she had felt a "dull, aching pain" in the lower part of the back which came on very gradually. Previous to this she had "been feeling fine." The pain, in the next few days, crept down to her right hip joint and expanded into that seen on admission. As the pain increased, she began to drag her leg, finally took to bed, and gave up all her usual activities. She could not recall any fall, injury, or other inciting item physical or psychological in nature that would account for the onset of the symptoms.

General History and Findings

The first admission examination recorded her past physical health as having been generally good. Two years before, she had had a hospitalization which reports indicated had been rather routine. She had been admitted with acute abdominal pain and a complaint of frequent sore throat. Records from this hospitalization are not available, but she underwent a laparotomy which was performed for an "appendectomy" and "floating kidney." A tonsillectomy was also performed. According to her story, recovery was rapid and she went back to work with no residual effects.

History of the physical health by systems also disclosed nothing of note. Catamenia began at age 14 and the periods were regular, heavy, and lasted for about five days. They were accompanied by some pain in the back, but she had no serious complaints and certainly the story did not sound unusual. She was unmarried and the introitus appeared virginal. Her weight was 200 pounds, and even though her skeletal proportions were large, she appeared a little overweight. In general physical appearance she was a "peasant" type. Her features were not unpleasant but she was certainly not pretty. Her movements were, of course, greatly constrained by her pain and she usually looked unhappy, both facial expression and posture conveying this impression. Her hair was graying and she appeared to be at least five years older than she was.

Early psychological testing with the Binet, Form L, showed her intelligence to be in the upper dull-normal region. Her MMPI pattern at that time had the code 312'49—6 8; 3; 9.[1] This profile did not in-

---

[1] For those not familiar with MMPI coding, the numbers refer to the nine clinical scales numbered in order (Hs is 1, D is 2, and on to Ma, which is 9). The code is written by putting the number of the scale with the largest T score first, the one with next largest second, and so on down to T score 54. All near-average

dicate a severe neurosis but was certainly clearly of the type observed
in hypochondriacal and conversion-type hysterical cases. The *Atlas*
(2) gives diagnoses of psychoneurosis; hypochondriasis, mixed; and
hysteria, in that order of frequency. Reactive depression and suicide
are often mentioned.

Hanvik (1) found functional low back pain cases to have a mean
profile with code 1′32478— 5; 4; 16. The code of the mean profile for
organic-type low back pain was ′123— 4; 4; 14 (Hs was only 58 in
this profile). On Hanvik's low back pain scale of 25 items, Ella's score
was 18. These data strongly indicate a functional rather than an organic problem. Of course, this refinement of MMPI interpretation
was not available at the time Ella took the MMPI. Only three scales
were then in use. The L score was abnormally high, and this was possibly a significant item in the psychological picture she presented. Later
MMPI data continued to show the same general pattern through several years. The L score always remained high. No test data except the
Binet and MMPI are available on the patient.

Ella's early family history was also without distinguishing events.
Her parents were devout Roman Catholics and she attended parochial
school for all of her school days. The teaching was in German and she
never lost her Germanic accent. Although the parents were usually
able to provide sufficient food for the family, they could not always
afford suitable clothing and necessities and there were few luxuries.

The mother, a passive woman, was never mentioned by the patient
in either critical or approving manner. Apparently she was a good
housewife and approximated the cultural patriarchal tradition in her
family life. The father, in accordance with this same tradition, was strict
but just. Neither parent had had much education and they are likely to
have been intellectually dull. The patient was never severely punished
although she was deeply inculcated with rules of conduct and, in mat-

---

scales are omitted from the code. After the dash the numbers of low T scores are
arranged from lowest upward to the average range. Scales with identical T scores
are underlined. Those within average range are omitted. A prime shows the point
in the order where 70 T score is located. Following the code the three validity
scores are given in raw score form in the order L; F; K. The first code given therefore signifies that that MMPI profile had the Hy, Hs, and D scales above 70 T
score. Of these Hs and D scores were equal but less than Hy. Pd and Ma scores
were in descending order from 70 down toward 54. Pa was below 46 and the other
three scales had values within the average range 46 to 54. For more detail on coding see the *Atlas* (2).

ters of interpersonal relationships, developed into a shy person who described herself as "kind of left out" in all social and especially in heterosexual activities. She pungently says of the family that they ". . . got up and worked and went to bed." She was kept out of school at times to catch up on the farm work, and it was expected of her and of her sisters as well as of the older brothers that they assume considerable responsibility about the farm. The patient, being large and strong, was frequently assigned to heavy outdoor work which she found burdensome. Her brothers were "mean" to her; according to her story, they considered her lazy and stubborn—an unjust description, she felt. She had no dates and no social life during this time but remembers that she wanted to be a nurse or a teacher.

At age 7 Ella started school in a one-room schoolhouse attached to the church. With difficulty she continued to the sixth grade, where she failed. After repeating this grade, she went into the seventh, failed again, and being of legal age to quit school she stopped and worked full time on her father's farm. During the five years from about age 15 to age 20, the patient continued working on the farm but was never happy. She began to "work out" on a neighboring farm. Religious responsibilities added to her unhappiness. Explaining "they were too strict about confession," she said that she often shook before a confession and afterwards the priest would scold her. At the same time she stated that she had never had any real sins to confess, she had had no heterosexual experience, and it was never clear to the examiners what the sins were for which she was scolded. She gave the general explanation that she was "too restless to settle down and didn't want to be told how to behave."

At age 20 Ella finally left home. Answering an advertisement, she went to another farm as a housekeeper. Shortly after this she gave up her association with the Catholic Church. Her family wrote her "mean" letters about her break, she reported. She never again returned to live with her family, protesting later that they were too poor to support her. There appeared to be no deep ties to any one of the family members although she kept in touch with a sister who had become a nun. She sometimes felt guilty at having abandoned her childhood church affiliation but became active in a small local Protestant church and appeared not unusually preoccupied with religion considering her background. She worked for one family for eight years. Ella was always well liked and apparently a hard worker. As mentioned above, this period seemed in retrospect to have been one of relatively good adjustment in all ways, considering her intelligence and training. In the latter portion of these years she accepted a job with a widowed farmer. This man had several children and she assumed full responsibility in the house. It was after a few months on this job that she went to the hospital for her first operation, the appendectomy and "floating kidney" repair. After the surgery she returned to the same farm and worked until the onset of the incapacity introducing the present illness, continuing there for a while as an increasingly dependent person to the point of the present admission.

As has been stated above, she had had very little active social experience although she was often a passive or auxiliary participant. Her first close association with a man occurred at about the time she left home, when she "was going with" a man who asked her to marry him. They were apparently rather congenial although he never put his arm around her or kissed her during the whole association. She started a hope chest and was fully expecting that she would be married, but on one occasion the man became very drunk, was abusive to his sisters, and fell into a drunken stupor. This so repelled the patient that she "gave him up." She said that in the next years there were no heterosexual contacts that she could remember although she often accompanied families for whom she worked to shows or other social events. When she was about 30, she went for six months with another man, a bachelor. He never kissed her or put his arm around her. In relating this she described herself as bashful and as ". . . a little cold on that line." Apparently no dramatic item interrupted this unexciting alliance; they simply did not progress with it and one may assume that the man found her not interesting.

She disclaimed any romantic attachment to the widower with whom she last worked. Actually there was no way to establish with certainty what this relationship was beyond her own statement. The man did marry during the time of Ella's first hospitalization of the present series. It did not appear unlikely, however, that she may have suppressed her feelings toward him and that in occupying the place of the dead wife she had seen herself as a well-established housekeeper. He may not have been inclined to give her encouragment or she may have been so shy and seemingly cool that he was never attracted to her.

Ella's manner was friendly, and examiners noted in her neither defensiveness nor hostility. She preferred to talk of her pains and continually repeated with great seeming sincerity that she would do *anything* to get well; that the only thing she wanted was to be self-supporting again. Her pain had made her dependent on others and this was humiliating and intolerable to her. She made a good hospital patient. With other women, especially those of her intellectual and socioeconomic level, she formed very good relationships and was usually waited upon willingly. An excerpt from a letter directed to the psychologist will tell much about her manner of speech and stream of thought: "I don't feel well at all today. My body ache so again. (*sic*) When I feel like this I don't care, for any thing. I have so much pain. . . . When I get this bad. I do wish something could be done. Instead going on like this. I been so discourage today. I can hardly make myself do anything. I feel sometimes there is no use. I been trying hard to keep going, and keep my courage up. Sometimes I can hardly stand it." In interviews, this kind of material was about all one could get. In spite of her emphasis of it, depression did not seem to be the dominant symptom except in reaction to the pain.

The complaint pattern and neurological findings, although inconclusive, led from the outpatient study to inpatient hospital admission for further evaluation. This admission turned out to be the first of ten admissions to the same hospital without inclusion of many interim outpatient visits.

Course of the Illness

The first evaluation led to a laminectomy in which the lumbar spinal canal was opened and some portion of the ligamenta flava excised. It was noted during the operation that although injection studies of the spinal canal had indicated that there was a prolapsed disc, direct examination of the site disclosed no apparent abnormality.

Following this operation her pains lessened somewhat, but within a few months they were so severe that her spinal canal was again opened. Further exploration was carried out and a little additional ligament was removed. Again the pains returned, and at the end of this hospitalization a cast was put on to immobilize her spine. Discharged with some relief, in a few weeks she was readmitted with return of essentially the same symptomatic pattern. This time the cast was removed and the incision was opened for the third time to carry out a fusion of several of the lumbar vertebrae. This fusion was successful but as usual the symptoms were relatively unaffected.

Returning to the farm where she had last worked, she learned of her employer's marriage and found the new wife to be cold and jealous. Her pains and general inability to work continued. In the successive hospitalizations she was treated in various other clinics. Dilatation and curettage and other gynecological procedures disclosed no convincing abnormality of the genital or endocrine systems.

These extensive physical procedures consumed about three and a half years. Finally she was admitted to the psychiatric ward. She received her first psychological work-up at that time and was positively recognized to be neurotic although the neurologists and neurosurgeons continued to feel that her condition was also in part due to some pathology in the spinal cord or its connections. Consequently during this admission the spinal canal was opened for the fourth time and a chordotomy was performed. This successfully cut the nerve fibers of the pain and temperature pathway from the right leg. Her symptoms still remained, and as a first active recognition of her neurotic illness she was discharged to stay in a rest home and entered into a group psychotherapeutic class that met several times a week.

The condition continued on much the same level and in the next four years Ella had as many more hospitalizations. She wore a brace for the last two of these years, and various other forms of psychotherapeutic and organic endeavor were undertaken. On the second of this series of admissions to the psychiatric hospital she was scheduled for the fifth major operative procedure on her back. It was intended that posterior radiotomy would be performed at several levels. The full recognition of the extent of her psychoneurosis, however, led to the alternative decision to really give her an intensive psychotherapeutic trial. She was still almost constantly bedridden and appeared a hopelessly dependent invalid.

This intense psychotherapeutic approach was initiated by a review of her history and by long, though not very fruitful, interviews. Several things stood out clearly. She was strongly characterized by moral rejection of any self-concept making her out to be an ill person except as would relate to demonstrable physical illness with organic findings. She seemed to genuinely wish to recover and to work, although she desired more interesting work that she had done before. She wanted a husband and children but felt this to be hopeless. All professional personnel concerned with her were briefed and continually informed about the intended therapy and all played parts in its effectiveness.

The more active therapy was initiated with rather painful faradic stimulation of the lumbar back and strong suggestive procedures that succeeded in a short time in getting her up and out of bed. She would proceed along the wall of the hallway leaning against the wall, gasping, and appearing in great pain. A number of observers independently pointed out that this pathetic picture was definitely less marked when she did not know that she was being observed. The staff was sympathetic but firm with her; they particularly refrained from waiting on her although she strongly evoked this impulse in nearly everyone. In the next two years she was given a great deal of psychotherapeutic attention. Various approaches were used. She was a laconic person who talked briefly and who could never be gotten to free-associate or coöperate more than passively in a verbal exchange. She dreamed only of banal topics that led nowhere. This lack of verbal color did not stem so much from resistance as merely from the restricted educational and social background and her dull intellectual level. Always friendly and coöperative, she would accept almost any plan for her betterment and appeared to be strongly motivated to get well. It was probably this factor that had kept her so long under organic treatment. She always fitted the lay observer's concept of a person suffering from an organic type of pain.

With the continued psychotherapeutic approach, her invalidism was arrested, not so much by any resolution of conflicts that one could discover as by marshaling all of her early inculcated attitudes to drive her toward making a more active struggle against her condition. That is, she was, on the one hand, led to see herself as whining and dependent and, on the other, gently exhorted to fight to take, with patient therapeutic help, the little forward steps that were necessary for her daily to increase her activities. It was always accepted that she would suffer from pain all the time, but it was pointed out to her that it did no good to relate this over and over, since everyone was aware of the matter. On the other hand, great value was placed on her becoming interested in things and actively attempting to get herself out of her dependent habits and social isolation. During all of this time depression was more marked than it had been; she cried frequently, often waking up in tears. It was recognized that she felt very inferior about her poor schooling; clearly her level of aspiration exceeded her actual capacities, and these she had not developed. During the period of treatment she was encouraged to study grammar, and she engaged in long practice sessions of writing and reading which were intended to improve her educational level. These efforts did lead to enough achievement to give her some satisfaction and make her a little more interesting in ways not connected with her illness.

To support herself Ella began to do piecework for a local garment factory; and although she needed some county help to support her in a rest home, she managed to make a little money and became gradually almost self-supporting. She never lost her complaints, however, and was almost wholly unable to do anything that required that she move about on her feet. She used crutches for a large part of the time. The results of the psychotherapy were in some ways meager, but at any rate the scheduled operation was never necessary and other costly hospitalizations were certainly prevented. Possibly more important, she was up out of bed and was no longer a helpless, bedridden invalid.

This general state of affairs continued for three or four years. When she was 45 years old, the welfare board received a letter from her which stated that she would no longer need to be helped. Characteristically, the letter contained profuse thanks for their help, but it gave no reason for her change in status. Until the present time she disappeared from our records. The illness from beginning to end occupied a total of ten years. Until the last note in the records, the pattern of her verbally described symptoms had remained relatively the same (modified, of course, by some changes due directly to the operative procedures). She still complained of back pain, radiating down her leg, and these pains were incapacitating so that she felt she could not work and this in turn resulted in depression. Of course the verbal complaint pattern was now in considerable contrast with her actual activities. She had effectively improved in other respects.

About six years after the last contact a follow-up study disclosed the denouement. During the last year of what we are calling her illness period, Ella had been living at a boarding home where she was, for much of the time, confined to a chair. Apparently in this home she made the acquaintance of a man who worked in a grocery store. They married, and it was at this time that she wrote the letter to the welfare agency. In the years following the marriage Ella had become increasingly better. She complained less and began to walk more freely and she is now doing her own housework and seems to be completely rehabilitated. The couple is harmonious, and a year or two after marriage they qualified for adoption of a child of seven years of age whom they are bringing up. Another bit of information obtained is that Ella has dropped out of all the church activities.

Discussion

A colleague has said, "Every case history book should have one of this type." Ella's story is not greatly different from that of many other patients with low back pain or related syndromes. Even when a program of psychotherapy is instituted early, it is usually protracted and costly. From the earliest outpatient contacts one finds that Ella's illness was recognized as having a "functional" component. The neurological findings, however, were intriguing although certainly not definitive. Her constant emphasis upon a wish to get well and her attribution of the depressive features to the physical disability seemed to be an adequate background for her invalidism and made her always an appealing patient for the neurosurgeon and internist. It is impossible today to estimate in what degree the symptoms may have been related to pathological factors commonly called organic. She improved after every operation, and injections in the region of the sciatic nerve tended also to give her relief. But always the relief was short-lived. The vigorous psychotherapeutic push that was initiated after she had taken to bed as a nearly helpless invalid did not greatly alter the basic symptom pattern and had to be considered successful only to the extent that it made her partially self-supporting and able to take care of her physical needs.

One could at this point criticize Ella's early treatment by pointing out that, although a psychological component was recognized at once, the treatment was nevertheless almost wholly directed at the assumed organic aspect—and the psychological element was permitted to continue for several years without a really convincing approach having been made to this aspect of her illness. She, like many patients, also early recognized factors of great importance in such psychological components as might exist in the disorder. Although she disclaimed symptoms of erotic deprivation, she was, in her own self-concept and as seen by the therapists, a person who would be expected to make a good adjustment as a housewife and mother. Yet, appealing as this lead seemed to be, there appeared little chance that anything could be done about it. She was not an attractive person and her relatively low intelligence and poor educational background did not lend luster to her physical and psychological attributes. It appears as a quite unusual outcome that she should have found a spouse with whom she could establish a compatible relationship at so late a period in life. Nevertheless, she did so, and the evidence is strong that her previous fair adjustment to life was restored in the beneficent light of the marriage.

It is intriguing to speculate upon the items illustrating the applicability of such terms as physical or organic treatment, psychotherapeutic treatment, environmental manipulation, and "experiments of nature" as these might be applied to the phases and stages in Ella's illness. When follow-up studies are made tracing the outcomes of psychotherapy and the outcomes of control cases that have not received psychotherapy, the data are often rather discouragingly indicative of little differentiation. It is quite possible that Ella's case gives some hint as to the reason for these findings. A minority of all persons who develop definite neurotic symptoms are identified as ill by asking for treatment from some recognized professional source. A great many unidentified patients accept their symptoms as best they can, or the brunt of the disability is carried by family and friends who accept it as having an organic basis. After the condition has lasted for a time, some internal process of healing or some change in the environment contributes the magic quality that permits recovery. This also happens to a large number of patients who do come for treatment but who receive little effective help. In a sense this means that the controls and other non-treated cases in a follow-up study have all been treated. The difference between the groups is mostly from artificial selection of the kind and name of treatment, professional or otherwise, and involving psychotherapy or organotherapy.

It is a matter for legitimate question whether we are sufficiently advanced to adequately understand and prescribe for cases like Ella's —whether our professional methods or concepts of the proper procedures are more effective in determining outcome than the highly varied environmental stimuli that play upon the person. These varied social and material events of the patient's daily life may ultimately strike a responsive note in him and lead him to recovery. He inherits money, gets a job, falls in love, gets a divorce, finds a deep faith in a patent medicine, or any one of a countless succession of powerful psychological events.

Speculation about the psychological background of Ella's illness must be based upon very uncertain data. Her home background was never found to have been particularly abnormal.. It is interesting that her siblings made an acceptable adjustment to life without known psychological upset. Although the marginal farm and first-generation immigrant background from which Ella came is known to contribute more than its proportion in the general population to the number of neurotics and psychotics in mental institutions, these factors are not definitive enough to be convincing.

It is easy to establish that Ella very early revolted against the heavy work and onerous religious demands. Quite out of line with her intellectual level she early aspired to be a professional woman, even after she had failed in school. This aspiration to rise above what seemed to be her basic capacities was a marked feature of her later psychological picture. One could say that the illness provided a respite in which she could be free of the direct responsibility to measure up to her self-concept; this also could be said of her desire to get married. It might be emphasized that the moderately strong psychopathic deviate component, characteristic of her early MMPI profile, was exemplified in her ability to leave the family and religion, apparently without great stress, and that other features of her illness displayed a certain amount of psychopathy.

Maloney (4) has suggested a relationship between "spinelessness" and the low back pain syndrome. Low back pain becomes a symptom of undigested submissiveness that has its roots in childhood fears. "The low back pain syndrome for the most part, then, is a physical attitude, a physical voice, a charade, which speaks louder than words. It says simply: 'I am a weak fellow, I can't stand up against reality. I must be coddled and babied. I don't dare become active or successful.' More simply: 'I am a weak-backed person.'" If Ella's complaints had this origin, they would seem to have occurred like the explosion of a time bomb. She should have had trouble earlier.

For those who are intrigued by the effects of repressed hostility, she makes a satisfactory example. A difficulty, however, is that such hostility was never at any time elicited in any form that could be clearly identified, and certainly there was no evidence that her ultimate recovery was an outcome of her having learned to express hostility. Again, it is quite obvious that her early moral and religious training led to the suppression or repression of free erotic expression. This could be thought of as a background for the development of the illness when she came to middle age and failed to marry the man who could make it possible for her to assume the role of wife and mother. Her denial of romantic interest in this man cannot be lightly dismissed; it was apparently sincere but could be considered as a distortion necessary to cover her frustration. At any rate the outcome of her case would appear to lend credence to this line of thought. It is important to recognize that neither the outcome nor the psychotherapeutic approaches would differ very markedly whatever one may believe about the causation of her illness. Psychotherapeutic procedures were very stringently limited in variety by her poor language facility and generally low level of interpersonal responsiveness. She herself would describe her reactions to therapeutic sessions by saying that she sat "like a bump on a log." With this the therapist could usually fervently agree. She always disclaimed suppressing anything during such sessions. Usually she said, and she appeared to be stating a fact, that she just sat there and "didn't think about much."

ADDENDUM

Back pain probably has been a problem to man since he assumed his upright stance, if not before, but the low back pain syndrome as a common, disabling aspect of psychological maladjustment has become an increasingly prominent problem in modern medicine. Every generation is marked by its peculiar pattern of frequency distribution among various psychosomatic disorders. Low back pain is a high-frequency item in the present day. In part such changes in popularity of syndromes are an outcome of advances in medical science. The low back pain syndrome may have been much facilitated by the recognition of the prolapsed disc and of other abnormalities of the spinal canal that lead to symptoms which can, in spectacular cases, be completely relieved by surgical intervention. Surgery itself has been greatly improved, and the surgeon dares to perform laminectomies, rhizotomies, leukotomies, and other cuts that were impossible in the preceding generation. With the development of such new skills, iatrogenic factors are bound to contribute to the syndromes that fit at all into the new and popular diagnostic categories. Early examinations and discussions in the presence of a patient obviously contribute to the patient's self-concept and, in what is broadly called suggestive influence, contribute to the expressed form of the symptoms and the emphases of their extent and quality.

Relative to such cases, Noyes (5, p. 438) says, ". . . If emotional disorders are mis-identified or mistreated as organic diseases the tendency of such disorders will not be toward recovery but toward chronicity. If, too, some incidental organic pathology is found the patient's anxiety is very apt to become fixed on the system involved. It should be remembered, also, that repeated tests and examinations tend to fix the idea in the patient's mind that he must certainly have a 'physical' illness, probably a mysterious one. He will then even more resist the idea that emotions may have had any part in the production or perpetuation of his illness." The patients exhibit an exceedingly stubborn resistance to acceptance of psychological mechanisms as important factors in their illnesses. This "organic mindedness" is almost always present and could account for the choice of symptom. Because of the patient's need to believe in an organic pathology, these iatrogenic influences are practically unavoidable and cannot be effectively dealt with by attempting to eliminate them at their source. A more profitable approach probably lies in the early, frank recognition of such possibilities in every susceptible patient and the coördinate institution of psychological management to offset a specialization in the organic approach that might encourage the distortion.

One useful suggestion for treatment comes from the foregoing point on "organic mindedness." It is frequently necessary for the psychotherapist to provide a final organic "face saving" if the patient is to recover. Another patient with a history similar to Ella's also became physically more active and generally much improved by psychotherapeutic work, but she likewise clung tenaciously to her symptoms. Finally, as a concurrent procedure, she went to another clinic where she was told that menopause (already far along) should be facilitated by X-ray. This procedure led to a marvelous recovery. The psychotherapist felt justified in claiming considerable credit although the patient, true to form, considered her belief in an organic cause to be finally and triumphantly vindicated. It may be argued by some that the issue should have been uncompromisingly fought on psychological grounds because the essential mechanism was in part intact or even strengthened. Expediency dictated otherwise. A two-year follow-up finds this patient also free of complaints (except for a belt of anesthesia resulting from a rhizotomy). Incidentally, this more recent patient was scheduled for lobotomy when active psychotherapy was begun.

A broad treatment program is proper even though the illness is clearly attributable to an organic type of disorder. Kraines (3, p. 349) says, "Thus a patient with a chronic and painful condition such as gout will tend to be irritable and have explosive outbursts, while his perhaps more intense suffering from a fracture of a wrist may in no way influence his reaction. Persistent stimulation of the cerebral centers by painful impulses will, however, soonor or later disturb the patient's personality."

Ella's case is presented to illustrate the difficulties in both the diagnosis and the treatment of these patients. Too often psychological study leads only to an elaboration of the mechanisms that the patients seem to be using and suggests little in the way of effective or practical therapeutic procedures. The unlovely and less verbal patient is repeatedly assessed, diagnosed as neurotic, given some half-hearted psychological help, then again abandoned. The fact that psychotherapists are such verbal persons means frustration by such patients. The patient who objects vigorously to the psychological approach is only too anxious to get back to the internist, neurologist, or surgeon. If Ella had been a recent patient, she would probably have had shock therapy and a lobotomy.

This case history does not suggest much to advance the effectiveness of psychological treatment. The main lesson is that we should make earlier positive diagnoses of the psychological illness and institute a vigorous program, mobilizing *all* professional contacts with the patient. In this way we may avoid the common errors due to independent and inconsistent management by different specialties. It is the psychiatric staff that should most appropriately assume responsibility for this coördination.

REFERENCES

1. Hanvik, L. J. MMPI profiles in patients with low back pain. *J. consult. Psychol.*, 1951, *15*, 350–353.
2. Hathaway, S. R., and Meehl, P. E. *An atlas for the clinical use of the MMPI*. Minneapolis: University of Minnesota Press, 1951.
3. Kraines, S. H. *The therapy of the neuroses and psychoses*. Philadelphia: Lea & Febiger, 1948.
4. Maloney, J. C. The effort syndrome and low back pain. *J. nerv. ment. Dis.*, 1948, *108*, 10–24.
5. Noyes, A. P. *Modern clinical psychiatry*. Philadelphia: W. B. Saunders Co., 4th ed., 1953.

CHAPTER SIX

Acute Paranoid Schizophrenia in a Veteran[1]

BY EDWIN S. SHNEIDMAN

The editors of this volume have charged each participant with the task of contributing "a description of a total functioning personality . . . [and] integration of materials obtained from the subject by various diagnostic methods with events in the life history to form a consistent picture of how the person got to be the way he is." This is a laudable goal, and a difficult one. There are at least three problems which must be faced in presenting such a case study:

1. *The problem of communicating the "flavor" of the particular case.* This involves conveying the patient's unique features—the "style of the man" as the characteristics which give his life its particular "stamp" and which distinguish him from all other persons.

2. *The problem of accuracy or validity.* In standard medical dictionaries an *anamnesis* is defined as (a) the faculty of memory and (b) the past history of any particular case. These two aspects of the definition are sometimes combined so that the anamnesis is thought of as the patient's own report (from his memory) of his condition up to the time of his illness (or up to the present). In this sense, the anamnesis is contrasted with the case history, wherein sources other than (or

[1] Appreciation is expressed to Seymour Pollack, M.D., and to Phillip A. Goodwin, Ph.D., who, as part of a larger project (supported by a research grant from the National Institute of Mental Health, United States Public Health Service) being conducted by Kenneth B. Little, Ph.D., and the present writer, obtained the anamnestic and psychological test data, respectively.

in addition to) the patient are used. Both the anamnesis and the case history raise the questions of the "truthfulness" (validity) and of the "repeatability" (reliability) of the data. It is well to realize that the anamnestic and case history protocols are not "facts" but, like their psychological test brethren, reports filtered by systematic perceptual, memorial, and other distortions.

3. *The problem of the possible confusion of cause and effect.* One must continually remind oneself that association and causation are not the same. For example, if an individual has had a rejecting mother and also later develops paranoid schizophrenia, this does not prove that the former caused the latter—although many, the present writer possibly included, would tend to assume that it did.

Orientation

A word to the reader about the writer's orientation is in order. Schizophrenia is a mysterious malady: we do not know how to cure it; we do not know what causes it; we do not even know what it is! This means that while clinical practitioners are forced to attempt to do practical things, researchers must continue to isolate the identity, etiology, and treatment of the disorder(s). At the present state of our knowledge, the only possible answer to such a question as "What are the causes of schizophrenia?" is "We do not know." This writer's personal preference is a psychological interpretation. In the following case history the possible hereditary, biological, morphological, and physiological factors in the etiology of this particular man's disorder will not be emphasized. They certainly may be there, but the choice in this case is to highlight the important psychological events (and their sequelae) that were involved. The basic psychological orientation will be one that emphasizes the unconscious meaning to the patient of important (to him) psychological events and his defensive reactions to them. We will take the view that mental status (to include both mental health and mental disorder) can be understood in terms of what has happened to the individual's striving for four basic psychological goals. These "four freedoms" are as follows:

1. *Freedom from rejection.* This is the basic striving. Every person wants to be loved. We often settle for less, but the goal is the same. We dilute or sublimate or distort or pervert the goal so that it comes out as striving for status, or grades, or prestige, or acclaim, or notoriety, or

attention, but basically each person wants to be accepted for himself —for "his own dirty, snotty little self."

2. *Freedom from anxiety, guilt, and fear.* We strive for equilibrium —homeostasis, if you wish. We are uncomfortable with psychological discomfort. Anxieties, guilts, and fears are the results of conflicts. We strive for freedom from this state. We try to resolve our conflicts. There are, unfortunately, psychotic and neurotic, as well as "normalic," ways to resolve conflict.

3. *Freedom from emotional impoverishment.* We love those who accept and comfort and succor us; we hate those who reject and thwart us. Anyone who is close to us—like a parent—does both. It is fine to say, "Mother, I love you," but not so acceptable to say, "Mother, I hate you." Yet both may be genuine feelings, one as honest as the other. The individual needs freedom to be able to "love deeply and to hate wisely." He needs freedom to be unafraid to form interpersonal relationships.

4. *Freedom from traumatic awareness of oneself.* One of the important functions of the personality is to protect itself from itself. In psychotherapy the magic mirror is held up to the naked unconscious *tachistoscopically* in a benign environment; if the individual were forced by exigencies of fate to look at too much of his repressed self he would run screaming into an extreme adjustment—suicide or psychosis. This may explain why so many paranoid schizophrenics appear to possess an almost uncanny ability to verbalize deep unconscious material and to understand the latent meanings in the behavior of others.

Let us now see how the lifelong search for these four psychological freedoms applies in this present case.

The Case of Elvin

The present case is meant to be an example of paranoid schizophrenia. Although this case illustrates many of the classical hallmarks of this disorder, it is also atypical in certain ways. In addition, it should be emphasized that it represents an early acute stage of previously untreated paranoid schizophrenia. Thus it presents a picture of the disorder in something of its pristine form, uncontaminated by the effects of, for example, electroshock treatment, the effects of having been (chronically) psychotic for a long period of time, or the effects of long-term psychiatric hospitalization.

Description of the Subject

Our subject—whom we will call Elvin—is a 24-year-old, single, white, native-born male. His maternal ancestry is Scotch-Irish; his paternal ancestry is Dutch and English. He is Protestant and is more than moderately religious in attitude and observances. He has no regular occupation, in that he entered the military service after completing high school. He has worked at several odd jobs for relatively short periods of time. A "verbal portrait" of him, as he appeared at the time he was admitted to a psychiatric hospital, is presented in Portrait 1.

Portrait 1: The Patient

Elvin is a handsome young man. He is well developed and well nourished and appears to be a few years older than his stated age. He has brown hair, hazel eyes, and a fair complexion. He is five feet, eight inches tall and weighs approximately 165 pounds. He has small hands and small feet. Elvin looks like a "clean-cut American boy." His hair is crew-cut. Typically, he is neatly dressed in clean, pressed denim slacks and a clean white shirt. His shoes are clean and relatively new, but not shined. He wears no tie. His hair is combed and his fingernails are clean.

He has a somewhat anxious facial expression. Elvin is pleasant toward people but is extremely anxious and tense and at times mildly agitated. His face flushes easily, he perspires readily, especially about the hands and forehead, and he has a moderately fine tremor of the hands. He often appears tearful and during interviews will occasionally break down and cry. He is not blocked in his speech, although his motor activity seems somewhat retarded.

The patient speaks in a very low monotone. He is coöperative and shows no overt hostility. His conversation appears connected and coherent except on a few occasions when there was a marked pressure and tension; then mild confusion becomes evident. Often he appeared to be depressed and on questioning he admitted he was depressed. He seemed, at least in part, to realize that this depression was intrinsic—from within him. Although he gives a history of auditory hallucinations, he does not show active hallucinations at this time. He appears fully oriented in all spheres and shows no obvious memory defects. He has partial insight and his judgment is fair. He is concerned about some of the patients in the hospital because he felt they were looking at him and spying on him.

(For a complete "album" of portraits of Elvin—from his baby picture to the present—the reader is referred to the "Chronological History" below.)

Presenting Problem

Although the patient's premilitary service adjustment showed no frankly bizarre features, he appeared to be somewhat withdrawn and showed something of a schizoid adjustment. At the age of 20, prior to his entry into military service, he already gave evidence of mild confusion, irritability, restlessness, and inability to plan for the future. He entered military service in 1950 and for the first six months appeared to make a satisfactory adjustment. From the beginning of his overseas duty in 1951 he began to show increasing confusion with bizarre personal experience. He felt that he was subjected to excessive and undue stress and responsibility by his military duty. Feelings of unreality developed. He was struck by the "awesome" beauty of his surroundings and felt that he had been there previously, whereas in reality this was not so. He became frightened by these feelings and also frightened by a premonition of events which seemed to occur in the manner and on the dates he had forecast, and he felt somehow that he had influenced these events and experiences. Following a homosexual experience in late 1951 and the psychiatric hospitalization of his best friend with hallucinations and bizarre ideas (the patient recognized him as frankly psychotic), the patient became increasingly more confused and frightened. He developed marked headaches, ringing in the ears, depression with fears of suicidal ideas, increased feelings of anger and resentment at the position which he held in military service, difficulties in thinking and concentrating, and a marked increase in nervousness and irritability. He was troubled with many conflicting ideas and was in a constant turmoil because of inability to commit himself to any action, weighing everything carefully and being unable to act. He began to have auditory hallucinations, specifically experiences of hearing people call him names and especially when he was in crowds. He also developed delusions that people were making critical remarks about him, looking at him, and talking about him. He suffered from insomnia, lost weight, and developed emotional instability with crying episodes.

He entered a military hospital but was discharged in two months and returned to active duty. Three months later, he returned to the hospital with an exacerbation of his difficulties: he was very suspicious of those about him, very anxious and tense, doubting his sanity and much more depressed. He was given a medical discharge in 1952. After a few months the patient came to live with his mother and became even more upset as a result of her difficulties with the stepfather. The anxiety state increased; he developed heart consciousness, palpitations, and chest pains in the heart area. He felt light-headed as if he were constantly febrile. The headaches became much more severe, and with these symptoms the patient applied for treatment at an outpatient clinic from which he was referred to the psychiatric hospital for admission and treatment.

Home in Which Patient Was Raised

The home consisted of Elvin's father, mother, older brother, and himself. "Verbal portraits" of the father, mother, and brother are presented in Portraits, 2, 3, and 4, respectively. The home was maternally dominated. The general reputation of the father is that of a chronic alcoholic who never adequately supported the family. The mother is much more critical of the father than is the patient. The patient says that the mother had complained that the father was completely unsatisfactory in his paternal and marital roles, whereas the patient himself feels that, although the father was a chronic alcoholic, he was "driven to drink" by the mother. The father was fairly wealthy prior to the financial crash of 1929, but he lost his money at that time and subsequently wandered throughout many of the midwestern states with the family doing varied jobs. The mother supported the family from the time of the patient's birth through the following years. The family moved very often until 1943, and the patient attended approximately twenty different schools during his childhood and adolescence. The home was apparently filled with sub-manifest tension produced by the father's alcoholism and lack of financial support and the mother's authoritarian, domineering, and nagging behavior. In the patient's early life he felt the mother to be quiet-mannered and self-controlled; only recently has he recognized her as having been temperamental and emotionally labile. The mother is described as being less warm than the father, and neither parent was considered to be affectionate and demonstrative. After many moves the family settled in a fairly large city in 1943, when the patient was 13 years old. They remained there for almost two years. This period was described by the patient as the happiest years of his life. They were certainly the most settled physically. During his childhood and adolescence the patient contributed to the family's support by doing odd jobs. Although his family was poor, and the patient had very little spending money, at no time were they destitute and there were always adequate funds for clothes and food. Late in 1945, when the patient was 15, the mother and father separated after the mother told the father to leave. The father at this time was in poor health and in very low spirits. The patient definitely identified with and felt drawn toward the father but remained with the mother. The father died in the downtown section of the city six months later of a heart attack accompanied by chronic alcoholism. The patient continued to live with the mother until the age of 19, when he moved into an apartment with three other schoolmates. He continued to support himself while he attended college and then at the age of 20 enlisted in military service.

Portrait 2: The Father

Elvin's father was a surveyor who died at the age of 52 of chronic alcoholism and heart disease when Elvin was 15 years old. He was of Dutch descent. His forebears had lived in the United States for two generations. He was described as tall, rather heavy set, distinguished— a good-looking man, powerful and robust. He was self-taught, with very little formal education. As a young man he was always attracted to adventure. He was not religious. He "lived and played hard." He was considered by the patient and the mother as self-willed, but also as affectionate and interested in the children. According to Elvin, his father preferred Elvin's older brother to him. According to the mother, the father was a charming man when sober; but when drunk (which was quite often), he was physically and verbally abusive to her and physically abusive to the children. The latter was denied by the patient; Elvin has a friendlier and favorable memory of his father.

The father married the mother in 1928 when he was 34 years old. He began to drink heavily following the financial crash of 1929. Until the father left home he worked for many different engineering firms as a surveyor and also took many odd jobs such as carpenter's helper, handyman, etc. The patient felt that the father was not the violent abusive man pictured by the mother, and that he was abused by the mother in her nagging, demanding, and domineering manner. She also constantly restricted the father's activities. Although Elvin described a few instances when the father appeared to be threatening the children, he felt he was never fearful of his father and never very angry with him. Elvin was aware of family dissension and marital discord from early life. He described his father as a man easily angered but one whose anger was reduced after its expression. The father had a full personal life and had friends in his own circle. However, he did not mingle with the mother's friends and spent very little time with the patient or his brother. When he was at home he spent most of his time alone. The patient recalls very few specific events when the father spent time with him.

Portrait 3: The Mother

Elvin's mother is 47 years old and is a teacher in a private elementary school. In the evenings she does tutoring and baby-sitting. She is described as being in fairly good health, although she calls herself ailing, without citing specific complaints. Her family was of English stock and her ancestors had lived in Pennsylvania from the early 1800's. She is a Protestant with metaphysical leanings and a very strict conscience. She is described as a restrained, cool, moderate, not affectionate or demonstrative woman, who has a martyr complex and likes to dominate and control. Elvin felt that she was overly domineering and authoritarian as well as overly restraining in her influence on all members of the family. She objected to many of the patient's hopes and activities, objected to the brother's marriage, objected to almost all of the father's activities, in particular those involving alcohol. She spent very little time with the family personally because of her need to work to support the family. The patient recalls a housekeeper during most of his childhood and early adolescence. Elvin's mother is described as having many good friends, making friends easily, but being "choosy" about them. With friends, she is very pleasant and usually hides the domineering, authoritarian characteristics which the patient feels are more typical of her. In the recent past the mother has been much more emotionally upset than he has ever seen her before. The mother attempted to push the patient into a professional career, and when he balked at this, she objected to his continuing with school. During most of his childhood and young adult life the patient objected inwardly to the mother's restraints and domineering approach. He felt that she actively tried to control and manipulate his life. The mother obtained her teacher's training before marrying and following marriage was a housewife for a very short time. She married at the age of 23. According to the mother, she refused to have sexual relations with the father from three months after she became pregnant with Elvin until the time they separated sixteen years later. She remained with the father only to continue a semblance of family life. She was not greatly upset at the father's death.

Her health continued to be fairly good until 1950, when she developed an arthritic knee pain. This disturbed Elvin considerably. For the first time he began to fear that the mother's health might not always be good and that she might fail.

All her life, according to the patient, she gave him misleading information about sex and made him feel very guilty about any sexual experiences. The mother's letters during his military service were close and endearing, and upset him by trying to control him, continually impressing him with the necessity of observing "good moral behavior." This accentuated his guilty conscience. The patient, during some of the interviews, openly stated that he hated his mother for her restraint and overbearing attitude but simultaneously acted as a submissive, dependent boy who obediently followed his mother's dictates. The patient described his feelings toward his mother as a continual fear that he would never live up to the standards she set for him. Until recently the patient felt she was a "Rock of Gibraltar." Only lately has he been able to verbalize to himself his feelings of antagonism and anger toward his mother. He fought her influence in his late adolescence when she wished to have him leave college to go to work. Also he fought her expressed interest that he enter into military service as his brother had done. In her conversation with the examiner the mother made a strong effort to exonerate herself of any responsibility for the patient's condition, indicating how bitter her lot in life had been and how hard she had worked in order to give the patient as much as possible.

Portrait 4: The Brother

Elvin's brother Bill is fourteen months older than he is. His birth weight was six pounds, two ounces after a full-term normal delivery. He is thought to look like the patient but to be very different in behavior. Bill is described as being very social, an extrovert, interested in athletics and social activities, and active sexually prior to his marriage. Bill, who was physically stronger and rougher than Elvin, allegedly had a "big brother" protective regard for the patient. The patient was always much more quiet and studious, less social and more introverted. Although the mother said the children were not jealous of each other, the patient described his relationship with his brother as being only "fair" and felt that the brother had excelled him in all respects except scholastically. He envied his brother's social, sexual, and athletic prowess and felt that he never knew his brother very well until a few years ago when both were in military service and shared a barracks. The patient felt that his brother was more intelligent but just not as interested in school. Bill was always more mechanically inclined. He almost always was much more like the father and was preferred by the father (according to the patient) on this account. The patient and his brother had very few mutual friends. While the patient worked from childhood to adolescence the brother worked very little and was much more interested in "having fun." The patient felt that he was working all the time while his brother was enjoying himself. Although the patient gave most of his money to his mother for maintaining the family, the brother worked solely in order to get money for his social activities. The patient and his brother did not do very much talking together and actually had little contact. They rarely fought with each other and communicated with each other very little, although they slept in the same bedroom until they were thirteen. When the father was forced out of the home by the mother, Bill was aware that the father wished that he would accompany him but instead he left home to enter military service. The patient allegedly had no strong feelings about the brother's going into military service at that time. The brother was in military service at the age of 20 and now has two young children. The patient feels that the brother can handle his affairs without getting too emotionally upset. Elvin feels he is closer emotionally to his brother in the past few years than he has ever been, although he actually has little contact with the brother now.

The patient expressed feelings of jealousy about the brother's resemblance to the father and about the father's preference for the brother. He felt that the brother was able to escape the mother's domination more than he had been able to because the mother had identified the brother with his father and did not exercise her pressure upon him with the same degree of fondness and positive expression that she had for the patient.

Physical and Laboratory Findings

The physical examination at the time of admission to the hospital was essentially negative. Visual examination revealed visual acuity to be 20 over 70 without glasses and 20 over 20 with glasses. Hearing acuity was found to be 15 over 20. Laboratory studies showed a normal complete blood count, a normal blood sugar, negative serological test for syphilis, and a normal urinalysis. Spine and chest and skull X-rays revealed no disease. The EKG showed a slight sinus arrhythmia. The EEG was normal with a good alpha activity and a basic frequency of 10 per second that was well defined. Hyperventilation EEG records revealed no abnormalities. Dental examination revealed dental caries and gingivitis.

Chronological History

1930: Age 0. Elvin was born in a fair-sized city in a western state. His mother was well during pregnancy. His birth weight was five pounds, four ounces. He was considered a good baby and was bottle fed. His mother returned to work when he was four weeks old because of the father's alcoholism and his inability to maintain the household. Elvin had an essentially normal developmental history. The family traveled and moved frequently from his early infancy. He and his brother were cared for by housekeepers.

1933: Age 3. Measles and mumps; not seriously ill. He and his family went to visit his maternal grandmother in another state. He remembers there was an accident en route. He was sitting in the back of the car and was not injured.

1934: Age 4. No unusual events except for constant traveling with father on his jobs. No enuresis. No neuropathic traits. Patient said to be a quiet, obedient boy who was sober and unemotional. The mother found it easy to discipline him. She would not let the father discipline the patient but did this herself. She felt that the father was too easy. The patient required little physical punishment. He appeared more attached to mother.

1936: Age 6. Flu epidemic in school system prevented patient from being entered in kindergarten. Remained home.

1937: Age 7. Started school. Enjoyed school. Tossed into fishpond by neighbor, but was not too disturbed.

Father discovered him in attic playing with genitals. Patient ran out of house nude and into field where he hid, very ashamed. As punishment by father patient was not allowed to put on clothes for two days and forced to remain by himself in great shame as a result. He felt himself unable to talk to mother and father for days after this experience.

Family moved to farm as a result of mother's wish but against father's desire. Up until this time family finances were fairly good. Following this time family had a much more difficult time financially.

1938: Age 8. Moved to another midwestern city. Mother working in school. In first grade with brother. Recalls windstorms and hurricanes. Enjoyed school. Liked art. Patient recalls pleasant experiences on farm. Mother read stories to patient and brother. Played games with brother and friends. Attended movies. Fell in love with Shirley Temple. Acted out exploits of movie heroes. At times felt close to brother, whom he envied because of brother's greater ability in social and athletic activities. Fell on rock and lost consciousness for one minute. No sequelae. Recalls color dream in which he killed his opponent in a sword fight. Felt remorseful about this but unable to change circumstances. Patient recalls no fears during these years. Able to go into dark areas. Not afraid of animals. Went into woods by himself without fear.

1940: Age 10. Frequent moves. Interest in airplanes. Very few presents for Christmas. Very little contact with either parent. Housekeeper in family until this year, after which patient and brother took care of themselves.

1941: Age 11. Moved again to far western state. Bicycle riding was chief hobby. Rode to school through fogs. Very much interested in airplanes and spent considerable time on airfield observing them. Learned about details of various airplanes. Enjoyed school. Liked to write stories and essays. Wanted to be writer. Goal later to become pilot and aviator.

First sexual experiences with girl aged 10 who lived next door. Brother had already had sexual experiences with her. Elvin played doctor with girl as patient. Three or four mutual exposures with attempted intercourse and questionable penetration. Patient enjoyed experience. Unable to accept this as wrong at the time, yet had very guilty feelings. Accepted concept of sex as bad from mother.

1942: Age 12. Had first seminal emission after sex play. Started masturbation. Seminal emission with girl friend.

Frequent moves with father while father was working on construction jobs. Patient and brother had much fun with father going swimming and meeting different people. Attended dances with father. Able to care for and to amuse self. Interested in mechanics of car. Interested in collecting animal life such as scorpions and snakes. Disliked brother's shooting lizards and other animals with air rifle. Felt bad about killing salmon caught in nets. Always on the go. Wished that family would settle down.

Masturbated by girl. Marked guilt feelings. Masturbation continued with guilt feelings for many years. Doing well in school. No grades lower than B, mostly A's. Frequent skipping of final examinations because his grades were good. Felt at ease with "brilliant students." Looked down on brother, who was less interested in academic achievements, but envied brother for social and athletic achievements. Interested in girls but fearful of being considered bad. Facts about sexual intercourse learned early but did not know pregnancy facts. Frequent daydreams about sex play with girls. Mother gave no information about sex but warned directly and implicitly about dangers of playing with girls. She kept patient in at night. Mother questioned patient about sexual behavior. Reminded patient he should have nothing to do with girls until he was married and permanently secure. Patient frightened by mother's aggressiveness.

Moved again with family. Enjoyed going from one school to another. Frequent bicycle riding. Made occasional friends. Daydreams about girls. One dream is recalled: he walked into a group of thirty to forty men of all ages. He had springs on his shoes and was jumping high. Jumped from one group to another. If they were young, he left them and said, "I will see you in a couple of years." He had many dreams of flying and fantasies of being a pilot. Interested in Tarzan and science fiction stories and other "escape literature." Swimming for ten to fifteen minutes with brother every morning before school. Almost drowned in ocean. Pulled out of water by a man. Felt helpless and frightened in riptide. Patient remained out of water for three months after this experience but had no residual fears subsequent to this time and now enjoys swimming. Has more respect for water, but is not afraid of it. While living on farm, patient and brother had their own rabbits and chickens. Raised rabbits for sale. Had dogs.

1943: Age 13. Gradual increase in height and weight. Patient slightly below average for height. No sudden spurts in weight or height. Patient one inch shorter than brother. Most of playmates were heavier and taller. He felt that he was temperamental. Patient had first job working in grocery store after school. Lifting heavy sacks and boxes. Felt strong. Moved again. Had afternoon and Sunday morning paper route. Played in old airplane. Helped polish airplane. Still interested in planes, rode for miles to see them, knew everything about them. Moved again. Saw first plane crash. Frightened and upset. Father and mother did not believe patient's story. Military plane crashed and gunner had head severed. Living in motel. Enjoyed beautiful school.

1944: Age 14. In seventh grade. Mother insisted that patient learn to play violin while brother played clarinet. Brother still plays whereas patient gave up after two semesters of music. Patient more interested in brother's clarinet than in his violin. Interested in ships and sailing. Moved again and regretted leaving old home. For about two years lived in old frame house in suburbs of city. Longest stay recalled. Enjoyed living and remaining in one place. Acquaintances and neighbors friendly. Very few close friends. Made deep attachment to this home. Regretted leaving this more than any other place. "Seems as if I spent my whole life there and would like to return there to make it my permanent home." Worked after school mowing lawns. Allowance from mother. Gave mother income derived from after-school work. Brother used his income for his social activities. Mother worked in store as clerk. Father working for construction company. Mother very nagging and demanding toward father. Undercurrent of unhappiness between father and mother. Occasionally saw father drunk and abusive to mother. Mother wanted to give patient and brother impression that father wanted to hurt them. On one occasion when father became abusive toward patient and brother, patient felt that he was goaded into this by mother. Patient declared that he was never frightened because father had never hurt him in reality. "If anyone ever made me feel that I should be afraid of father it was mother. Not father. I wanted to be like my father. He meant a great deal to me." Patient felt that nothing was ever right as far as mother was concerned if the father did it. Mother never let father forget about his failings. Mother very impatient, although tried to control herself.

1945: Age 15. Moved to California. Lived in an apartment which was maintained by mother. Mother told father to leave home. Mother told children she had intended to separate for several years but had remained with father in order to keep family together. She had been biding her time and now felt it was appropriate for father to leave. Patient inwardly upset and felt sympathetic toward father but did not openly express feeling. Father ill physically and depressed mentally. Patient felt father should have been in hospital. Father did not want to leave family. Patient felt intensive barrage of propaganda by mother against father. Father died of chronic alcoholism and heart attack in county hospital six months later. "How happy mother was after father died. There were no bills and nothing more for her to worry about." Patient had no overt expression of regrets or sorrow. Did not attend father's funeral. Was interested in getting father's car and father's effects but was prevented from doing this by mother. Felt that "whole affair was handled in cold blood." Subsequently felt revolted by mother's attitude toward father. Father had expressed interest in having brother live with him prior to his death but brother had refused. Brother had taken opportunity to enter military service, leaving high school before graduation. Entered military service to avoid unpleasantness of refusing father. Brother also sympathetic toward father but unable to stand up against mother. Elvin still working after school. Patient paid mother for room and board. Life consisted of regular grind for the next four years and patient resented this very much. Up into seventh grade patient had been outstanding student. In seventh grade patient ran for the office of school secretary against his best friend, who was also very smart but was more outstanding in athletics. Patient won the election but lost his friend. Patient felt many people in school disliked him because he spent much of his time studying and away from them. He promised himself that he would never allow himself to be outstanding scholastically but would rather be only an average student. In eighth grade patient deliberately reduced time spent in studying and attempted to be "with his schoolmates more." At times he would answer questions on examinations incorrectly in order to reduce his score. Patient stated that school work during these years was always easy and that he studied because he enjoyed it rather than because it was necessary for him to study. This impression was contradicted by the mother, who felt that the patient had to study considerably for his good grades.

1946: Age 16. Affair with Claire, sister of Elvin's boy friend. Patient seduced by her. Attempted intercourse. Frightened by her look of blissful rapture. "Afraid of what I could do to her to make her get into that state." Patient still likes Claire but avoids her. Brother left home to enlist in Air Force. Elvin envied brother's active social and sexual life. Patient concerned about brother's friends, who were much rougher and who might "get the brother into trouble." At the same time patient jealous of brother's activities. Patient working most of the time while going to school and felt as if he were "drugged." Interested in social and heterosexual activities but never had time for dates.

1947: Age 17. "Drugged life; school and work." Decreased scholastic achievement without compensatory social activities and without time for heterosexual social activities. Angry and resentful. Living at home with mother and resentful toward her, but unable to express feeling.

1948: Age 18. Met Sonya at summer-school session. Very much interested in her. Took her on fishing trips. Sonya interested in same goals as patient—writing and literature. Steady dates with Sonya. Frequent correspondence. Occasional dating because of limitations of school and work activities. Saw her as frequently as possible. "Clean-cut romance. Mother approved of this." Patient began to reduce activities in school and work in order to make time for Sonya.

1949: Age 19. Graduated from high school. During this last year patient felt increasing resentment with mother. Wanted to spend more time with contemporaries and to be accepted by them. Strong desire for social acceptance. Wished to be active in school activities but unable to find time. Upset by high school's bad reputation. "School filled with roughnecks." Felt that boys in this school were gangsters and girls were all streetwalkers. Patient moderately active on school newspaper. In last year of high school left mother's home to get apartment in nearby suburb and changed high schools. He did not wish to graduate from the "bad" school. Increased his work activities in order to maintain himself. Decreased dating with Sonya; anger and resentment about this. Diminished his social activities. Heard only infrequently from brother. Little contact with mother during this year. Cooked own meals and ate alone. Patient wished to go to college and wanted to take liberal arts course and become a teacher. Still interested in writing. Began to distrust self and his abilities. Unable to decide about plans. Primarily interested in continuing with school. During all of patient's childhood and adolescence mother had stressed her desire for him to be a physician. After patient left home and went to another high school against mother's wishes, mother began to press for patient's quitting high school as brother had done to go into service. Mother attempted to maintain closer relationship with patient. Patient tired of her restraint. Not tired of school but increasingly upset about poor grades, B's and C's. Patient felt that mother's early ambition for him to become a professional man was spurious and that mother had been hypocritical. Patient had very strong feelings about going into military service because of mother's pressure. Most pleasant time was when he was in school. Only time when he felt at peace. Four months before graduation, patient left school (with understanding that he would graduate) and went to visit his old home in another state "to see old friends and see how they had turned out." Patient felt that many of his friends had not turned out as well as he had.

Patient worked in rodeo during summer. Liked being around horses. Unable to decide as to future plans. "Looking for something but did not know what for." Maintained contact with Sonya by letter. Sonya now working in department store and going to night school. He did not expect to see her much but still interested in her. Had not talked with Sonya about his plans. Followed rodeo through western states. Patient attached to kitchen unit. Few older women with rodeo and patient had very little contact with them. No sexual relationship.

1950: Age 20. Returned to city where mother lived. Started to college. Mother wanted him to work and not go on to school. Mother resented patient's running away and his desire to go to school. Patient felt that mother was balking his every move. "Every time I tried to do something at school it was stopped by my mother. No one was really interested in me or in my going to school. Why should I?" Patient still uncertain about future. Felt he needed help. Unable to look to anyone for help. Patient did not want to live with mother but was talked into it by mother, who asked him to help her with expenses. Patient working in grocery store as cashier after school. Had little contact with mother. Finally left mother to live with another boy. Felt restless. Felt he had to go somewhere but unable to decide where. Patient had to quit work because of increasing restlessness. Strong urge to move and do something. Urge to better himself by scholastic activities but unable to decide. Increasing pressure by mother to enter military service. Patient strongly against this. "Had a phobia against military service." Two weeks after patient had expressed himself most strongly and definitely against military service, he enlisted in the Air Force.

Patient explained his complete change of attitude by a dream he had a few months previously about a military attack upon the city. Increased emotional upset about Asiatic war. Felt he went into service for patriotic reasons. Patient enjoyed basic training, the physical exercise, and being with other fellows. Had felt increasing mental confusion during previous six months at college and enjoyed "not having to think any more." Had never shot rifle before but enjoyed getting marksman's medal. After eight weeks of basic training patient transferred to medical unit as medical corpsman. At first objected to this because felt he had not enlisted for it, but then enjoyed training as medical corpsman. Good social relations with other men. Made several good friends. Became drunk for first time. Felt good. Great celebration. Never concerned about drinking. Mother concerned about patient's becoming a chronic alcoholic and drunkard as father had been.

Home on furlough. First sexual relations with Sonya. Markedly' upset. Patient felt that he was the aggressor but Sonya told him that this was not her first sexual experience. Patient emotionally upset about learning that she had had previous sexual relations without having been emotionally involved. "If she were emotionally involved it would have been all right." He had idea that he would marry Sonya before going overseas, but after he had had sexual relations with her he objected inwardly to marrying her. Patient felt markedly disillusioned. He wished that Sonya had refused to have sexual relations with him.

"I felt cheated. I could have done the same thing with a whore and it would have been okay." Because he was emotionally involved with Sonya he felt that he should not have sexual relations with her. Very much upset by her not being a virgin.

Brother at home on furlough during same time. Patient and brother in same barracks and patient had more cordial relations with brother than he had ever had previously. Got to know and like brother better than he had previously.

Went overseas to Pacific theater. Eager to go. In many respects patient felt he "got what he bargained for." Attempts to force self to enjoy military service. Arrival in Orient. Excited by beautiful scenery and unusual appearance. Felt awed by scenic effects. Assigned to Medical Administrative Corps to work in hospital. Assigned to work under sergeant who was very pleasant and coöperative, but who was very much involved with his marital and social activities. He shunted responsibilities onto patient. Patient felt much influenced by commanding officer of hospital. Felt pressured by commanding officer to work. First month in Orient very much interested in sightseeing and getting acquainted. Borrowed friend's motorcycle and traveled around. Confused impression of faces and events. Much Christmas activity and New Year drinking.

1951: Age 21. Purchased second-hand car from friend for travel. Attended many night spots, bars, and sports activities with friends in service. Played a little baseball. Interested in getting off the base to visit spots in Orient.

Increased pressure of work. Patient's immediate supervisor left for furlough and patient forced to accept full responsibility. When supervisor returned from furlough he remained inactive and allowed patient to do all the work and assume all the responsibilities. Supervisor drank heavily. Patient resented increased responsibility and increased pressure. Work and responsibility were piling up. Supervisor gave patient very little help after first few days, when he taught patient a few rules and regulations. Patient studied regulations after hours. Felt regulations were difficult. Had responsibility for compiling reports. Wanted more help but none available. Felt system was antiquated. In the evening after hours patient began to drink in bars. Patient liked supervisor and supervisor's young wife, but resented his shunting responsibility to patient. Felt that supervisor had been waiting for someone like patient to come along and take over. Felt he got along fine with the men in outfit, although had no personal attachments except for two friends.

Assigned to venereal disease control clinic in large Oriental city. Patient had to accompany civilian officers to houses of prostitution and private dwellings where prostitutes were working in order to close houses and in order to identify the girls. Given access to records. Saw many prostitutes and taxi dancers. Patient invited by girls to visit them to have sexual relations rather than close houses. Patient returned a few times to visit one girl and remained with her all night on one occasion. Spent a number of hours with her subsequently. Stopped having sexual relations with prostitutes allegedly because of pressure of work, but recognized strong guilt feelings about sexual activities. Did not have to pay for prostitutes. Felt that girls were none that mother would approve of. Mother writing letters very often to patient pointing out how attached she was to him and what a fine young man he was.

Intensified work. Regulations increasingly hard to understand. Supervisor increasingly more careless and less responsible. Supervisor secretly being treated by doctor for alcoholism. Patient rented room for himself in town in order to get away from base in evening. Drove around town in car. Increased drinking activities, visiting bars with acquaintance. Drunk very often. Very few hangovers. Increased feeling of loneliness. Patient increasingly more irritable and nervous. No personal contact except with one friend who was very religious. Long talks with this friend about religious activities. Increasingly resentful about unchanging climate and unchanging scenery. Felt that he wanted a change from people, things, and activities. In travels patient felt that colors of Orient were particularly brilliant and upsetting. Scenic settings very upsetting to patient. Weird feelings of beauty. In letters to mother remarked that everything appeared very familiar as if he had been there previously. Feelings of repeating life experiences. Increased odd feelings. Patient had feeling that he could anticipate events which would occur. Frightened by his premonitions. Felt that his ideas in some way influenced events and was frightened because he wished to feel that events occurred without his influence. Attempted to dismiss premonitions from his mind. Colors of scenery appeared vivid with electric effect. Increasingly frightened and bewildered.

Patient's one friend talked with him about religious events and ghosts, life after death, and supernatural events, which patient began to believe in. Patient recognized bizarre features in friend's behavior and friend's emotional disturbance when he began to hallucinate weird, bizarre, and supernatural things.

Patient on drinking spree picked up by sailor and had homosexual experience. Suppressed experience from memory for many months. Very much upset. Felt that this was greatest sin. Attempted to stop drinking but continued moderately. Increased pressure of work. Within a few weeks after homosexual experience felt that everyone in his office had found out about it and that he was being watched and observed by all. Patient increasingly suspicious of those about him. Ringing in ears started at this time. Felt that he had done wrong and that he had no excuse for it. Felt upset because of possibility of his desire for homosexual experience. Still unable to excuse behavior. Increased feelings of bewilderment and confusion. Everything becoming a nightmare with work piling up. Patient talked to chaplain and attempted to tell him about experience but unable to understand what chaplain said to him and does not recall clearly what he talked about. Started taking benzedrine. In the evenings, when patient left work he felt that people were watching him. Began to hear his name called when in crowds. Very upset about sexual experience and sexual ideas about women that he considered perverse and abnormal. Thought of suicide and at times attempted to slash wrists with razor blade or take medicine with suicidal intent but unable to complete activity. Bizarre feelings about scenery. When talking with friend patient began to question the value of religion and felt that religion was wrong. Friend attempted to kill self and now openly hallucinated. Patient initiated friend's entry into hospital, where he was diagnosed as schizophrenic. Patient felt that he was very much like friend. Patient has continued friendship with this man to this day. Later met same friend at the present hospital.

Increasing difficulty with superior officers. Feeling that he was living in an unreal world and unreal situations. Reported to superior officer and entered into hospital for observation. Chief complaint he gave was ringing in ears. Patient concerned about lack of work activity and supervisor's removing responsibility from him. Suspicious of hospital personnel and questioned them as to why they were treating him as they were. In hospital for three weeks, with increasing anger and resentment. Diagnosed as "anxiety reaction" and returned to active duty.

Increased feelings of confusion, bewilderment, depression, and emotional upset. Felt useless. Suicidal ideas. Had many ideas which bothered him. Return of all ideas and feelings noted above. Constant self-arguments with pros and cons on all issues. Had to weigh everything he wanted to do very carefully and then ended with sudden impulsive idea or behavior. Discharge from penis; treated self for venereal disease. Concerned about having contracted gonorrhea. Ringing in ears became accentuated. Ideas that people were talking about him and watching him. Often heard name called. Felt unable to continue with work. Returned to hospital for treatment of "anxiety reaction." Following observation, patient was returned to United States hospital. Asked for discharge and given medical discharge. Not concerned about pension. Patient offered job by fellow patient in hospital. Upset about reasons for his discharge when given papers with diagnosis of "schizoid personality" and "planlessness." Felt he should not have been discharged because of nervous condition but that it should have been a straight honorable discharge. After discharge, patient accepted offer from fellow patient to go into real-estate business with him. Patient wrote to mother and borrowed money from her as well as small loan from brother to help to go into business with this man. Went to Chicago with him. Patient unaware at this time that friend was a "confidence man." This man came from a wealthy family and allegedly was living off family and friends in unscrupulous manner. Finally patient recognized that real-estate business was a blind and friend admitted that he was a criminal attempting to get friends to invest money in spurious ventures. Patient had given all of his money to him to invest and thus lost it. Felt stuck. Patient increasingly upset following discharge. Felt that he was being watched by detectives set upon him. Felt constantly that he was being watched and talked about. Heard people talking about him. Felt unable to get out of trap. Very careful about to whom he spoke. Felt angry with himself for having become associated with a criminal. Hardly enough money to get back home. Unable to throw off feeling that he was being watched. Unable to tell who was his friend and who was not. Recognized that he was upset emotionally but unable to decide what to do about this feeling. More depressed and disturbed.

Mother wrote to him of difficulty she was having with her fiancé. Mother had wanted to remarry but the man had not been successful in obtaining divorce from his previous wife. Mother had asked patient to come home to intercede for her.

1952: Age 22. Living with mother. Insomnia and headaches. Felt very irritable about mother's difficulties. Disliked mother's attitudes and her childishness. Mother increasingly emotionally disturbed in patient's presence. Saw mother crying for first time. Patient upset about Sonya, whom he occasionally saw and who accused him of being unfaithful and of not being interested in her. Interested in entering school but uncertain of ability to carry through his plans. Feeling of being pressured and unable to manage life. Suicidal ideas. Felt tense and "trapped." Suspected that mother and fiancé were sleeping together because of fiancé's clothing left in mother's bedroom. Angry with mother as a result of mother's attempts to get patient to talk to fiancé and have fiancé marry her. "I have my own problems and she throws her problems on me." Angry at self for being "weak" and for not leaving mother. Unable to decide on course of action. Exacerbation of ideas that people knew about him, his mistakes, and his ideas. Felt they were watching and talking about him. Very suspicious of all people. Heard name called particularly when in a crowd. Upset about his thoughts of suicide. Fear that he would not be able to control his behavior. Development of long crying spells and difficulty in controlling these. Went to a Veterans Administration Regional Office for examination and request for treatment. Referred to a neuropsychiatric hospital for examination.

Entry into neuropsychiatric hospital for present hospitalization. Mother was unaware of patient's extreme emotional upset and of his decision to enter hospital. Mother opposed to patient's hospitalization and opposed to patient's receiving any shock treatment in hospital.

Following entry, patient showed fewer ideas that people were watching him and feelings of being talked about. Very suspicious of fellow patients and of doctors. Sporadic fluctuations in tension state. Markedly upset by mother's visits and opposed to idea of returning to live with mother.

Patient left the psychiatric hospital AMA (Against Medical Advice) at the instigation of his mother. She refused to recognize the patient as emotionally disturbed or mentally ill. She stated to the doctor: "There is nothing wrong with my boy. He is just a little nervous. I understand him better than any psychiatrist." She would not sign permission for the insulin coma treatment that the hospital had recommended. The patient attempted to influence the mother in order to obtain treatment or to stay in the hospital but was not successful and, at the mother's request, he left the hospital to return to live with her.

Diagnosis

The diagnosis of this case established by the psychiatric staff was schizophrenic reaction, paranoid type. This condition followed the early acute undifferentiated type of schizophrenic reaction. The patient first showed confusion of thinking, emotional turmoil, perplexity, ideas of reference, weird and peculiar ideas, and feelings of awe and premonition. Auditory hallucinations at first were mild and unclear and never developed into very clear-cut hallucinatory phenomena even in the more fully developed paranoid state. The outstanding psychiatric condition early manifested was the perplexity and emotional turmoil with increased ambivalent feelings and confusion of thinking. Subsequently, thinking became more unrealistic and autistic with a more definite development of delusions of persecution and ideas of reference. Behavior became more impulsive and unpredictable, and the underlying anger, resentment, and aggressive feelings were obvious. Also, somatic symptoms of headache and scattered physical pains developed. An anxiety and tension state continued throughout the months of the development of the schizophrenic reaction. The loss of contact with reality and the development of the bizarre symptomatology makes the diagnosis unequivocal.

ADDENDUM OF PSYCHOLOGICAL TEST RESPONSES

The test summary, based on a group-administered battery (consisting of the Shipley-Hartford Scale, the Draw-A-Person, Sentence Completion, and MMPI), was as follows:

The patient was in good reality contact at the time of testing and on most of the tests he showed adequate control and an absence of bizarre or disorganized thought processes. The over-all test results, however, clearly indicate a schizophrenic process of paranoid type.

There is a generalized impairment of abstract reasoning ability; the pre-psychotic level was superior and the present level of intellectual functioning is high average. While problem solving ability is reduced, memory functions are relatively intact. On simple tasks, he works quickly and accurately, but when he is given his own opportunity to make an interpretation of a task, his perceptions become distorted and his responses become over-elaborate and fanciful. In spite of the fact that he is both anxious and depressed, his responses show noticeable self-inflative and mildly grandiose attitudes.

The patient clearly reveals his attitude of resentment toward a domineering and over-protective mother and shows a lack of a strong relationship with a father.

On the personality inventory, he admits of hallucinations, delusions of persecution, feelings of estrangement, suicidal and homicidal impulses. The picture is that of a person in the early stages of a schizophrenic process of paranoid type with high level of anxiety, depressed mood, and acting out tendencies which suggest possible suicidal risk.

On a personality questionnaire, the Minnesota Multiphasic Personality Inventory (MMPI), given at the time of his admission to the hospital, he admitted to the following items, which are presented below in abbreviated and paraphrased form:

—His sex life is unsatisfactory.
—Evil spirits possess him at times.
—He has been in trouble because of his sex behavior.
—His head hurts.
—He hears queer things.
—There is a tight band around his head.
—He believes he is being plotted against.
—He has indulged in unusual sex practices.
—He sometimes feels he must injure himself or others.
—He has the wanderlust.
—He has periods of unremembered activities.
—He thinks there is something wrong with his mind.
—He is afraid of losing his mind.
—He hears voices.
—He thinks people are trying to steal his thoughts.
—He thinks he is a condemned person.
—Someone is trying to influence his mind.

—Peculiar odors come to him at times.

—He has anxiety about something almost all the time.

—Sometimes he wishes he were dead.

—He feels as though things were not real.

—He has strange and peculiar thoughts.

—He hears strange things when alone.

THEMATIC APPERCEPTION TEST

No. 1 (*Boy Contemplating Violin*)

There's a young boy . . . a young boy looking at a violin, wondering whether he should take the violin or not. He doesn't want to. He doesn't like it in the least. He doesn't like the idea. But his mother has told him to take the violin. Therefore he must take it. And he doesn't see any way to get out of it. So he's sitting there thinking about chopping the violin to pieces if he can get away with it, or destroying it, or perhaps thinking whether he should go to his mother and tell her "I refuse to take the violin," but he knows he can't do that so he'll just think about it, and he'll look at the violin and hate it. (How will the story end?) He'll probably take the violin until he gets to a point where he's old enough to do what he pleases.

No. 3BM (*Huddled Form on Floor*)

It's a sad and very dejected person. Probably . . . probably had a great calamity in his life, the loss of a mother or better yet I . . . is that a razor blade in there or is that my imagination? (It can be anything.) As long as it doesn't make me look like a suicidal person. I see perhaps a person that's very depressed for reasons, I can use myself if you want the reasons. And a . . . a feeling of hopelessness. And in this position he's in now he cannot tell about his future at all, whether it is good or bad.

No. 6BM (*Elderly Woman with Back to Young Man*)

I see a son that could never live up to his mother's expectations. She'll . . . in this picture she is past the age where she could change at all, that is, to help her son by understanding. She's very set in her ways. She can't do much for him. She can only be surprised and a little hurt, perhaps startled at some of the things he does. It's a pretty poor ending for her but the boy or the young man don't give a damn.

No. 13MF (*Man Standing Downcast; Figure of Woman in Bed*)

I see a young man and a woman . . . young woman. Perhaps his first . . . her first . . . especially her first love experience He has probably come back from overseas and has probably had experience with women before but she hasn't. She has still been a good girl in school and he has an . . . the thought that she wasn't as innocent as she believed . . . as he believed she had been . . . so he was going to . . . he might as well make love to her now instead of waiting until after they were married. There's nothing to it. He does. And after finishing the experience, he realizes how innocent she had been. How much of a child she really was, and he realizes that he had made a . . . a great mistake in mistrusting her and to perhaps hurting her physi . . . psychologically by perhaps his roughness that he brought back from overseas. The future for the young man, I guess, I believe that she'll probably see her family doctor and he'll explain it to her about that was a fairly natural thing and the boy really cared for her and he did and does and they'll probably marry and have a fairly good life. The psychological shock to her at this point, she does seek medical advice.

No. 18GF (*Woman Choking Another Woman*)

This picture of a . . . very . . . hard faced, hatchet faced woman with bobbed hair . . . she looks a little insane. And ah . . . the other form, I can't tell whether it's a man or woman, looks more like a woman, suggests a woman, shape and the hair, and she is strangling the woman. The story . . . perhaps the hatchet faced person is an older sister and the younger sister is much prettier than she is, and she dislikes the younger sister so intensely and especially one night when she comes home with a beau that . . . the older woman had taken an attachment to from afar, but had not made any advances or tried to get in touch with the beau . . . the beau came one night and the older sister watched young girl being kissed very passionately by the man, and she smacked her lips, and she waited until the man had left . . . and waited in the shadows by the stairway and when the girl came home the older sister started making . . . ah, insane implications . . . a dark past for the young girl, and the young girl was, of course, surprised and innocent but she is also afraid of her sister . . . her older sister and didn't understand her. And she waited passively as the older woman came close and just expected an argument and a harangue and the older woman would go away and she would go . . . be sent to her room perhaps. Instead the older woman went berserk and strangled her. The younger woman did not have a happy ending. She died.

Four Picture Test

Order: IV, II, III, I

I start with the fourth picture, the scene where the whole family is sitting out in the . . . perhaps in the back of their . . . their manse, near their tennis court. Very comfortable group. They're well-to-do. There's the mother and the father and the young man and young girl. This story takes into consideration the young man in the . . . in the family. He's a protected individual, he's well educated. He leaves school at . . . he finishes his college at a very early age and goes out into the world with a bachelor's degree but no actual experience in life. And, I go on to the second picture, the bed, the picture of the bed where he runs into a young woman, who is a streetwalker and, although she is a streetwalker she looks like a movie star, she's well dressed, she's quiet personality and she's very understanding, she's perhaps five or six years older than she (sic) is, and she takes him up to his . . . her room where . . . her hotel, and she really falls for the young fellow and . . . she doesn't have the fellow pay for the room, although she admits that she had intended to have him pay, but because she really liked him, tried to set him straight in a few things, he was ashamed of the act, of the sexual act with her and he told her and she said she was trying to comfort him and tell . . . tell him that it was nothing to be ashamed of. I go to the picture of the lamppost. The young man takes a great deal of time out of his life to think about those things. About the prostitute, about the sheltered life he lived, and the . . . the mother . . . and the parents . . . the high standards he had to live up to. And . . . he's depressed. And he doesn't want to work, he doesn't want to eat, he doesn't want to sleep, he feels like a . . . a hobo, more or less, and he can't understand his feelings. He really enjoyed the experience with the prostitute, but he knew his mother . . . his *charming* mother wouldn't approve, and he is thinking about it and brooding about it and it's cold. Pretty soon the cold . . . he's standing against the lightpost and everything is cul-culminating to the point where the brooding is . . . he would like to commit suicide. But then it starts to get cold and snow. And the exhilaration . . . the feeling of snow is like a . . . sort of wakes him up. He is given a sort of sense of value that he has to keep warm. First he wants to keep warm now, get warm and to stay warm, and he wants to seek companionship, and he wants to have a job and live his own life, that it wasn't so important his mother and father couldn't determine whether could starve to death or stay in the position that he was in now standing against the lamp-post brooding about his past experiences . . . so he gets out of the storm. He walks into a building. First he probably sought aid. He probably went to the Salvation Army just to get a bowl of soup, even though he could have gone back to his own home, the wealthy family, he chose the Salvation Army just to get something warm inside of him, so that he could feel energy again, in himself, and then he starts on his own to build up his own success, which I go to the final picture. I say he's a president or vice-president of a business, now. He's solved all his problems, he's happily married. Now . . . I'd say he's about fifty-five in this picture. He has a home and a couple of kids and he has taken a great deal in his stride over the years and become a fairly successful man, he'll never be as wealthy, or he'll never be able to emulate his father, what his father did and his father's successes, but in his own small way he . . . is . . . has done his share to meet his responsibility as a citizen.

MAKE A PICTURE STORY TEST

Street (Used Figures M-4, F-3)

Now let me see. Picture of a street. Vacant. I guess it's dusk. A serviceman walking down the street. Ah yes, this prostitute . . . she is making herself obvious to the Air Force . . . let's call him Corporal, and . . . she is out entirely for his money. The Corporal is fully in accord with what she is standing on the corner for. She takes him up to her room. That's the end of that. (Can you tell more of an ending?) I guess the Corporal . . . will, when he's discharged, will go back to civilian life and take up with his old . . . girl friend where he left off, perhaps who he went to school with. And the ending for her, oh, she'll probably, ah . . . become old before her time. (What might you call this?) "The Street" or "The Streetwalker."

Dream (Used Figure F-2; used and removed I-2, S-2)

Well, this is a picture of . . . this suggestion of a face . . . I'll make it the head of . . . of myself. Be my face. Let's see what will go in my . . . go on in my mind, if I can find the characters for it. This is a difficult one. What would go on in my mind . . . that you have here in feelings. Okay, put this in, a man . . . a young man who is, ah, looking into the future. His own future, perhaps. Perhaps he sees all of it at once and it makes him very depressed. He sees himself as a young man but he can't see himself as . . . any further than that. I don't know. This is a difficult one. Blank. This picture I put in there is just a cartoon outline of a man . . . try to put it down as aged, or 40 years, 50 years old, or . . . I can't find anything that would suit it. And ah . . . let me see. Oh, well. This is good enough. Take the first two out and then change to a young woman. The woman is perhaps his girl friend and he . . . the woman is his girl friend and taken the . . . perhaps, I'd say the . . . he's now recalling his first time he ever had intercourse with the girl that he loved. The pictures are there. The episode. I don't know what to call it. It's . . . I'd say, "Thoughts." (How did the thoughts end?) The first one was depression. The looking into the future depressed him. Seeing perhaps all the good things and all the bad things at once, rather than taking them singularly, took them all at one time, it depressed him. The second one. Perhaps the future's a question mark. But he knows that . . . he has a feeling that things will turn out right. The third one is . . . that with this girl, is a memory of the past. He's thinking of the past then, thinking over the experience with a girl which was a good one. That's all I can say.

Bridge (Used Figures M-5, F-4)

This is a picture of a bridge and a foggy day. I imagine it would be San Francisco, the San Francisco Golden Gate Bridge. And the girl is looking out over the bridge at the water and she is . . . is depressed. She is in a world of her own, her own thoughts. And she is looking out and she sees the buildings and she is . . . through the haze of the fog, but she really doesn't see them. She notes patches of light on the water where the sun has filtered through the clouds, but she doesn't actually see the light either. But the scene fascinates her because . . . floating with her thoughts it coincides with many thoughts that are running through her mind without any direction. The second figure in the picture is a policeman who is walking by, has no idea what the girl is thinking about, but he suspects that she is trying . . . she has thoughts in her mind of killing herself and the young man stops, talks to the girl and tries to steer her away from the bridge and perhaps send her along to the place where she can get some help. Psychiatric help. (Laughs.) And the episode is the "Bridge." (How would it end?) She'll go back to being a prostitute. She won't commit suicide but she'll live the sort of life that she always led. The policeman will forget all about the episode afterwards.

Raft (Selected by Subject) (Used Figures M-14, M-16, F-2, N-7)

Well I see a raft and a very still ocean. Hot day. Now let's find someone to put on the raft. Ah . . . who to put on a raft? (Pause.) There are four figures on the raft. Obviously, there has just been a shipwreck and the raft is off the freighter that had hit a reef on the South Seas somewhere, I'd say off the coast of . . . off the northern coast of Australia in the Coral Sea, and the occupants of the raft are all C deck. They came out together. The girl was in a hurry, she was unable to dress, she could only dress in her shorts and her bra. The men were more fortunate, they had been dressed or maybe they weren't fortunate, I don't know the circumstances actually, but we have for the occupants of the raft an old man, a . . . let's say a doctor, let's say a retired . . . a psychiatrist, retired psychiatrist, and he is from the school of Freud. The second man is a married, a middle-aged married businessman who has four kids back home, back in the United States. He was on his way to Japan on business. And the third man is a shy nineteen-year-old fellow, a student, who has found himself in a very embarrassing position that the girl is his age and he has . . . had taken a liking to her before the accident, before the wreck, and here he is with two other men, besides her, and in his way he had thought of having a wreck, hoping that they would have had a ship-wreck and that she would be on a raft with him or on a lifeboat with him. Oh, it happened, but the appearance of the other two men, the psychia-trist and the businessman, sort of upset his plans, but they are going to drift for days and days and days until almost all hope is abandoned and the psychiatrist is going to convince the young man that to . . . if they're really in love, and if she loves him for them to forget the other occupants of the raft. And the businessman has ideas of his own. He is an expe-rienced man and he tries to get into the woman's good graces, and she won't have it. She likes the young man. How it ends up? They . . . well I can't say they . . . let's put it that they are picked up by a ship just before they have their relationship . . . they would have, because the psychiatrist had them understood that they were young and they should have their fun. And the ship picks them up. The young man and the girl are married aboard this other ship and have a happy life. The psychiatrist is happy and pleased it's his last case. Actually his last case is helping this young man. The businessman is frustrated because he has to go back to a wife who is nagging and the four kids. The episode, "The Raft."

C H A P T E R   S E V E N

Aggression and Self-Realization in a Young Woman[1]

BY ARTHUR BURTON

Introduction

Rita L. might in any ordinary situation pass for a dark-eyed, diminutive, 33-year-old woman undistinguished by other than a certain appealing charm. On casual contact it would be difficult indeed to forecast that this tiny person carries within her the deep conflicts not only of a culture but of her own identification in a world she sees as hostile and depreciating. Rita is in many ways typical of the woman of today; but she, unlike other women, has been unable to compromise her needs and accept with definitiveness any role which would make her existence meaningful. Wherever she has gone her appeal for help has met immediate and universal response—and she has received the best where there was often little to offer—because somehow Rita struck chords which touched all people alike. This is a case history of the struggle for self-realization in the modern world—of love, hatred, fear, self-punishment, and flight—an odyssey of a desperate attempt to find oneself.

If one needs justification in a clinical sense for a biographical study such as this, it is that the opportunity for longitudinal examination of life experiences permits us to validate our fundamental personality theories in a way that transcends the abstractive quality of the labora-

[1] I am grateful to Robert P. Quirmbach, M.D., for making this study possible and to Mrs. Sue Kalua for certain of the test results.

tory experiment. Life histories are in a sense the primary datum of clinical psychology, and it is in this way that basic postulates of behavior are both formulated and validated.

Rita was seen by many psychiatrists and treated by several. Their diagnostic, therapeutic, and personality statements were available and could be tested in the crucible of her own maturation, and in the systematic observations we could make over a four-year period. Her therapeutic response gave substance to some theoretical formulations, but not to others—it tended to validate certain therapeutic interventions but gave no support to others. It is in life histories involving such diagnostic and treatment elements that systematic postulates can be made in regard to aggression, coping mechanisms, reality organization, etc., which can then be subjected to more controlled experimental design, or at least to the therapeutic manipulation and validation of later clinicians.

Family History

Rita was born in Poland, a country noted as the reservoir of orthodox Hebrew tradition and the political and military battlefield of world ambitions in the last several centuries. Her family was Jewish and, as such, a part of the ghetto life now so well documented. While our data on the early family background are limited by a geographic span involving three continents, and a certain reluctance on the part of family members to deal with this period, some reconstruction of the facts is possible.

Rita's father, a tailor, went to live in the home of his future wife. Whether this occurred because they were first cousins or because his trade was the same as that of his father-in-law is not clear. Since Mrs. L.'s parents were reputedly wealthy, it may be that they saw in him a future heir and thus wanted to further his economic circumstances. At any rate Mr. and Mrs. L. were thrown together in this way.

Mr. L. was from the first observed to be temperamental, distrait, and lacking those qualities necessary for economic success. Mrs. L. reported many years later that even then her husband was inclined to be suspicious, to have violent outbursts of temper, and he may even have had hallucinations. Nevertheless, the attachment between them grew and they were married over the later objections of her parents. Now, Mrs. L. likes to believe that this marriage was arranged for her, and that she was rather a passive partner in a plan between two sets of parents, a custom not unusual for the times. It would appear from this vantage point, however, that she was more of a participant than she is willing to admit or can recall. At any rate, Rita's mother, an intelligent and ambitious person, immediately began to shape a career for her husband and plan for family happiness, As it happened, Rita was born the following year.

As was apparently predestined, the marriage was unhappy from the start. Mr. L. could not measure up to his wife's achievement needs, and quarrels and emotional displays were frequent. Because of family tension, the lack of economic success, and probably the advent of anti-Semitism, Mr. L. left for a British Commonwealth nation where a relative of his resided. Three years later Rita and her mother joined him. There he continued working as a tailor, but with characteristic ineptitude. His relative, a man of some means, was not inclined to assist him further at this point and Mrs. L. had to take in boarders to eke out a livelihood. In the meantime Anna was born and a third child, Sam, was conceived.

They appealed to a paternal uncle residing in the United States and he sent funds for transportation. For reasons yet unknown, the father went on alone, although the separation was to be temporary. In the United States his economic failure became more pronounced and his emotional illness flourished so that hospitalization in a state institution was necessary. It so happened that the hospital was located in the city in which the paternal uncle lived. The records at this facility make no mention of a diagnosis but report symptoms as varying as ideas of being poisoned and a suicidal attempt by drowning. Mr. L. was finally discharged from the hospital after one year of treatment. The state of his health at discharge is not reported.

Mrs. L. in the interim packed up her brood and followed her husband to the United States. The following events are not clear in terms of either records or statements of several of the interested parties. The father returned to Europe, was hospitalized there, and then dropped from sight. It is believed that he died or was killed during the Hitler regime. One version has it that he was deported by immigration authorities as a mentally ill indigent—his wife and uncle refusing to support him. The other is that he voluntarily returned to be with his parents.

There is some evidence that the uncle, a domineering, egocentric, and possessive person, played a prominent part in the decision made in regard to the father's future. It may have been that Mrs. L., troubled by her plight and somewhat at the mercy of her relative, made no great effort to maintain her faltering marriage. Even now the father is a guilt-laden subject which she, if not all members of the family, shies away from with considerable anxiety and discomfort. Rita at one point in treatment inveighed against her uncle, pointing out with great vehemence that her mother always defended him rather than her children, and this seems related in her thinking to her father's sudden departure.

The paternal uncle was a moderately wealthy man, a bachelor, and accustomed to having things his way. He immediately assumed a father-surrogate role in his new-found family. However, beyond providing subsistence, he apparently offered none of the emotional support and warmth growing children require. He not only dictated disciplinary practices to the mother but prescribed special conditions under which they had to live so that Rita and her siblings were never free to make friends and bring them home. On cosmetics, dancing, and athletics he was particularly rabid, interpreting them as immoral. Not unexpectedly, severe friction soon developed between siblings and uncle.

Anna revealed the greatest vigor in resisting her uncle, and finally he insisted that she be placed outside the home. She went to a Jewish sheltering home where fortunately, as we shall see later, psychiatric assistance was available. Rita sought more devious and unhealthy ways of making an adjustment. She finally also left; but it was to go to a neighboring city with the first manifestation of the symptoms which were later to characterize her illness. That the uncle was himself the victim of ambivalence is noted by the fact that at his death Mrs. L. and two of the children were found to be heirs to his estate. Rita was disinherited completely—a significant event for the understanding of the patient.

Because Mrs. L. was available only at a stage of the therapeutic relationship where it might have been detrimental to Rita's treatment to see her, she was not seen by the therapist, even though she requested it. However, she was interviewed by a staff psychiatric social worker. This worker describes Mrs. L. as a small, dark, dependent woman who underneath her need for constant reassurance is really quite a demanding person. It is said that she needs a full-time worker herself in terms of the number of requests she makes for information and reassurance. Actually she has had little contact with Rita in the hospital, having been satisfied with reports from the social worker. This has come about in part from Rita's periodic refusal to see her, but also because she is genuinely afraid of her daughter. After an absence of more than three years, it required a psychiatrist to bring them together when, after much reassurance, she finally visited the hospital. However, the intensity of the "repetition need" for her daughter is illustrated by the number of people she approaches and the frequency with which these contacts occur.

Mrs. L. received some training as a teacher in the old country and is obviously above average in intelligence. Apparently, because of personality needs, she was never able to make consistent use of her abilities. Recently she has bewailed the fact that her children have not turned out as she expected. In some fashion she would like to be surrounded by them and revered as a mother who sacrificed her own goals in life for their benefit. Her systematic alienation of each of them, and their consequent escape from her maternal surveillance, has left her a little puzzled and also frightened and alone. For reasons peculiar to herself, she has never been able to put these defections to the test of insight. At the height of Rita's illness she escaped to the Middle East— the ancient homeland of the Jews—and, although she returned two years later, she took up residence in another state and thus geographically removed herself from the area of conflict. This ambivalence and flight are characteristic, and the selection of the Holy Land for her hegira was probably not without dynamic meaning.

Mrs. L.'s probable expectations are that absence will bring her children to book. This failing, she points up her impoverished health, her loneliness, and an extensive repertory of other techniques which, this far at least, have not had the desired effect. She will write to anyone who will give her audience to point out her self-denial, her willingness to go even further in self-sacrifice, and the consistent lack of gratitude she receives. At times this assumes a frenetic quality and is certainly overdetermined.

The mother's positive attitudes toward Rita are not so easily come by—possibly because no opportunity was afforded to know her directly—but they were nevertheless present. Rita, for example, is magnificent in her capacity to demand exorbitant quantities of love and affection, and she is highly sensitive to implied defections. It is questionable whether her irrational needs for affection could be met by anyone, and this was verified by her stormy demands of the therapist. Mrs. L. undoubtedly attempted to offer her daughter what she could in the way of positive feeling, but she soon found herself unequal to the burden. The following letter from Rita to her mother indicates the intensity of her feelings:

Don't think that a box of candy rectifies your complete neglect. If it were possible, I would have returned it unopened. How can you live with your own conscience? Leaving your daughter to stagnate in an insane asylum. If I waited for your so-called help, I'd die here. Can't you get it through your stupid head that I can't make a move without funds? Can't you comprehend anything at all? You have always run away from your responsibilities and still are. You have never stood by when I needed you much and I'll never forgive you. You're not fit to be a mother. I hate you more than words can express. As far as I am concerned, you are dead.

It was mentioned earlier that Anna was forced out of the uncle's home at his insistence. Her exact age at the time of this occurrence is not known. She was placed in several foster homes but reportedly did not do well. Finally, at the age of 16, she went to live in a residential home for neglected and dependent children. There she remained for approximately five years, when she returned to her mother—after the death of the uncle.

The early years did little to prepare Anna for group living. From the outset she revealed an inability to relate to other children and to incorporate herself as an entity in this surrogate home. School became a burden, so she absented herself without meaningful interpretation. Temper tantrums were frequent. Finally she made a suicidal attempt and was referred to an analytically oriented clinic for evaluation and treatment. There she was given a battery of psychological tests as well as being interviewed by a psychiatrist. The diagnostic formulation was "character neurosis with hysterical and obsessive-compulsive features." The presence of aggression—directed both inwardly and outwardly—was considered unusually strong. Murder and suicide were highly abundant themes in fantasy material. Anna, it was noted, was badly in need of affection, but she confused attention with love.

Anna was seen at the clinic for ten therapeutic interviews. At the end of this period she had given up several of her symptoms, found a boy friend, and asked to discontinue treatment because she felt better. It was after this that she returned to her mother. Incidental information reaching us concerning later developments indicated that Anna subsequently married and had a child. The marriage was tenuous, but it survives to date.

Anna has always said that she was much like Rita and that their problems were similar. In later years this similarity has not served to bring them into any closer relationship, and before this there were active rivalry and hostility. Rita's references in therapy to her sister have all revealed chagrin that her sister has turned out so well. She is particularly envious of her sister's marriage and deprecates her husband at every turn. He has responded to this by refusing her admittance to his home.

Less is known of Sam, the male sibling, than of any other member of the family. He is ten years Rita's junior, and two years younger than Anna. Sam was born with a physical handicap, a clubfoot, but surgical repair was successful so that he was able to meet military standards. After the uncle left him a substantial sum of money, he matriculated at a university and was drafted from there into military service. He is said to be the best-adjusted member of the family, partly because he has maintained physical and emotional distance from them. Repeated entreaties for funds from Rita have left him unmoved. Although close to her place of hospitalization he has shown no interest in coming to see her. Rita on occasion speaks wistfully of him, but in a tone which recognizes that no response is to be expected.

The Presenting Problem

It is against the background of the familial setting that Rita's problems are best understood. For this reason we have reserved until this moment her specific complaints. Possibly these are best presented in her own words through a fragment of a group therapy protocol taken soon after her first admission. The group consisted of ten women with non-psychotic diagnoses, and was coördinated with a carbon dioxide inhalation treatment program being done on the female admission ward.

MRS. T. (*therapist to group in general*): What do you want from the group, what does it mean to you?

RITA: I'm so lost; I need something to hang onto I guess—you don't feel so alone.

(Group talked about being transferred from the treatment ward. It has a double meaning: one, that you are better and is in a sense a promotion; two, that you've lost the close contact with the therapists and other patients.)

RITA: I'd come back if I could (to the treatment ward). As Mrs. T. says, you're not alone, but . . .

(Discussion of the fact that patients do the same work in the hospital, such as work in the kitchen, as at home, but they feel differently about it.)

PATIENT A: I think I don't like to work alone.

RITA: I don't have energy.

(Discussion of people looking better than they feel and thus not getting help because others think they aren't so sick.)

PATIENT B: They say if I look like that, why couldn't I do it; but I went at it and went until I came back pleading to be let in.

RITA: You've no choice. Let's face reality. Leave here and it's like a prison record. If I told employers, I wouldn't have a chance.

PATIENT B: I did.

PATIENT C: I did.

RITA: Talk about no help outside—it's different with a sanatorium and here. (Rita becoming emphatic and excited in contrast with usual ambivalence.) It's like serving a term in a prison.

PATIENT B: (cutting Rita off): You didn't get the point.

RITA: You upset me.

(PATIENT C talked about Abraham Lincoln having been sick and still being President.)

RITA: Why do some overcome it and some not? . . . I've nothing to live for.

PATIENT B: You have hands, feet, eyes . . .

RITA: But I'm emotionally crippled and that's worse.

PATIENT B: There are those that enjoy poor health.

PATIENT D: Are you looking at Rita or me?

PATIENT A: I think I do—so I will have something obvious to complain about.

RITA: Some people say it is to get attention . . . I don't feel I have a reason for living. Nobody cares.

GROUP RESPONSE: We care.

RITA (*evading*):   I don't mean here. I don't have a husband, etc., who cares. If you have deep feelings of inadequacy and yet everybody says you have everything, there is a feeling there, in yourself, like a brick wall . . .

PATIENT B: Walking in quicksand!

RITA: It's your own self-esteem, but if you don't have it, why don't you? You can follow a pattern, you are your own worst enemy—but what can you do, it's like a power you can't control.

MRS. T.:   But if it's within you, there is the potentiality of control.

RITA: If no one cares, you feel worthless because no one does . . .

(PATIENT D is quoted as saying, "You've done a lot for me, you're so normal.")

RITA: Maybe if you have self-love—but I hate myself.

PATIENT D: I did, but here I feel more self-respect.

RITA: Come here and fall in love with yourself (*laughed*).

(PATIENT D ignored this.)

RITA: The more you do the more you can, the less you do, the less you can.

Rita came voluntarily to a state hospital in the spring of 1950, at age 29, as a matter of desperation, but also upon the urging of psychiatrists with whom she had been in treatment. Over a four-year period she had made the rounds of private and clinic facilities in a large city but terminated each relationship on the grounds of increasing depression and hopelessness. Several reports from these sources indicate that she was never able to penetrate the veneer of her feelings even though she had the best of psychiatric help. There is consistent mention of these interviews as a "broken record" and it is quite probable that each relationship was manipulated by Rita so that its ultimate failure was assured. This left her with strong feelings of hostility toward psychiatry. Quite characteristically in the psychotherapy at the hospital she periodically accused the therapist of being incompetent, of promoting human misery for a livelihood, and of being incapable of sensing her practical needs.

She told the admitting psychiatrist on her first admission:

I had seen psychiatrists but had no incentive, so didn't get anywhere. No, I'm not a psychotic—I don't imagine things—they are all tangible. It's just that I felt rejected—ever since I was a little girl. Extremely inadequate and inferior, whether there is reason for it or not, I feel it. I just hate myself. I've just been pushed from pillar to post and can't take it any more. I feel that I need a leaning post—seems like I am all alone—nobody cares—I don't care either—pushed around—seems as if I've been running around in the same circle. Life is so futile—meaningless—maybe I've been too much of an idealist—life during the war was too glamorous. I don't know what's behind it. I thought I had a good deal of insight—maybe I don't.

Documents accompanying her, or secured in the course of diagnostic study, revealed that she had been employed as a legal secretary for a high governmental official in a large city when she began to complain of depression, suicidal thoughts, difficulty in concentrating, and increased irritability. She was placed in a private sanitarium and was released in 86 days as recovered. Four years later she became restless, left her job, went to another city, worked for two weeks, and then sought psychiatric help because of inability to work and feelings of depression. Then commenced a veritable odyssey, in which she continually traveled between two western cities and also the one in which her mother lived. The patient herself said that she has ridden every distinctive train and airplane available between these cities and presented a list itemizing them. She could also enumerate the many hotels in which she stayed. Finally she attempted suicide by opening the gas burners on her kitchen range. She was then returned to the private sanitarium in which she had previously been treated. There she was given six E.C.T. treatments and again released. She continued her travels, made another suicidal attempt, worked briefly at numerous jobs, saw many therapists, stayed in bed continuously for lengthy periods, and finally came to the state hospital, the first of three admissions. She remained 6 months on the first admission, 14 months on the second, and 25 months on the third. The interruptions between hospital stays were directly related to the psychotherapeutic process and the pattern of flight established earlier. Her adjustment outside the hospital on these occasions was precarious and not dissimilar from that manifested before she came to the hospital.

Course in the Hospital

From the first, Rita's plaintive and urgent demands for help interested a variety of clinical personnel so that some sort of traffic management soon became necessary. This occurred because she aroused interest in all who came in contact with her, and because she was very agile in manipulating staff members. Not only staff but also patients soon dedicated themselves by offering raiment, cosmetics, a place for week-end leaves, etc. Invariably, she interpreted these ministrations in the direction of her own needs—"that she was alone and that no one wanted to help her." At any rate, Rita received the best the hospital could afford. This included the most favorable ward milieu, individual and group psychotherapy, carbon dioxide inhalation therapy, social service contacts of many kinds, industrial and recreational therapy, dental reconstruction, etc. The history of most of these therapeutic procedures was the same. Initially she responded and participated enthusiastically. When, however, she could not incorporate the treatment into her "repetition compulsion," she discontinued it. This was also true of individual psychotherapy, with the important exception that she always left a way open to return and was accepted when this happened. Two excerpts of psychiatrists' notes from the hospital record will illustrate fairly typical reactions to treatment.

This patient refused to continue CO_2 inhalation therapy which was interrupted after her fifth treatment. The patient has been mostly uncooperative and sarcastic and consistently tried to stir up the other patients, especially during group therapy, revealing morbid ideation.

Says she has been transferred five times in two months and it is asinine. Says no consistency in her treatment; all they do is push you around and make a complete wreck of you. Doesn't want to go to group therapy. Feels pushed around as though she is in a penal institution. Feels no one is interested in her welfare. Agitated, depressed.

All treatment of these kinds was evaluated by the staff as relatively unsuccessful. Thus her ward psychiatrist described her at one time as "the kind of patient which nothing helps." In retrospect, it can be assumed that such inconsistency was a necessary prelude to the opportunity for working through interpersonal conflicts in psychotherapy. In light of her past history we can conclude that psychotherapy could not have proceeded successfully on an outpatient basis.

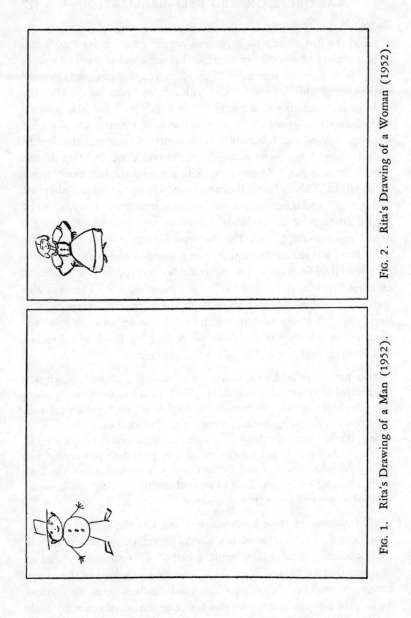

FIG. 2. Rita's Drawing of a Woman (1952).

FIG. 1. Rita's Drawing of a Man (1952).

Repeated physical and neurological examinations were consistently negative.

A great deal of attention was paid to the patient's diagnosis—probably in part because the prognosis and treatment indications were so complex. The diagnosis seemed to vary somewhat with the particular cross section of time in which she was seen. Her rapid alternation of well-being and depression, intense and unremitting hostility, obsessiveness, lack of energy, withdrawal, etc., were all noted as possibly psychotic in degree and intensity. But she was never officially listed on the roster as having more than a psychoneurotic condition.

Psychodiagnostic Study

Rita objected to being tested as she did to all other forms of assessment but was particularly adamant about projective tests. She could never quite verbalize her feelings, but patently they involved fears of revealing too much. She was receptive to such devices as the Draw-a-Person and Bender Gestalt, which are relatively innocuous in appearance, but resistant and hostile toward the Rorschach. Despite her attitude, a considerable number of tests were administered over the period in which we knew her.

Draw-A-Person: Two sets of drawings were obtained about two years apart (1952 and 1954). Let us consider the earlier set of drawings (Figs. 1 and 2) first.

Immediately striking are the placement of the drawings on the page, and the differences between the male and female. Quite obviously this is a person who is fearful of entering the stream of things and who must remain sheltered and secluded. This is confirmed not only by the placement of the figures but also by their size. Both figures have a childlike, puppet quality as though they were objects of manipulation and could not themselves initiate life or purpose. They are helpless in the face of the one who pulls the strings!

The male is primitive; the female highly structured. The feet and hands are exceedingly rudimentary in the male. He is incapable of movement—imprisoned—and thus not dangerous. Much attention has been given to the ears, which are exceptionally prominent. The ear is a receptable and not without sexual significance. It is the only masculinity allowed him but, as is known, the ear is often symbolic of the female genitalia. Our patient has thus castrated the male figure by endowing him with a vaginal orifice. In this connection the patient related in therapy how it pleased her to arouse men sexually and then enjoy the spectacle of their discomfiture. She resented men and said they felt important because they carried a special organ. It would appear that a "masculine protest" and confusion in sexual role are depicted in this drawing.

Some note must also be given to the oral emphasis in both drawings. The mouth has received disproportionate pencil pressure. This gives

FIG. 3. Rita's Drawing of a Man and Woman (1954).

us some clue to the patient's oral-nurturant and oral-sadistic needs which were so prominently revealed in treatment.

When we examine comparable drawings made two years later (Fig. 3) representing current (1954) functioning of the patient, some interesting comparisons occur. The female is strikingly similar to her earlier counterpart, but the male has become more complex. Actually, the patient drew the skeletonized male first (Fig. 3A). When asked whether it was a he, she said, "He's an it." However, she was able to go on spontaneously to draw Figure 3B.

This drawing indicates considerable progress in feminine identification, for it admits the male to the species and gives him a scope equal to, if not larger than, that of the female. His stance, and thus his stability, is improved; he seems more interested in and capable of action, and considerable attention has been paid to his clothing. That he is not yet completely male is seen by the still prominent ear symbols and the rigidity of the arms.

If human figure drawings, as projective techniques, reveal fundamental personality organization, then there is better object cathexis, role identification, and ego integration revealed in the post-treatment drawings.

Bender Visual Motor Gestalt: These were administered in 1952, and again in 1953, with the standard presentation, a speed or pressure administration, and a recall trial.

The performance was rather good. No gross abnormalities or perceptual dysfunctioning of the kind measured by this device were noted. There was an impulsive quality which grew stronger as the demands on her increased. She belittled her performance and on the later figures sacrificed accuracy and detail in order to get the anxiety-provoking task over with. There were no distortions, rotations, or fragmentations as seen in schizophrenic protocols, or the peculiar rigidity and disrupted gestalten of the organically brain-damaged individual. The angulated hexagons in the series (Cards 7 and 8) were correctly copied but were exaggerated in size. Possibly their symbolic value as phalli mobilized anxiety and resulted in an enhancement of their size.

Pressure and recall trials were not such as to alter the generality of the observations made above in regard to the performance proper.

Rorschach's Test: Rita was given three Rorschach examinations during our acquaintance with her. After the initial administration

(1950), admittedly unsatisfactory because of inadequate limits testing, two protocols (1952 and 1953) were obtained to evaluate functioning with psychotherapy. So that the actual flavor of her responses can be noted, the 1950 and 1953 protocols are reproduced in the appendix to this chapter.

Rita's helplessness in interpersonal situations which have emotional impact is quite clear in the Rorschach. She must again and again assault the bastions of what is to her the core of existence—people— but her immobilization is characterized by her frantic search for "insects" on the chromatic cards. Invariably, her concepts involve "two" —as though ego and alter were in some way inextricably intermingled as the social unit and personal existence (the self) cannot be countenanced alone. But the alter—and thus the self—invokes anxiety and so instinctual needs must be repressed and anxiety arrested at its source. Thus, a real achievement is that the protocols taken after therapy do show anxiety in the form of anatomical concepts and hazy substances which were not manifest before. There is less need to imbue human figures with animal connotations, but she is still very tentative in her relationships and falls back upon "witches" and "dwarfs" and, in moments of severe stress, denial of human concepts altogether.

The Rorschach was a trial to Rita, as the many incidental references in the protocol reveal. Her hesitation was no doubt related to the basic fear that all patients have of being overwhelmed by some finding or interpretation they are unable to defend against. In fact, the extreme repression and sublimation on the "father" and "mother" cards clearly indicated trauma in basic identifications and extreme sensitivity in regard to interpersonal relationships. Her very great need for a mother figure upon which to pattern femininity is revealed as "lambs" on Card VII, but she becomes disturbed at the long ears of the lambs. Is it far fetched to believe that in this instance the lamb's ear has properties of masculine and feminine genitality—that her mother herself could fill neither masculine nor feminine role but straddled both? Could it be that Rita found herself first in one role and then another, and is only now through therapy seeking clarity?

Despite the extensive repression and control mechanisms the tremendous instinctual forces and hostility reveal themselves. These are to some degree balanced by a fantasy life which is, however, insufficient as a defense against her libidinal needs. It has sometimes also appeared that the persistence with which these fantasies are held in the face of reality factors may be prognostic of a serious divorcement of a schizophrenic kind. It is not necessary in this connection that distortions and bizarreness, as reflected by F — perceptions, be present in the Rorschach for such an interpretation.

A dragon symbolizes the father and a lamb the mother, but Rita cannot integrate them. One is either a dragon or a lamb, but one cannot be both. This fragment may be related to a fantasy she periodically reiterated in therapy. A knight on a white horse would come riding one day and sweep her up to happiness. He would provide wealth, adoration, and surcease. It appears on the evidence that in Rita's fantasies the mythical knight represents both the lamb and dragon and thus her parents as a unity in terms of her needs.

The later Rorschachs confirm the impressions gained from therapeutic hours and independent psychiatric evaluation that more energy had been freed for interpersonal relations; that instinctual forces are less readily expressed as canalized aggression against family figures, or substitutes; that anxiety is available for therapeutic purposes; and that reality testing had less of a borderline character.

Minnesota Multiphasic Personality Inventory: Three MMPI's were administered, the first in April, 1950, fourteen days after the first admission, the second approximately one month later, and the third in September, 1952, in connection with her third admission. It was planned to administer seriatim MMPI's as a measure of growth in therapy but, as it turned out, Rita was not receptive to repetitive testing and it was felt that to insist in this instance would be an impediment to psychotherapy.

Figure 4 illustrates the first and third administrations. Disregarding for the moment the changes over the two-and-one-half-year period, we find the following of interest in terms of our understanding of the patient.

1. The records are dysphoric with three scales in one instance and four in the other exceeding the two sigma deviation from Hathaway and McKinley's normative group (1). Several additional scales approach this critical score. The patient thus expresses herself as significantly ill on the MMPI in these several areas.

2. While both the neurotic and psychotic ends of the profile are elevated, the former is much more prominent.

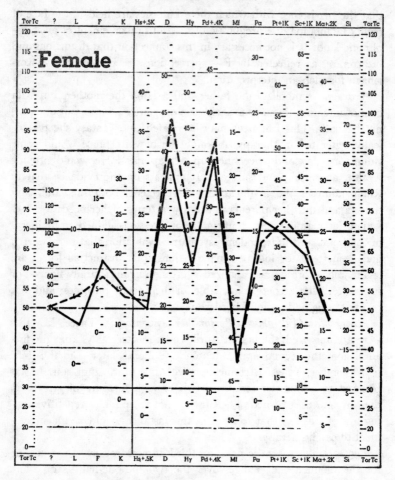

FIG. 4.   Rita's MMPI Profiles. (Solid line, 1950; hatched line, 1952.)

3. Depression (D) and Psychopathic Deviate (Pd) scales are extreme—even for patients in a psychiatric hospital—and deviate four to five sigma from the mean T score.

4. The Masculinity-Femininity (Mf) and Psychopathic Deviate scales are opposed, being low and high, respectively.

5. The Schizophrenia (Sc) scale remains within normal limits.

6. The Hypomania (Ma) scale—usually not subject to wide de-

viations in the profiles we have seen—is below the mean T score for the normative group.

7. The validity scales indicate that the patient is neither exaggerating nor minimizing her problems.

This is not, as one might ordinarily suspect from the Pd elevation, an acting-out individual motivated by pleasure-seeking such as one finds among certain addicts, alcoholics, and sexual deviates. These profiles represent rather a failure to establish an ego-ideal on a parental model, i.e., identification with parents, or parental surrogates, so that a harmonious integration of id, ego, and superego prevails. Thus, in a breakdown of the Pd scale, Social Alienation (feeling of alienation from others—lack of identification—schizophrenic flavor) and Familial Discord provide the dominant sub-scale loading.[2]

The MMPI predicted the course of the transference in which the ambivalence and hostility of faulty model-building was canalized upon the therapist and indicated the patient's tremendous investment of energy in the resolution of oedipal conflict. That this occurs at some cost is seen when the Depression sub-scales are analyzed. Activity Level —slow psychomotor tempo, no participation in social activities or very slow participation—has the heaviest loading. Mental Alertness—psychic retardation, feeling of dullness, unresponsiveness—is next. Joie de Vivre—pessimistic about life—nothing is interesting, inertia, poor morale; Brooding—dwells on past, mulls things over, thinking rather than doing; Low Threshold for Social Irritation are next in order. Her conflicts leave her without energy for dealing with her problems, and too exhausted to do anything but the simple interactive requirements of daily living. This is confirmed by the history of her staying in bed for long periods and refusing to leave at all if anyone could be pressed into service in assisting her in meeting minimum physiological needs. This behavior has led a number of psychiatrists to conclude that she was clinically depressed and to consider her a manic-depressive.

The Hypomania sub-scales lend substance to the interpretation of restricted object libido. This is really an attempt to avoid examination of her feelings through limitation of energy output. She prefers to see people as essentially amoral, and for her the "firstest with mostest" applies in human relations. Because of her inhibited aggression, how-

[2] Unpublished research by Dr. Robert E. Harris, University of California Medical School, on a set of sub-scales for the MMPI.

ever, she is unable to act upon this philosophy and amass worldly possessions. A pattern of hostility-guilt-depression soon comes to operate in most situations of emotional involvement. The Schizophrenic sub-scale loadings very properly fall into place with *conative* and *social alienation,* i.e., drive and object loss, as indicated problem areas.

In summarizing the diagnostic contribution of the MMPI, we might say that while the profile at first impression seems more neurotic than psychotic, dynamically the findings indicate that the disturbance in object relations, in self-identity, energy distribution, and aggression-passivity is such as to probably involve more than the limits of neuroticism.

The interval of approximately two and one-half years between administrations, in which hospitalization, psychotherapy, and an attempt at adjustment in the community, as well as other treatment factors, intervened, produced little change in the MMPI profile. In fact greater mobilization of anxiety and feeling-disturbance are indicated in the later profile. This may well be due to the ongoing psychotherapeutic process.

The Course of Psychotherapy

The criteria for the selection of a patient for long-term psychotherapy are not well understood, and much remains to be done in this area. Certainly the needs of both the patient and the therapist must be considered. Appraisal by available tests is helpful—it can reveal strengths and weaknesses of ego functioning, capacity to relate, the level of anxiety, intellectual resources, the force and direction of aggression, and similar facets. Whether the patient actually enters psychotherapy, and whether formulated goals are attained, is at this stage of our development dependent upon nebulous but nevertheless highly important feelings between patient and therapist. Special reservations on the part of the therapist, the stage of his own therapeutic growth, his capacity for handling affection and aggression, and, more basically, his identification with emotionally ill people are all critical elements in whether or not therapy is actually carried to a conclusion. By no means of small importance are the special attitudes and feelings of the therapee toward the therapist and therapeutic process.

Rita had a long history of therapeutic failure. The prognosis was uniformly expressed as unfavorable; her immediate reaction to hospitalization was such as to appear that she would be unable to use its resources; her first approach to psychological referral was negative in quality; and there was the possibility that her refractoriness masked a psychosis. Still, behind the façade and anger there was a substantial plea for help—and the promise that if only one could sustain the massive fire of her aggression (her prime defense) a therapeutic relationship could be established. This she unmistakably said in symbolic fashion in the first interview. There was also the ineffable quality mentioned above which impelled the therapist, like other staff members, to help her. It seemed also that, if she was to be helped at all, it would need to be at this point, where hospitalization was not yet a way of life, and when anxiety and hostility were driving her toward resolution of conflicts.

The test data we interpreted as favorable to intensive psychotherapy of an uncovering sort. There was first of all sufficient affectivity available for therapy. Fantasy-sublimative capacities were in abundance and this was of course correlated with a good intellect. The disturbance in personality organization—the nature of the defenses—was not such as to rule out the possibilities of a transference relationship. Of importance, also, was the apparent absence of a clinical depression of basically psychotic proportions.

The possible goals, and the various roles the therapist would play, were considered. These cannot always be determined in advance and depend in great part upon the vicissitudes of the therapy. However, it was known that Rita's hostility was a protective cloak which separated her from other people and that her feelings would become more intense as therapy progressed. A repertory of flight reactions and severe disruptive behavior of hysterical or psychotic-like nature might also be expected. If such predicted events could be survived, then she might come to learn the basis for her loneliness and hostility. Obviously, significant roles of the therapist would involve mother, father, and uncle either individually or overlapping in time.

Thus individual psychotherapy was started in June, 1950, and continued until July, 1954, with such lacunae as were made necessary by the patient's absence from the hospital. A total of 206 hours was thus given Rita.

The *beginning* stages of therapy were spent by the patient in defining her problem—her despair, hopelessness, and lack of progress toward mature goals. She felt that by coming to the hospital she had doomed herself to the same pattern as her father. She iterated and reiterated the desertion by her family—primarily her mother—and her conviction that psychology and psychiatry were futile. (She had herself once been a psychology major and claimed special knowledge of the field because of this.) Again and again she said it was futile to see the therapist—that nothing could be gained by talking—that it was practical help that she needed. She then brought up the fantasy given earlier of a knight in armor who would provide her with a castle, coach, and the most beautiful of raiment. The reality equivalents of this fantasy were a young, blond, handsome, and worshipful man providing a custom home, a Cadillac, and clothes from the most lavish of shops. (Even without means she had contrived over the years to buy the best of apparel and she bitterly resented the clothes made available by the hospital or other patients.) Rita was up to the last period of therapy fully convinced that this would some day happen—that she was worthy of it, and that it was her due.

The therapist's passivity soon infuriated her. The rare interventions which he attempted were scornfully rejected. She urged him to be more active and to give practical advice. When he maintained his position by pointing out that the answers lay with her and that they could be found with exploration, she berated him as an "intellectual fool" and attacked psychology, and the hospital itself. She was astute in seeking out the therapist's weaknesses and capitalizing upon them.

Such periods were often followed by tears, self-reproach, depression, and statements that it was easier to die than live this way. There were times when she would not come to therapy, pleading fatigue or illness. As could be expected, her hostility generalized to the ward so that nursing personnel complained of her behavior. Consequently she was transferred from an open ward to one offering closer supervision. She was assigned choice industrial therapy positions, but on one basis or another alienated the supervisor and patients and thus forced termination of the assignment. Rita refused to attend the dances because she thought the patients were beneath her. On the ward she insisted she was not a "scullery maid" and did a minimum of kitchen work. She scorned the assistance of a social worker from an independent Jewish agency and would not identify with the Jewish patients in any way.

Her mother was a frequent subject of the therapy hour. Rita felt that she had been deserted by her mother, who had gone to the Middle East during this period. She refused to read her letters, to write to her, or to accept her gifts. She frequently said that as far as she was concerned her mother might as well be dead. One Christmas she wanted to destroy a package from her which she had not even opened. This was not permitted by hospital personnel and she was obsessed with the injustice of it for weeks. At other times she would urge the therapist and other people to write to her mother requesting money for various purposes. This was a constant theme in many therapeutic hours; it was only with great difficulty that she came to understand that money was a medium of affection and the latter rather than money itself was the issue. Minor regressions in the final stages of therapy inevitably involved a continuation of demands that money be obtained from her mother.

It was only natural that Rita should inveigh against the therapist, who, as she saw him at this period, was someone who focused her pain but did nothing immediate and practical to alleviate it. This was an aspect of the *transference* and *magical maneuver* which are the crux of the transference process itself (2).

Rita recalled as the happiest period in her life the time in a large eastern city when she was 19 to 23 years of age. It was during World War II and this city was adjacent to a large Army air base. She was employed as a secretary to a key governmental official and found herself in great social demand by military men and others. She was particularly proud of the fact that she had entree to the Officers' Club. Each evening brought a new swain, possibly a new gown, and a place of high entertainment. She fell in with the mood, drank a great deal, and was involved in numerous temporary alliances of a sexual nature. The latter Rita never quite enjoyed. She had little emotional reaction to the act and considered herself frigid. She believed, however, that sexual relations were a necessary culmination of any friendship between man and woman, that it was expected of her, that it was one of the few things of value she had to offer, and that if she refused she would not be dated.

While Rita recalls this as a happy period she also reflects on her promiscuity with some guilt. She wishes this period both reinstated and blotted out. What she cannot so easily put aside is the serviceman who asked her to marry him. She saw him regularly, grew somewhat fond of him, but could never bring herself to accept his proposal. In fact, violent quarrels ensued when she had other dates—and she insisted upon them. Before military service he had been studying to be a psychologist, and she made frequent references to this fact in the therapy. This was her closest relationship to any male who was not a relative, but on one basis or another she terminated it. Years later, when her illness flowered, she returned to him wishing to reinstate her earlier role, but he had married in the interim and was no longer interested in continuing their relationship. Rita believes that he played a significant part in her illness, for it was shortly after terminating their friendship that she left the city and began her travels. It was to be expected that in the course of therapy this significant relationship would be reinstated and that the therapist would be projected upon in this way.

The *middle course* of therapy saw the release of tremendous resistances in the form of hostility and depression. She tried but could not stay away from therapy. On a few occasions somatic symptoms allowed her to rationalize not coming. Rita was almost impossible to live with on the ward and she began to be shunned by fellow patients. At one point the ward physician ordered seclusion overnight. She was sobered by this experience, since she had always maintained a conceptual distance between herself and "mentally ill" patients.

Unconsciously she was attempting once again to terminate therapy before a transference could be effected. Investment of libido in a positive way was so threatening as to be avoided at all costs. There was undoubtedly an incestuous basis to the developing transference for she reported a fantasy in which her uncle made advances to her in return for his sufferance. The memories of her father were the most severely repressed, and even free association throughout the many hours of therapy was not successful in bringing much to light about him. Later requests for information about him were met impatiently by Rita with statements that she was too young to remember him. The two fragments that did come to light were (1) that he was handsome, and (2) the fear she experienced when he escaped from the state hospital. This thoroughgoing repression is significant because of the energy devoted to maintaining it over the years. The "pull" of these residual memories indicates the ambivalence of the oedipal relationship. "The 'handsome one' was taken away by madness," she must have reasoned. "But how does madness come about? Am I to blame or is my mother?" That some such reasoning actually took place is seen in her frequent reference to "following in [her] father's footsteps." Having made her father ill was it not also natural for her to become ill in the same way? But principally her mother—her rival—must bear the burden for this deprivation. Not only did Mrs. L. possess the loved father, but she destroyed him by making him ill and, as we shall see later, put Rita in his place.

The *transference maneuver* involving the acting out of oedipal desires was of course a necessary part of therapy, but so great was the intensity of the conflict that the patient actually interrupted treatment. This she did by leaving the hospital on two different occasions.

The tremendous need to incorporate, to receive, to be the object of beneficence is not entirely uncharacteristic of a personality which cannot give or yield in human relationships. To interact mutually implies identification with bestower as well as recipient. But to give was alien to Rita and she pitied all humanitarians. "One must first take care of oneself" was her watchword. (We suspect in this connection that her strong feeling against social workers was in part because of their giving qualities.) This aspect of her character most certainly came about from severe frustration of oral needs, and all the children bore its stamp. Mrs. L. for all her piety, self-sacrifice, and martyrdom was unable to give what Rita needed most—a part of herself in the form of nourishment at the time when it counted most. The reasons can only remain conjectural at this time.

Nourishment deprivation became especially fixated at an oral-sadistic stage and, at higher symbolic levels, found its equivalent in biting sarcasm, food intake, a tenacious social quality (which often stood her in good stead), and the like. One incident bears this out. Rita related the peculiar gratification she obtained from sexually arousing male companions and then denying them satisfaction. This was a frequently recurring pattern and frankly castrative in import. The oral phases of this demasculinization process were symbolically seen in bold relief in the interviews.

These formulations lead us to the patient's conception of self. Here a dualism in Rita's nature is apparent. Never having experienced a fundamentally satisfying relationship she was sensitized to the rejecting qualities of her environment. But in her fantasies she was the most alluring of creatures and no one could afford to reject her. This partisan appreciation of self involved reflections of reality testing. It was in actuality a *schizoid maneuver* and a part of her larger fantasy of omnipotence (3). The manipulation of the transference involved working through such dynamic conversions of reality and also what Silverberg calls *magical maneuvers*—the seeking of omnipotence through projection of this quality upon the therapist within a framework of magic.

One could expect that a patient with a schizoid or schizophrenic orientation would use mechanisms of this sort in the resolution of conflicts. It is not, however, the presence of these mechanisms which leads to such speculations, but their strength and the manner in which they were rooted in the personality which is crucial. The success or failure of treatment often depends upon such questions.

One area Rita invariably avoided was ethnic and religious membership. Rita claimed to be either an agnostic or an atheist. More properly this position was a flight from the religion of her parents rather than any philosophical position. In the hospital, social services by a Jewish philanthropic group were available. These included case work, religious services, financial assistance, etc. Rita made one or two abortive efforts to meet with the workers and thereafter would have nothing to do with them. Even during moments of direst need, when she was seeking to leave the hospital, she could not bring herself to accept their assistance.

Rita was born and spent her formative years in Poland, the refuge of millions of Jews. Here they lived in ghettos and were tolerated until periodic pogroms stirred their anxieties and uprooted them further. With the coming of Hitler they were either dispersed or systematically destroyed. In this part of Europe the age-old dream of leaving the Diaspora and finding a homeland beat fast in many hearts. Here it was that Zionism, if not actually created as an idea, received its major impetus. The shame, fear, and indignities of centuries were no longer tolerable and they sought roots in soil promised long ago by Holy Book, legend, and prophecy. For many, however, it was more expeditious to suppress their lack of identity and feeling of not being wanted.

Rita's paternal grandfather was a rabbi. It was the rabbis and Talmudic scholars above all who held fast to Hebraic religious and cultural values where assimilation and conversion were often thought to give immunity to persecution. They were at once the bulwark of resistance and the herald of the new life, and they permitted in themselves no compromise with tradition and did not brook it in others. It is quite probable that Rita did not go untouched by these currents. But the burden of being a Jew added to her other problems was something she could not accept. The finality of these early and troublesome feelings she summed up succinctly in this particular way: When asked early in treatment where her father might be, she said with a shrug, "He was deported to his home in Poland and killed in a concentration camp by Hitler."

In the search for identity these deep-rooted membership feelings were not easily reinstated and in the *middle period* of therapy they were hardly touched upon at all. One can speculate that these are as deeply rooted as the earliest stages of development and will be worked through as one of the later stages of maturation. There was some evidence near the close of treatment that self-realization involving freedom of impulse, object cathexis, and reality organization involved Rita's identification as a Jew, which she came more and more to accept. It is difficult to see the resolution of her identity conflict without also involving her ethnic membership.

What we consider the *ending period* of therapy was signified by a diminution of hostility in the interviews and in the hospital milieu. She was able to say to the therapist that her hostility toward him was unjustified but that she could not help feeling that way. This occurred gradually as a transitional stage and it was a harbinger of positive feelings to come. She found it less and less necessary to maintain a role which forced rejection by the therapist.

The number of interviews per week had been manipulated as a means of furthering movement in accordance with her capacity to handle the insight and anxiety they provoked. At this point they were increased to three hours a week. She came to understand her feelings toward her mother as competitive and as wanting to be cared for within a pattern of mutually destructive forces. For the first time she saw her mother as someone with her own problems, and she was able to gradually think of herself as someone not entirely alone and differentiated from her mother. She began to talk of the outside world and how pleasant it could be. The fantasy of the "knight" was less and less frequently invoked.

Rita still made occasional demands of the therapist for practical help and said that no good could come from merely talking. But she said this with a trace of laughter. She was given an industrial therapy assignment which she held continuously. Her work was thoroughly acceptable and she made several friends among the employees and patients. Her improvement was independently noted by psychiatrists so that pre-leave planning was instituted.

Most fundamental of all, Rita was systematically able to work through her relationship to male figures other than the therapist and to understand her self-defeating behavior. While her behavior toward men on several visits outside the hospital still involved castrative components, she was aware of it and took steps to change it. A recent relationship of this kind indicated that she could now see and accept herself as a woman without condemnation by mechanisms which led to rejection or to offering herself as a sexual object.

While the patient had made gains at the close of psychotherapy, we did not construe this as a completed job. There were obviously many areas yet untouched. Since the patient herself did not show an inclination to deal with them, we were content to leave them for the time being. The obvious next step was for Rita to test her new-found insights and strengths outside the hospital and to continue psychotherapy on an outpatient basis.

ADDENDUM

We have described the life history of a patient whom it was possible to observe and treat over a four-year period. This was a woman who had a tremendous need to interact with others but who was unable to do so. She lacked identity and could play no satisfactory personal or social role. Guilt, hostility, depression, dependency were all prominent symptoms.

If we were to formulate the patient's dynamics in capsular fashion we would point primarily to parental images formed in a setting of personal and ethnic dislocation. Rita's mother was never able to offer her the security and affection which she needed in the oral stages of her development. This left her with a basic defect upon which to build later social relationships. Mrs. L. was herself the victim of severe conflicts, with a passive-suffering personality orientation, and when her husband no longer met her masochistic needs, she placed her children successively in this role. It was necessary for her to have someone ill to nurture, but in this way also she was able to rob them of strength so that her own deficiencies seemed less in contrast. It has been said by an independent observer that what Mrs. L. really demands is that Rita take care of her. More properly it appears to us that what Mrs. L. is seeking is a weak, emotionally disintegrated person to whom to relate and in this way to gain strength. With special sensitivity Rita responded unconsciously and homeostatically by hostility sufficiently intense to frighten Mrs. L. and remove her as a threat. This was an elemental act of defense of the personality although rather complex in mechanism. It was of course accomplished at a price, as we have seen. The evidence for oral aggression indicates that the process was begun very early in her development.

Rita approached the oedipal period with a fixation upon a father who himself was struggling with his identity. Unfortunately, we know so little about him as to make any statement of his motivations conjectural. However, his departures from reality, self-destructive attempts, and vocational incapacity all point to a disorganized personality. It was probably difficult, if not impossible, under the circumstances for Rita to survive this important developmental period without trauma. That trauma did occur we see clearly from her present attempts at feminine and sexual definition and her unconscious incestuous conflicts.

The improvement which came with psychotherapy occurred in conjunction with formulations such as these derived from test findings and observations in the therapy itself. While improvement may well have been independent of such formulations, or related to still other variables, they were the conceptual tools the therapist employed and have meaning in this sense.

Our presentation has been rather free of concern about an exact diagnosis, which, in a sense, is the specific function of this volume. In actuality, more concern was given to diagnosis in the hospital than the material here would imply. At least one of the psychiatrists who had seen Rita before she entered the hospital and who retrospectively assessed the case material after several years considered her schizophrenic. Our earliest test material did not necessarily rule out the possibility of an ambulatory schizophrenia, and this possibility still exists. However, the urgency of a diagnosis no longer exists. We have instead some understanding of anxiety and defenses and these seem of greater importance for the patient's welfare than a diagnosis. Diagnosis, also, as a ritual can be an empty thing and even at times misleading. It can, for example, cause the clinician to abbreviate his diagnostic and prognostic understanding, and bias the therapist away from treatment. If our description of this particular personality has been meaningful in terms of the patient's future welfare, then a diagnostic label at this point would be merely a postscript.

APPENDIX
Rorschach Responses (1950)

I.	30″	Two people waving
		D M H
	110″	

II.	55″	Two roosters clapping wings together
		W FM A
	90″	

III.	23″	1. A butterfly
		D F A P
		2. Two birds tugging at something
		W FM A → P
	100″	

IV.	23″	A dragon upside down
		W F → FM A
	120″	

V.	75″	V An eagle's beak
		d F Ad
	170″	

VI.	10″	1. Cat's head
		D F Ad
		2. Rug—from an animal
		W F Aobj
	95″	

VII.	15″	1. Dwarfs
		D F (H)
		2. Couple of lambs
		D F A
	130″	

VIII.	19″	1. Two rats
		D F A → P
		2. Cow heads—bulls—at least bovine animals
		D F Ad
	80″	

IX.   90"   Two deer heads
                D F Ad
        170"

X.   70"   1. Insects
                D F A
                2. A snake
                D F A
        180"

Rorschach Responses (1953) [3]

I

36"   Oh, I can't go through this, I just can't take it, what if I refused to take it, what will you do? (Examiner did not answer)

1. It still looks like two human beings waving. D M,FC' H

D4 The skirt body, sort of like those black—silhouettes—hands right here.

2. Or is it one human being? D F H (contam →)

D4 I did? Well, let's leave it the way it is, it has to be two if these are the heads unless it was a two-headed human.
It just looks like an ink blot. D6 V

3. Sort of looks like two faces, I mean what do you call those black outlines? d F Hd

4. I don't know what a bat looks like so I don't know whether it looks like a bat or not. W F A P
I don't see anything in them anyway, I don't have a very good imagination, I just face reality.

I've heard so many people talk about bats so I think I have to see bats. These could be wings these whole sides (D2) and this would be the head.

5. It could be a map of a country with the four great lakes. W,S F Geo

(Recounted her previous responses.)

Only there should be five (referring to the Great Lakes of the United States). I don't know why, just the whole thing. (Question besides shape) The white looks like lakes.

[3] Location areas are from the Integral Research Company cards.

Legs, dress, heads, hands,
that's all.
I don't see much of any-
thing—except an ink blot
(laughed).

272"

II

22"   (Sighed) You'll probably
get exactly the same an-
swer you got before. I
just detest these.

1. Well, I guess it looks
like two old witches
clapping hands, play-
ing peas porridge hot.
W M (H)

Nose, face, then their (top)
bodies don't look human at all,
actually just heads. D4 Looks
like hands.

2. I think the last time I
said roosters.
D CF A

Something about the red reminds you of the mane, do you
call it the mane, honestly I've
lost my vocabulary, it would be
the mane of a horse not a
rooster.

I should have brought
my glasses, it seems
so silly.

3. They look like two
lambs.
D F Ad P

This shape looks like the head of
a cow I guess, sheep, lamb, just
the head.

4. Or dogs or something.
D F Ad
Anyhow two heads,
some kind of animal.
I think you're real
cruel, I'll never speak
to you again.
(Laughed)

These two heads,
neck, shoulders, not
necessarily lambs,
some kind of animal,
cow or dog.

I remember on one of
these seeing Scotties,
that's not the one was

it, it doesn't look like Scotties now, they can't change. I want to see the Scotties and I can't see them.

241"

III

3"

1. The middle one looks like a butterfly.
D   F   A   P

D3   Shaped like one. It could be either a butterfly or a moth.

2. Looks like they're having a tug-of-war but they're not human they look like birds.
D   F   Ad   (see #4)
And the middle one looks like a butterfly.

The head looks like it has a beak, the rest doesn't really look like a bird.

3. This sure looks like two heads with a little bit—a beard and a head (laughed) funny looking head.
D   F   Hd

VD4   Like an old man with a beard, funny shaped head. (Why old?) because usually old men have beards.

4. Birds couldn't be having a tug-of-war.
W   M,FM   H,A
(contam   →   )

They look like they're pulling. The position they're standing in looks like they could be pulling against each other, actually the body doesn't look like a bird, it looks like a person. It doesn't look like a bird and doesn't look like a person. Take away the head and it looks like a person, persons with birds' heads having a tug-of-war and the rodents and butterflies watching, could be building a fire or could be taking the eggs out of the nest. If you want me to write you a story.

Did you ever take these, how many responses did you see?

It doesn't really look like a head.

5. These could be a pair of socks (laughs).
D   F   Obj   O

D5   The foot, top, the heel and toe.

| | 6. Maybe more like fish than socks with a tail and head and fins. | D5 The tail here, head and fin. A |
| 158″ | Do you ever tell anybody the results of these tests? | D2 Could be the tail, and body of some kind of rodent. D F Ad |

IV

19″	If you knew how much I hated this you wouldn't do it to me.	
	1. Still looks like a dragon's head, the head and wings and part of the body's gone. W F A	D1 The head, D2 wings, could be the dragon's legs I guess (D4) D3 His tail.
	2. The middle part, I don't know much about anatomy but it looks like an X-ray or some part of the anatomy. dr F At	The middle part (in D5) right here, sort of looks like it may be a spine, just this little section, it's all so vague. Isn't a defined picture of some part of the body.
	3. These two things sort of look like two boots. D F Obj	D7 Outline. This is a foot like great big boots, they have with big tops on them. Actually just see the definition of a foot.
	4. I should think this should look like something, it could be two arms with hands on the ends, no it couldn't either but it's not attached to a body just one on each side.	D4 Really doesn't fit into anything, there's no body there. (Rejected)
134″		

V

| 13″ | 1. Looks like a big moth. Or a butterfly, no a moth I guess. W FM A P | Some kind of thing that flies. D4 the wings D7 the body. It's so much bigger and there's no color so it's more like a moth, it just looks more like one. |
| | 2. These two things look like eagles' heads, beaks and things. d F Ad | VD3 Beak, not necessarily an eagle. (Question) Two beaks, wait a minute could be one head with the beak open but I first saw two. |

I don't know, doesn't look like anything else but I keep having the feeling I should see something.

d, S F Ad

3. These two little jiggers look like Christmas socks, children's that is.
dr Fm Obj,Sym

D2 (part) Just looks like socks hanging up for Christmas, just the legs, it doesn't go on to anything, seems like you should see the rest.

Is the time it takes to see something important? Seems to me I saw more before, seems like insects and centipedes.

116"

VI

4"

1. Cat's head.
D F Ad
2. Could be one of those bear rugs.
W F Aobj P

D3 The head really looks like a cat, whiskers and ears.
The whole thing, head and rug all spread out, it's just the closest thing.
(Anything besides the shape?) Could be a dead cat skinned I guess, the head looks like a cat. (Anything besides outline?) The middle looks like a spine, no just the outline. (Apparently no shading used)

I don't know, I just don't see anything else. (Repeated her two previous responses)

I don't know, I don't see a thing, not a thing, I see less than last time, is that a good sign or bad sign.

3. The middle, I don't know, something about it makes me think of an X-ray.
D F A +
I guess that's all.

D10 Actually nothing definite like in anatomy but something about the middle part of it looks like it, I don't know how to explain it.

173"

VII

8"

1. Oh.
   This one is the one
   with two Scotties'
   heads, dogs.
   D F A

   VD2 Head, body and tail.

2. Top thing looks like a
   moth.
   D F A

   VD4 Middle and wings, I can't
   think of anything else it looks
   like.

3. I remember one—that
   looks like two lambs.
   D F A

   ΛD2 The closest thing I could
   think of I guess.

I supposed if you'd kind
of—in the other direction
you could see it looks
like two lambs.

All I see is Scotties and
the moth. If I turn it,
could be lambs except
this is too long, lambs
don't have long ears do
they, or any?

93"

VIII

10"

The colored ones I re-
member I saw less on
them than the others.

I like pictures that have definite
shape and look like something.

1. Two, ummmm, rats,
   what's another be-
   sides insects and cen-
   tipedes? Rodents I
   mean.
   D F A → P

   D1 Some kind of rodent. (Alive
   or mounted?) I guess it could be
   alive (question) I don't know,
   you have too analytic a mind.

2. Sort of looks like two
   cows' heads.
   D F Ad

   VD2 Could be steers' heads,
   horn, nose and eyes.

3. And the whole shape
   looks like a butterfly,
   I've seen a lot of them,
   it's colored so make it
   a butterfly instead of
   a moth.
   D FC A

   D2

4. Two flags.
   D Fm Obj,Sym

   D5 It's square and sort of gives
   the appearance of flags flying
   but there are no handles.

5. A Christmas tree or one of those trees that look like Christmas trees.
D   F   Pl,Sym

(What makes it look like a Christmas tree?) (Patient laughed) How can I answer? Because that's the closest shape it appears.

I think I saw a snake, I wonder.

(Snakes?) A snake. It seems like I saw insects before but now I can't see any of them.

Oh.

140″   Maybe the insects are in this one, maybe they're coming yet.

IX

53″   That's a conglomeration.

20″   It doesn't look like anything.

1. Oh me, well it sort of looks like anatomy I guess, the middle. I don't know anything about anatomy.
dr   F   A +

VD5 This middle thing looks like part of the body. (Area below the pink) I don't know, maybe it's intestines or part of the stomach, vaguely—it's very vague.

2. The middle sort of looks like two deer heads here and here, sort of obliterated.
D   F   Ad

>D2 Not at all defined just in a cloud, very vague. (Diffusion not certain)

3. The orange could be a couple of witches.
D   Fm   (H)d
I try so hard to see something and I just don't see it.

It's awfully vague, this sort of looks like the head and the rest is—they're just floating like ghosts.

Well, I should think with all those colors you should see lots of things.

Did I say that top thing looked like a butterfly? I'm seeing too many butterflies. (What makes it look that way?) It doesn't really, it's just this pink thing. (D6)
D   F   A

Some people see lots of anatomy and part of the body.

How any of this stuff can mean anything is beyond me.

205″

You'd think with all those colors you should see lots of things.

X

3″   Oh yeah, here they are.

1. Yeah, these two things sort of look like snakes or caterpillars.
D FC A P

D4 The head and tail. (Which?) Caterpillars more than snakes. (Why?) Because I think they have green caterpillars and I don't know about green snakes.

2. The blue things sort of look like spiders, I don't know whether they really do or not, I want to say something looks like something and that's the closest.
D F A P

Other than the insects or caterpillars the rest doesn't look like much of anything.

I think you should tell me what the result is after I go through all this torture.

D1 Don't really look like spiders but that's the closest.

3. These two little gray things look like something, body, legs, this thing could be the head I guess and this the body and legs, but I don't know what kind of animal.
D FM A

D7 I don't know what kind, could be antelope but the head doesn't look like it. The body and the thin legs here, the head just doesn't look right, just the body, the head doesn't look like it. (Why antelope?) Ah, I don't know, the bodies and legs look like something running but the head doesn't look right. Let's say a headless antelope.

Immediately I see the rodents and insects, some kind of insects, I don't know what kind, two of them.

183″

RORSCHACH SUMMARY (1953)

R = 38	M = 3	H = 4
W = 7	FM = 2 + 1	Hd = 3
D = 26 + 1	M = 3	A = 14 + 2
d = 2 + 1	F = 28	Ad = 7 + 1
Dd = 3	FC = 2	Aobj = 1
S = 0 + 2		At = 3
		Obj = 4
		Pl = 1
		Geo = 1
		Sym = 0 + 3

$$\frac{\text{Total F}}{R} = 74\%$$

$$\frac{FK + F + Fc}{R} = 74\%$$

$$\frac{A + Ad}{R} = 50\%$$

$$P = 7$$

$$O = 1$$

$$(H + A):(Hd + Ad) = 18:10$$

$$\text{Sum C} = \frac{FC + 2CF + 3C}{2} = 1$$

$$M:\text{Sum C} = 3:1$$

$$(FM + m):(Fc + c + C') = 5:0$$

$$\frac{\text{VIII, IX, X}}{R} = 29\%$$

$$W:M = 7:3$$

$$W\% = 18; \quad D\% = 68; \quad d\% = 5 \qquad Dd \frac{\text{and}}{\text{or}} S = 8\%$$

REFERENCES

1. Hathaway, S. R., and McKinley, J. C. *Manual for the Minnesota multiphasic personality inventory.* New York: Psychological Corp., rev. ed., 1951.
2. Silverberg, W. V. The factor of omnipotence in neurosis. *Psychiatry,* 1949, *12*, 387–398.
3. Silverberg, W. V. The schizoid maneuver. *Psychiatry,* 1947, *10*, 383–393.

CHAPTER EIGHT

An Adult Neurotic

BY LAWRENCE S. ROGERS

Introduction

Joseph F. Miller, a white, married, Catholic, male veteran, 36 years of age, requested treatment shortly after his transfer to this city. His work consists of servicing complicated machinery as a field representative for a nationally known firm, and it is necessary for him to be transferred from time to time. He had been seen for fifteen treatment interviews at a clinic in another city and wanted to resume treatment as soon as possible. The veteran is about six feet tall and weighs close to 155 pounds. In general, he may be described as a rather slender but handsome man. He is always well dressed and gives the impression of a successful salesman or junior executive.

During the intake interview, the veteran enumerated a variety of symptoms: loss of appetite, nausea, and frequent attacks of colitis. He complained of repeated episodes during which he suffered from extreme feelings of panic. He associated these panic feelings with situations in which he was a member of an audience whose attention was focused on, for example, either a speaker as in a church or a screen as in a movie. He also related that he occasionally felt an urge to take a knife and kill his wife. While driving he was preoccupied with impulses either to drive into other cars or drive off high places. He was terrified at the thought that these impulses might materialize. At the intake interview, the worker noted that despite obvious anxiety he spoke freely and easily. Although he recognized his emotional problems, he still felt strongly that there must be some physiological basis for his symptoms and requested assignment to a physician. He was convinced that only a medical person could possibly give him the reassurance he needed. The veteran gave the impression that he was looking for a magical formula to solve his problems. The intake worker also predicted that despite the patient's superficial interest he would present much resistance to psychotherapy.

The history and background, as presented below, were obtained during the course of the therapeutic interviews. The patient was referred for psychological evaluation after the tenth therapy hour. He was seen for 52 interviews but moved to another city before treatment could be completed.

Childhood and Adolescence (Up to Age 21)

The patient, an only son and the oldest of four siblings, was born in a large western city in 1918. When four years old, he developed asthma after an attack of "whooping cough." The asthma occurred at a time when his mother was pregnant with the next child, and the patient had been sent to visit relatives in a nearby city. The asthma persisted until he was of high-school age. The veteran described himself as a rather sickly child who was never very strong or big.

There was apparently little communication between Mr. Miller and his parents. Rarely was anything discussed with him; rather, he was simply given orders as to what to do or not to do. In general, he described his mother as a very compulsive, over-protecting, rejecting woman. She was the dominant figure in the home, made the necessary decisions, and handled the money. She took care of his material needs, and nursed him when he was ill, but devoted the rest of her time to the house. As far back as he can remember, he recalls his mother scolding him for not being more tidy and neat. His mother felt so strongly about having her home dirtied that she forbade him to bring any of his friends into the house. The veteran attributed his lack of friends primarily to his mother's attitude and still feels somewhat bitter about it. The father was equally rejecting. The veteran could not recall any discussion with him that did not end in an argument. His father was severely critical of the patient and when, on occasion, the patient would rebel, corporal punishment resulted.

Mr. Miller's relationships with his sisters were always quite distant. He never had much to do with them and always felt that they were favored by his parents. He recalled that his oldest sister usually got the clothes she wanted, whereas his requests were customarily denied. The veteran had a strong fear of water, would not go swimming, and would tremble when near a dog, whereas he described his sisters as healthy girls who did not share his fears. He recalled some instances when the girls and his parents had a gay time at the beach while he felt miserable.

The veteran as a youth felt different from other boys. He recalled vividly that he did not receive birthday presents, even though he once asked for them. He felt ashamed because his classmates, who were no better off economically, could boast about the presents they had received. Too, the patient felt odd because he was made to wear short trousers for a long time after boys his age had graduated into long ones. The veteran's academic record was fairly good although he was too timid to volunteer in class. His social adjustment was poor throughout elementary school but was more adequate in high school. He had wanted to go to college, but his parents flatly refused him permission. His disappointment was very great, but he could not recall any discussion of the matter, nor did he remember any reasons being given him. The veteran still does not know why he could not go to college. Nevertheless, he did manage to take some evening courses in drafting and engineering. After he finished high school, he worked at various odd jobs until he went into military service.

The patient did not receive any sex instruction at home, nor was sex ever mentioned. The patient was sent away from home when his siblings were born and given the story that they were brought by the doctor. When he was about nine years of age he learned the "facts of life" from a friend. He recalls how startled he was about this information and how he immediately spread the word to other less informed boys. One boy's mother complained to the patient's parents. The patient was told in no uncertain terms that he was a horrible child and he was severely whipped. He was quite confused by this experience because no one had said that he had told any lies nor was he told why he was being punished except that he had committed a sin. Since then, he has always envied homes in which sex is discussed, and people who can talk about sex freely.

The patient began masturbating in his early teens and continued this practice until his marriage. He always felt extremely guilty about his masturbation and relates he first experienced panic in church when he felt the priest was referring to him in a sermon on sin. He occasionally frequented burlesque houses and this activity intensified his feelings of guilt. The patient consistently denied any kind of homosexual activity although he relates he was approached once or twice in later life. He was embarrassed and upset by these incidents. The veteran's relationships with members of the opposite sex were infrequent and quite casual. He occasionally dated girls but did not get involved in any necking or other sexual activity.

Military Service (Age 21 to 27)

The veteran had served in the National Guard for several years prior to World War II and had won his commission. He entered military service in 1941 when the Guard was nationalized. His overall service record was fairly good, although he received only one promotion during his five years of service. For the first two years the patient was in good health, but in 1943 he was hospitalized for a "nervous stomach." Shortly afterwards he was sent to the European theater, where he served nine months before being hospitalized for a recurrence of his asthma. The veteran attributed this attack of asthma to the change in climate and denied there were any emotional factors involved. However, it was brought out in treatment that he began getting tense, upset, and fearful when he was shipped overseas. He was seasick and frightened all the way across and was certain he would not live to see land again. Shortly after he entered the hospital, his unit was moved up to the front lines, but the veteran vehemently insists he was unaware that such a move was contemplated. He was sent back to the United States and hospitalized for six months. After this he was placed on limited duty and assigned to a midwestern city.

Mr. Miller related that after his return to duty he felt more inadequate than ever. Being on limited duty lowered him, he thought, in the eyes of his fellow officers and the enlisted men. He felt incompetent to plan the work of his outfit and found it very difficult to give orders. He was continually worried for fear the work would not get done in time or mistakes would be made and he would be criticized by his superiors. He attributed his good fortune in being able to do a satisfactory job to his noncommissioned officers. The pattern of comparative social isolation continued, and he felt there was no one on whom he could really depend. He had no close friends and described himself as being different from the other men. One major area of difference was his attitude toward sex. He never told dirty stories and was embarrassed when he heard them.

He rarely went out with women and had not had sexual intercourse until he met his future wife in 1944. He had had a number of dates with her but, according to the patient, had not progressed to the point of sexual play. Mr. Miller was very fond of her and thought of proposing marriage. When she admitted to him she had an illegitimate child he was startled. However, he claimed this made no difference in his attitude toward her. But he insisted she have intercourse with him since she had done it with at least one other man. She agreed, but the patient became so upset emotionally he could hardly perform the act. He immediately felt extremely guilty and worthless, went into a panic state, and was hospitalized in a neuropsychiatric ward for two weeks. The veteran could not bring himself to discuss with his physicians the real reason for this depressive episode. He was given symptomatic treatment, recovered rapidly, and was returned to duty.

They were married shortly afterwards at the veteran's insistence. Mr. Miller has given various reasons why he insisted upon the marriage. At first he said he was in love with her and wanted to marry her; later in treatment, he stated he felt he had to marry her because they had had sexual relations; still later he admitted he felt he ought to marry her because no other woman would have him. Shortly after their marriage Mrs. Miller insisted they adopt her illegitimate daughter. The veteran protested, but capitulated when his wife threatened to leave him. He was terribly embarrassed because he strongly suspected his parents knew that this child was his wife's illegitimate daughter. He has never discussed this problem with them. About two weeks after his marriage the patient first had the urge to pick up a knife and kill his wife. This impulse reappeared frequently during the following years. It was Mrs. Miller's custom to spend one evening a week "with the girls" when they were first married. The veteran took this as a rejection, and felt that she could not love him if she could leave him alone. He was also jealous and suspicious despite the fact he was certain there were no other men involved. When he objected, she stopped going out without him. She offered no objections to his going out alone, and this too he has interpreted as proof that she did not love him.

Mr. Miller had planned to make the Army his career because it would offer him a secure future. But after the war was over, when there was little for him to do, he became dissatisfied and tense. His asthma recurred after not bothering him for nearly three years. He was hospitalized again in 1946, at which time he requested his discharge from military service. While in the hospital, he began feeling tense, upset, and depressed, and lost his appetite. He was finally transferred to an NP ward and given insulin to help him regain his appetite. His symptoms disappeared and he was discharged a few weeks later. He received various diagnoses while in service including "psychoneurosis, mixed type," "hysteria," and "obsessive-compulsive reaction." He was subsequently awarded 20 percent compensation by the VA for "psychoneurosis, mixed type."

Post-Service History (Age 27 to 36)

After his discharge from service, Mr. Miller moved back to the western city in which his parents resided. Experiencing difficulty in finding employment, he went to work for his father, a licensed plumber. Since he could do nothing that would please his father, this was a trying period. He was subject to constant criticism; either he was too slow, or was using the wrong tools, or was not doing the job the way his father would have done it. His father became particularly incensed if the veteran was late for work. Despite his efforts to get to work on time, the veteran was frequently late, and this precipitated more difficulties for him. In treatment, the patient was able to recognize the purposive aspect of his lateness. Finally, the patient began to develop "tight feelings in the chest" and decided to seek other employment.

Mr. Miller was able to secure training in mechanical work and subsequently went into business with a partner. The business went very well but the patient coud not tolerate his partner's wife, who, he felt, was interfering too much, giving orders, and preventing her husband from doing his share of the work. Consequently, the patient gave up this lucrative business to take a position with a large firm. Here he did well and was promoted to an administrative position but had considerable friction with his co-workers. He felt they did not like him, that they were jealous of his promotion, and that they thought he was not doing a good job. The patient developed dizzy spells and again reported loss of appetite. He was hospitalized twice, for a week each time, for "stomach condition."

In 1952 he joined the firm with which he is presently associated as a field representative and took a training course to learn the company's machines. While awaiting his first assignment, he noticed that other men with less seniority were being sent out to the field. His feelings of inadequacy increased, and he thought he was being ignored by his superiors. His colitis appeared during this period, becoming so severe he could not drive to work without stopping to relieve himself several times. About this same time he first experienced panic while driving or riding as a passenger in a car. Finally he received his first assignment but the symptoms did not disappear. He had visited numerous private physicians in attempts to get relief from his symptoms, but the physicians were unanimous in reporting no organic pathology. He then sought treatment at a mental hygiene clinic.

The veteran felt very inadequate on the job. He claimed he did not understand his machines thoroughly, he did not have an engineering degree as did most of his co-workers, and he did not have enough background to fully comprehend the theories of physics on which the machines operated. When anything went wrong, he could not sit down and figure out the source of the trouble; he had to work on the machine and do it by trial and error. This procedure, while highly successful and apparently satisfying to everyone else, left him very unhappy. Since he did have much free time, he was in a constant state of anxiety for fear he was not doing everything he should on the job. Exploration of this area in therapy revealed that he had, in fact, done everything he had been asked to do or could have thought of doing. He was tense because he felt that the other men looked down on him and had little respect for him. He thought that his superiors in the home office did not understand his problems, did not appreciate him, and sometimes had even forgotten about him. He resented the fact that the home office did not answer his letters promptly, although he frequently could not bring himself to reply to their inquiries or to file his reports on time. From all external indications, it seemed that he was doing a job that was satisfactory to the home office as well as the company to which he was assigned.

Although he did not mention it at the time of the intake interview, it later developed that one of Mr. Miller's primary problems was in the area of interpersonal relations. This problem was highlighted by the psychologist's report before it was brought out by the veteran, and only then was the patient able to focus upon and express it. The form of expression is exemplified by his discussion of social difficulties in his various types of employment. As the patient described the problem, he had no difficulty in making friends and keeping them for a short period of time. But always the same thing happened; he would do or say something that he felt had angered a friend and then was unable to accept the fact that this person would continue to be friendly to him. There were many times that, for no apparent reason, he found himself saying or doing something that must have been irritating to his friends or co-workers. The veteran consistently denied that he expected retaliation in any form from them; rather, he felt that they had lost interest in him and would not want to have anything further to do with him. Usually this led to increased feelings of inadequacy and anger at himself. These feelings were worked through with the patient, and he was able to accept the interpretation that they frequently had little basis in reality but were rather determined by, or aroused out of, his own feelings. He recited numerous examples of interactions between himself and his co-workers which contained no objective basis for his feelings. The possibility of fear of homosexual relationships was explored; but the patient brought forth material which seemed to be more characteristic of a dependency-independency conflict. He described his relationships in terms of expecting his friends to do more and more for him, and in terms of how their failure to do so occasionally led to the behavior described above.

His relationship with his wife can be described in similar terms. Essentially he wanted her to take over, run the household, the children, and himself. Failure on her part to do so resulted in his feeling that she did not really love him. He used each instance in which she did not do what he asked of her, or in which she did not do what he merely thought he would want her to do, as further evidence of her lack of love. He spent considerable time in treatment criticizing her, but he came to recognize that if she had done the opposite he would have felt just the same way. For example, when she did not protest his spending every evening and most of the week ends working on his hobbies, he took this as a sign she did not love him. However, he admitted that if she had protested he would have interpreted this behavior the same way. It is certain that if she pressed him into doing too much of the housework he would have been as disturbed as by her reluctance to have him do any.

The patient reported that his sexual adjustment with his wife was satisfactory; they had relations two or three times a week. He was always the aggressor and this bothered him; he never knew if she really wanted intercourse, although she usually had an orgasm and seemed to enjoy the act. However, she, a non-Catholic, insisted that contraceptive devices be used, and this added to Mr. Miller's feelings of guilt when he tried going to church for he felt he could never face the priest. Once, when assigned temporarily to another city, he had an extramarital affair. He described the woman involved as a dominating, aggressive person who took the initiative, made the dates, and provided an apartment for him. Although tremendously guilty, he looked back wistfully at this affair because it was so satisfying for him. Yet, he could never have married such a woman; he could not have trusted her and would have been extremely jealous. He never told his wife about this affair, although he suspected that she guessed what had occurred because he had mentioned the other woman's name in his sleep.

Sex plays an extremely important part in Mr. Miller's life. Despite his feeling that no woman but his wife would have him, he had almost constant fantasies of himself as a dashing Don Juan at whose feet beautiful women would fall. During the treatment period he had the occasion to return to his home office for two weeks. He had deliberately taken along things to do in the evenings because he feared his sexual desires, but found he was extremely restless in his room and could not concentrate. Despite these fears, he visited bars with the expectation of meeting some women but, contrary to his fantasies, became practically tongue-tied in the presence of women, and gradually the discomfort and tension mounted so that he had to leave and return to his room alone. Since his extramarital affair, if a woman ever did make any approach to him, he would take this as an attempted seduction and flee. Even in innocuous situations, as when one of the women at the home office invited several male field representatives to dinner, the patient felt he was being placed in a compromising position even though he knew there was no basis in reality for this feeling.

Mr. Miller's marital adjustment remained poor. He perceived his role in the family as the one who made the money and caused trouble by constant carping criticism. He and his wife differed completely on their desires for recreation; she liked movies and driving, neither of which he could enjoy because these situations produced his feelings of panic. He liked to visit friends or to go to bars and drink. Occasionally one would yield to the other, and plans would be made to spend an evening out. The results were invariably the same; supper would be late, the dishes not done, the house in a mess, Mrs. Miller would not be ready on time, and the veteran would become furious before they left the house. As a result, they rarely went out. Instead, he would work on his hobbies evenings and week ends while his wife would continue with her housework. The veteran has become most eager for his wife to go out without him despite his former resentment at such behavior on her part. Among the reasons for his change in attitude are a denial of jealousy on his part, an attempt to ease his guilt feelings for going out alone, and his inability to enjoy the things she likes to do.

Another area of difficulty has been the veteran's attitude toward his children. He resented his wife's illegitimate daughter and did not attempt to hide his feelings. He came to realize the child was not at fault and suspected that his resentment toward her was a way of expressing feelings toward his wife. The veteran could not bear to be in the presence of anyone who knew the child's real father. In contrast, he claimed his wife more than offset his resentment toward this girl by favoring her over their own two children. He perceives this girl as more intelligent and better adjusted than his own daughter and this augments his feelings of resentment. His child was shy, bashful, and very slow in all her activities, given to periods of crying and subject to psychosomatic stomach complaints. At first, he blamed his wife for the manner in which this child developed, but through treatment has come to accept some of the responsibility for her present state.

The veteran was aware that his own childhood was a most unpleasant experience for him, and it shocked him to realize that in many respects he was treating his children in the same manner in which he had been treated. He was usually cranky and irritable around the house and barked orders at his children, particularly the two girls. He said little about his son, who was only two years old and whom he dismissed as being just a baby. He was unable to discuss anything with the girls and tried to get his wife to do this for him. He refused to permit them to have bicycles or roller skates for fear they might hurt themselves, in spite of his realization that this made them as different from other children as he himself felt as a boy. As he put it, he always "expected the worst for them."

He always expected the worst for himself too. He was fearful of death and took elaborate steps to protect his health. When his sister was ill with an infectious disease in 1948, he refused to visit her; after she died, he refused to attend the funeral even though he knew this would antagonize the rest of the family. On two occasions during treatment he came in contact with sprays used for exterminating garden pests and each time sought medical care because he thought he absorbed some poisons through his skin. He was afraid to be alone because, as he put it, "Something might happen to me, and there would be no one to help me." He fears his panic states will result in death. As he described the development of a panic state, he becomes uncomfortable in a situation and this discomfort is followed by the feeling that he has exhaled all the air from his lungs, and there is a tightness of and pressing sensation on the chest. The veteran consciously then has to breathe deeply as if forcing air into his lungs since he is acutely aware that failure to do so might result in death. Getting out of a difficult situation by leaving a movie or stopping his car usually alleviates the panic state. His anxiety is best reduced by his wife's comforting him and patting him on the head saying, "There, there, everything will be all right."

Results of the Psychological Evaluation [1]

The patient was referred for psychological evaluation after the tenth interview. By this time the therapist was able to formulate more clearly the questions he wanted answered. One question was related to the possibility of paranoid ideation. The veteran had mentioned his feelings that people look at him in a restaurant, that he felt panicky when he was a focus of attention and was unable to form close friendships with men. The therapist also wanted to get some additional informa-

[1] The psychological evaluation was done by Phillip H. Chase, clinical psychology trainee.

tion concerning the patient's interpersonal relationships with important members of his family. He had indicated his attitude toward his wife and father only, up to this point, and had not mentioned his mother despite efforts to have him talk about her. Another question raised by the therapist concerned his hostility, the objects toward which it was directed, and the manner in which it was provoked.

At the time of testing, the psychologist who was asked these questions knew only the face sheet information about the patient. The complete Rorschach and some of the TAT stories are given below. The patient was also given a Sentence Completion Test (Michigan). He was unable to complete the latter, leaving out 20 of the 100 items, but the omitted items did not seem to form any particular pattern. The psychologist's report reads:

Test results emphasize a basically characterological problem with currently hysteroid defenses. Impairment of his ability to make adequate use of independent and creative fantasy, associated with emotional lability and naïveté, are characteristic of him. He has difficulty in repressing his unacceptable feelings and wishes, and is in the unfortunate position of being unable to make adequate use of fantasy as an alternate control. In fact, it appears that the very attempt to use fantasy typically results in preliminary success followed often by hopelessly inadequate endings that seem not to reduce, but to increase his anxiety.

Anxiety is easily evoked and seems to be primarily related to problems arising from his difficulty in developing close interpersonal relationships. Due to a markedly passive-aggressive character make-up, in which the infantile dependency needs are continually warring with his hostile tendencies, it is not difficult to understand his current conflict over sexual expression. Sexually, he is probably basically passive, and yet may be as demanding of his sexual partner as he is in other types of relationships. It is apparent that such behavior, which in this patient is likely to be marked, would lead to difficulties with and probable rejection by, any long-term sexual partner. There is a strong element of fearfulness in his conception of sex.

It is possible that much of his difficulty is historically connected with his early relationships and identifications with his parents. Although the father is perceived as a satisfying figure, there are many indications that his relationship with an apparently aggressive, demanding and dominating mother was most difficult for him. His current relations with his wife do not appear to represent an improvement from the earlier ones with his mother. Any failure on her part to give in to his demands probably leads to hostile feelings on his part—hostile feelings that he finds most difficult to express for the fear of loss of love. In general, his attitude toward women as a whole is a hostile one. His relationships with them have probably never been satisfying to him.

Feelings of inadequacy are coupled with strong status needs and with many indications of self-doubt and deprecation. Some increase in self-esteem is sought through fantasy, often frankly sexual in nature. No matter how satisfying the beginning, however, conflict and guilt often prevent a satisfactory consummation of the fantasied situation. No evidence of paranoid thinking was found.

RORSCHACH

I

W(S)	FM.FC'	A	P	(5") Well! A butterfly—bat. Weird bug. It looks like something ready to bite something right there (points to D1).

II

D	CF.mF	Exp		(9") That looks like something on fire, huh? It looks like this is an explosion here in this part. (D3)
W	F +	A		Besides that it still seems to look something like this (points to card I) weird bug.
Ds	FK	N		Well, I was thinking it reminded me of a hole—a cave—cave in a mountain. (Ds 6 + 5)
D	CF	Hd Sex		Something else. The vagina of a woman. (D3)

III

D	F +	A		(7") They seem to have a butterfly effect still. (D3)
D	M	H	P	It looks like two people looking at each other. I think that's it. (D9)
Add D	Fk	X-ray		This part right here looks like an X-ray of the pelvis. (D6)

IV

W	Fc	Aobj	P	(14") That looks like the skin of an animal on the floor—a rug.
W	F +	A		To me it still has a butterfly appearance. Does it matter which way you hold it? It's a terrible

looking animal. Or a bat. Could be a butterfly with a hideous head. The head looks like the head of a weird animal. I suppose they all have that appearance where they are a blot.

V

| W | F+ | A | P | (3") This is another butterfly again. S'all. |

VI

| W | F+ | A | | (15") Another weird bug (weak laugh). That's it. |

VII

| Ws | FK | N | | (8") Ah—the impression I get is that this is a road I would be traveling through towering cliffs on each side. |

| W | M.FC' | Hd Sex | | Huh! It reminds me of pictures I've seen of a woman with her legs spread out. |

VIII

| W | C/F | At | | (12") This gives me a resemblance of these charts that a medical school might have of the insides of the body. Heart, lungs, etc., up to the shoulder. |

| D | FM | A | P | It looks like an animal on each side here, walking over high parts of a hill or a mountain—looking down.
(D1 + D5 + D6 + 7) |

IX

| W | C/F.kF | At | | (8") Well, this reminds me somewhat of the same as the first one. Medical charts look like the spine here. Combination of an X-ray with it. Lungs, heart, and the spine down here. |

| D | CF | Art | | Holding it upside down like that it looks like a painting—odd painting of a tree. Colorful green and red. That's not counting the |

				orange part. It looks like somebody doing a watercolor painting. (D11, 6)
D	FM.CF	A		Holding it here, this looks like a large deer running through the woods. That's just an impression. It doesn't look much like it. That's about it. (D3 + D7)

X

D	F +	A	P	(15") Well, here in the blue it looks like some terrible spiders. I don't get anything more on that. (D1)
Add D	F +	At		I also see the esophagus going down toward the lungs. (D11)
Add D	F +	A		There again, a deer. (D7)

SUMMARY OF RORSCHACH FINDINGS

W = 10	M = 2	H = 1	P = 6
D = 9 + 3	F + = 6 + 2	Hd = 2 (Sex)	O = 0
	FM = 3	A = 9 + 1	
	Fk = 0 + 1	Aobj = 1	
	FK = 2	At = 2 + 1	
	Fc = 1	N = 2	
	CF = 5	Art = 1	
		Exp = 1	
		X-ray = 0 + 1	

W% = 53	F + 90 = 100	A% = 47	P% = 32
D% = 47			

M:C

2:5

FM:Fc

3:1

$$\frac{\text{VIII} \quad \text{IX} \quad \text{X}}{\text{R}} = 32\%$$

Selected TAT Stories

3BM. This little boy—the past—has done something—something they didn't like. Disliked it enough to punish him—say something to him. He's brooding over, possibly the punishment. They're taking away his doing whatever it was he wanted to. Pretty soon after a lot of brooding or just a little brooding, he will find something else to do. Or, somebody would have given in to him on what he wanted or was doing. That's the story briefly. (Q.) Yes. I'd say he does. (Get into trouble often.) (Q.) Probably not. (Get his own way usually.)

4. This fellow has been working as an illustrator or painter where he uses models to work with. Or, he has been doing this: He's been acting in a manner which the model has tended to like him and she's now making sort of advances toward him and he's shying away from them. The future (laughs) can go two ways. Let's say he doesn't—just—doesn't get together with her—refuses her. That's where it ends. (Q.) Well, he probably likes her, but doesn't care to get mixed up with her. He could have somebody else, or be married, or feel that it might affect his work, or it could be that she has connections that he doesn't want to get involved with.

6BM. Some of these pictures could have happened to me or make you think of things you could tell stories about. I'd say this picture here is about a story of a man who had been taking care of his mother—living with her. She's probably alone, depending upon him for income—for income and company. They'd been very close, and he's telling her that he has a job away from home and must leave home. They both appear to be quite unhappy. But— he's going to go anyway, regardless of what she says. He goes away, does well on his job, and takes care of her quite well. Their relationships have been strained due to the parting. I feel as though it would do them both good. That's it. Do you copy this word for word?

7BM. Well, hmmm—I'd say the young man has had troubles of some sort, financial or family, with his wife, and he's talking over the situation with his father. His father is passing along his thoughts on how to take care of the situation. If it's financial, he will help him. If it's with his wife, it's just a word of wisdom. The young man uses his father's aid, financial or advice, and everything turns out good.

12M.   This is a story of a girl who has gone to some lonely cabin or area where she can have a vacation or nice weekend, fishing, swimming, horseback riding. When it came evening she, of course, was tired and she relaxed on a couch that was in a cabin; her friends having gone elsewhere and left her behind. An intruder comes in the cabin, a man, overcome by her charms, and puts his hand on her mouth so she wouldn't scream and proposes to her for a seduction. Here, he finds he runs into a great deal of difficulty and flees from the cabin. That's the end of the story. I don't know what else to tell. (Q. Why didn't he make out?) Well, it could have gone either way and I chose that way. One thing, I just can't see that kind of a girl giving into that kind of an approach anyway, unless she herself is not fully coherent.

Course of Treatment

Treatment began very slowly. As predicted by the intake worker, the patient resisted working on his emotional problems. The first few interviews were concerned almost entirely with a recital of symptoms interspersed with discussions relating to his employment. Feelings were not mentioned spontaneously by the patient nor were they acknowledged when pointed out by the therapist. During this phase of treatment, arrangements were made for a medical work-up at the request of the veteran but he failed to follow through and saw his private physician instead. This incident provided an opportunity for discussion of the patient's feelings about being assigned to a psychologist for treatment after he had specifically requested a physician as his therapist. His negative feelings toward the therapist, as well as toward mental hygiene clinic treatment and VA medical care, were discussed and explored. As he gradually came to see that he could express negative feelings and still be accepted, he was able to talk more freely about his emotional problems.

At this time the patient was referred for psychological evaluation. He was ambivalent toward the referral. Although psychological testing had been discussed with him on several occasions, he persisted in regarding the referral as a sign of rejection on the part of the therapist. At the same time, he hoped that the testing would provide the answer to all his problems. He was eager to have the results of the psychological study discussed with him, but was fearful lest the psychologist's report lower him in the therapist's eyes. He was apologetic for not completing the Sentence Completion Test, for not giving better stories on the TAT, and for the "silly things" he saw on the Rorschach. Mr. Miller was helped to recognize that these feelings stemmed from himself, and that neither the psychologist nor his therapist had given him any basis for them. It was apparent that these feelings arose from guilt about the hostility he had had toward the referral. The patient's attitudes about the psychological report were exhaustively explored with emphasis on his mixed feelings that somehow he had failed, and on his hopes that a magical solution to his problem would be forthcoming. His feeling was that somehow the therapist would be able to clear up his difficulties with a few chosen words and with little or no participation on his part. After working through these feelings, portions of the test write-up were discussed with him.

It should be noted that the psychologist's report agreed exceedingly well with the therapist's impression of the patient after 52 interviews. The one major discrepancy concerns attitudes toward the father; the patient had always felt his father rejected him, whereas the psychologist described the father as a satisfying figure. There was no doubt that the latter was the sort of father-ideal for whom the patient was searching, an individual who would love, protect, and care for him. To a certain degree, he had found the therapist to be this type of paternal surrogate and leaned very heavily on him. On several occasions, when particularly distressed, he called the therapist at home on a Sunday. In the extra sessions the therapist merely listened to the patient and, more in manner than words, provided reassurance and evidence of interest. This attention was enough to enable the patient to gain relief from his overwhelming anxiety.

It was possible to use the psychologist's report in several ways. First, it reaffirmed some of the impressions of the therapist, namely, the importance of the patient's dependency needs, the hostility that was evoked when these needs were not met, and the extreme importance of sexual problems. It further eliminated the possibility that the patient was a paranoid schizophrenic. As mentioned earlier, the report emphasized the importance of the conflict in the area of interpersonal relations. Each time a section of the report, referring to a particular type of behavior, was revealed to him, one or more hours were spent discussing it. The evaluation of interpersonal relationships, an area about which the patient had said but little up to that time, led him into a long discussion of his past and current difficulties with people. While this material would have, without doubt, been forthcoming sooner or later, the psychologist's report certainly facilitated its appearance at that time.

The patient, while superficially coöperative, could not readily identify feelings. He did not accept or reject interpretations, saying instead, "It could be so." He would frequently fail to hear important interpretations which were threatening to him and often discussed his problems in a rather dissociated way, as if they referred to a third person. These attitudes were never fully worked through and kept reappearing throughout treatment. However, in the later interviews he was able to recognize this type of behavior himself, both in and outside of treatment.

While considerable insight was developed during the course of treatment, behavioral changes were only beginning to show themselves at the time of termination. There were two primary reasons for the lack of movement. Firstly, there was but little motivation for change; the symptoms produced some secondary gains in terms of extra care and attention from his wife, the therapist, and some of his co-workers. Secondly, the patient's intellectualization and dissociative tendencies enabled him to acknowledge the sort of person he was, but he could not express or identify his feelings. For example, he could never remember dreams, or recall his fantasies when in a panic state. He could describe the panic vividly but only in terms of the somatic aspects.

Nevertheless, some improvement was noted. The generalized tension diminished considerably, and his feeling of well-being increased with support and reassurance. Concomitantly, his colitis disappeared. He became a little less demanding of his wife, somewhat more giving, and able to participate more in family activities. His ability to get along with friends and co-workers markedly improved, while his feelings of inadequacy became less intense. He was able to evaluate his hostile behavior more realistically. While the panic states remained the same in intensity when they did occur, the stimulus for the panic had to be much stronger than originally. He was able to tolerate longer automobile drives; only under the stress of heavy traffic or mountain driving would he occasionally develop the panic attacks. He could comfortably view drive-in movies but not regular movies, and he was able to attend some meetings. The veteran's panic at the time he left this city was much less disabling than when he was transferred here. At termination, he felt it would not be necessary to resume treatment immediately in the new city. He thought he would see how he got along without additional help for a while.

Discussion

The veteran's symptom picture dates back to his early childhood. He probably felt the rejection by his parents even before his asthma developed at the age of four. The asthma first appeared when the patient was sent away from home at the time his mother was pregnant with the next sibling. Fenichel (1), Gerard in Alexander and French (2), Marx (3), and many other writers have pointed out that asthmatic attacks seem to be a reaction to the fear of separation from the mother or to the loss of her love. The other two attacks of asthma mentioned by the patient also occurred at crucial periods in his life: when he was sent overseas (another physical separation from mother) and when he was being separated from the service (in which he had hoped to stay because of the security it offered).

The patient described himself as a sickly child. He was always concerned about his health and has maintained the self-concept of a sickly person, and is acutely aware of his bodily sensations. The therapist obtained the impression that the patient, through his illness, tried to secure the attention from the parents that could not be gained through any other means. He still uses his illness as a means of securing attention, but there seems to be an additional factor involved. When he becomes ill, or has been exposed to some illness or poison, he develops a panic attack. He cannot conceive himself as having a mild illness but feels that any illness must necessarily be fatal. Death is not perceived as coming in the distant future, but as imminent. His constant fear of death might arise from his feeling that it would be just punishment for his behavior or thoughts.

From the patient's reports, it is apparent that he never had an opportunity to develop emotionally satisfying relationships with members of his family. His history revealed that in his school days, in service, and in adult life he had not been able to form any close relationships. Even his marriage cannot be considered close. The veteran expects an inordinate amount of attention and consideration from his acquaintances and relatives. When his expectations are not fulfilled, feelings of hostility are aroused. He acts as if these feelings are immediately recognized by others and consequently that people will no longer have anything to do with him. The end result is increased feelings of social inadequacy and isolation.

The patient has never felt equal to or as competent as others, nor has he ever felt that he could satisfy authority figures. He could never do anything that met with his father's approval and felt his every action was subject to criticism. In school he was afraid to volunteer or answer questions for fear he would be wrong and then be ridiculed. In service, as in later years, he felt incompetent; he thought other men were doing better than he and he constantly expected the wrath of his superiors. He attributed many of these feelings of inadequacy and incompetency to the fact that he was not sufficiently trained or given adequate supervision, or to other factors external to himself. It also appears that the veteran, without conscious intent, provoked his superiors by one means or another; for example, he frequently reported late when employed by his father and did not file reports when due to his superiors. It was the therapist's impression that the veteran was seeking adequate justification for his hostile feelings toward these authority figures.

The veteran's marital conflicts appear to be an outgrowth of his attitudes and feelings toward his mother. After his rejection by his mother he developed an attitude of hostility toward women in general. He was taught that sex was too sinful to be talked about. His marriage to a woman with an illegitimate child and his acceptance of the child into his home may be attributed to his need to have some basis for his feeling of hostility toward women. It would seem he blamed his sisters for usurping his mother's love. Currently, his daughters prevent him from getting what he considers his just share of his wife's love. As treatment was being terminated, he was beginning to develop insight into his marital relationships and to recognize that in a variety of ways he viewed his wife and his mother in almost identical fashion.

Probably all the factors mentioned above play a part in his phobic reactions. He is inadequate, cannot satisfy authority figures, has strong feelings of hostility, has no one to look after him, and fears death. It should be noted that the panic attacks began at the time his asthma was disappearing, and since the attacks have become intensified the asthma has not reappeared at all, almost as if these reactions have been a substitute for the asthma. The panic attacks first appeared in church and later were generalized to movies and automobiles. There is a large element of guilt and fear of punishment in his attacks which can be alleviated best by retreating from the situation or reduced through an excessive amount of dependency gratification.

It is apparent that the patient's difficulties all stem from his basic feeling of parental rejection and the concomitant lack of adequate dependency gratification. His mechanisms of defense have varied from time to time. He unsuccessfully attempted to utilize illness to gain dependency gratification. He also has exhibited marked feelings of hostility when these dependency needs were not gratified, which in turn led to fear of punishment or retaliation. When this fear mounts, it results in a panic attack and he fears imminent death. At this clinic, in view of the symptom most disturbing to the patient, the diagnosis was "phobic reaction."

REFERENCES

1. Fenichel, O. *The psychoanalytic theory of neurosis.* New York: W. W. Norton & Co., 1945.
2. Gerard, M. W. Bronchial asthma in children. In Alexander, F., and French, T. M. (eds.) *Studies in psychosomatic medicine.* New York: Ronald Press, 1948.
3. Marx, J. R. Treatment of veterans with asthma in a Veterans Administration Mental Hygiene Clinic. Unpublished paper presented at American Orthopsychiatric Association Meeting in New York, 1954.

A Hysterical Character Disorder in a Housewife

BY DAVID SHAPIRO

The patient, Mrs. L. P., was a tall, attractive 34-year-old housewife and mother, who retained distinctly some of the tomboy about her but in dress and much of her general manner was quite "ladylike." When she was first seen at a private psychiatric sanitarium, she was extremely tense and burst into tears quite easily. She had experienced for many years, and with increasing frequency and severity during the past year, outbursts of anger and tears followed by feelings of guilt and mild depression. Her disturbance had increased greatly during the past summer, when she refused, with her husband's consent, to follow their custom of spending vacations with her in-laws. She took several brief holidays during the summer but found that they did not produce the relaxation she had hoped. She experienced greater tension during these holidays and was bothered also by a good deal of pain in the leg and back. There was also some sensation of numbness in the leg. She had had such pain in milder fashion off and on for some years. Upon returning home from her vacation and finding the house (which was being renovated) "in a complete mess," she had outbursts of even greater intensity. From that time until her admission to the sanitarium several weeks later the tension was continuous, and it reached an explosive peak on the Sunday morning before her admission.

Family Background

Her father, now 68 years old, is described by Mrs. P. as a large, rather handsome man, intense in his emotions ("wham bang, like me") although cool and undemonstrative as far as the patient's mother was concerned. He is apparently a hard-driving and extremely ambitious man. His mother died when he was 12, and the patient's grandfather, an Army officer and "terrible disciplinarian," placed the patient's father with an aunt and uncle. He left their home at an early age, put himself through school, and became a quite successful business executive. He had adopted Catholicism at the time of his first marriage and is still a Catholic. His first wife died two years after their marriage, and about eight years later he married the patient's mother. Three years after mother's death, when the patient was 16, he married for the third time. At the time the patient was seen, her father was expressing dissatisfaction with his third marriage saying that he was now in love with his secretary.

The patient's mother had died of cancer at the age of 53. She was from an English family, in the upper class socially and economically, which had settled in a western city and had at one time considerable wealth in the form of various business holdings. This money had been largely dissipated, however, although the patient still received a small income from an inheritance. The mother was described as a "very sweet," retiring person, "almost too ladylike." Mrs. P. did not recall ever having been kissed by her mother or ever having seen her parents kiss each other. From the time the patient was about 6 years old her mother was seriously ill with cancer until she died ten years later, and she spent much of her time in a darkened room. Mrs. P. remembered very little of her childhood and what is known was mostly reconstructed by her from information she had heard in later years. She was cared for largely by a succession of nurses and maids until she was about 10 years old. Of these she has no memory whatsoever, with the exception of a vague impression of one nurse whom she remembers as a foreign woman who was very strict and whom she did not like. She recalls practically no contact with her mother. The atmosphere in the home was always subdued, and in that sense the patient considers it to have been a reflection of the personality of her mother. It grew even more subdued as the mother's illness became progressively worse and as the mother was forced to spend all of her time in a sickbed.

The principal relief from this atmosphere at home came from the patient's father, who, though cool in his relationship with his wife, was gay and affectionate with the patient. He took her out frequently to various sports events, etc., seeming to prefer her company to that of his wife. At the same time it was because of her father's convictions that the patient received some religious training in Catholicism. Her mother, although not herself a Catholic, evidently did not object to this. Mrs. P. states that she never cared for Catholicism, and she and her husband now maintain a nominal affiliation with a Protestant church.

She dates romantic interest in boys from about the age of 12; before that she was quite a tomboy and "thought mostly about boys in competition with them." She recalls some masturbation from a few years earlier. There were very few parties and no dates during the following several years, since they were not permitted by her mother. When she was 15 and 16, parties were more frequent, always well chaperoned, and tended to be somewhat formal. She was rather awkward and gawky during this time, somewhat overweight, and was never permitted to wear lipstick. After her mother's death, when she was 16, the patient began to date frequently, was quite popular, and enjoyed her popularity very much. She rejected the physical advances of the men she went out with until she was 19. Then she fell in love with a young man who was disapproved of by her father and whose drinking frightened her as well. She terminated this relationship with some regret, began dating Mr. P., and dated only him after that. Her first sexual intercourse was with her husband.

At this time and until her marriage at 22, the patient lived with her father in a small house to which they had moved after her mother's death. Her father had begun to suffer financial reverses about this time; but the patient was never told about this and when she did notice her father's concern she was entirely uninterested. Her life at this time was most exclusively given over to coming-out parties, formal balls, and the like. A few years before the patient's marriage another woman, an acquaintance of her father's, moved into the house, ostensibly as a roomer. It was not until much later that the patient realized that there had been an intimate sexual relationship between this woman and her father.

More Recent History

Mrs. P. said about her husband, "I don't think I've ever really been in love with him . . . though I love him very dearly." He seemed a quite passive man and very much under the domination of his mother. Although she always found his company congenial, and had found him quite attractive, she felt that the comfortable atmosphere of his family home, which was dominated by his mother, was also of considerable importance to her in her decision to marry him. She readily accepted her mother-in-law's arrangements for the wedding, as well as her mother-in-law's decoration of the house into which she and her husband were to move. Shortly after occupying the house her dissatisfaction with these and other interferences became felt. Discussions of the issue with her husband seemed to accomplish little. The problem was heightened some months later when her husband returned from the hospital after minor surgery and chose to spend a convalescent period at his mother's house.

During the ensuing years the mother-in-law issue continued to be prominent and was made still more acute by the fact that the patient's husband worked in the family-owned department store, and while this was run by his father it was actually dominated by his mother. At the time of the birth of her first child, and again when her husband entered the service sometime later, the patient moved into her mother-in-law's home, each time of her own volition, but then quickly feeling intense resentment. Her second child was born shortly before her husband went overseas. The boy was born with severe brain damage resulting in deaf-mutism and feeble-mindedness; but for some time the deficiency was not understood or was not accepted as real by the family. The patient did not inform her husband of her concern for the child for several years, at which time her husband returned to this country and found her physically under par and extremely overwrought. She was not certain as to why she had not informed her husband earlier, but it seems clear that one factor was that she felt she might in some way have been responsible for the condition. During the very disturbing period immediately prior to her husband's return when she had definitely been convinced of her child's deficiency, she felt a great need to buy clothes and to make herself attractive. During this time she met several men to whom she felt physically attracted, but she finally rejected their physical advances.

After her husband's discharge from the service the patient's life continued much as it had before. Two more children were born without complications, and the child described above was institutionalized. She and her husband bought a home directly across the street from his parents, continued their custom of spending vacation periods with them, and Mrs. P.'s conflict with her mother-in-law gradually increased. She seemed to accept the institutionalization of her child as well as could be expected, although she was very much disturbed when about a year before admission the child had to be transferred to a different institution. About this time, after one of her visits to the institution, the patient had a complete loss of memory for a very brief time.

About a year before this the patient's father, who for some years had been living in the West, returned to the city in which the patient lived. Within a few months, Mrs. P. began to feel intensely "disillusioned" and to feel strong resentment toward him. He no longer seemed, as in the past, someone to whom she could always turn for help. On the contrary, she bitterly resented his attempts at relating to her, his sharing of confidences, and in particular his revelation of intimate relationships with several women. He continued nevertheless to see her, to press his confidences upon her, to exhort her to embrace Catholicism, to tell her how much he needed her, and so on.

During the spring before her admission the patient decided, and for the first time her husband agreed, that they should spend their summer vacation away from their in-laws. She went away first with the children but found that she was becoming more than ever upset. She returned home and made then another short trip alone with her husband. The results were the same. During this time the outbursts of temper and tears increased in frequency and severity. They were directed at various times at her husband, her father, her mother-in-law—though in her husband's presence only—and less frequently at one of the children. General problems of running the household, and particularly the problem of household budgeting, seemed to loom very large. During this time she felt increased dissatisfaction with the quality and appearance of her home and their general living standard, and much envy of friends who were better off. Notwithstanding these things she has during this past year in some ways felt considerably closer to her husband, and she reports that her sexual gratification has increased despite continued frequent impotence on the part of her husband.

Test Results

The test battery that was given consisted of the Rorschach, TAT, and Wechsler-Bellevue.[1] No attempt will be made here to present a complete test analysis. I will instead indicate a few aspects of the test material which either were important confirmations of the diagnostic impression or served particularly to clarify certain features of the patient's character.

The Rorschach Test scores gave immediate and strong support to the general diagnostic picture of hysteria. The Rorschach psychogram follows: [2]

W	14	F +	15	A	12
D	28	F —	2	Ad	5
Dd	1	F ±	4	H	
Dr	2	F ±	8	(H)	1
De	1	M		Hd	2
S	1	FM		Obj	3
s	1	FMs	1	At	8
Do	2	FC	3	Pl	1
Do	1	F/C	1	Geog	6
	51	CF	1	Sex	5
		C/F	3	Art	2
		CC'F	1	Cl	2
		C		Footprint	1
		F(c)	1	Expl	1
		(c)F			
		F(c)C'	1		
		FC'			
		C'F	1		
		C'			
		FCh	2		
		ChC'F	2		
		ChF	3		
		Ch			
			49		

W%	29	R	49	EB	.5/7
D%	57	F%	59/78	A%	35
DR%	8	F + %	66/69	P%	12

[1] The original test interpretation and administration were done by Dr. Roy Schafer.

[2] The Rorschach scoring used here follows that described in D. Rapaport, R. Schafer, and M. Gill, *Diagnostic Psychological Testing*, Vol. II. Chicago: Yearbook Publishers, Inc., 1945 and 1946.

The extreme emotional lability, characteristic of hysterics, and the repressive emphasis are suggested in the M:sum C balance of .5/7. Her intense affective reactiveness is also indicated in her characteristic verbalizations throughout the tests; e.g., almost every Rorschach card or TAT picture was greeted with an "Oh, my heavens!" or "Oh, my goodness!" Her concern with the body and bodily functions as reflected in a large number of At responses—a particularly large number when one considers that most of her Sex responses fall also within the broader At category—suggests the possibility of conversion symptoms, although this by itself by no means constitutes a definite indication.

Occasionally in her verbalizations and test responses there is a suggestion of the kind of naïve fearfulness that is usually associated with phobic tendencies (e.g., one response to Card IX of the Rorschach was "spook eyes"). Clinically, however, there were no clear-cut phobic symptoms observed, although there did seem to be a certain amount of generalized fearfulness.

It may be that certain aspects of her character worked against or, so to say, permitted her to control the fearful and passive tendencies which are often conspicuous in hysterical characters. Specifically, the tests suggested also certain compulsive features, which seemed in turn to be associated with some tendencies toward a more aggressive, masculine identification. It seemed in this patient, as it often appears in such patients, that a certain degree of compulsive organization and masculinity lent her a quality of firmness and resilience which stood her in good stead. In the tests such qualities appear, for example, in the fact that she gives 51 Rorschach responses—quite unusual in an otherwise impressively hysterical and repressive record. Similarly she gave a relatively large number of good "whole" responses. Clinically these features of her character are manifest in a certain determination and forthrightness rather clearly associated with the residues of her aggressive tomboyishness. To consider an example from her history, it seems noteworthy that she was able, whatever the reason, to keep the burden of the knowledge of her child's deficiency completely to herself for several years. However neurotic the reasons for this may have been, the fact remains that it took more than a little strength and firmness. Confirmation of such an assessment of this aspect of her history seems to come also from a TAT story in which she describes a mother of a sick child who "has just been told that the child will live but will not be well . . . she is desolate . . . [but] is attempting to *gain self-control* so that she can return to his room cheerfully. She is able to do this. She takes care of him happily—er—not happily, with a great deal of *will power* for many years." [3]

Her behavior in therapeutic interviews also showed clearly this quality of "will power" or "self-control" and determination. She would often approach an issue with the fearfulness and embarrassment of a somewhat childish kind so frequently found in hysterical women, but after a short period of exclamations and statements that it would certainly be impossible to talk about this or that, she would then say, "But I know I simply have to" and proceed doggedly to speak rather fully about the issue in question.

These traits of Mrs. P. which have been described in the preceding paragraphs, and which seem to reflect those compulsive features in her character, should not be overstated or exaggerated. Compulsive features did not appear clinically or in the test material to an extent which, for example, would warrant a diagnosis of mixed neurosis. Nevertheless they seem to be worth noting because though outweighed, so to speak, by the hysterical and generally more passive aspects of her character, the compulsive features yet seem to make an important difference. Probably this is so because conflict and vacillation between the more passive, hysterical position and the more aggressive, compulsive tendency seemed likely to constitute an important issue in its own right. Within the hysterical context, the compulsive features constituted a favorable prognostic factor. It was in fact due to her surprising firmness, even stubbornness, in the face of considerable family pressure to discontinue treatment that she was able clearly to establish her right to continue long-range treatment after the more acute disturbance was over. Clinically it certainly seemed that these traits enabled her to resist temptations toward the role of the chronic invalid, a role for which both her mother and her child provided models.

The Wechsler-Bellevue results provide further confirmation and some clarification of the general character picture. Her scores (on Form I) are as follows:

[3] Italics mine.

SUBTEST	WEIGHTED SCORE
Information	8
Comprehension	9
Digit Span	10
Arithmetic	6
Similarities	13
Vocabulary	13
Picture Arrangement	13
Picture Completion	10
Block Design	12
Object Assembly	14
Digit Symbol	12
Verbal I.Q.	104
Performance I.Q.	123
Total I.Q.	114

The markedly lower Verbal I.Q. seems strongly suggestive of the repressive orientation and the steering away from reflectiveness which are found in hysterical characters. It is interesting, however, that Mrs. P. generally gave an impression of greater verbal intelligence than her Verbal I.Q. score would support. There may be some explanation of this impression in the relatively high Vocabulary and Similarities scores. It is likely that these scores reflect relatively superficial verbal facilities and accomplishments consonant with her social background, education, and social ambitions. The fact that she was able to achieve a relatively good vocabulary and capacity for some types of conceptual verbalization, however superficial these may be, in spite of the generally repressive emphasis, probably testifies again to those traits of doggedness and persistence described above which, for example, might cause her to make a point of looking at least lightly through the newspapers every day. Her low Arithmetic score, which in other contexts might be interpreted as a serious impairment of concentration, seems here to have other meanings. Primarily it seems to be another reflection of her rather narcissistic and repressive orientation. Schafer (2) has observed that narcissistic characters, particularly women, when faced with the Arithmetic test, frequently tend to protest their inadequacy or lack of interest rather than face the anxiety-provoking task. An additional factor for women from a social background like the patient's and with characteristic snobbishness is that to do well in arithmetic does not represent an accomplishment, but rather approximates an insult similar to having callouses on one's hands. Mrs. P. approached the Arithmetic test with statements of "I can't" and continued thus in a childish and helpless way (in the simplest problems she counted on her fingers). She said helplessly that she didn't know how many feet there were in a yard, but when pressed for this information she came forth with it nevertheless.

Probably the least important contribution of the test material to the understanding of this patient was the information the tests provided concerning Mrs. P.'s view of the parent figures. Nevertheless this did tend to confirm what might well have been guessed on the basis of the personal history alone. There is some suggestion in the TAT material of the father figure still as a rather heroic person and some suggestion, also, of an unusually strong sexual attachment to him (e.g., in the TAT Card 13MF, which almost always evokes a story involving lovers, a marital situation, or the like, Mrs. P.'s story involves a father and daughter). The mother figure is pictured, in general, as "proud" and "cold."

Analysis of such aspects of the TAT content as the patient's view of important family figures is usually far less reliable but at the same time less important than the use of the stories to understand more about the manner of handling various types of situations and impulses. In this function the TAT content can often fill in and enrich some of the more formal leads provided by the other tests. In addition, of course, various formal aspects of the TAT stories, such as length, style of verbalization, lucidity or lack of it, and the like, are of considerable value in conjunction with the other tests.

This patient's usual typically hysterical style of verbalization ("Oh, my goodness!") has already been commented on. Most of her TAT stories were characterized by a repressive, unreflective, sweetness-and-light quality, particularly in their endings. Evil characters almost miraculously change into good people, unpleasant and difficult situations suddenly and without real explanation became pleasant and comfortable, etc. At the same time, here and there in her stories there were sparks of distance from herself when she would occasionally poke fun at her own Pollyanna-like tendencies.

At times in the TAT stories the attraction of the role of the sick one or the invalid as a solution to difficult situations is evident (the invalid role appears in several stories but perhaps most clearly in one in which the identification figure is afflicted with the same disease that actually killed the patient's mother). Yet at other times, in several stories, the identification figures meet difficulty with "will power" and "self-control," emphasizing the more aggressive traits mentioned, which were not so immediately apparent clinically.

Other aspects of the TAT content throw light on the narcissistic aspects of her character. Such a TAT story as one (Card 5) in which a woman is annoyed because "someone spoiled the effect [room arrangement] which she tried to create" is of value in this respect. The emphasis on "effect" in this story seems to go along with the suggestion in the Wechsler-Bellevue of a desire to give an appearance of intellectual interestedness, without much actual interest in intellectual things. Such TAT content also brings to mind the emphasis in her personal history on the appearance of her home, keeping up with her friends, and the like, particularly evident at the height of her upset. At the same time, the fact that in this TAT story she indicates displeasure with this attitude on the part of the principal figure—the woman is described as "disagreeable"—suggests again, along with the other test and clinical data, that she does not go along altogether uncritically with these tendencies but can probably be counted on for some self-critical distance from them.

The appearance in the TAT stories of these various attitudes and styles seems again to bring into more prominent relief several important aspects of her character and at the same time to point up some of the difficulties and some of the favorable factors that are likely to influence the therapeutic work.

ADDENDUM

There seems ample evidence in the personal history that the patient's father selected her as his companion, in later life his confidante, and the special object of his "wham-bang" emotions. To some extent this was done in preference to his "subdued" and "ladylike" wife. It seems likely, also, that the mother's illness and her increasing withdrawal from family participation would have intensified the relationship between father and daughter from both sides. The history, as well as some of the content of the TAT stories, strongly suggests that in this situation the patient's normal oedipal wishes were stimulated. In adolescence, when these issues would naturally have been intensified, the patient's mother became gravely ill and died. The patient's reaction seems to have been, at first, heavy dating, a privilege which had previously been denied her by her mother, but then a marriage to a man whom she did not love.

Her solution seems to have been primarily repressive. The repressive orientation is very much in evidence in the test material. In the Rorschach, for example, there is the almost complete absence of M responses, but perhaps the most striking representation of her repressive orientation appears in the sharply lowered Verbal I.Q. on the Wechsler-Bellevue. Such a lowering, if it is to be explained by repressive influence at all, can be understood only as a consequence of a very long-standing and already relatively well-established repressive orientation. There was also much clinical evidence of the repressive influences. Aside from such transient episodes as her very brief amnesia following a disturbing visit to her institutionalized child, there is the characteristic amnesia for a considerable part of her childhood, the complete absence—at least during the earliest part of her treatment—of any dream recall, her striking naïveté, as exemplified in her simply "not seeing" some of her father's relationships for what they were, and the like.

By way of historical understanding it is possible to offer only vague speculation concerning the somewhat masculine, aggressive, compulsive traits suggested by the test material and also by certain aspects of her present behavior. There is some hint that in certain respects her father also treated her like a son (e.g., taking her frequently to sports events with him). We do know that at one time of her life, before puberty, she was a tomboy. She describes herself as having been very competitive with boys and in that and in other respects quite aggressive during this period. It may be imagined, then, that particularly during this time she sought a solution not only in repression but to some extent also in an identification with her aggressive, ambitious, hard-driving father.

The dependent needfulness and the antagonism she must have felt toward her mother seemed, in later life, to be transferred to her dominating mother-in-law. She was satisfied and did not protest, at least at first, taking up residence across the street from her mother-in-law and moving in with her when her husband went into the Army, spending their vacations with her, and so on. She remembered, in fact, that during the time when her husband was courting her the "comfortable atmosphere" of his home, dominated by his mother, was very attractive to her. Her antagonism to this woman grew, however, to considerable proportions, no doubt partly stimulated by the close relationship between her husband and her mother-in-law, which immediately placed the two women in rivalry for the husband's affections.

The exacerbation of her illness leading to the period of hospitalization seemed, at least in part, related to the return of her father from another city, his pressure to renew their close relationship, and the consequent rearousal of her ambivalence toward him. Other disturbing factors, such as the necessity for moving her son to another institution, no doubt also made a contribution. Finally, her attempts during the summer just before her hospitalization to assert her independence of her mother-in-law and to claim, so to say, exclusive rights to her husband may well have been the last straw.

At the same time it must be admitted that the clinical history provides us, at most, with a general time of exacerbation of her illness for which all the factors responsible are not altogether clear. It does not seem possible to speak here of a real precipitation of neurosis. Certainly, with the possible minor exception of the leg and back pains— and these have not been definitely established as conversion symptoms —there is a conspicuous absence of either real conversion symptoms or crystallized phobias. It seems, therefore, appropriate to describe her condition as a hysterical character disorder rather than a symptomatic neurosis. In the matter of deciding between a diagnosis of hysterical character neurosis and hysterical symptom neurosis, the tests appear to have little to offer. Certainly by far their major function is already fulfilled if they help to outline the major lines of character organization. Beyond this it seems possible only to say that there were no clear indications of specific symptoms in the test material and there was conspicuous evidence that the major neurotic features had been in existence and had been well stabilized over a long period of time.

REFERENCES

1. Rapaport, D., Schafer, R., and Gill, M. *Diagnostic psychological testing*. Chicago: Yearbook Publishers, Inc., 1945 and 1946.
2. Schafer, R. *Clinical application of psychological tests*. New York: International Universities Press, 1948.

CHAPTER TEN

Neurotic Depression and Masochism

BY LESTER LUBORSKY, RICHARD SIEGAL, and GEORGE A. GROSS

Any case history must be selective. At best, one can be clear about the biases that show up in what is highlighted and know enough about the patient to indicate what has been neglected. We could have chosen to point up the sources of the patient's anxiety, methods of controlling hostility and orality, tendency to be withdrawn, or psychosomatic symptoms. Instead, we drew on all these to comprehend two major symptoms, depression and masochism, which were important in causing the patient to apply for treatment.

The main body of this study consists of the initial evaluation of the patient by a "team" (including social worker, psychiatrist, psychologist, and others), the psychological retest report at the end of the psychotherapy, and a separate comparison of the initial and terminal test batteries. We will draw on this personality study and the events in the psychotherapy to answer these questions about the major symptoms: (1) How did it come about in this patient's life that she relied on these symptoms as a way of dealing with her problems (the genetic question)? (2) What was the patient reacting to at the time she applied for treatment that led to an increase of these two symptoms? (3) What changes took place in the patient during treatment that lessened her reliance upon these symptoms? The last should help us comprehend the disease process; we will learn not only how the symptoms were created in the first place but what process had to be employed in order to make them less necessary.

Initial Evaluation (Including Psychological Test Report)

1. *Identification of the case.* Mrs. Dorothy M. was a 25-year-old divorced college student who wrote requesting an outpatient examination.

2. *Statement of the problem.* The patient outlined several problems with which she wanted help. She said, "My relationship to boys is all fouled up." She was involved in a triangular affair with two men, both of them under psychiatric care. She was concerned about the fact that she had "never been able to accept my responsibilities." By this she referred to her relationship to her child and her financial responsibilities. Another problem was her difficulty in studying.

3. *Historical data.* The patient felt that her illness began after she wrote to her mother describing how happy and well satisfied she was in her work and living conditions at school. Immediately after this she began to have feelings of depression and difficulty in studying, and she began going out every night. Her difficulty in concentration was something new to her and quite disturbing. She had been planning to go into nurses' training, and changed to a bacteriology major. Neither the reason for this change nor the time it occurred is clear. Along with difficulty in studying, the patient had a rather marked nervous tension, difficulty in sleeping, a feeling of a knot in her stomach which prevented her from eating the way she wanted to, and occasional nausea with no vomiting. The patient had been in the habit of taking an occasional bromide tablet but at this time she began to take bromides three or four times a day and seconal at night to sleep. She continued to take this medication.

For about ten months the patient had been going out with two young men, both of whom were quite disturbed emotionally. The relationship had been very stormy. These boys, one an incipient schizophrenic and the other having a character disorder of some sort, had pushed her back and forth from one to another. She did enjoy their intellectual discussions about world events, and so forth, but neither had been able to provide her with a satisfactory and warm relationship. She went into rather minute detail in discussing her relationship with each of them and was quite disturbed about the fact that she seemed to be a pawn between them. She expressed guilt about coming between these two friends.

The patient is the second of three children (the oldest, a son, died in infancy) born in a rather unstable home. Her father is restless, demanding, excitable, a semi-professional man who has never gotten along with his two daughters. The mother is a very stern, demanding, rigid woman who the patient said has always emphasized her own difficulties and never paid any attention to the problems of her daughters. About eight years before the patient's admission her father gradually became interested in a neighbor woman, and this matter was discussed openly in the presence of the patient and her sister. The patient's mother remained by her husband and never wanted to get a divorce. The patient was very bitter toward her father because "he does not love me." Her attitude toward her mother was one of hostile, demanding insistence that the mother take care of her needs such as financing her way in college, taking care of her son, and so forth.

The patient's birth was uneventful. However, it was noted that she was extremely jaundiced immediately after and remained so for several weeks. At the age of $3\frac{1}{2}$ she was described as having a "neurological difficulty" based on a long family history of various neurological disorders. At the age of 5 she was diagnosed as having "chorea"; the diagnosis was based on jerky movements of her head, difficulty in holding objects, and frequent fainting episodes. The mother's attitude was to "not form any abnormal mental reaction to it" and she tried to ignore these movements. However, the patient became very self-conscious about them and apparently continued to be so. She continued to have these jerky movements of her face and difficulty with fine movement of her hands such as in writing, dishwashing, and doing laboratory work.

The patient got along fairly well in school and was a rather outgoing person, with many dates. Her sexual history included affairs with several men prior to her marriage at the age of 18. This marriage took place soon after she had broken an engagement with another fellow and only about two weeks after her husband had returned home on a furlough prior to going overseas. The marriage was a very stormy one, with numerous separations, reconciliations, and extramarital affairs on the part of both the patient and her husband. A boy was born who was five years old at the time of admission and had been living with her parents. She described her difficulty in getting along with men: "I always get them to feel sorry for me by playing on their sympathy and after I become sure of them I like to leave them. This does not make me happy at all." After her divorce two years before admission the patient had serious affairs with three men and numerous minor affairs. She started to college, planning to take a nurses' training course. She had had a secretarial course, and off and on during the past six or eight years had done secretarial work in a very unsatisfactory way. She had difficulty in typing because of muscular incoördination and also difficulty in getting along with her employers. She had never been satisfied with the quality of work she turned out and frequently mentioned this. The patient was reared in the Episcopal Church but said she was now a Catholic; by this she meant that she went to Catholic services but had never been accepted as a member of the Church.

4. *Examination data.* The physical, laboratory, and X-ray reports are omitted here. The neurological examination revealed jerky involuntary movements of the head and choreiform movements of the hands.

Psychological data were as follows:

The patient is a rather slender woman of about 5 feet, 3 inches with light blond hair, blue eyes, and long eyelashes. She wore dark glasses into the examination room and when asked about these expressed the idea that she somehow or other felt that other people could "read my thoughts through my eyes." When the dark glasses were brought to her attention she immediately removed them. Her general facial expression was a mixture of depression, bitterness, and pouting. She showed some reluctance in speaking at first and sat with her hands clasped tightly in her lap. There were continuous rather bizarre jerky movements of the head. She showed some difficulty in grasping what was being asked of her and would go into a rather detailed description of her immediate problem without apparent realization of what had been asked. There was some suggestion of confusion but when she was brought back to the point at hand this tended to disappear momentarily. She was correctly oriented in all spheres. There was no evidence of hallucinations. She gave a description of depersonalization episodes in which she felt that she was floating and detached from the immediate situation. Her intelligence appeared to be somewhat above average and her ability to think abstractly as tested by proverbs was keenly intact. The general fund of information and knowledge was above average and her memory was intact in several test situations. Her judgment seemed to be defective in that she had difficulty in formulating a life plan and felt that her school work was aimed primarily toward getting in a financial situation independent of her parents. She was unable to relate her confusion and depersonalization to her present relationship to the boy friends. There was a marked lack of spontaneity in the patient, and she tended to present her problems in a rather disjointed, poorly organized, and sometimes contradictory fashion. There was considerable evidence of obsessive thinking especially in regard to her school work and her relationship to men. Several times her answers were rather irrelevant; however, this seemed to be a reflection of her general state of confusion. The thought content seemed to be centered around her triangular love situation, and to her symptomatology which included tenseness, confusion, and difficulty in studying. Her rather frequent fantasies included thoughts of her child being severely injured or dying and she said, "All my daydreams are bad. People are being murdered, dying, and things like that." There was little evidence of truly delusional thinking; however, the rather blatant assumption that her mother and father would find a way to finance her schooling indefinitely or that she could obtain some money from a rich aunt in New York seemed to border on the delusional. It was difficult to ascertain the validity of her frequent accusations directed toward her mother and father. Her emotional level seemed to be that primarily of a depression; however, she frequently came through with a friendly smile. She expressed considerable fear and worry about how she was likely to be hurt by other people, especially men. In her interpersonal relationships she showed a marked preference for the company of men and at the same time felt rather unhappy about these relationships. They seemed to be very intense and to cause considerable emotional disturbance both to her and to them before they were finally broken off. There was some suggestion of promiscuity at various times of her life. Her choice of male friends included some rather emotionally disturbed fellows.

Psychological tests administered were the Wechsler-Bellevue, Rorschach, Thematic Apperception (Self-Interpretation of TAT) [1] and Word Association.

General impressions of the patient were the following: She spoke evenly, slightly dragging out the words, and with very little expression

---

[1] The use of this test as a clinical procedure has recently been described (3).

in her face. She said nothing unless she was asked and seemed to react automatically to what she was told to do. The only evidence that she had feelings about what she was doing was her quiet comments, almost to herself, about the difficulty of a task or the strain it was to do it. Her general attitude seemed to be one of resigned compliance and low mood. Throughout the test examination whenever a situation was anxiety-rousing, choreiform movements present in her head, neck, and arms would increase. The patient made no sign that she was aware of this. (These movements seemed severe enough to perhaps interfere with the fine motor coördinations required by her bacteriological work.) It was also clear to the examiner that he had to raise his voice in order to be heard. Again, if the patient recognized that she was having difficulty hearing, she gave no sign of it. In both cases, her choreiform movements and her apparent hearing difficulty, she must have been denying to herself the extent of their severity by trying to act as if they did not exist.

The patient's personality structure and dynamics were revealed in the tests. It was clear from the test results that the patient was involved in a severely disturbing life situation to which she responded by depressive reactions and strong guilt. Her superego structure was such that it required strong external controls. For example, in her response to *Why are laws necessary?* she said, "Because you live in a group of people you can't be strictly uninhibited." She had a strong tendency toward self-punishment, was constantly making derogatory comments about her own abilities and condemning herself for transgression, and saw condemnation in many places where it did not exist, even in the definitions of words she did not know; for example, she said for the word *traduce,* "It's the opposite of like a reprimand, I don't mean reprimand, I mean condemning."

In her TAT stories she told succinctly, largely in their manifest content, about the immediate problems that concerned her and her feelings about herself. She told a story of a young boy who was realizing talent which the father never was able to actualize. "There is a girl whose parents are ambitious for her to have a good education that they were denied. She goes to school and gets farther away from her former associations and finally cuts herself off completely from them." "Woman in complete despair, of a lower middle class, who had an unhappy childhood due to poverty and uncongenial parents. She married young, thinking that would be an escape from her former way of life, now she finds herself with small children for whom she is responsible and her husband has apparently deserted her, she doesn't know where to turn for help." "A girl who was rejected by her husband and commits suicide." In the last story she was concerned with the complete futility of life, saw nothing but blankness in the future, contemplating eternity and wondering about suicide. The main problems that arose were despair over the future, her need for support from her parents which was lacking, her poor economic background, her disappointment to her parents because her husband was unacceptable.

Characterologically she can be described as having had obsessive-compulsive as well as repressive defenses. Her obsessiveness was entwined with a great deal of self-doubt about her abilities. In the Wechsler-Bellevue, for example, a great many of the answers which were correct were still given with the qualifications "I suppose" or "I don't know" or "maybe," or with a shrug of the shoulders. The patient's compulsivity, intellectualizing, and generalizing abilities were effective. The patient had a notable problem in handling her hostility, a great deal of which went into self-criticism and depression. Much of the hostility also was directed toward men. Her association to *men* was "dog" and to *father,* "fight." In the TAT story the idea of suicide came up in connection with having been deserted by her husband.

The patient became upset and anxious relatively easily, however. For example, in the Arithmetic test, to which she had an especially strong reaction, she became completely stopped and said she couldn't do it, couldn't even think. Her way of handling the anxiety was to try to improvise an answer even though she couldn't focus her thinking on the correct solution. Another anxiety manifestation was seen in biting her nails and chewing her fingers. She at such times explained to the examiner that "things like this upset me." She further explained that her way of dealing with such problems in the past had been to memorize the answers without understanding them. Later on in the examination, during the Rorschach, she became anxious. For example, after she saw in Card VII "tropical fish with long tails" she began to feel sick to her stomach but was willing to continue the testing. Her anxiety when not handled by the previously mentioned obsessive-compulsive and repressive defenses tended to go into motor expressions involving accentuation of choreiform movements and oral activities like nail biting and chewing of her fingers, or into gastrointestinal upsets.

In terms of conspicuous symptoms, a *mixed neurosis* was an applicable diagnostic formulation. Principally, it was largely a reactive depression, with secondary psychosomatic concomitants. This was seen in a character structure of fairly well-developed compulsive intellectualizing and some repressive defenses with poorly sublimated passive and masochistic tendencies. The patient had a strong feeling of guilt. She intensely denied her aggressive impulses but showed hostile feelings which were especially strong toward men and also, strongly denied, toward her child.

Concerning the future she felt lost, deserted, hopeless. In her depressed state she had considered suicide (according to her Self-Interpretation) but concluded that "it would have been an ignominious death." However, she still had a strong suicidal potentiality.

There were some indications of sources of strength, however: (a) her ambition to succeed, together with above-average intelligence (I.Q. 120–123, in the superior range, with Verbal I.Q. of 123–126 and Performance I.Q. of 113) and fairly effective compulsivity, and (b) a willingness to try to analyze her problems (as shown by the TAT-Self-Interpretation).

5. *Case summary.* This patient, who was raised in an emotionally unsatisfying environment, had constantly sought rather intense but temporary relationships outside of her home. Her bitterness toward and feeling of being rejected by her father and the marked hostility which she expressed toward men in general had produced in her considerable guilt feelings and feelings of inadequacy as a woman. The more direct expression of this hostility as reflected in her castrating behavior toward men was near enough to consciousness to produce a great deal of anxiety, guilt, and depression.

1. Medical and surgical diagnosis: Chorea, "congenital," moderate.
2. Characterological diagnosis: "Mixed" personality structure, obsessive and hysterical features.
3. Psychiatric syndrome diagnosis: Neurotic depression, moderate.
4. Social diagnosis: A divorced mother and student who has turned over the care of her child to her parents.

6. *Treatment recommendations.*
   a. It was felt that this patient needed a supportive relationship with

a woman who would be much less demanding and ambition stirring than the patient's mother had been (which characteristics had been a tremendous, overwhelming disappointment to the patient) and a much more accepting figure with whom the patient perhaps could arrive at a more tenable identification. Such support could be given by a psychiatric social worker one to two times a week with the principal aim of affording the patient an opportunity for the above and helping her restructure her reality situation on a much more stable basis. The patient might then develop the ability to utilize a more definitive exploratory psychotherapy or psychoanalysis. At present, however, it seemed that her reality situation was so unfavorable and her object relationships particularly with men so complicated that more definitive psychotherapy was contraindicated.

b. It was thought that the patient should be encouraged to consider temporarily dropping her school work, for two reasons: to relieve the pressure she probably felt to achieve great success in her school work without a clear idea as to her goal in going to school, and also perhaps to disentangle herself at least to some extent from the potential dangers of her complicated relationship with two maladjusted fellow students, with one of whom she was in danger of making an impulsive and probably again unsatisfactory marriage; and to become self-supporting so that she could undertake treatment.

c. The question of hospitalization was a very difficult one particularly since the parents appeared to be thus far unwilling to recognize the severity of the patient's problems and to coöperate in any way and since the patient's resources in general were so limited. It was felt that the patient had obtained some relief as a result of entering into the evaluation and that the danger of suicide, although still present, was somewhat less, at least to the point of warranting an attempt to take a calculated risk on an outpatient basis. However, the question of conveying to the parents the reality of the patient's need for help was one which would have to be worked out further with the patient.

d. There was no treatment indicated for her chorea. It was a chronic nonprogressive type. The only treatment was rhythm training through typing, dancing, etc., which had been carried out earlier in her life.

7. *Prognosis.* The prognosis for this patient was still guarded; supportive counseling-type psychotherapy at frequent intervals seemed the

best treatment under the circumstances. The patient might become more disturbed and require hospitalization in the future. She might show better response to intensive psychotherapy than to counseling. However, this was not feasible at the time.

8. *Discussion of recommendations.* The recommendations were discussed with the patient twice. She was resistive to the idea of a woman therapist. It became clear that this attitude was related to her mother's cold reception of her problems. The patient was told that these were things she must work out with the therapist.

She was encouraged to drop out of school but told this decision would be left up to her. She was anxious about her inability to get a job and felt that the sooner she finished school the sooner she would become independent of her family.

These initial studies are not only evaluative; the treatment begins in these interviews, often in the "working through" of the recommendations with the patient and his relatives.

The patient began seeing a woman therapist for weekly interviews but in the course of the next month became more anxious and hopeless. The psychiatrist believed the patient's suicidal thoughts needed to be taken seriously and the patient was hospitalized for the next month. She then definitely decided to give up school and on leaving the hospital found a job.

A few months later, just after marrying one of the two boy friends, Mrs. M. started psychoanalytically oriented expressive psychotherapy with a male psychotherapist. Perhaps in the expectation of beginning psychotherapy, she had improved somewhat in the interval before the psychotherapy, although the problems she presented were almost the same as in the initial evaluation. Now she was terribly afraid of a repetition of marital failure. Although she said she despised her present husband and claimed all the problems of the marriage were his, she was even more afraid to say the happiness of the marriage was in question. The psychotherapy continued for a little more than three years with two one-hour appointments per week (a total of a little more than 200 hours).

Psychological Retest Report

(This section is based upon a readministration of the same psychological tests at the termination of psychotherapy. The assessment was done "blind," i.e., without knowledge of the patient from other sources, including the initial tests.)

From the present test picture one would not expect neurotic symptomatology in this patient at this time. Neither pressing problems nor marked anxiety is seen. It does appear, however, that the character structure is one which would provide fertile soil for the growth of a depressive symptom picture with obsessional, projective, and perhaps agitated features. Intellectualizing defenses, isolation and denial, appear to be the primary mechanisms of impulse control, together with secondary obsessional mechanisms. One suspects that feelings, in the past, have been experienced in rather diffuse and displaced ways, and that obsessional-ruminative thinking has to a great extent supplanted free, spontaneous warmth and emotionality.

This is the character setting, the underlying picture, so to speak. However, certain significant additions must be made. It should again be pointed out that neither depression nor anxiety is apparent now. In addition, the marked intellectual over-control (particularly evident in the Rorschach) is punctuated by sporadic releases of warmth and almost spontaneous expressions of affect.

There is a quality of acceptance and understanding of her own feelings (particularly past feelings, though certainly she experiences much greater comfort with present feelings than she probably did previously) evident in the tests. She is obviously more able now to secure and accept gratification from her immediate environment and from her commonplace day-to-day routine. Her sources of gratification appear to be, appropriately, the realities of her daily life. One might speculate that feelings of inadequacy and a sense of deprivation are now memories rather than present realities.

In addition, there seems to be a kind of confidence in her ability to handle herself in anxious situations. This is at least partially justified, in that her intellectualizing efforts, though they are accompanied by tension and a loss of intellectual efficiency in stressful situations, are effective in getting to the root of the anxiety-producing situation. If tension has not already mounted to extremes, she is able, by methodically and systematically isolating aspects of the total problem in turn, to take action directed at the root of the difficulty. At least, she does feel that action directed toward changing the situation is a desirable step, and, since she neither is impulsive nor has judgmental difficulties, alleviation of the tension may well follow. Similarly, when she is caught on the horns of an obsessive dilemma, she feels impelled to break the impasse (or by-pass it) with the realization that emotional and interpersonal appropriateness should guide her rather than trivial meticulousness. Again, one might speculatively infer that thinking has become less egocentrically oriented.

There is another aspect to this general constellation of self-acceptance and confidence in her own methods of personal problem solution. This is a tendency toward resignation and acceptance of problems. Her TAT story of a tired, lonely, depressed, and thoroughly resigned woman who accepts her "fate" and continues on her lonely way is an example. While she (the patient) accepts her situation, herself, and her potentialities for securing gratification, there are few signs of zest or enthusiasm accompanying the calmness.

The record in general is rather constricted for one of this intellectual level and there is (except in a few scattered instances) a lack of pleasure in creative fantasy. It is *as if* the confidence in herself is obtained at the expense of limiting her thinking and activity to spheres in which she feels safe and unchallenged. This gives the test picture an inhibited, guarded, and mildly depressed flavor; not that depressed mood is present but that she is unable to quickly enter fully the testing situation as a challenging one. Part of her confidence would seem to stem from the feeling that she has experienced depression before, is familiar with it, and therefore is not afraid of it.

Her thought content, too, has this accepting, resigned quality. She feels that her parents were not interested in her, that she has not had the love or attention due her, and though she rather wistfully wishes things had been different, she is able to accept things as they are now. Certainly what she describes as her efforts to hang on to people in the face of rejection seem to have abated with the realization that other sources of gratification are and will be open to her. Her TAT stories indicate this strongly. In one she tells of a brief visit home by a son and his father's pleasure at seeing him, which is not marred by the son's impending departure. In a self-interpretation of one of her stories in which a woman is trying to hold on to a rejecting lover, the patient says quite matter-of-factly, "I've had unhappy relations with fellows where I was the one holding them and they were pulling away from me. Maybe I felt I couldn't find a better one . . . I did . . . I had an unhappy marriage that lasted four years and . . . now I have a happy one." (Perhaps this reflects something of her feelings upon leaving therapy.)

With the exception of potential depression no direct outlet for hostility is seen. Somatization, which one might expect in this sort of character picture, is not in evidence in the tests. One would feel the patient must have been a rather angry person whose values were at least superficially rebellious and defiant. These, while she is not content to accept completely conforming, conventional attitudes, have been softened by a greater acceptance and knowledge of past feelings, to the extent that she can be aware of the conventional viewpoint and fit her actions appropriately into it. She apparently is able to act independently and make her own decisions but she values highly support from parental figures. From this and the content of some of her TAT themes one would feel that she has viewed her therapist as an interested, supporting father figure who encourages her to find independent solutions to her problems. The relationship must have been a gratifying one to her, yet she is realistically able to relinquish it with the confident expectation of finding other relationships to replace it.

Summary. Though intellectualizing defenses are strong, they are probably not as rigid as formerly and appear to be more integrated into an adjustment which allows more experienced feeling and gratification. Tightness, inhibition, and guardedness are seen but perhaps the patient needs time and distance from the therapeutic situation to become somewhat more relaxed. The changes which apparently have occurred and the insights gained do seem deep in the sense that for the most part they are felt and rather confidently accepted. What the patient has learned she knows well and intimately and she is not, nor will she be, content with empty intellectual formulas. She has a much more vivid self-concept and idea of what her life should be and what role she would like to play in it.

All things considered—her termination of therapy, the recent birth of her child, and the impending change in her life routine—her adjustment to these major events is calm, and hopefully confident. In consequence one might say that the inhibition seen in the tests represents a characterological background which is a limiting factor perhaps, but which nevertheless allows her sufficient freedom for investment of energies in appropriate object relationships to maintain, if not an excitingly creative life, at least a calm, stable, and relatively productive one.

Comparison of Initial and Termination Test Batteries

Though there are great similarities between these two sets of tests almost four years apart, the differences are rather striking. It would be fascinating to devote time to a detailed content analysis of the tests, since many of the patient's responses appear particularly rich in clues as to how she structures her world. Instead of this minute response-by-response analysis, several striking changes and the overall trends and directions of change will be examined in the belief that in this way the major test (and personality) differences can be clearly seen.

In the area of the patient's symptomatology the changes are quite clear and striking. Depression, despair, and futility have disappeared and have been replaced by the idea of continuing and successful struggle against helplessness. In addition, anxiety is markedly diminished. This can be seen not only in the kinds of comments she makes (compare, for instance, her comment on the first testing in regard to Arithmetic, "Things like this upset me, I just can't think," with her comment to the same test now, "I never could do these in school [laughs]") but also in slightly improved performance. Weighted scores on Digit Span and Arithmetic previously were 6 and 7 respectively; now they are 9 and 10. Somatization and somatic concern, which were noted in the first report, are not evident now.

There are many evidences of her interest in and the gratification she receives from her family now. (Her story, four years ago, to the blank TAT card told of future blankness, futility, and hopelessness, while this time her story told warmly and glowingly of her newborn daughter's future.) It is obvious that much of her energy is devoted to her family and much of her gratification is obtained from it.

On the whole, there is much less of an intellectual façade now. Whereas before she quoted a couplet by Pope in response to the "Bad Company" item on the Wechsler, she now answers in much more personal terms using an example from the current political scene. Her answers on Similarities reflect this change also. Whereas previously wood and alcohol were alike "in that they're both hydrocarbons," now their essential similarity is that they are "both things that are frequently used by human beings . . . in ordinary living." Praise and punishment were previously "stimuli to behavior"; now "they might both be forms of directing an individual in a certain way."

It is quite true that at the time of the previous testing the patient was a junior in college, while now she is a wife and the mother of two children. One might expect her interests and attitudes to have changed by virtue of this fact alone; however, the direction of changes is congruent with changes in her emotional life, her attitudes toward interpersonal relations, and her methods of impulse control, so that one may say they represent not only a situational change but primarily a personal one. Her interest in people and the gratification she can accept from them is much increased. Behaviorally, one might speculate, these changes would be manifested by increased friendliness; less sarcasm, hostility, and shyness; decreased immediate concern with the impression she will create in ordinary social contacts; increased cheerfulness; and an increased willingness to allow herself to enjoy the present moment.

Striking changes in the Rorschach are seen. The decrease in obsessive, anxious intellectualizing and depression is quite clear. (At the same time the slight constriction or inhibition mentioned in the "blind" report is evident in the change in the "experience balance" from 3/1.5 to 2/0.5.) Despite the drop in response to color, one might say the repressive, hysterical elements have come slightly to the fore as evidenced by the patient's responses to the colored cards (and her comments on the TAT) manifested by lengthened reaction times to the cards.

Changes in the content of Rorschach responses are interesting and in general support the hypothesis of increased spontaneity, emotional freedom, and empathic ability. (On Card III what was "bent over men" is now "men pulling away from each other with big noses and pointed heads." On the same card, what was "circus girls climbing ropes with one missing leg" is now someone doing a "swan dive.") She now also sees some sexual responses which were absent before and whereas on Card X she saw four very common responses she now gives seven responses including a fanciful reference to a comic strip character.

In regard to the basic mechanisms of impulse control, then, the situation does show some change, primarily a change in degree. Although she is still a person of mixed character structure, the various intellectualizing, obsessive-compulsive mechanisms are neither as strong nor as overworked as previously. Feelings are more freely and directly experienced, yet there remains in this area (as well as particularly in the area of hostile outlets) a characterological problem (or perhaps limitation). Hostility is less directly in evidence (in the content of the Word Association Test, for example), although the potentiality for depression still exists. (Her previous response to the word "man" was "dog"; now it is "boy." She has brought him further up the evolutionary ladder but he still has some distance to travel.)

Other Word Association responses show a change in sexual attitude (from "penis"—"men" to "penis"—"man") and reflect a greater preoccupation with her role as a mother.

Changes in her feelings toward her parents and toward the question of genuine independence for herself are marked. These appear particularly in responses to the TAT and self-interpretations of her previous responses. For one thing, it seems as if she is no longer "taken in" by "spurious" or "superficial" parental regard. She says now, "I used to feel my mother was rather bored by being a mother." Before she felt, "My mother always took a great deal of time in talking to me of things that were of interest to her and that she thought would be of interest to me." A previous story was of a mother reading to her daughter "trying to give her child the things she missed at that age . . . she grows up realizing her mother is ambitious for her and she makes an effort not to be a disappointment. After her mother dies she marries a man her mother disapproved of and is very happy with him." Now the story to the same card tells of a mother who "looks like a pleasant woman who enjoys what she's doing" reading to her daughter, who is daydreaming about "the time when she grows up and is reading to *her* children" and who "grows up to have a happy life, happy marriage and be well-adjusted." From this and other indications it would seem that the patient accepts and enjoys her womanly role in a way that would have been impossible for her four years ago.

This change has come about partly as a result of a much greater emotional clarity and insight. Looking back at the feelings she had, she can accept them and at the same time understand them, although they are no longer with her. She says now, "Many of these feelings that I see expressed on these pages have been long forgotten—they return as a surprise. This [TAT story] seems to indicate a preoccupation with evil and death. I think my interpretation was accurate. I was frightened of so many things then—school, men, therapy, etc."

The greater clarity about her feelings and at the same time the greater distance she has achieved from them result in less rigid social attitudes (increases in Comprehension and Picture Arrangement on the Wechsler, for example) and in a more flexible self-concept. She can now, for instance, accept her hearing defect and comment, "My hearing must be worse than usual today" in contrast to making no mention whatever of it during the first testing.

On the basis of the attitudes displayed in the first testing and the present sessions, one might infer that the transference relationship probably was one in which possessiveness and demandingness (when she became able to allow herself to express these qualities) were worked through until she became able to operate on a basis of mutual trust and affection without therapeutic (parental) interference or directiveness. She has learned, she feels, to identify and distinguish genuine affection and coöperation from "benevolent" over-protection and interference.

Summary. The changes evident in the comparison between these two sets of tests four years apart show the disappearance of disturbing anxiety and depression, the diminishing of obsessional intellectualizing, the increase of direct emotional expression (with perhaps some intensification, or bringing to the fore of the repressive elements in the character structure), and many changes in basic attitudes toward her own role in interpersonal relations and in life in general. She is a more giving and accepting person, is less possessive and possessed (more independent) and yet can accept gratification from sources which she previously had denied herself. The changes, not "flashy" and dramatic and thus not open to the charge of "transference cure," seem stable and integrated into the character structure.

Depression and Masochism

Symptoms have a purpose. They are substitutes for or a failure in direct gratification and often combine in themselves both the abortive gratification and punishment for it. The terms "depression" and "masochism" are used here in a fairly widely accepted sense. Depression is a state resulting from defensive reactions in which hostility, instead of being directed onto the object of the anger, is turned onto the self (1). Masochism is a concept referring to a type of psychosexual adaptation in which an increase in "unpleasure" (pain) is a necessary condition for sexual satisfaction. Obviously these two concepts do not stand in any simple relation to each other.

How did Mrs. M. develop these symptoms? It is easy to find examples in her past life of attempts at gratification leading to masochistic behavior and then a period of depression. Once at about the age of 19 on a date with a young man (the husband of a friend) she was sitting in the car with him and must have desired to pet but got very frightened and mistook his approaches as attempts to choke her and fled in panic down the dark deserted street. As a younger adolescent she often had the fantasy that some day she would grow up, get married, and have a child and the man would abandon her with the child and she would live unhappily thereafter.

One of the simplest ways to comprehend the purpose of the neurotic symptoms is in terms of a schematic picture of relationships with her parents and her own attempts to eventually achieve independence and heterosexual maturity. Although she often resented her mother, mother was the main person who could be relied upon and Mrs. M. felt deeply her need for her. Mother always emphasized to her daughters the peculiarity and unreliability of the father and held up as a living and verbal ideal "A woman should be cool to men" and should "never be a millstone around his neck." Mrs. M. tried hard to live up to this ideal; she was ambitious scholastically and agreed with her mother about the father. She went even further; she was tempted, at least unconsciously, to be like father and take his place. Both daughters joined mother in despising the father and found it especially easy to threaten him by referring to his liking to do cooking and laundry and such feminine tasks. Apparently the patient thought of being independent as close to being masculine. To be masculine in this way must mean to compete with father. Father confirmed the competition by making it clear that he was upset by certain evidences of what he felt were masculine impulses in his daughter. One day she wore a pair of slacks and it infuriated him so that he took a knife and made a slit in them while she was wearing them. The fear and striving toward masculinity was also illustrated by the patient's statement that her sister was "just like her father." Mrs. M. sometimes even feared that the choreiform movements of her neck were proof of her being like father.

There was a mixture of abhorrence and envy in these statements. To be like father in this way of course meant on one level to compete with him for mother, and certainly the two sisters competed tremendously in this respect.

Yet scholastic success meant more than not having to depend on a man; it meant also a way to become independent of her mother. And this leads into the other side of her feelings toward her parents. Many times as a child she had ventured comments on positive aspects of the father, only to be, as she felt it, set straight by her mother. She could not show any of her positive feelings to father and hardly even to herself. To keep away from a man of this kind and join mother in condemnation of him was a way of pleasing mother; to be interested in a man of this kind she experienced as a competition with mother. Almost all her choices of men have been those whom she saw as unreliable and physically or verbally hostile. Before she married her first husband she knew that he had once hit his mother with a beer bottle.

The net effect of such choices was to make her relationships with men a failure or a punishing fate—which brings us up to the time she applied for treatment. She had concluded her first marriage by living out her adolescent fantasy of being left by a man with a child. She had then given the child to her mother—she often said it seemed more like mother's—and returned to school to work further on her (and mother's) ideal of making herself independent of men.

On the face of it, it appears to be a paradox that, after writing to her mother how happy and well satisfied she was with her work and living conditions at school, she began having feelings of depression and difficulty in studying and began going out every night. But behind this "face" we know that at the time of the letter she was struggling with seesawing forces and had only managed to keep down one side of them momentarily.

To complete school would enable her to be independent of mother, which she doubted that she was ready for. And devoting herself entirely to school work meant to her not trying to solve her heterosexual problems. As we know, she tried a new solution; unable to concentrate on her studies, she went out with boys every night even though they seemed dangerous to her and her mother would and did object to her choices. She achieved some sexual gratification but was even more disturbed by her inability to respond sexually and more and more oppressed with the feeling of having degraded herself. Mrs. M. felt angry alternately at the two boys and her mother for what they had done to her and, as usual for her, took it out on herself and became depressed. She followed the example and advice of the two boy friends and sought psychiatric treatment "to straighten out her relationship with boys." She had also become during this brief period very dependent upon them for advice and admired their intelligence—a "new" experience for her.

What changes were brought about during the treatment? One of the most crucial was that she no longer was so afraid of her mother; she could occasionally now see another side of her husband. She was less dependent on her mother and more on her husband; many of the old problems with the mother now emerged with the husband. She was extremely afraid to reveal to her husband that she wanted to visit the mother—supposedly because it was such a threat *to him*. By the end of the treatment she was able to distinguish better her worry about how the *husband* would react from her own worry about whether it is really dangerous *for her* to have such impulses toward her mother. She had frequent arguments with her husband and later was able to express her feelings with more self-respect and without feeling pushed around. The fights with the husband became less severe; they did not go to the ultimate of each daring the other to pack his bags.

She admitted to the therapist in the last few weeks of treatment that she did not feel her father was so horrible as she always used to when she was younger. She still had a hard time talking with him, but she felt he was more benign now. Now she just wonders what to say to him, rather than being so afraid to say anything to him. About her husband she has undergone quite a marked change in attitude. She can say now that she admires his intelligence without having to say it in a way which shows that she's bitter and envious about it. She often still feels about little matters that the husband will be completely rigid and unchangeable and she will never get her way, and always have to either give in or steal her way. But this attitude is much more difficult for her to stick to because of the many evidences of the husband's being able to change and accept what she wants. She still finds it somewhat difficult to unqualifiedly express admiration and love and respect for him.

With her son she became able by the end of treatment to feel more like a parent, rather than, as she had before, like another child. She now can be firm on matters that affect his welfare without such fear that she is being hostile. This change came about also when she was less worried about whether or not she was being like her mother (whom she always saw as hostile and demanding).[2] She is in general less worried about the destructiveness of her hostility and is therefore less likely to get her husband angry at her so that he kicks her around when *she* feels angry.

In the last year of treatment she had much less concern over her sexual adequacy and responsiveness. About three months before the end of treatment it was mentioned once for a time after the baby girl arrived—a very common time for such problems to arise.

Psychosomatic disorders are much rarer. In the early part of treatment there were lots of "accidental" injuries such as cutting of the fingers; these have vanished. Mrs. M. looks better, is healthier, is less often anxious. Even the choreiform movements around her neck have disappeared and are not evident at all in her hands. And her hearing seems to be better—at least she has less difficulty hearing the therapist.

The reader will notice that the initial evaluation was too pessimistic in predicting the outcome of treatment. Perhaps the examiners were too much impressed by the mixed-up state of her life at the moment. But it was clear at the beginning that major personality changes could not take place without long-term treatment. Perhaps not enough attention was given to the stable and strength-giving aspects of her personality and the fact that the patient had gotten along fairly well in school and prior to her first marriage. This episode was the first one in which her disturbance with men began to generalize to other areas of her life, so that she could not concentrate, showed great anxiety and depression, and so on. She had come for treatment during one of the worst phases of her illness and young enough so that the pattern might still have some chance of being altered.

Many changes, of course, cannot be attributed to the treatment directly. The patient's husband was in treatment at the same time. Surely though, without treatment the marriage, which started out so inauspiciously, could not have endured. In marrying this man she could also be proud of his intelligence and share gratification in his

---

[2] Greenson (2) describes the treatment of a group of similar patients who had extreme difficulty in identifying with the parent of the same sex.

achievements, which are close to the kinds of achievements she once wanted for herself. He proved to be stable enough so that she could transfer to him some of the dependency she had felt toward her mother, and, the crowning satisfaction, she was able to get what she had longed for so deeply, a child who was her own and not mother's.

REFERENCES

1. Freud, S. Mourning and melancholia. *Collected papers,* Vol. IV. London: Hogarth Press, 1925, pp. 152–170.
2. Greenson, R. The struggle against identification. *J. Amer. Psychoanal. Ass.,* 1954, *2,* 200–217.
3. Luborsky, L. Self-interpretation of the TAT as a clinical technique. *J. proj. Tech.,* 1953, *17,* 217–223.

CHAPTER ELEVEN

Hysterical Deafness in a Young Girl[1]

BY ROBERT B. MALMO [2]

This is the story of Anne Burns, a classic case of conversion hysteria. Such patients used to abound in the days of Janet but they are now very rare. Anne, a very pretty, unmarried girl of 19, had a stormy late adolescence, which was distressing to her middle-aged parents. A year ago she had a baby, and at the hospital it was discovered that Anne had syphilis. Anne insisted that she had intercourse with one man only, and only once with him. This evidently was a casual affair because he dropped out of her life without even learning that he had impregnated her. The baby was given up for adoption, and Anne returned to her job as bookkeeper for a fur company.

There she soon became involved in the embezzlement of some $300. She swore she did not take the money, but her father was convinced she was guilty and paid the company. Bill Burns, her father, was a house painter who, at the age of 60, could ill afford this expense. It so happened that Anne was not living at home at the time he made the payment. Following disputes with her parents over how late she should stay out on dates she had moved out temporarily and was staying with another girl.

She had been away from home a week when this matter came to a head and her father paid his money to the furriers. One afternoon a

[1] Preparation of this chapter was aided by the Research and Development Division, Office of the Surgeon General, Department of the U.S. Army, under Contract DA-49-007-MD-70.
[2] I should like to express my gratitude to Dr. S. Barza, Dr. J. F. Davis, Miss Fern J. Cramer, and Mrs. Joan Spindler for their invaluable help in collection of data, and for reading the manuscript.

week later Anne returned home looking very pale, complaining that she felt dizzy and faint. She was put to bed and because she seemed ill was spared the questions and criticisms which she otherwise would surely have faced. On the following morning she consulted the family physician, who prescribed some pills, which she took according to directions for two days. On the second day she complained of buzzing in the ears (which later investigation showed was not due to the medication), and on the third morning she awoke to find herself deaf. Immediately all the other symptoms of faintness, dizziness, and tinnitus disappeared.

The patient's attitude toward her symptom was typically *la belle indifférence*. With her hearing gone she could no longer work, and something would have to be done about this thing which had happened to her. She was promptly referred by her physician to an otolaryngologist, who could detect no organic basis for the illness. The ear canals were clear, drums were intact, and all normal landmarks were present. The airways were clear, there was no purulent discharge in either meatus, the tonsils had been cleanly removed, the pharynx was healthy, and the nasal pharynx clear. Cold water in each ear produced brisk nystagmic response on both sides, indicating an intact vestibular apparatus. The audiometer was then introduced to test the patient's hearing. This was the first of a number of disturbing situations in which the patient felt that her claim to deafness was being challenged.

The patient insisted on seeing the lips of anyone interviewing her. She told how she had faced the mirror diligently again and again, watching her lips as she formed words, teaching herself to lip-read. Later her psychotherapist was able to put her lip-reading ability to various tests (e.g., forming words without sounding them) and he was convinced that the ability was genuine. This was one of the objective indications that the patient was not a malingerer. Anne was able to carry on a conversation quite easily in this manner, except that occasionally she repeated a question to make sure she had understood it correctly.

The patient became annoyed with her psychotherapist when he failed to make lip reading easy for her: "I'm sorry, but I can't see your lips clearly. I know you're saying something but I can't understand." Whenever the patient felt that she was being accused of malingering or whenever it was implied that she was responsible for her deafness she wept: "Do you think I want this?" Sometimes amidst tears, sometimes with anger, "Why should I say I can't hear if I can? It's not funny, you know!"

In the audiometric test the patient said she could hear nothing until very low-pitched tones (125 and 250 cycles per second) were presented at high intensity (70 to 75 decibels on a standard A.D.C. audiometer). Then she did not admit to hearing but described a feeling of vibration. This report of feeling without sound was quite plausible because those particular stimuli at such high intensity were very close to the threshold for feeling. But any sensation connected with sound seemed very disturbing to Anne, because after describing the vibratory feelings she began to sob, wept for several minutes, and denied any sensation whatever when 125 and 250 were repeated at 75 decibels. This defensiveness is typical of the hysteric when threatened by loss of the symptom, and is accompanied by anxiety, sometimes of panic proportions. It seemed quite clear in this case as with other similar cases of hysteria that the patient did not in fact hear anything. It appeared that the whole world of auditory experience had been completely removed from consciousness. The otolaryngologist, recognizing the hysterical elements in this case, referred the patient to the psychiatric clinic. There, a psychiatrist made the diagnosis of hysterical deafness and began the series of psychotherapeutic sessions which, combined with special conditioning procedures, eventually led to symptomatic recovery.

Anne was admitted to the Day Hospital. She went to the Institute each morning and returned home in the evening. Her mother feared that her deafness might make it unsafe for her to cross busy city streets alone, and therefore some member of her family (usually her mother, sometimes her sister) always accompanied her on these two trips each day. By this time the family were deeply worried about her and obviously anxious to do whatever they could to help her get well.

From the patient's history, which was taken when she was admitted, the following information was obtained. As a child she was shy and a feeding problem. It is perhaps significant that at Anne's birth her mother was nearly forty. Considering her age and the fact that she already had two daughters aged twelve and five, it was unlikely that Mary Burns wanted another child. Mrs. Burns volunteered that Anne was "the hardest of her daughters to get along with." Progress in

school was satisfactory until she reached ninth grade. She was not promoted, and left school for a job in a small insurance office. At that
time she was sixteen. She held this job for two years but frequently
complained of feeling depressed and lonely because her employer came
to the office so little. She liked her next job as bookkeeper in a wholesale fur company much better.

The shyness of her early childhood had by this time been completely
overcome. Anne was now known as a girl who mixed well and enjoyed
people. She had many friends. She enjoyed dancing and was good at
sports. Her friends thought of her as a person who dressed well, and
she was in fact particularly attentive to her appearance. She was also
known as one likely to "work herself up" and make a big commotion
over minor trifles. Since her deafness, however, she had become more
withdrawn and felt self-conscious in company.

The parents never got along well and the home atmosphere was
always strained, with the mother complaining bitterly and crying frequently. Anne felt that her mother was the one who provoked the
trouble and she always sided with her father. Her older sister, Kay,
sided with the mother. For years the father had been becoming more
and more passive and he had now withdrawn to the point of allowing
his wife to completely dominate the family. He had been a noisy
drinker at one time, but in later years his alcoholism had diminished
along with his assertiveness.

There was no question that the father was the patient's favorite.
"He was always kind to me, gave me everything I wanted, but he was
never warm or affectionate. I cannot ever remember his kissing me."
Strong underlying hostility was the prevailing attitude toward the
mother, although there was considerable ambivalence in her feelings.
Mary Burns is a tense, domineering, overcritical woman who is superficially demonstrative. With Anne she was highly over-protective in a
"smothering," nagging way: "Mother nags me incessantly." For as
long as she can remember the patient has felt rejected by her mother.
She has always looked upon Kay as her mother's favorite. Kay, 24 and
unmarried, is not a pretty girl like Anne. Perhaps as a compensatory
activity she takes college courses at night. College work was unusual
enough in this family for Kay to reap considerable kudos. All of this
added to the patient's resentment, and to her feelings of rejection.

It was in this family setting that Anne experienced the series of events which had at least participating significance in the matter of her present symptom picture. Mary Burns was shocked to think that her daughter was pregnant. But having faced it she promptly rallied the whole family to meet this new situation. She rented an apartment in another part of the city and arranged for Kay to take Anne there during the last two months of pregnancy. Anne had little or no money and the mother arranged to pay the extra expenses from family savings. For this aid the patient was duly grateful; but there was that ambivalence of feeling which was always present where her mother was concerned: "As soon as I get better, I'll have to pay her back the money. . . . You don't know my mother." She felt, too, that her mother was partially to blame for never having given her any sex instruction. The patient always insisted that the pregnancy and contraction of syphilis resulted from her first and only act of coitus. In this situation, as always, the mother took complete charge, delegating only passive and minor roles to the father. What the patient resented most was her mother's determination to have the baby given out for adoption, completely against the patient's wishes. We may assume that Anne's unrealistic wish to hold on to the baby was partly determined by the wish to embarrass her mother. The mother, of course, would not listen to Anne's pleas; and it was typical of Bill Burns that he did not so much as discuss the question of adoption with his daughter. This was a matter for his wife to handle.

With Anne and Kay back and all four people once again under the same roof, hostilities and resentments which had been checked now appeared in full strength. Friction between the patient and her mother was greatly increased. "I felt she didn't trust me any more. She got angry if I ever stayed out late, and she kept watching me like a hawk. She kept harping on the 'trouble' I had caused and the money it had cost. She kept picking on me and blaming me for everything. In the evening she sat and talked to Kay. Whenever I came into the room they'd shut up. I'm sure they were talking about me."

The following transcript from a recorded interview is revealing with respect to the interactions between the patient and her mother and her sister.

DOCTOR: You used to hear your mother and Kay talking about you? (Pause. No answer.)

DOCTOR: Where were you when you'd hear them talking?

PATIENT: Usually in my bedroom.

DR.: That's pretty far, isn't it, from the kitchen where they're sitting?

PT.: No, it's not very far. The hall isn't very long.

DR.: What would they be saying about you?

PT.: Oh, most likely mother would be telling my sister that she shouldn't have bothered doing something for me. But what I really disliked was that they never used my name. It was always, she, she, she. You'd think I didn't have a name. Everything was "she" or "her." One of these days she'll get around to calling me "it."

DR.: That got you angry, did it?

PT.: Well, I didn't like it. She never called Kay "she." Of course, if she had mentioned her name just before that, well, she might say "she." But my name was never used.

DR.: You felt you were being given a raw deal, didn't you?

PT.: Well, I didn't see why I shouldn't be treated as well as she was. My mother is always throwing up in my face about how much I cost her, and about having a baby.

DR.: How much money do you owe your mother?

PT.: How much money do I owe her? I don't owe her anything. She never told me that I had to pay her back. But I'll pay her back every cent that she ever spent on me.

The following, a part of the same recorded interview, is interesting from the standpoint of the malingering question, and it also provides an excellent example of repression at work. The Saturday interview which is referred to was conducted after the patient had been injected with sodium amytal. Hysterics often lose their symptoms under sodium amytal, whereas malingerers go on pretending even when they are under the influence of this drug. Reference to the patient's hearing during this interview will be noted in the transcription, as will the haziness and vagueness characterizing the patient's memory for the painful events.

DR.: You were very upset last week, Anne—last Saturday—because you thought that during the interview you were able to hear. Do you remember this? I don't care whether you did or you didn't but you were upset about it anyway. I looked at you throughout the interview just as I am looking at you now, but afterwards you said, "I don't remember reading your lips, so I must have been hearing you." And you were crying.

Pт.:   I can't remember anything about it. It's something to worry about if I thought I could hear you.

Dr.:   Well, I don't know if you did or didn't; it's just that you were upset over things. You forgot all about Saturday, did you?

Pт.:   No, it wasn't that I forgot about it; I didn't want to forget. I just couldn't remember it.

Dr.:   You didn't want to forget?

Pт.:   I don't think so. There's no reason why I should want to forget about it. I've been trying to think about it, but can't reach it. I don't know what happened.

Psychological Tests on Admission

In the testing situation the patient was friendly and coöperative. She seemed entirely at ease and absolutely unconcerned about her deafness. There was very little trouble in getting her to follow instructions. From time to time she announced pleasantly that she could not understand and asked to have the question written down.

Intelligence on the abbreviated Wechsler-Bellevue Scale (VIBS) was in the average range. A high Digit Span indicated absence of severe free-floating anxiety. Bender Gestalt performance was accurate and completely within normal limits. Figure Drawings (see Fig. 1A) were small in size (approximately 3½ inches high), and were placed in the upper left-hand corner of each sheet. The male figure was drawn first. She referred to it as "like something from the middle-ages, a caveman." Strong egocentricity and avoidance of problems were indicated in the drawings. The improved drawings in Figure 1B were made following treatment. Post-treatment testing will be dealt with presently.

The Katogram (see Fig. 2) shows a very good beginning, but blocking and difficult progress occurred just as the task was nearly over. Being faced with a new situation (mirror drawing) seemed to evoke impulsive behavior with initial lucky success which carried nearly, but not quite, to the goal. Sudden blocking just before reaching the goal, with crossing, spiking, and wavering of lines suggests a panicky display of helplessness. On the AMI Level of Aspiration Test the patient was very cautious. Fearful of failure, she was careful not to set a goal any higher than one which prior experience had convinced her she could easily attain.

The TAT stories were brief and rather banal in theme. There was

FIG. 1. Figure Drawings. A. Before recovery of hearing. B. After
recovery of hearing.

a certain glibness and superficiality about them—a moralizing quality
—as if the patient knew what was wanted, what the correct response
should be, and gave the "pat" answer. Some general themes running
through the stories included the following: (1) impatience, shirking
of responsibilities, and desire for immediate gratification of wishes; (2)

shifting of responsibility for actions; (3) postponing and avoiding decisions. Aggressive wishes were prominent; but they were repressed (e.g., attributed to some external influence).

In the stories it is not difficult to perceive a mother who, even in her kinder moments, repels the patient. Death wishes against the mother figure appear repeatedly. The patient's desire to take the mother's place with her father comes out several times. With Picture 6GF, for

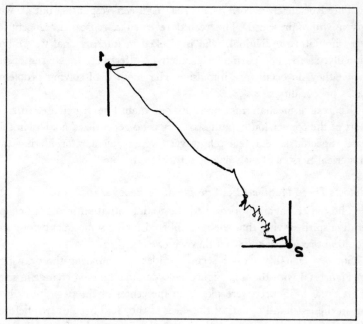

FIG. 2.   Mirror Drawing Record. Note block near goal.

example, where it is unusual to see the young girl as wife of the much older man, the patient began her story: "In this picture we see a man and his wife having an earnest talk about their children, who lately have not been doing exactly as they should." It is of interest that the father in her story shocks his wife by wanting to spank the children. The patient's own father is passive, inconspicuous, and completely dominated by the mother. There are some hints through the stories of shifting identification from man to woman, wife to husband, daughter to mother, even doll to daughter. Wishes for change in the mother to a less castrating figure like the father seemed to be part of a very ambivalent pattern of conflicting needs (e.g., *n Aggression n Succorance*). Strong oedipal wishes seemed manifest in several stories. The story about the farm scene in Picture 2 begins in the usual way, but immediately after the first sentence the girl with the books has actually become the older woman leaning against the tree watching the husband (father) working.

The Rorschach record was brief, eighteen responses, but it was given with fair speed. The record revealed a repressed, egocentric, very immature individual, who is blocked in interpersonal ties. Emotionally, she is not particularly reactive; affectively toned responses, when they do occur, are impulsive. Her method of solving problems lacks practicality.

Repressive mechanisms constitute one main line of defense. In support of the conversion hypothesis, there is no generalized anxiety in this case. Specific sexual fears, however, were present. Considering the hysterical personality it was not surprising to note "color shock."

Retests Three Months After Symptomatic Recovery

The patient again approached the testing situation in a very coöperative spirit, saying that she remembered taking some tests before but could not recall exactly what they were.

Some personality growth seemed evident. Comparing the drawings in Figure 1B with those in Figure 1A we note a marked change in size. This time the figures were placed in the center of the page instead of up in the left-hand corner of the sheet as they had been drawn before. The shift from naked to clothed figures is a very significant change, and the order of drawing the sexes was reversed: the female figure was drawn first this time.

These changes are encouraging, suggesting some growth in ego strength, in feeling of security, and in satisfaction with her role. Recovery from depressed mood is very evident. She seems more concerned with relating well to others, and more aware of social opinion. Behavior toward others is more outgoing (note that arms of both figures show a bend outwards, as compared with the former rigid side arm posture). Growth has not proceeded very far, however. There is still the picture of the dependent, bewildered child, afraid to face the responsibilities of adulthood and hesitating before the dangers of mature heterosexual relationships.

The patient declared she didn't remember taking the ink-blot test before, although she recalled having been tested during the summer. The record was again a brief one, fifteen main and four additional responses. One encouraging sign was the less constricted psychogram (a decline in F% from 61% to 33%, and a rise in FM from three to five, plus three additionals). The patient now is considerably more spontaneous, less on the defensive, and much more willing to face new situations. There were some signs of improved emotional control. Other encouraging changes indicated were some decreases in egocentricity and a shift toward more practical approaches to problems. There was no evidence of blocking to sexual cues in this record. Some of the responses showed a warming up, a freer expression of feminine traits, and need for affection.

Muscle Potential Recording During Auditory Stimulation

Reaction to loud sound. Six weeks after admission the patient remained totally deaf. The therapist felt that he had made some progress in helping her achieve better insight, but what of the conversion symptom? Would it suddenly disappear to be immediately replaced by another, even more alarming, symptom? Could this possibly be an atypical early schizophrenia with deafness as the last defense before a psychotic breakdown? Was it wise to focus on the symptom? Still, the deafness had become very troublesome to the patient, and it now seemed clear that she was most anxious to be cured. Probability of schizophrenia did not seem very great, and most considerations favored making a direct attack on the symptom at this time.

It was at this point that her therapist decided to suggest to her that through special electrophysiological studies we might learn how to restore her hearing. She was told that we wished first to take records of her muscle potentials while stimulating her with loud sound. He then brought her to our electrophysiological suite, saying that he would be nearby in case he was needed.

After attaching electrodes we asked the patient to lie down on the hospital bed. We then placed earphones on her head. She lay quietly, without apparent fearfulness (although her heart rate was quite high), obediently following the directions of the girl technician. The patient

was told that her therapist would be in the adjoining instrumental
control room during the test. Actually, the therapist could see the
patient through a one-way-vision window.

Auditory stimuli were 700-cycle tones approximately 90 decibels
above auditory threshold. There were ten stimulations. Onset of stimulation produced a very loud click of brief duration; tone continued
for three seconds.

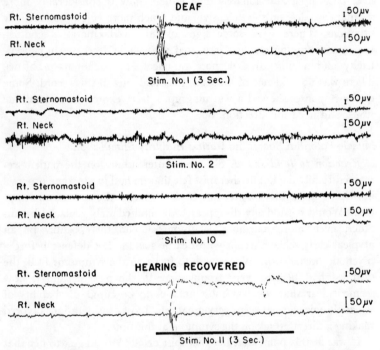

FIG. 3. Muscle Potential Reaction to Strong Auditory Stimulation.
Observe startle reaction to the first stimulus in the deaf state, and note
complete absence of any reaction to the second stimulus. Lower record
shows that after recovery of hearing, the patient was still responding,
even after ten prior stimulations.

The first stimulus had visible effect; it was plain to see that the
patient had been startled (see recorded muscle potential reaction in
Fig. 3). Soon after the immediate startle reaction her head began to
tremble, and the trembling spread to the rest of the body. When the

patient began to weep, her therapist entered the room to give reassurance. To the question of whether she had heard the sound, Anne replied that she had heard nothing but that she had felt pain in her head "as if something hit me on the head." Later, after the test, she added: "It felt as if the top of my head was going to blow off."

The second stimulus, which came one minute following the first, failed to elicit any reaction, nor did any of the subsequent stimuli produce any reaction which could be detected in the electromyographic (EMG) records (see Fig. 3) or by the observer. Each time the observer heard the stimulus, she asked the subject if she had felt anything. The reply, each time, was that she had felt nothing and heard nothing. Because of the weeping, which brought on frequent blinking, it is difficult to say much about the blink reaction to sound, although from the observer's notes it is probable that the blink may have remained as a residual reaction. The functional localization of this reaction in the brain is not known; it is subcortical apparently, but in any event seems dissociated from the head reaction in startle and completely resistant to all forms of inhibition: normal habituation (trained marksmen never lose it), hypnosis, and—most probably—hysterical inhibition.

Anne's therapist remained until after the third stimulus, when he left the room and resumed his observation through the one-way-vision window. Sobbing had stopped at this time.

Hearing recovered. In the repeat test, one week after Anne had recovered her hearing, she reacted to every stimulus. Control tests with normal individuals show that strong head reaction to stimulus 1 followed by no head movement to stimulus 2 does not occur. Normally there is a gradual and progressive falling off in the size of reaction from trial to trial.

Heart rate. Resting heart rate in the period before stimulation in the first test showed that in the deaf state there was greater apprehensiveness than later, in the second test, after hearing had been restored. Resting heart rate was from 94 to 102 beats per minute in the first test, compared with 71 to 76 beats per minute in the second. The fast rate the first time may have been partly attributable to primacy (facing an entirely new situation). But undoubtedly the main factor producing the accelerated heart rate was the threat to the patient's defense against sound. Actual penetration of the barrier of silence (first stimulus) produced an additional immediate rise in heart rate of thirteen beats per minute. During weeping, heart rate was, of course, high; it gradually decreased as emotional disturbance subsided. No rise in heart rate was noted on any other stimulus in the first session.

Comment. Anne's symptom defense was broken through by means of intense auditory stimulation. The penetration of the symptom barrier was achieved, no doubt, through using a very novel form of stimulation. Startling noises in everyday life situations were ineffective. For example, the therapist's attempt to produce a startle reaction by clapping his hands behind Anne's back had failed to elicit any response.

She reacted to the novel situation in our test with emotional disturbance, had a brief fit of weeping which subsided when her therapist came into the room and reassured her. Then—and this is the most remarkable thing—in the sixty seconds which elapsed between stimulus 1 and stimulus 2 her defense against sound somehow strengthened so that it was effective again, even against the same stimulus.

Somehow, impulses coming in over auditory pathways (which had in the first instance effectively carried through to the skeletal-motor pathways) were blocked centrally upon repetition of the stimulus. This must mean that central reorganization took place, and in a remarkably short space of time. An understanding of the neural mechanisms involved in such rapid alteration of central nervous action would seem to lead to basic explanation of typical hysterical phenomena, such as sudden onset and disappearance of conversion symptoms and repression of certain thought sequences. These observations logically lead us to consider phenomena of central inhibition in relation to our observations; and because there is not space to deal with this question here the reader is referred elsewhere for a discussion of this topic (1, pp. 194 ff.).

Conditioned Finger Withdrawal to Sound Stimulus

We come now to the most interesting procedure of all, especially from the point of view of therapeutic change. Having failed to produce any lasting effect with strong auditory stimulation, it seemed worth while to try conditioning. There are a number of published accounts of successful CR therapy in the literature, and as early as 1912 the Russian reflexologist, Bechterev, claimed successful treatment of hysterical deafness with conditioning techniques.

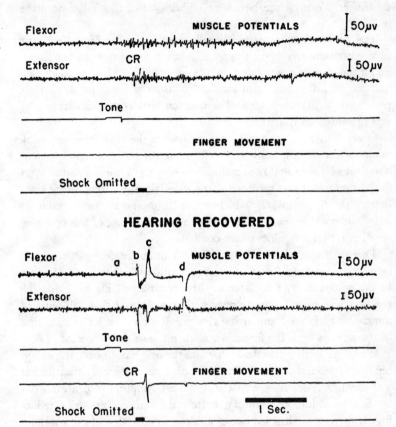

FIG. 4. Conditioned Responses on First Test Trial, in Session 1 When S Was Deaf and in Corresponding Test Trial, Session 2, After Hearing Had Been Recovered. Electrical artifacts in muscle lines of lower record are (a) relay switching artifact, (b) closing shock circuit connected to S (who felt nothing because shock voltage was zero), (c) artifact due to S's removing finger from electrode which was grounded, and (d) artifact caused by return of finger to button electrode.

Conditioning was carried out in the same duplex suite. Details of apparatus and procedure are presented elsewhere (1). Only the most essential items will be described here. The subject's forefinger rested on a silvered button which served both to give a shock at appropriate times and also to record any movement of the finger, either pressure of the finger down on the button or withdrawal of the finger from the button.

The subject was instructed simply to raise her forefinger from the silvered button every time she felt a shock to her finger. In conditioning, a tone was presented first, and this was followed by the shock one-half second later. Some two hundred pairings of tone and shock were presented during the session. The first test trial (tone without shock) was presented on trial 150.

Observe in Figure 4 what happened when the tone came on. Look at the upper record, labeled "Deaf." Note the burst of muscle potentials, but also note that the reaction was covert; that is, no actual overt finger movement was recorded. Note especially the strong motor reaction in the flexor muscle, which was antagonistic to the direction of the withdrawal response. The most probable meaning of this opposing reaction is that it signifies motor conflict.

Thorough analysis of all the CR data from the deaf subject (pre-recovery) revealed a flexor-extensor opposition which was not a feature of the post-recovery CR. Note in the lower part of Figure 4 that the reaction was overt (actual finger withdrawal) and that the burst of muscle potentials accompanying response is somewhat lower than that in the records from the first session, when the subject was deaf.

When the subject was deaf what was the origin of flexion, the antagonistic reaction? It seemed clear from analysis of the data that flexion was identified somehow with the hysterical symptom of deafness. According to conditioning theory, hysterical symptoms are drive reducing. If drive is the learned one of anxiety, interruption of the symptom would have the effect of raising the level of anxiety. We saw a good example of this arousal of anxiety in experiment 1, when the loud novel sound penetrated the symptom barrier.

Now finger extension in anticipation of shock would actually represent symptom interruption because it would imply ability to hear. It follows then that extending the finger or even the initiation of finger extension might be anxiety arousing. Here anxiety assumes the status of drive. It thus appears that, when the symptom was present, there were two coexisting and interrelated mechanisms of conditioning leading to conflict. These mechanisms may be outlined as follows:

	CONDITIONING A	CONDITIONING B
Drive	pain	anxiety
Cue	tone	motor cue (lifting finger to tone, in anticipation of shock, signifies hearing)
Response	finger withdrawal (extension)	movement opposed to finger withdrawal (flexion)
Reinforcement	avoidance of pain	avoidance of anxiety

Recovery of hearing. It was on the morning following this session that the patient's hearing was restored. Following the CR session the patient smilingly asserted that she still could not hear. The therapist then repeated his suggestion that hearing would return on the following morning, after a night's sleep. The therapist made certain that the patient read his lips correctly. On the next morning, Anne was crossing a busy street, on her way to the Institute, when a driver who had narrowly avoided hitting her blasted his horn and shouted at her. Her hearing suddenly returned, and has remained intact.

It may be significant that this was the first time since her deafness that the patient had attempted to cross a busy street alone. The propinquity of events makes it appear very likely that the CR training was a factor in removing the symptom. Just how it occurred we cannot say, although the records were very revealing in giving us a picture of certain aspects of the symptom mechanism.

Follow-Up

All the fears of a shift to another symptom or of a psychotic break following recovery of hearing proved groundless. The patient's family were considerably relieved by her recovery, gave her more support, stopped harping on the old friction-producing topics; and to make things even easier her sister Kay left the home. Symptomatic cure was achieved without further complications. The patient has since married and thus far appears to be making a satisfactory adjustment. Anne's fiancé had been patient and considerate all through her illness. But he undoubtedly was an important factor in the dynamics of recovery, for the patient feared she might lose him because of her deafness.

Anne is still a rather egocentric, over-dependent person with many personality weaknesses. While there have been some gains in strength of personality, the main therapeutic achievement was removal of a troublesome symptom. Contrary to belief in some quarters, therapeutic focus on a symptom may be useful, provided it takes place in the setting of general psychotherapy. Apparently a conversion symptom may outlive its usefulness as a defense and go on autonomously causing the patient much distress, sometimes for many years (1, p. 190).

ADDENDUM

In this chapter we have reviewed a classical example of conversion hysteria. We have focused mainly on six weeks of a woman's life when as an Institute patient she was the subject of intense study. At this time she was deaf, and was using lip reading to communicate with others. Interviews and projective tests provided indispensable data for understanding the basic dynamics of her personality. Special conditioning techniques brought out the patient's unconscious reactions to sound: muscle contractions so minute that they could be detected only with a very sensitive electromyograph. The same techniques seemed to be instrumental in restoring her hearing.

REFERENCES

1. Malmo, R. B., Davis, J. F., and Barza, S. Total hysterical deafness: an experimental case study. *J. Pers.*, 1952, *21*, 188–204.

A College Freshman with a Stuttering Problem

BY WENDELL JOHNSON and WILLIAM D. TROTTER

Ann is a 20-year-old freshman who attended the Speech Clinic of a midwestern university. This report covers her first four months in the Clinic.

History of the Speech Problem

In most adult stuttering cases it is extremely difficult, and often impossible, to determine the exact time of onset and the precise circumstances surrounding it. In the present case neither Ann nor her parents have reported any instances of stuttering before the second grade (seventh year). As Ann told the story during preliminary interviews, she first experienced stuttering on about April 1, 1941. On that day the second-grade teacher asked her to stand before the other children, call their names, and quiz them over some examination questions that had been used the previous year. She said she did all this without any difficulty, except that she had "not been able" to say the name of one boy. Later intensively close questioning brought out the fact that this boy was her chief rival for the position at the head of the class. Her mother had been a schoolteacher. Her older brother and older sister were making very good records in school. In general, Ann seemed to have been strongly motivated to excel scholastically, and to compete as successfully as possible with the boy in question. The close questioning indicated that Ann might have simply refused to call on the boy and that she might have felt some guilt about this later. It indicated that if she did "stutter" she had no memory of what she had done or experienced in the way of actual speech behavior. If it was a considerable blockage—an "inability" to say the boy's name—her failure to recall any previous difficulty of even slight degree, or any reaction by the other children or by her to this sudden and, as one might suppose, more or less dramatic "inability" to speak is essentially incredible. Moreover, close questioning of Ann and her mother and an aunt brought out no report of further "stuttering" until about six weeks later, at which time Ann says she had "trouble" telling her teacher about the family's new refrigerator. She says she had "trouble" saying "refrigerator," but it is not clear whether the difficulty was distinctively different from what other children of the same age might have had saying that sort of word.

At about this same time, but probably a week or so later, an incident occurred which she remembers as being very upsetting to her. She had been selected to play the leading role of the Queen of Hearts in a school program. Her mother had made her a beautiful costume for the part and Ann was looking forward to this big occasion in her life with a great deal of enthusiasm. A few days before the program was scheduled to take place she became ill with the measles. This was a deep disappointment to her, but, in addition, she was keenly hurt by the behavior of a close girl friend of hers. This girl showed little concern about Ann's illness, and the day she found out Ann was ill she arranged with the teacher to take her part. Then she tried to persuade Ann's sister to obtain Ann's costume without letting Ann know about it. However, Ann found out that her friend had tried to get her costume without permission and was deeply affected. As it turned out, there were two performances. Ann missed the first one, but although still quite sick she was taken by her mother to the second performance and participated in it. Neither she nor her mother can recall that she had any difficulty in speaking during the program or during the stressful few days that preceded it. Both Ann and her parents say, however, that she began to "stutter" shortly after this incident. What is probably more accurate is that the upsetting incident made her more non-fluent. It is to be duly considered that this period of presumed excessive non-fluency might have passed if it had not been for the parental concern and disapproval of her speech that appears to have begun at about this time. The parents report that they began to tell Ann to "stop stuttering," "slow down," "take it easy," etc. It appears that this eventually resulted in her developing self-consciousness about speaking.

It is to be emphasized that very intensive questioning on several occasions, on one of which the mother and an aunt were present, failed to establish the facts concerning onset. This is generally the case

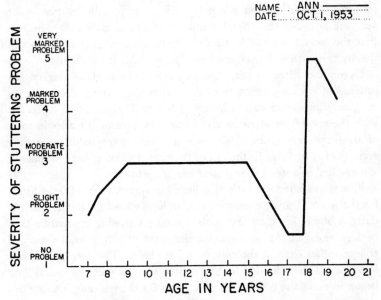

FIG. 1. History of the Severity of the Stuttering Problem as Rated from the Memory of the Stutterer.

with adult stutterers. It implies that stuttering is as a rule not very dramatic or sudden in its mode of onset, and that whatever the speech behavior is that first attracts the disturbed attention of the parents, or teachers, it must not be very severe or unusual, or consistently disabling. Research (8, 4, 3) on the onset of stuttering in very young children, with histories taken soon after onset, support these implications, as will be indicated in a later section of this paper.

Ann was asked to draw a graph of the severity of her stuttering problem from the time of onset, as reported by her, to the time when she began her therapy program at the University of Iowa Speech Clinic. This graph, reproduced as Figure 1, shows that the problem increased gradually in severity from the seventh to the ninth year. When she was about 10 years of age she received treatment from a chiropractor for about six months. Her physical condition, which had been poor because of a prolonged attack of influenza, apparently improved during this same period. The speech problem was not affected. All during high school she received treatment from student speech correctionists sent out from a nearby university and during her senior year she attended the Speech Clinic at this same university. She says that the speech therapy had no effect on her stuttering and explains this by saying that she refused to coöperate with the therapists.

During her fifteenth year Ann's speech began to show marked improvement. It was during this period that she started to become an extremely important person in the high school. She was very popular with the rest of the students and eventually became a leader in most of the important clubs. There was a concomitant reduction in the severity of stuttering. In the fall of the year, following her graduation, she enrolled in a small college near her home town.

Five weeks after she entered college her speech took a marked turn for the worse. During her senior year in high school she had frequently dated a boy in her class and in the summer following graduation they became engaged. At his insistence she enrolled with him at the small college rather than at the college of her choice. Two weeks after college opened they decided to get married the following June and Ann began to make the necessary preparations for the wedding. During this period Ann's stuttering was so mild that, according to her report, very few people regarded her as being a stutterer. Then, one night in October she was visited by her fiancé, who, without any previous warning, told her he was no longer interested in marrying her and asked her to break off their engagement. The only reason he gave for this request was that she had insisted on too long an engagement. However, according to Ann, this reason was evidently not the real one because she had wanted to get married at Christmas, but he had put the marriage off until June in order to pay for a new car he had recently purchased. Her first reaction to the request to break off the engagement was that he was ashamed of her stuttering, but when she questioned him about this he denied that her speech had anything to do with his actions. His parents later also told Ann that her speech was not a factor in breaking the engagement.

This incident had a very traumatic effect on her speech. As the graph indicates, the severity of her stuttering increased from a "mild problem" to a "very marked problem." She immediately dropped out of school and until about a year later she remained at home helping her mother with the household duties. Concerning this period she states in her autobiography, "I lost all confidence in myself. I didn't feel good about myself any more." It should also be noted that the social prominence she enjoyed in high school, which was temporally associated with her speech improvement, was now missing.

During the year she remained at home her stuttering problem continued to be severe. The following October she began work as a clerk in the supply room of a large hospital. Some time later she obtained a better position as a secretary-receptionist in the office of an optometrist, a position which she held until she left to attend the Speech Clinic. During this time she underwent psychiatric treatment for one half-hour a week for a period of six months. Although this treatment made her "feel better," as she explains it, no noticeable change in the severity of the stuttering was apparent. She does report that the stuttering was less severe by the time she left the optometrist's employment to enroll in the Speech Clinic, but she thinks that this was due to the amount of talking she did in connection with her office duties.

Family Relationships

In Darley's (3) study of the attitudes and relationships of the parents of fifty stuttering and fifty non-stuttering children he reports, "A general conclusion which may be drawn is that the two groups are markedly similar on the vast majority of items studied." Clinical observation seems to support this finding. The relationships of stutterers with their parents are usually not outstandingly different from those of non-stutterers. In Ann's case, however, there appears to have been at least one major source of conflict in the home. Until about four years ago her great-grandmother and her great-uncle lived in the home, and Ann's parents insisted on keeping the house quiet for them. The result was that Ann was not allowed to bring friends into the home. For the most part, however, so far as Ann is capable of reporting it, the relationship with her parents seems, at least on the surface, to have been a fairly happy one.

Ann's parents, by their own testimony and according to Ann's memory, have made little attempt to correct her speech by their own personal efforts since she was about eight years of age. They seem to have relatively good empathy for her feelings about her stuttering. This is shown, for example, by the fact that when she talks they always allow her to finish what she has to say without attempting to supply words for her. Ann claims they do not show signs of impatience or disapproval when she is having a particularly difficult time with her stuttering. They have not been indifferent about her speech, however, because they have always taken advantage of any opportunities for speech therapy that were available in the community.

Status at Beginning Period of Therapy

1. *Problem profile.* The person most closely acquainted with Ann's problems is the speech clinician, with whom she has had frequent individual conferences. This speech clinician is a graduate student specializing in speech pathology. She is not a clinical psychologist, although she has had some psychological training. Her major professional training is in speech pathology. As Ann's clinician she has played an important role in evaluating the severity of Ann's speech problem at the beginning and end of the period of therapy.

On the basis of clinical experience it has been found practical to divide a stutterer's problems into a number of somewhat arbitrary categories: (a) speech, (b) speaking time behavior, (c) feelings about stuttering, (d) personality adjustment, (e) reactions to treatment, (f) social adjustment, (g) school adjustment, (h) family adjustment, (i) vocational adjustment, (j) physical adjustment. Ann's clinician was asked to evaluate the severity of her problems in each of these at the beginning and end of the therapy period, according to a specified procedure (11). Ann's problem profile is given below essentially as completed by her clinician. Some further material has been added in order to clarify the clinician's statements. The quantitative rating given in each of the areas of the profile is in terms of a five-point scale ranging from 1 (no problem present) to 5 (very marked problem present). This profile was completed at the end of the eighth individual conference and represents the severity of Ann's problem at the end of the second week of therapy.

1. *Speech Problem*
   Rating: Marked Problem (4)
   Reasons for Rating:

   a. Percentage of stuttering while talking to clinician alone.   5
   b. Percentage of stuttering while reading to clinician alone.   5
   c. Rating on Severity of Stuttering Rating Sheet (7) while talking to clinician alone. This rating sheet employs a seven-point scale of severity ranging from 1 (no stuttering) to 7 (very severe stuttering).   4
   d. Rating on Severity of Stuttering Rating Sheet while reading to clinician alone.   4

2. *Feelings About Stuttering*
   Rating: Moderate Problem (3)
   Reasons for Rating:

   At the present time Ann shows the avoidance behavior characteristic of stutterers. Most stutterers have a strong motivation to avoid the unpleasantness they experience when they stutter and consequently they tend to avoid speaking situations in which they feel they will stutter and to substitute non-feared words for feared ones. Ann was asked to record for four days any speaking situations in which she avoided speaking as much as she would have liked to, and any times she substituted words. In four days she recorded an average of ten such situations, and an average of ten substituted words, per day. She also worries considerably about people being ashamed of her because she is a stutterer.

   Many stutterers show embarrassment during stuttering by looking away from the listener, or blushing, for example, but Ann seldom shows such signs.

3. *Speaking Time Behavior*
   Rating: Moderate Problem (3)
   Reasons for Rating:

   The majority of stutterers speak much less than non-stutterers, but according to the detailed speaking time records which Ann kept during the first week of therapy she spoke an average of about 25 minutes a day. According to the unpublished research done on this

problem by the junior author, her speaking time is below that of the average non-stutterer. Ann tends strongly to avoid speaking situations involving strangers.

4. *Personality Adjustment*

   Rating: Moderate Problem (3)

   Reasons for Rating:

   According to the behavior that the clinician has observed and Ann's own verbal reports, her personality adjustment appears to fall well within the normal range. However, according to the results of the MMPI test (see below) there appears to be a moderately severe adjustment problem present. The rating of "moderate" is given on the basis of the test results rather than on the basis of any behavior observed by the clinician.

5. *Reaction to Treatment*

   Rating: No Problem (1)

   Reasons for Rating:

   Up to the end of the second week of therapy she has participated fully in the therapy program. She has done all her assignments conscientiously and has taken a very active part in the group therapy.

6. *Social Adjustment*

   Rating: No Problem (1)

   Reasons for Rating:

   Ann has an excellent ability to make friends and in the short while that she has been here she has become a member of several social groups.

7. *School Adjustment*

   Rating: Moderate Problem (3)

   Reasons for Rating:

   She is doing relatively well in her university course work, but she tends to worry considerably that she will not make good grades. She did well in high school but has been out of school for two years and seems to be finding some difficulty in adjusting herself to the routine of studying.

8. *Family Adjustment*

   Rating: No Problem (1)

   Reasons for Rating:

   At the present time there appears to be no problem in this area. The parents seem to be understanding about Ann's speech problem. There is no evidence that they reject her because of her stuttering.

9. *Vocational Adjustment*

   Rating: Moderate Problem (3)

Reasons for Rating:

The rating of "moderate" is given because Ann has no definite vocational goals, although she is making some effort at the present time to remedy this situation. She has had two jobs in the past which required considerable speech, and her employers seem to have accepted the fact that she stuttered. Her attitude toward her speech, which is generally one of frankness and cheerfulness, makes her stuttering less of a handicap than it otherwise would be because her stuttering is actually severe enough to interfere to some degree with effective communication.

10. *Physical Adjustment*

Rating: No Problem (1)

Reasons for Rating:

Ann appears to be in good health and has no physical problems.

2. *Detailed speech evaluation.* In addition to the speech evaluation made by Ann's clinician, a more detailed analysis was carried out by the junior author. He obtained recorded samples of Ann's speech at the beginning of the therapy period, following the procedure used in the Hill Foundation fluency norms study (5, 6). The procedure consisted of recording Ann's speech while she (a) talked about her "present job," "past job," or "future job," (b) constructed a story in response to Thematic Apperception Test Card 10, and (c) read a 300-word passage.

These speech samples were analyzed to determine the number of each of several types of non-fluency. Ann's speech was compared, in terms of these measurements, with speech samples obtained from fifty female non-stutterers and fifty male stutterers of Ann's approximate age level. Normative data are not yet available for female stutterers. Only the speech samples for the "job" situation are considered in this report.

Table 1 gives the number of non-fluencies per hundred words in Ann's speech in the "job" speaking situation. A detailed description of each of the types of non-fluencies will not be given here, but most of their names are relatively descriptive. In the second and third columns are given the decile ranks for the female non-stutterers and the male stutterers that are closest to Ann's non-fluency counts. Ann's speech, as indicated by Table 1, is very different from that of female non-stutterers of her own age. She is somewhat more non-fluent than the average male stutterer. For six of the eight categories the number of

TABLE 1. NUMBER OF NON-FLUENCIES OF EACH SPECIFIED TYPE PER 100 WORDS IN ANN'S SPEECH AT THE BEGINNING AND END OF THE THERAPY PERIOD, AS COMPARED WITH NON-FLUENCY DATA FOR 50 MALE STUTTERERS AND 50 FEMALE NON-STUTTERERS

TYPE OF NON-FLUENCY	BEGINNING OF FOUR-MONTH THERAPY PERIOD			END OF FOUR-MONTH THERAPY PERIOD		
	NUMBER OF NON-FLUENCIES PER 100 WORDS IN ANN'S SPEECH	NEAREST DECILE RANK FOR FEMALE NON-STUTTERERS	NEAREST DECILE RANK FOR MALE STUTTERERS	NUMBER OF NON-FLUENCIES PER 100 WORDS IN ANN'S SPEECH	NEAREST DECILE RANK FOR FEMALE NON-STUTTERERS	NEAREST DECILE RANK FOR MALE STUTTERERS
Interjections (sounds, syllables, words, phrases)	8.0	10th	5th	4.2	7th	3rd
Repetitions (sounds, syllables)	13.3	10th	8th	11.1	10th	7th
Repetition (words)	3.1	10th	5th	2.1	10th	4th
Repeated phrases	2.7	10th	9th	0	1st	1st
Revisions	3.1	10th	10th	0	1st	1st
Incomplete phrases	0	1st	1st	0	1st	1st
Broken words	0	1st	1st	0.7	10th	8th
Prolonged sounds	12.4	10th	9th	17.4	10th	10th
Total	42.6	10th	8th	35.5	10th	9th

Ann's non-fluencies is greater than the number recorded for any of the female non-stutterers. The two categories of "Incomplete phrases" and "Broken words," in which she has no non-fluencies, account for less than 3 percent of the non-fluencies in the speech of non-stutterers and stutterers. Ann has more non-fluencies than at least 50 percent or more of the stutterers in six of the eight categories.

Ann stuttered 21 percent of the words in the "job" speaking situation. On the basis of this measure she would be classified as a moderately severe stutterer.

3. *Problem questionnaire* (11). Six weeks after the beginning of therapy Ann filled out the "Problem Questionnaire." This questionnaire covers 75 "dimensions of improvement," or aspects of a stutterer's total problem. Ann was asked to complete the questionnaire twice, two days apart, using two different sets of instructions. The first time she was given the following instructions:

Rate the severity of your problem with respect to each of the factors listed on the questionnaire—in terms of the problem scale—as you think it was two weeks after you began your stuttering therapy program at the University Speech Clinic.

The second time she completed the questionnaire with the following instructions:

Rate the severity of your problem with respect to each of the factors listed on the questionnaire—in terms of the problem scale—as it is at the present time.

The problem scale referred to above is a five-point scale ranging from 1 (no problem) to 5 (very marked problem).

The 75 items of the "Problem Questionnaire" are divided into three major categories and eighteen subcategories, and the mean rating was calculated for each of these. Ann's mean ratings are given in Table 2. They indicate Ann's own evaluation of the severity of her problem and also show how her evaluations of the severity of the problem changed over periods of six weeks and four months.

Some of the ratings by Ann disagree with those given by her clinician on the "Problem Profile." The detailed explanations for these differences in ratings are too long to be given here, but in general the discrepancies may be accounted for by the fact that the clinician underestimated the strength of Ann's feelings with respect to these problems.

TABLE 2.   ANN'S MEAN SELF-RATINGS ON THE CATEGORIES AND SUB-CATEGORIES OF THE "PROBLEM QUESTIONNAIRE" AT THE END OF TWO WEEKS, SIX WEEKS, AND FOUR MONTHS OF THERAPY.

CATEGORIES	2W [a]	6W [b]	4M [c]
General			
Total stuttering problem	3.0	3.0	3.0
Feelings about stuttering	3.9	2.1	2.1
Reactions to treatment	2.2	1.3	1.6
Personality adjustment	2.0	2.0	2.0
Social adjustment	3.0	2.0	3.0
Family adjustment	1.0	1.0	1.0
School adjustment	3.0	2.0	2.0
Vocational adjustment	1.0	1.0	3.0
Category means	2.4	1.8	2.2
Difficult Speaking Situations			
Frequency of stuttering	5.0	4.0	3.0
Severity of stuttering blocks	5.0	3.7	3.3
Speaking time behavior	5.0	2.0	3.0
Feelings about stuttering	5.0	3.0	3.2
Control of stuttering	5.0	3.2	3.2
Category means	5.0	3.2	3.1
Easy Speaking Situations			
Frequency of stuttering	3.0	3.0	2.0
Severity of stuttering blocks	3.7	2.0	2.7
Speaking time behavior	1.0	2.0	2.0
Feelings about stuttering	3.2	1.6	2.0
Control of stuttering	3.8	2.0	2.4
Category means	2.9	2.1	2.2
Means of the three category means	3.4	2.4	2.5

[a] 2w, end of two weeks.
[b] 6w, end of six weeks.
[c] 4M, four months of therapy.

4. *Speech Situation Rating Sheet* (2). The "Speech Situation Rating Sheet" consists of a list of forty speaking situations. Each is evaluated by the stutterer in terms of four different five-point rating scales. These scales concern the tendency to avoid the situations, degree of enjoyment derived from speaking in the situations, frequency of stuttering, and frequency with which the situations are met. Ann's mean scores for these scales were 3.68, 3.82, 3.84, and 4.1, respectively, which values indicate that she avoids more of these speaking situations, enjoys speaking in these situations less, stutters more frequently in them, and meets the situations less often than 75 percent of stutterers (2).

5. *Iowa Scale of Attitude Toward Stuttering* (1). This scale is designed to measure the stutterer's attitude toward his stuttering. The following is one of the questions:

1. If a person at the family dinner table is about to stutter on a word, he should substitute another word for it and go on.

| Strongly agree | Moderately agree | Undecided | Moderately disagree | Strongly disagree |

The stutterer encircles the response which best reflects his own attitude. The "preferred" answer to the sample question is "strongly disagree" because this response indicates a more tolerant or accepting attitude toward stuttering than do the other responses. Ann was asked to complete this scale in terms of how she *actually behaved in* or *actually felt about* these situations. Her score was 2.48, indicating that she had considerable intolerance of stuttering (1).

6. *Minnesota Multiphasic Personality Inventory*. The MMPI was administered to Ann shortly after she began her therapy program. The results of this test were interpreted by a representative of the University Student Counseling Service as follows:

This 20-year-old college freshman would appear, on the basis of her initial MMPI profile, to be a rather depressed and introverted person. She expresses considerable concern about herself and her future. She regards the future as rather hopeless, appearing quite passive and apathetic. Clinically, she would appear tense, anxious and self-ruminative. Her worrying and irritability probably leads to impaired social relationships, further complicating her problems of adjustment.

This disagrees with the evaluation represented by the problem profile constructed by Ann's speech clinician. It is to be expected, of course, that the problem of stuttering would give rise to certain anxieties because of the social and vocational handicaps it involves. Ann's speech clinician believes that the maladjustment indicated by the test did not seem to interfere with effective stuttering therapy.

7. *Intelligence test.* A representative of the University Student Counseling Office administered an intelligence test to Ann and made the following report:

Observations: Ann was apparently not enthused about taking the test since she made several remarks to the effect that she couldn't see why it was necessary for her to take the test. However, she adjusted to the idea quite quickly and rapport was easily established. Ann was very attentive to the tasks and showed very satisfactory effort. She displayed an attitude of self-depreciation, commenting several times that the test would show how "stupid" she was. Ann expressed herself well despite severe stuttering, at times.

Results: On the Revised Stanford Binet, Form L, Ann's C.A. was 20–1, her M.A. was 17–11, giving her an I.Q. of 119. This indicates a high average intelligence level, surpassing approximately 85 per cent of her age group in intellectual ability. A basal age was established at XIII and a ceiling age at Superior Adult III. Ann's stuttering did not seem to have any significant effect on the results. The test appears quite valid and no additional testing is recommended.

Therapy

The general therapeutic approach employed in this case has been described by Johnson (7, 9) and Van Riper (13). Therapy was given principally through the media of (1) individual conferences with a graduate student speech clinician, (2) group therapy with a graduate assistant acting as the leader of the group, and (3) group therapy conducted by the senior author. The student clinicians in this program are trained in the specific area of stuttering therapy by the senior author in a three-semester-hour didactic course involving considerable clinical observation. The students have previously taken courses in speech pathology and audiology, voice and phonetics, general speech, general psychology, psychology of adjustment, introduction to clinical practice in speech involving participation in an outpatient speech clinic, voice and articulation disorders; the majority have taken a course in general semantics, and all have had relevant courses in addition to those listed here. In the clinical practice with stutterers, cases are staffed, logs are kept, and case summaries are prepared, and by these means as well as through the group therapy conducted by the senior author and his assistants, and through individual conferences, the student clinicians are provided with supervision and continuing instruction.

During the therapy period covered in this report Ann spent 18.5 hours in individual conferences with a graduate student speech clinician, 24 hours in group therapy supervised by the senior author's assistant, and 48 hours in group therapy conducted by the senior author. The general therapeutic approach and the adaptations of it that were made in consideration of Ann's specific characteristics and needs are indicated in the following sections.

Individual therapy. Stuttering is not regarded at this Speech Clinic as a symptom of a neurotic state. Stutterers who are thought to have marked personality problems are referred for counseling to a clinical psychologist. Stuttering in the adult is treated on the hypothesis that the stutterer has anxieties concerning the unpleasant experience of his stuttering and it is this anxiety which is the direct cause of his stuttering at the present time. Without anxiety concerning the stuttering, there would be no stuttering. The therapy is, therefore, directed at reducing the strength of this anxiety.

Stuttering therapy with Ann consisted of a combination of directive and non-directive counseling. The therapy was non-directive in the sense that the therapy session was regarded as a situation in which Ann could talk with the therapist in a highly permissive atmosphere regarding the anxieties she had about her stuttering. The therapy was directive in that Ann was expected to follow a program designed by the clinician to reduce the strength of the unpleasant emotional reaction to her stuttering and thus reduce the severity of the stuttering.

Summary of Conferences 1 to 10. The first ten meetings were primarily devoted to the following activities:

1. Information concerning various aspects of stuttering was given to Ann and discussed with her. This information included known facts and current hypotheses concerning the onset of stuttering, the patterns and dynamics of its development after onset, the conditions under which the severity of stuttering appears to increase and decrease, prob-

lems associated with stuttering and the various positive approaches to them, and general and specific approaches to therapy. Ann was asked to read material dealing with these matters and the senior author devoted part of the time in some of the group sessions which Ann attended to a presentation of relevant information and to discussion of it in specific relationship to the problems presented by members of the group. Like the majority of entering cases, Ann was almost completely uninformed regarding the problem of stuttering. In the clinician's judgment the information presented to Ann helped to reduce the intensity of the unpleasant feelings she had about her stuttering. She told the clinician, "What I've learned about stuttering since coming here has made me feel less ashamed of it."

2. The clinician encouraged Ann to verbalize the feelings she had about her stuttering. Her feelings were generally like those reported by other stutterers. She very much disliked stuttering and had been accustomed to avoiding situations in which she felt she would stutter. However, apart from these feelings regarding her stuttering she appeared, as has been indicated, to have no outstanding personality problems. Ann said with respect to the attempts to verbalize her stuttering, "This is the first time I've really been able to tell about my stuttering. I've never been able to talk to anyone else about it like this and it really makes me feel good."

3. During this period Ann quite thoroughly analyzed her stuttering problem. She spent several hours in front of the mirror studying what she looked like and what she did specifically when she stuttered. Ann says of this, "After a while it didn't look half as bad as I always thought it looked to people. I always imagined that I looked terrible when I stuttered whereas actually I don't look too bad at all." She was asked to describe thoroughly what she did when she stuttered, which muscles she tensed, precisely what she did with reference to lip, tongue, and jaw movements, and restrictions of movement, breathing and vocalization, and any associated activities of head, arms, hands, or other parts of the body. She was asked to describe her feelings while doing these things. The purpose of the mirror work was to make her attitude toward the problem more objective and to reduce the intensity of her feelings of fear and dread concerning her stuttering.

Ann also kept a record of the speaking situations that she participated in and the amount of time she spent in actual speaking in each of these situations. This record indicated that she was avoiding certain speaking situations completely and probably restricting her speaking in many other situations. The possible and probable reasons for this avoidance behavior were thoroughly discussed with Ann.

4. She was given assignments to carry out in order to give her increased confidence in the fact that she was physically able to speak normally. For example, she was asked to read in unison with several other stutterers. To Ann's surprise she discovered that she, like practically all other stutterers, could speak without stuttering under these conditions.

Summary of Conferences 11 to 25. The anxiety that Ann felt about her stuttering was further reduced by subjecting her repeatedly to feared speaking situations, under conditions in which she was able to reëvaluate her anxieties about her stuttering in more realistic terms. For example, Ann had acute anxiety about stuttering to strangers and tried consistently to avoid speaking to them. Whenever she could not avoid talking to strangers, as in shopping, for example, she tried to avoid stuttering by substituting words she felt able to say for words on which she feared stuttering. The clinician assumed that if anxiety reduction concerning stuttering could be achieved in this type of situation there would be considerable carry-over to other speaking situations in which the fears and avoidance tendencies were not as strong.

In the eleventh conference the clinician told Ann that she thought she was ready to work more directly on the anxiety by having her participate in speaking situations involving strangers. The clinician's report on the first assigned situation follows:

I took Ann down to the bus depot in order to find a situation where there would be some strangers. On the way down I told her that she was to go in to the depot and ask the ticket agent for the fare to Marion and to inquire about the possible connections at this place to Chicago. Ann seemed somewhat reluctant about entering this situation and I asked her why she thought she felt this way.

ANN: I suppose because I am going to stutter. I just know I am.
CLINICIAN: Why do you think that?
A.: Whenever I think of asking for that ticket I can feel myself getting tense in the chest and face and my hands are sweating and my mouth feels awfully dry. Whenever I feel this way about speaking in a situation I know I am going to have a bad time with my speech.

C.: Why do you think you are anxious about stuttering to this man?

A.: Well, I don't like the way people look at me when I have a bad block. They seem to be thinking, "That poor girl, she can hardly say a word. She's such a nice-looking girl, it's too bad she has such a terrible handicap." If there's anything I dislike it's having someone pitying me.

C.: Do you know this ticket agent?

A.: No.

C.: Then how do you know how he is going to react to your stuttering?

A.: Well, I don't exactly, but I've heard people pity other handicapped people and I suppose all people feel the same way.

C.: You heard one person pity the handicapped so you know for certain that every time you stutter the person you are stuttering to is going to pity you.

A.: Well, I don't know for certain.

C.: It's difficult, don't you think, to tell what people are thinking of your stuttering?

A.: I suppose it is.

C.: Do you think if you didn't worry so much about what people are thinking about your stuttering, that you wouldn't be so anxious about your stuttering?

A.: I suppose so, but I can't help thinking that they pity me.

When we arrived at the bus station Ann approached the agent and asked for the necessary information. She stuttered fairly severely, but not as severely, I think, as she usually does to people she doesn't know very well. There was no reaction on the part of the man as far as I could ascertain from his expression and he waited patiently until Ann was finished with what she had to say. After she was finished I asked her if she felt as bad about stuttering to this agent as she thought she would.

A.: I didn't like to stutter, of course, but I didn't feel half as bad about it as I had expected.

C.: Do you think the man pitied you because you stuttered?

A.: You couldn't tell whether he did or not. He didn't look as if he did.

C.: Why do you think it was less unpleasant to stutter to this man than you had expected beforehand?

A.: For the last two years or so when my stuttering became severe, I have always avoided speaking in situations like this. I've come to regard them as some sort of a monster that will devour me if I come too close to it. Every time I avoided speaking in one of these situations I seemed to have become more afraid of them. When I actually went in and stuttered in one like I did just now I found it only about half as bad as I thought it would be. I guess that's why I feel pretty good about doing it.

C.: Do you think it would be a good idea to do a lot of this type of thing?

A.: I think it would. I'd like to try another one or two right now.

The next stop was the railway station, where Ann inquired about the rates for a berth to Los Angeles. She had a difficult time trying to say the word "berth" and the agent tried to fill in the word for her. When he did this Ann told him in a polite way that she didn't want him to try to say the words for her and that she was able to say them all right, but that it took her a little longer than most people. The ticket agent apologized profusely and told her that he didn't realize that she didn't want to be helped. He had always thought that stutterers wanted to be helped when they had trouble getting a word out. This started a conversation about stuttering and they talked for five minutes about the best way to treat stutterers when they came to his window at the station. When they were finished I told Ann that I thought she had done a fine job of handling this speaking situation.

A.: I really feel good about what I did just then. If there's anything that gives me a pain in the neck, it's having someone try to fill in a word for me and I felt that this was as good a time as any to start doing something about it. It made me feel good to tell that guy that I didn't want him to say the word for me. He turned out to be a nice fellow, actually, once I explained a part of my problem to him.

We did two more of these situations that afternoon and after each one Ann seemed to be pleased about what she had accomplished.

The remainder of the conferences during this period were devoted to this type of situational therapy. In addition to the speaking situations which she did with her clinician Ann was assigned to do many more of these situations with other stutterers in the clinic accompanying her, and also to do many by herself. By the end of this period of therapy her anxiety regarding her stuttering had been reduced in almost all speaking situations to the point where she was willing to stutter in even her most difficult situations without a great deal of the accompanying anxiety. She remarked to the clinician, "Not only do I feel better about my stuttering when I'm actually doing the speaking, but I also feel much less afraid of the situation before I enter it and I have stopped brooding about the stuttering after I do it. That is, I don't feel too badly about the stuttering while I'm doing it and I think about it hardly at all either before or after."

During this time Ann had some important school adjustment problems which had nothing to do with her stuttering, but which the clinician spent considerable time discussing with her. It has been found by experience that a stutterer works most effectively on his stuttering when he is relatively free from anxieties concerning other facets of his adjustment. Ann had very inept methods of studying for her examinations, and the clinician attempted to instruct her in more efficient procedures. She was also perfectionistic about her studies and set high standards for herself that she could not possibly achieve. The clinician assisted her in reëvaluating these excessively high goals. She appeared to have no other major problems that interfered with her therapy program.

Conferences 25 to 37. Therapy during this period was concentrated upon teaching Ann how to stutter more simply. The first step in the simplification of Ann's stuttering pattern was to have her deliberately imitate her own stuttering whenever she was talking to her clinician. Ann had been working on this in mirror practice more or less since therapy had begun and she was now able to do it to the clinician quite successfully. She was able to imitate her own stuttering without the tension that usually characterized it. She found by doing this that she rarely experienced "real" stuttering, because when she stuttered on purpose she felt little or no tendency to be anxious about whether or not she was going to stutter. She remarked to the clinician, "When I go ahead and stutter on purpose like I am doing now I'm not all tensed and bothered about whether I'm going to stutter or not. Since I am not bothered about whether I'm going to stutter I don't seem to have any tense uncontrolled blocks." Ann went on to imitate her own pattern of stuttering in a wide variety of speaking situations. At first, she was not very successful in stuttering on purpose in more difficult speaking situations, but gradually, after considerably more practice in easier situations, she began to be more successful in the ones where she ordinarily stuttered quite severely. This is not to say that therapy was a smooth progression from one step to another. Like stutterers generally, Ann had periods in which she was more or less depressed about her progress. The clinician described what happened when Ann came in one day and told her she was feeling disappointed about her stuttering.

The first thing that Ann said when she came into my office was that she felt very disappointed with how things were going with her speech.

CLINICIAN: Disappointed?

ANN: Yes, I just finished making a phone call to a friend of mine and I stuttered all over the place. I forgot all about imitating my stuttering and my speech went to pieces.

C.:   When you say your speech went to pieces you mean that you stuttered as severely as you did when you first began your therapy?

A.:   No, I don't think it was quite as severe, but it certainly was bad enough.

C.:   Well, at least you're not back to where you were when you came here. Did you have any speaking situations in which you experienced some success with imitating your stuttering today?

A.:   I had about six situations today so far and come to think of it I did all right about my stuttering in about half of them.

C.:   Do you think it would help if you kept account of the numbers of successes and failures you have with respect to your stuttering so that you would know how often you are being successful and how often having a failure?

A.:   I suppose it would. It would let me see whether I am making any progress or not.

C.:   When you first came in here and said you were very disappointed it sounded to me as if you had been having failures with your speech in every speaking situation, whereas actually only two situations out of the six were failures. Do you expect to have success in every speaking situation at the present time?

A.:   It sounds as if I do, doesn't it?

C.:   You seem to be behaving as if you expected success in all situations whereas, as you know from the discussions we've had about this before, you can't be successful in every situation all at once.

The clinician had many discussions with Ann about such problems because she was inclined to become depressed after a failure without stopping to consider the number of successes she had experienced.

Ann was next asked to produce a more simple pattern of stuttering than her own. This consisted of an easy prolongation of the first sound or syllable of the word. She first did a great deal of listening to her own recording of this on tape and watching her performance of it in the mirror. After she had arrived at the point where she seemed to be adept and at ease using this pattern of stuttering in clinical situations she began to employ it during conferences with her clinician. After considerable practice in these conferences she then introduced it into her easier outside speaking situations and by the end of the therapy period covered in this report she was employing it with a fair amount of success in difficult situations.

Group therapy. As has been previously mentioned, Ann participated in 48 hours of group therapy conducted by the senior author and 24 hours conducted by the senior author's clinical assistant. It is difficult in the space available to give an adequate account of this type of therapy, but a general indication of the procedures employed will be attempted.

GROUP THERAPY MEETINGS CONDUCTED BY THE SENIOR AUTHOR

Group Meeting One.[1] Dr. Johnson discussed the purpose of group therapy and defined it as "individuals meeting together to work out problems." He said that he was not there in the role of a teacher and wished to be considered as a member of the group. He suggested that the group begin by trying the group interview technique in which one of the stutterers stands before the group and is asked questions by the other members. This technique not only gives each member of a group an opportunity to become acquainted with the other members, but also involves their doing something which is therapeutically useful so far as their stuttering is concerned. Each person who is being questioned has a choice of answering or not answering a particular question and can also decide how far he wishes to go in answering.

The first stutterer to volunteer to be questioned was Bob. One of the first questions asked was whether he thought his grades in his speech course would be higher if he wasn't a stutterer. Bob said they would be. This precipitated a great number of questions from the group concerning why he thought this. At the end of his questioning Bob seemed less sure that his stuttering was interfering with his grade in the course.

The next interviewee was Norman, who was asked some questions about what he was planning to do with his college education. He said that he was hoping to get into medical school if it was possible for him to do so despite the fact that he is a fairly severe stutterer at the present time. There was considerable discussion by the group as to how much of a difference stuttering would make to a doctor and it was generally agreed

[1] This and the following descriptions of group therapy sessions are taken from the logs of student observers.

that severe stuttering would certainly make a considerable difference because of the person's inability to communicate effectively with his patients. The group members were of the opinion that moderate or mild stuttering would make little difference to a medical career provided the person was not ashamed of it and did not try to hide it.

Ann, the present case, was the next to be questioned and they asked her how she felt about her stuttering when she was on a date with a boy. She said that she almost always tried to hide it as much as possible because she was afraid the boy would not ask her out again if she stuttered. Ann said it was hard for a girl not to hide her stuttering when she was on a date because most boys' ideal of a girl was something that resembled a Hollywood movie star and that such girls do not stutter. Jim disagreed with what Ann had said, saying that *his* ideal of a girl was not the movie star type and that he thought Ann was generalizing too much about people. Jim said that he himself would not mind going out with a girl who stuttered. At this point the group laughed at what Jim had said and George remarked that if Jim wasn't a stutterer it would probably bother him some to go out with a girl who stuttered. Jim said that he didn't think so and he asked the group how many shared Ann's opinion about boys. Less than half the group agreed with Ann and the other half agreed that some boys might have as their ideal a movie star, but certainly not most of them.

Group Meeting Fifteen. Several members of the group had asked Dr. Johnson to talk to them on the general subject of "slumps" in stuttering therapy. "Slumps" are periods in a stutterer's therapy program when he finds it difficult to do any work on his stuttering problem. Dr. Johnson said that "slumps" resemble depression periods of non-stutterers. The reasons people get depressed are probably the same reasons stutterers have "slumps." Depressions are generally the result of expectations being far removed from reality. The majority of stutterers expect too much improvement in their speech in a short time. When they don't improve as fast as they think they should they become depressed about it. Also, many stutterers have a non-realistic idea of how smooth their progress should be from day to day. They seem to think that they should get a little better each day. Progress in stuttering therapy, in reality, is far from smooth and it is a series of improvements and setbacks. The reason a stutterer has a "slump" is that his ideas of his therapeutic progress are so far out of line with reality. (This is a highly condensed report of Dr. Johnson's talk on this subject, but it serves to illustrate the type of therapy that is carried out sometimes in these meetings. The general aim of all such talks is to get the stutterer to understand better his own behavior and its probable motivations.)

Group Meeting Forty-One. Dr. Johnson asked each member of the group to prepare a three-minute talk on some topic in which he was interested, and to give this talk in order to practice doing something to change his habitual way of stuttering. The stutterers were told not to try any changes that hadn't been thoroughly discussed and approved by their individual speech clinicians.

Ann was the first to speak and she talked about some of the social activities she had participated in since she came here. While she was talking on this topic she practiced imitating her own habitual pattern of stuttering.

Charles was the next speaker and he discussed his hobby of photography. While he was doing this he tried to keep himself from substituting non-feared words for feared ones.

Six more stutterers gave speeches and the meeting concluded with a discussion as to the value of this activity in stuttering therapy. All the stutterers agreed it had been helpful.

Group Therapy Meetings Conducted by a Clinical Assistant

Group Meeting Two. After a short period of general conversation each person introduced himself to the group. A topic of discussion was brought up; it was "normal non-fluencies."

Questions such as these were discussed: What is a normal non-fluency? Who makes them? How does a non-fluency differ from stuttering? Do stutterers experience normal non-fluencies? What relationship do they bear to a stutterer's problems?

Briefly, normal non-fluencies were defined by the group as any kind of "bobble." They were said to occur in the speech of everyone, including stutterers, and they were said to differ from stuttering in that fear and anxiety were not present when they occurred.

It is difficult to evaluate the insight, if any, gained by the group through this discussion, but they did seem to enjoy and be interested in what was said. Most of the group members participated actively in the discussion.

Group Meeting Sixteen. The meeting was opened by each stutterer introducing himself.

A list of unfavorable listener reactions to stuttering was written on the blackboard. The following seven reactions were considered unfavorable by the group: (1) laughing, (2) avoiding eye contact, (3) impatient behavior (fidgeting, etc.), (4) cutting off the stutterer by such phrases as

"I understand," (5) filling in words which are blocked, (6) ignoring the stutterer, and (7) walking away while the stutterer is still talking.

After a discussion of these reactions the stutterers were divided into pairs. One member of the pair took the part of the stutterer and talked to the other member, who took the part of a listener who demonstrated one of the unfavorable reactions which had just been discussed.

Status of Case at End of Four Months of Therapy

1. *Problem profile.* At the end of the therapy period under consideration the clinician reëvaluated the severity of Ann's adjustment in the various areas in which there were problems at the beginning of therapy.

PROBLEM PROFILE

DESCRIPTION OF PROBLEM PROFILE AT END OF THERAPY PERIOD

Improvement was noted in all areas in which there had been problems at the beginning of therapy except those of Personality Adjustment and School Adjustment.

1. *Speech Problem*
   Rating: Slight Problem (2)
   Reasons for Rating:
   The severity of the speech problem has decreased from marked to slight. This is based on the following information:
   a. The percentage of stuttering while talking to the clinician alone has decreased from 5 to 3.
   b. The percentage of stuttering while reading to the clinician alone has decreased from 5 to 1.
   c. The rating on the Severity of Stuttering Rating Sheet while talking to the clinician alone has decreased from a rating of 4 to a rating of 2.
   d. The rating on the Severity of Stuttering Rating Sheet while reading to the clinician alone has decreased from 4 to 2.
2. *Feelings About Stuttering*
   Rating: Slight Problem (2)
   Reasons for Rating:
   The severity of the problem in this area has decreased from moderate to slight. Her dislike of stuttering has decreased remarkably. She rarely substitutes non-feared for feared words and rarely avoids a speaking situation. She worries much less about people being

ashamed of her because she is a stutterer than she did at the beginning of therapy. She has learned to accept her stuttering problem to the point where she has addressed several large groups of people on the subject of her stuttering. Her sense of humor about her stuttering has improved and she often makes jokes or light-hearted remarks about it.

3. *Speaking Time Behavior*
   Rating: No Problem (1)
   Reasons for Rating:
   There was a moderate problem with respect to speaking time four months ago. There appears to be no problem now. Her speaking time has increased from an approximate average of 25 minutes a day to an average of about 40 minutes, and she participates in all assigned or available types of speaking situations.

4. *Personality Adjustment*
   Rating: Moderate Problem (3)
   Reasons for Rating:
   The rating of "moderate" is given on the basis of the MMPI test results [see below]. According to these results little change has taken place in Ann's general adjustment. From what the clinician has observed of Ann's behavior during the course of therapy there has been little verification of the test results.

5. *School Adjustment*
   Rating: Moderate Problem (3)
   Reasons for Rating:
   Although she made relatively good mid-term grades in her college work she still tends to worry a great deal about her school work. Several times she has remarked to the clinician that she dislikes school but thinks it is necessary to get a college education. The clinician has counseled her about this problem on several occasions, but it seems to have had little effect on her behavior.

2. *Detailed speech evaluation.* The junior author obtained recorded samples of Ann's speech after four months of therapy, using the same procedure employed at the beginning of therapy. These new speech samples were analyzed in the manner previously described. Table 1 shows the frequency per 100 words of each type and of all types of Ann's non-fluency at this time.

As has been indicated, Ann has been doing "imitation" or "deliberate" stuttering, as part of her therapy, using at present a prolongation of the first sound or syllable of the word. An examination of Table 1 shows that the "Prolonged sounds" category is the only category in which there has been an important increase in the number of non-fluencies. The increase in this category is from a mean of 12.4 non-fluencies per 100 words at the beginning of therapy to a mean of 17.4 four months later. This specific change is a direct function of a particular clinical instruction, previously described, and indicates that the instruction is definitely being carried out. One of the apparent results is that in all other categories, with the unimportant exception in the case of "Broken words," the number of non-fluencies has decreased. The prolongations that Ann is now performing are different, of course, from the prolongations she exhibited at the beginning of therapy. They are generally easy or effortless, free from the tension that was present four months ago. Our measures of severity—that is, the frequency counts shown in Table 1—do not take into consideration these changes in the tension with which Ann's prolongations are performed. In measuring the severity of the stutterer's problem it is necessary, obviously, to take into consideration not only the frequency of occurrence of stuttering but also the severity with which the stutterings are performed. That it is possible to do this has been demonstrated by Trotter (12), but the procedure Trotter used has not yet been adapted for clinical use.

It has been mentioned elsewhere that the conventional manner of measuring the severity of stuttering is to count the number of stutterings. By this measure, the percentage of stuttering has risen from 21 to 34, an increase of 13 percent. This rise in the percentage of stuttering may be accounted for by the same explanation as was given for the rise in the number of non-fluencies.

3. *Problem questionnaire.* At the end of therapy Ann was asked to complete the questionnaire according to the following instructions:

Rate the severity of your problem with respect to each of the factors listed on the questionnaire—in terms of the problem scale—as it is at the present time.

An examination of the ratings of Table 2 indicates that according to Ann's own self-evaluation there was some improvement in almost all aspects of her stuttering problem after she began receiving therapy and that the most pronounced changes had occurred by the end of six weeks.

4. *Speech Situation Rating Sheet.* Ann was administered this test at the end of therapy. Her scores on the three scales which are con-

cerned with measuring (a) tendency to avoid speaking, (b) enjoyment derived from speaking, and (c) frequency of stuttering are 1.75, 2.48, and 2.98, respectively. Compared to other stutterers these figures place her at the 25th, 50th, and 75th percentiles, respectively. This represents considerable improvement over the scores obtained at the beginning of therapy. According to the test results there has been little change in the frequency with which she meets speaking situations.

5. *Iowa Scale of Attitude Toward Stuttering.* Ann completed this test at the end of therapy. Her score has decreased from 2.48, which indicated considerable intolerance of stuttering, to 1.13, which indicates considerable tolerance of stuttering. According to this test Ann now has a more healthy attitude toward her stuttering problem.

6. *Minnesota Multiphasic Personality Inventory.* The MMPI was administered to Ann again shortly before the end of the four-month therapy period. The results are as follows: "The second profile, collected four months later, reflects little change. She appears somewhat less anxious and the future seems more hopeful. While the changes from the first to the second profile are quite small, these changes are all in the direction of better adjustment."

7. *Ann's evaluation of her improvement.* Ann was asked to write out an answer to the following question: "Would you describe the ways in which you feel your stuttering problem has improved?" She answered:

I stutter with less tension and do not fear certain situations like I once did. Before I came to the Clinic, I would sometimes have such severe blocks, that they would cause pain between my shoulders. For some time it's been very hard for me to say my name. Now I can usually say it with little difficulty. My attitude toward my problem has changed. I now realize that it is not such a terrible thing to stutter. I do not feel ashamed or embarrassed about it, as I once did. I feel now that I can succeed in most any profession I choose.

General Discussion of Ann's Case History [2]

Considerable research in the beginnings and early development of stuttering (**8, 4, 3**) has been done in the last fifteen years, and it ap-

[2] Parts of this section have been abstracted from an article entitled "Stuttering," by Dr. Wendell Johnson, which is to appear in the forthcoming work by G. M. Coates and H. P. Schenck (eds.), *Otolaryngology*. Hagerstown: W. F. Prior Co., Inc., 1955. Reproduced by permission of the publisher.

pears quite clear that (1) it is practically always first diagnosed by laymen, usually the parents, especially the mothers, rather than specialists in speech; (2) what these laymen diagnose as stuttering turns out, on close and thorough investigation in cases studied very soon after onset (or, better, after diagnosis), to be the normal repetitions and hesitations characteristic of early childhood speech; (3) once the parents have come to look upon these normal repetitions and hesitations as stuttering—that is, as undesirable or abnormal—they worry about them so that their general relationships with the child are disturbed, which makes the youngster feel insecure. Moreover, as they begin to show disapproval of the child's speech, as such, either in unconscious gestures, postures, and facial expressions or outright by asking the child to go slow, stop and start over, stop and think, etc., the child becomes self-conscious about his speech and naturally, therefore, speaks more and more hesitantly. In spite of his parents' "help," he gets worse. Such aggravation leads in time to tension in speaking, and the easy repetitions and slight hesitations, normal in childhood, give way to strained blocking in gradually intensifying forms.

Research has shown that normal children between the ages of 2 and 5 years repeat, on the average, 45 times per 1000 words. They repeat syllables, or whole words, or phrases. All children so far surveyed do some repeating, and the normal range extends to over 100 instances per 1000 words. There is no question but what this is the sort of thing that laymen mistakenly diagnose as "stuttering," and, having done so, they react to the youngster's speech in ways that disturb his previously normal speech. In Ann's case the diagnosis of the stuttering may have occurred at a later age than it usually does, but this is not known for certain because Ann's and her parents' reports are ambiguous and not clearly dependable.

Stuttering is now widely regarded among speech pathologists as a learned behavior pattern that is perpetuated and reinforced by the stutterer's fear of its recurrence. Having stuttered at one time in a given situation, he is afraid he will have similar trouble in the same or similar circumstances another time. So he tries to avoid the stuttering which he expects and dreads, and in trying to avoid it he does the things that we call stuttering—such as holding his breath, clamping his jaws together, and compressing his lips. He does these things in a sort of struggle to keep from going ahead and attempting words with which he expects to have trouble, and he does such things instead of calmly coming to a full stop simply because he is being strongly motivated to speak by the situation in which he finds himself. But the things he does "to keep from stuttering" are exactly the stuttering he is trying to avoid. In this sense, then, the harder the stutterer tries to keep from stuttering the more things he does that we call stuttering.

In general, the more important it is for a stutterer not to stutter the more severely he is likely to stutter. The history of the severity of Ann's problem illustrates this point. When she was a success in her high-school group it did not matter too much whether she stuttered or not. Consequently the stuttering decreased in severity. But when she was suddenly rejected by someone she loved and suspected that such rejection might have been based, in part, upon her stuttering, it suddenly became very important for her not to stutter. As a result, the stuttering increased markedly in severity.

Treatment varies with stage of development of the stuttering, character of the individual, family and school circumstances, and other relevant factors. Very young stutterers are nearly always best treated indirectly by means of properly detailed counseling of the parents. With rare exceptions, no speech training for the child would be prescribed. In some cases techniques such as play therapy may be indicated. Modifications of aggravating parental attitudes and policies and details of home management are of chief importance. The majority of very young stutterers respond well and fairly rapidly to such relief of environmental pressures, provided they have not yet developed well-established anxiety tensions.

Stutterers who have developed marked anxiety tensions, such as Ann, respond less well to treatment, but worth-while relief can be achieved in most cases, and complete or nearly complete recovery is not extremely rare. Chronic stutterers almost always require therapy, together with such environmental modifications as can be managed. As has been demonstrated in Ann's case, direct treatment divides generally into (1) psychological counseling and (2) directed changes in habitual speech performance. Properly instructed, most stutterers can learn to do their stuttering more simply, with decreased tension and less emotional disturbance.

Ann applied herself well in the therapy program. The majority of adult stutterers, although they wish to get over their stuttering, do not work impressively hard at it. An important reason appears to be that, although the goal of therapy (i.e., less stuttering) is a pleasant one for them, the therapy itself involves specific experiences that are obviously not enjoyable.

REFERENCES

1. Ammons, R., and Johnson, W. Studies in the psychology of stuttering: XVIII. The construction and application of a test of attitude towards stuttering. *J. Speech Disorders*, 1944, *9*, 39–49.

2. Cherhavy, I. An evaluation of the Iowa Speech Clinic stutterers speech situation rating sheet. Unpublished M.A. thesis, University of Iowa, 1949.

3. Darley, F. L. The relationship of parental attitudes and adjustments to the development of stuttering. In *Stuttering in children and adults*. (W. Johnson, ed.) Minneapolis: University of Minnesota Press, in press.

4. Davis, D. The relation of repetitions in the speech of young children to certain measures of language maturity and situational factors. *J. Speech Disorders*, 1939, *4*, 303–318; 1940, *5*, 235–241, 242–246.

5. Fluency of college students. Unpublished report submitted to the Louis W. and Maud Hill Family Foundation by the University of Iowa Speech Clinic, 1954. Available at University of Iowa Speech Clinic.

6. Fluency of stuttering and non-stuttering male college students. Unpublished report submitted to the Louis W. and Maud Hill Family Foundation by the University of Iowa Speech Clinic, 1954. Available at University of Iowa Speech Clinic.

7. Johnson, W. *People in quandaries*. New York: Harper & Brothers, 1946.

8. Johnson, W., et al. The onset and development of stuttering. *J. Speech Disorders*, 1942, *8*, 251–257.

9. Johnson, W., Brown, S. F., Curtis, J. F., Edney, C. W., and Keaster, J. *Speech handicapped school children*. New York: Harper & Brothers, 1948.

10. Johnson, W., Darley, F. L., and Spriestersbach, D. C. *Diagnostic manual in speech correction*. New York: Harper & Brothers, 1952.

11. The stuttering therapy program of the University of Iowa Summer Speech Clinic, 1953. Unpublished report submitted to the Louis W. and Maud Hill Family Foundation by the University of Iowa Speech Clinic, 1954. Available at University of Iowa Speech Clinic.

12. Trotter, W. D. A study of the severity of the individual moments of stuttering under the conditions of successive readings of the same material. Unpublished Ph.D. thesis, University of Iowa, 1953.

13. Van Riper, C. *Speech correction: principles and methods*. New York: Prentice-Hall, Inc., rev. ed., 1947.

Note: This report is based in part on research supported by the Louis W. and Maud Hill Family Foundation, St. Paul, Minnesota.

CHAPTER THIRTEEN

A Compliant Alcoholic

BY ROY M. HAMLIN

David P. Selby, a 34-year-old professional man, recently married for the second time, was referred by his employer to a community mental hygiene clinic in a southern industrial city some eight years ago. His excessive drinking and absence from work had increased in the past few months but had long been a periodic problem. He came originally from a small crossroads town some fifty miles distant and was the only living child of conscientious, devoutly religious Methodist parents, who were now in their seventies but still active and much concerned about their son's problem.

Three Interviews at Age 34

The notes in this section are condensed from three of fifteen interviews conducted by the author, who was then on the staff of the clinic. These interviews were recorded in detail at the time and may therefore suffer less than more remote background material from the selection and distortion that are an ever present source of error in the case method. It is for this reason that the sample of interviews will be presented first with minimal reference to early development, which will be filled in later. After the sampled interview material, brief summary reports will be presented on the patient three and six years later. These summary reports are more interpretive, and depart further from directly observed data, but are also centered around recent observations. Next, samples of the patient's performance on projective and similar techniques will be considered. Then background and developmental material will be summarized, and finally some formulation will be offered in the Addendum.

Interview 1. David Selby stands six feet tall, a thin stooped man with a small head and face, who appears weak and physically ill. It is hard to believe that he weighed over 180 pounds not long ago, and that he had been something of an athlete in high school and college. As he begins to talk, he mentions that he has had a drink earlier although it is now only ten o'clock in the morning. He does not give the impression of being intoxicated, but the smell of whiskey is on his breath.

His hands show a skin condition that has not had even ordinary care, with open sores which have been scratched and tend to run. They need bandaging or at least cleaning up, and after the interview he is sent directly to the dermatologist, although ordinarily an appointment would be arranged for another day. Even if he expressed no complaints verbally, his hands complain for him, demanding that someone do something for him at once.

He is known to be a highly intelligent law-school graduate and talks and behaves in keeping with his intelligence. Yet he seems as weak in personality as he looks physically and his superior record in law school raises a question, since it would be easier to believe that he had started law school but never finished. Again, however, his employer, an intelligent and efficient man who puts a high premium on schedules and production, describes patient as a keen and able worker except for his drinking and missing work. Patient has worked with this man for four years, with promotion to a responsible supervisory position. His income in work that utilizes his legal training is more than adequate.

Patient's speech, manner, and attitudes are complaining and superficially disorganized. He is undoubtedly distressed and helpless, but what he says is not as disorganized as it seems, since he expresses himself clearly until asked a question, then becomes vague or confusing. He might be saying: "I am too sick, too miserable. How can you ask me questions? Do something for me." He suggests that he be hospitalized and fears that he is developing a "Korsakoff's syndrome." His condition gives support to his request, but five brief hospitalizations in the past three months are already on record. Just as his hands speak for themselves, so the presenting picture demands prompt hospitalization. Above all, he seems determinedly helpless in caring for himself, his hands, his drinking, his problems, and his job. The staff have already decided, in terms of overall knowledge, that an effort will be made to avoid hospitalization.

He soon begins to rail at his present wife, who told him this morning that he didn't "have a wife any more." He says they have had no sexual relations for some time, but that this is "all right" with him since she does not want to become pregnant again and has no desire to be intimate with him anyhow. He then adds that she is a "good wife" in other respects, but does not say what other respects. Instead he goes on to an incident, not located in time, when she induced an abortion because she did not want a child by a "drunken father." Her rejection was apparently direct and brutal, and he resented it deeply.

However, in this interview, he does not say specifically how he responded, but soon reports another incident which may indicate what he felt like doing. On this other occasion, when he was staying at his parents' home, his mother said she wished he were dead. He then jumped out the window, breaking three ribs and a shoulder bone, and the doctor said he was lucky not to have killed himself. As he relates this incident, he seems truly depressed, self-accusatory, and also resentful. He goes on to say that he has not seen his parents in six weeks, apparently a long and important lack of contact to him, even though they live some distance from the city.

All material from this interview is spotty and seldom entirely clear. At the most cautious question, he shows evasiveness, complaining irritability, and suspicion manifested chiefly by a prompt retreat into superficial confusion and helplessness.

He does say that his wife works and adds, with a suggestion of disdain, that she was his secretary before they married. He was hospitalized recently, underwent an operation for hemorrhoids, and received some other treatment which he feels might be related to incipient stomach ulcers. He says that when he is sick he cannot go home to his wife, since she would find out that he had not been at work. He goes to a movie or bar until time to go home.

Interview 9. Seven intervening interviews are not reported here. Between the second and third, patient fell through a large pane of glass propped up on his porch. He cut his hands severely and needed prompt medical care, missing an appointment at the clinic. At the time he fell, he had been denied his request for hospitalization and had been drinking. The specific similarity between falling through a pane of glass and jumping out a window may be far fetched. As will be indicated, his tendency to fall and injure himself became marked in his later adjustments. In any case, after cutting his hands he showed steady superficial improvement, drank little, and showed increasing concern about missing work to come to the clinic. The ninth interview, three weeks after the first, follows.

Patient's general appearance and attitude have continued to improve. He is no longer quavering, helpless, and confused, but rather seems calm and businesslike. The interview is the first that is focused throughout.

A week ago, after leaving the therapist, he went immediately downstairs for a blood test, about which he expressed considerable apprehension. The therapist told him in effect: Leave now, go downstairs, get it over. He did so. However, he had already supplied himself with spirits of ammonia in case he became faint.

In this interview, patient reports that he went to visit his parents for two days last week end. His wife refused to go with him and thought he would not go by himself; but he went out to Elmwood, a part of the city where there is a railroad station, and telephoned from there that he was taking a train. He feels that he showed some strength in going by himself and displays malicious satisfaction at having bested his wife. After he reached his parents' home, she telephoned twice and was conciliatory.

He goes on to talk about his wife, saying that she was sick a day or so ago and telephoned him to leave his work and come home, apparently for moral support. Her illness was associated with menstruation and with her induced abortion, which patient now dates for the first time: it occurred four months ago. He states that he is not sure she was ever pregnant anyhow; that he is not sure she attempted an abortion; that if she did, she succeeded. He says he began his last episode of heavy drinking at this time. She used mustard and quinine and, when he remonstrated with her, threw mustard in his eyes. He told her that she was committing a felony.

His wife telephoned him again today to be sure he comes home on time—to take her to the dentist. Since he visited his parents by himself, she has been less "dominating." Before the visit, he played pinochle with her and her father one night, and she slapped his face regularly, blaming him when she lost. After his visit, they played pinochle again and she was not so unreasonable. Patient adds that he likes to play bridge, but she prefers pinochle.

He had to go out Wednesday night to shop for Thanksgiving dinner. They ate with his wife's family, but he bought the turkey. Patient then makes a cryptic remark to the effect that his wife "has heard" that his parents try to manage him too much.

During this session, patient is consistently better organized than in previous interviews and seems to be expressing a certain attachment for the therapist. He expresses emotion readily, but in a normally controlled manner, without the insistent undertone of pleading and complaining which has been prominent before.

Interview 11. Patient comes in although he is not scheduled until tomorrow. Therapist's supervisor has suggested that patient may be forming an over-attachment to him.

Patient seems sober; at the last interview he had had a drink or so. He refers to the fact that he is an only child and adds that his father was most severe toward him. For example, his father threatened to put him in jail if he even got a traffic ticket. His father was Justice of the Peace and would never give anyone an excuse for accusing him of favoritism. His father beat him severely with a three-edged ruler for smoking grape leaves.

However, his father's attitude changed somewhere around the time patient reached his junior year in college. He even served drinks at home, allowed patient to smoke, and permitted other freedoms. Patient says he was puzzled by this change.

Patient is rather calm today when asked to say a little more about the occasion on which he jumped out the window. This incident occurred ten months ago, when he and his second wife, Lili, were staying with his parents. Lili and his mother were "snapping at each other." When asked about his part in the quarrel, he says sulkily that it was a "three-cornered fight." His mother was "sick" at the time, and he was "sick" also. It was "just one of those things." With some pride, he repeats the doctor's opinion that it was a "wonder he didn't kill himself." If he had jumped in the usual manner, he would have killed himself; but he dived head first.

His parents suggested recently breaking off all contact with him.

His wife and "one other person," connected with Alcoholics Anonymous, persuaded his parents to make the suggestion. He shows marked resentment as he talks, and expresses extreme hostility toward Alcoholics Anonymous and his wife. They felt he was "too tied to his parents." His parents wrote that they were selling their home and the store and intended to move where he would be unable to contact them. Patient says this was a bad way to handle the problem even if he *is* too attached to his parents.

He goes on to say that he and his wife live directly above her parents. She can't be happy away from them; he is pleased in pointing out her dependency. Her sister and family visit about every second week end. They have a noisy child, and his in-laws in general do not appeal to him. He dreads these visits, when he is drawn into the family.

Patient finally comes out with the opinion that coming to the clinic is a reflection on his own adequacy. He can see no need to come.

These three interviews at the age of 34 suggest a pattern of behavior. He demands help and acceptance but distrusts any move that he sees as an attempt to change him or to know him better. His relation to his second wife may reflect attitudes toward his mother; and his relation to his employer may reflect attitudes toward his father. When he forces his mother to reject him, he jumps out a window. When he forces his wife to reject him, he begins an episode of extreme alcoholism. Actually, of course, his wife rejected him because of his drinking, which increased when she became pregnant. When the clinic will not hospitalize him, he becomes sufficiently intoxicated to fall through a pane of glass and cut himself severely. Yet, when he is still not hospitalized, this "accident" is followed by marked but superficial improvement. He soon gains weight, demands less, feels that his visits keep him from his work and are a reflection on his adequacy. He wants no further help and indicates that he can handle his own problems.

Complete acceptance of his unreasonable demands or exacting supervision are the closest relationships he can accept. He drinks to ease his constant irritation and uneasiness and enters an episode of heavy drinking as an expression of rage and disappointment. He punishes his wife, mother, or the therapist by hurting himself and by rendering himself in need of care.

Hospitalization at Age 37

These next notes represent a sample of somewhat different material: a brief summary of hospitalization, psychiatric formulation, and treatment, presenting the patient as he appeared some three years later at the age of 37. The patient was hospitalized many times, usually for a period of a month or two: the available records report fourteen hospitalizations between the ages of 33 and 40. This particular hospitalization and one other have been selected since they occurred three and six years after the interviews at age 34, providing equally spaced follow-up material. Also the hospital notes are still close to the patient's behavior as actually observed, and soon afterwards recorded.

At this time, when the patient was 37, he was referred to a university psychiatric hospital under circumstances and with complaints paralleling those of the mental hygiene clinic referral three years earlier. As with the earlier referral, the same paternalistic employer showed great concern for the patient's welfare, took the initiative in arranging the best possible care for him, and enlisted the aid of others in effecting the patient's admission. As before, the patient's physical and psychological collapse demanded immediate attention; this time he was placed in a general hospital for a week and then transferred to the university hospital, when a bed was available. As before, his extreme drinking followed the pregnancy of his second wife, Lili. On the earlier occasion, the pregnancy did not continue to full term. This time, their first child, a daughter, was born a week before patient's admission to the hospital. Again as before, hospitalization was brought to an end, as were the clinic contacts, after some six weeks, when patient's physical condition improved rapidly and he regained his superficial confidence, insisting that he must return to work in order to keep his job and support his family. The hospital did arrange for a pattern of continued outpatient treatment which the patient was able to accept for a time.

When admitted at the age of 37, patient comes directly from another hospital where he has been under treatment for eight days. He has already begun to show physical improvement, has gained back a few pounds of weight, and may have quieted a little in his frantic anxiety to be cared for. Otherwise, he presents much the same picture as he did three years earlier. He looks thin, sickly, poorly nourished, and pallid. His gait is unsteady, and he shows numerous fine tremors and minor impairment of coördination and sensation. His conversation is intelligent and relevant. Chiefly he seems discouraged and hopeless. In his own words: "This time I feel I'm really at the bottom. If there is anything worse than this I don't want to know about it." He is concerned primarily with his problem of alcoholism, how he can cope with it, what causes it, as well as with family problems. He gives as his chief concern the fact that he can no longer remember taking "the first drink." He will "come to" after having had three or four drinks and then "it is too late." His rationalization is that this "amnesia" makes it absurd to rely on will power to stop drinking. He wants some physical treatment initiated to prevent further drinking. He also claims complete inability to estimate how much he drinks.

He readily states the connection between his wife's pregnancy and his drinking. It was shortly after he learned of her pregnancy that he became "particularly sick." He says this was partly due to his wife's reaction. She became an "entirely different person, threw things and made life miserable for me." He also refers to the constant friction between his wife, his parents, and his son by his first marriage. Typically, he is vague in regard to details of this friction, but his wife, Lili, adds some information from her point of view.

She states that he is very dependent on her. Even if he goes out to play golf, he wants her to go with him although she does not play. She waits for him in the car until he finishes his game. Except at his work, he does not socialize readily with anyone unless she can be with him or unless he is drinking. When she became pregnant, he "began to go downhill very fast." She feels he is extremely jealous and insecure about the newborn daughter. At first, she felt, he accepted this second pregnancy well, and they were both anxious to have a child. However, when his parents learned of her pregnancy, they were "furious," and patient has been upset about it ever since. Lili feels that patient is hopelessly dependent on his parents, goes home a great deal and is usually upset when he returns. He never really lived away from them until he married her, and cannot detach himself from their influence now. They have interfered with his whole life, dominated his first marriage, and are a continual source of friction now. As an expression of resentment about her pregnancy, patient's father is now "threatening" to send the fourteen-year-old son by patient's first wife to live with them. This "threat" and the timing of it may be particularly effective, coming as it does with the arrival of the new baby and with Lili's giving up her job, which has always been an additional source of income.

In any case, patient became more and more distressed and began to drink heavily again about seven months ago. The pattern of anticipated rejection and increased responsibility resulting from his wife's pregnancy, followed by an outspoken reminder of his inadequacy, this time from his father, again preceded his increased drinking. According to his wife, he had been drinking in moderation, and for periods not at all, for more than a year before her second pregnancy. During this time he had been seen for regular supportive contacts by a psychiatrist, who had persuaded him that it was safest to "observe the same regulations as an alcoholic." Patient had been adjusting well to work, had gained weight and weighed 185 pounds shortly before he began to drink again. Soon after his wife's pregnancy, however, he broke off his contacts with the psychiatrist and returned to his alcoholic "binges." In a few months he was either intoxicated or recuperating all the time and was completely unable to handle his job. By the time he entered the hospital, his weight had dropped to 120 pounds; he was bruised and scarred from numerous recent falls; and his appearance was much as described when first seen three years earlier.

Hospital examinations included extensive studies, all negative, to rule out once more any possibility of epilepsy. Gradual intellectual impairment and impairment of liver function were considered, but were not deemed alarming. With special diet, vitamin therapy, and insulin sedation, patient soon showed physical gains and a striking return of self-confidence and assurance. He gained twenty pounds in weight before he was discharged, at his insistence, after six weeks in the hospital. In psychiatric interviews, areas explored included "the patient's great dependency needs and the resultant conflict arising out of his dependency both on his father and wife; the threat to the patient's security which his recent child represents; the patient's feelings of inferiority and inadequacy and his resort to compensatory habits such as alcoholism; conflicts arising in the course of the patient's work," involving his relationship to his protective employer, and his dread of making responsible decisions.

The patient's insistence that he must return to his job was accepted by the hospital staff readily enough but after careful consideration. His inability to accept help in a close therapeutic relationship was recognized. Insulin sedation had been begun soon after he entered the hospital and seemed particularly effective, in part because the patient put great faith in it. This treatment relieved his tensions, but also fitted in with his dependency needs and with his extreme distrust of close personal influences, which for him always reactivated his problems with his parents. It was therefore decided to continue him on an outpatient basis—have him come to the hospital each Saturday for insulin sedation and have him seen twice a month for limited supportive psychiatric contacts.

For several months this arrangement met with superficial success:

> With no exceptions this man has returned each Saturday for sedative insulin therapy since his discharge three and a half months ago. He seems to benefit by the continuing support which this connection with the hospital gives him. He reports that his work is going well, that he feels better than at any time he can remember and that his domestic life is a happy one. Patient has been seen two or three times monthly for brief supportive sessions at the time of his insulin sedation. Earlier this week the patient's father stopped by the hospital to say that he was most happy at the result of his son's treatment, adding that his son has not missed a day's work and seems to have made a good adjustment to his wife and child. The patient visits his parents about once every two weeks and seems to have been able to sever the strong ties with his father to a satisfactory degree. . . . Patient will be continued on insulin sedation once weekly for an indefinite period of time.

However, six and a half months after discharge, patient himself discontinued the weekly sedation treatments. Except for a one-day episode, he had not been drinking during these six months. According to later information from his wife, he was able to control his drinking for another eight months after he broke off the sedation treatments. Then he began an episode in which he was "dead drunk" for three days and later "deathly sick," followed by eight months of moderate drinking or minor "binges" before the next month-long episode that required hospitalization. The tensions which triggered various episodes of drinking are not all recorded, but a number seemed to follow the usual pattern of threatened rejection and threatened adequacy. For example, on one occasion he was admitted to a hospital "in a highly excited state"; he had been drinking, "wanted to kill his father-in-law, and was very hostile to his wife." Another time, he had finally been demoted from his responsible job because of a cut in staff and had been drinking heavily for several weeks.

Hospitalization at Age 40

The notes in this section will summarize one more hospitalization briefly to suggest the continuing pattern and changes over a six-year period. At the age of 40, patient was admitted and stayed twenty days in a general hospital where he had been treated at least five times previously over the years. He had been discharged from the same hospital two and a half months earlier. Again the precipitating causes were associated with his wife's pregnancy and the birth of their second child, another daughter. His presenting complaints, run-down physical condition, and helpless disorganization are also the familiar periodic picture.

When admitted at this time, his weight has dropped to 125 pounds. He looks chronically ill and is suffering from malnutrition and avitaminosis as a result of his drinking. He is unsteady in gait and tremulous, but neurological examination is relatively negative. His upper teeth have been extracted and he has a denture. His legs and chest are discolored with bruises from recent falls. In the last year he has broken two more ribs in a fall but these have healed well. His liver is tender and moderately enlarged, again suggesting the possibility of cirrhosis of the liver; but after examination the consultant reports that such a diagnosis is not yet warranted.

Patient complains of falling, frequent nosebleed, inability to sleep, depression, and fear of insanity. He feels he may have a "Korsakoff's syndrome," claiming inability to think and loss of memory. He believes he should be committed to a mental hospital. Actually, his thinking seems clear and his conversation relevant and coherent. No obvious memory loss is apparent.

In mood, he is depressed and preoccupied, and with increasing age he seems more demanding and helpless than ever. He has been out of the hospital less than three months before this readmission and has continued to drink. However, in a rather resentful, paranoid manner he rationalizes his difficulties as due to something other than drinking. He believes the doctors should be able to find something physically wrong with him other than alcoholism and should give him medication to cure him. He bases his argument in part on the fact that insulin sedation helped him. He also argues that alcohol cannot be the problem since recently he has been able to take only a drink or two before becoming sick. Therefore, he hasn't had much to drink in the past two weeks. His main problem is still his alcoholism, although deriving, of course, from his passive dependency and periods of marked anxiety.

The circumstances preceding his most recent downfall are of some interest, since he had made some apparent superficial progress in the year and a half before the birth of his second child. His wife, Lili, reports that he himself had taken the initiative in buying a house and moving away from the home of her parents. He had also made the decision to buy a car. In the past, she felt that either she or his father had had to make any final major decision for him. His periods of heavy drinking had been infrequent and had not lasted long. He showed increased assurance, was doing a fairly consistent job at work, and had made some efforts to establish a small additional private practice. Even when she became pregnant this time, he was not too upset and did not begin to drink excessively.

However, the pregnancy did not go well. His wife bled for a month before the baby was finally delivered by a Caesarean operation; and she was still in the hospital when patient was admitted earlier this year. It was shortly before the birth of this second daughter that he went to pieces again and began to drink heavily. By the time he left the hospital earlier this year, he had surrendered his home and his car. His son, now 17, was placed with his parents, and Lili and the two daughters with her parents. Patient went to his parents' home and took care of his father's little store until his continued drinking and frequent falls resulted in the present readmission.

Whether he might have continued to make at least a marginal adjustment for several years more, it is impossible to say. The most recent stresses were somewhat more severe than on some occasions in the past. The loss of his car and his home, symbols of adequacy to him, and the return to complete dependence on his father made his defeat all the more thorough.

Intelligence

Patient was given the Wechsler-Bellevue at age 34 and again at age 37. The discussion here will be limited chiefly to the question of intellectual impairment. The patient shows some temporary impairment due to recent drinking, some permanent loss of intellectual efficiency, and some unevenness of abilities that has no doubt always been characteristic of his unbalanced development. The weighted scores of the two Wechslers are presented in Table 1.

TABLE 1. WECHSLER-BELLEVUE AT 34 AND 37

	AGE 34	AGE 37
Information	17	15
Comprehension	11	13
Digits	13	9
Arithmetic	10	12
Similarities	14	16
Vocabulary	15	17
Prorated verbal score	67	68
Verbal I.Q.	124	126
Picture Arrangement	9	10
Picture Completion	10	6
Block Design	8	10
Object Assembly	11	not given
Digit Symbol	10	10
Prorated performance score	48	45
Performance I.Q.	103	103
Prorated total score	115	113
Full Scale I.Q.	115	116

Both Wechslers were given as the patient was beginning to recover from an episode of heavy drinking, and for this reason some care was taken in administration. For example, the earlier Wechsler was given in the first contacts when he was at his worst; and no subtest was begun unless he seemed attentive and coöperative. In general he enjoyed the tests and was pleased to display his knowledge but had real difficulty in mobilizing and sustaining his capacities with any consistency. He became uneasy and defensive, "coöperatively hostile," whenever he could not succeed. His phraseology became more pedantic, and, as an instance, when he failed only a few of the last Vocabulary items, he introduced a vocabulary test of his own for the examiner consisting of highly technical legal terms. The readiness with which his feelings of inadequacy are aroused and his compliant hostility were both apparent.

When the Wechslers were given he was still tremulous, anxious, and uneven in his functioning. His Figure Drawings, signature, and Bender Gestalt show obvious effects of tremor and uncertainty. In addition, one or two items on the Bender suggest that he cannot maintain a consistent level of efficiency: there are slight breaks in quality that are not easily explained as due to an unsteady hand. This variable inconsistency must be considered in evaluating poor scores on specific, unreliable Wechsler subtests. For example, the one weighted score of 6 on Picture Completion, and of 9 on Digits, should not be over-interpreted.

On the other hand, the consistent discrepancy of more than 20 points between verbal and performance I.Q. deserves further comment. It is not entirely due to temporary inefficiency; his handling of the material argues against this possibility. At least some degree of permanent loss is suggested, but his whole history of adjustment should be considered as well. All of his successes and satisfactions, and all of his defenses and rationalizations, have been intellectual and academic. In social and everyday competence he shows a lifelong history of inadequacy, in spite of some early participation in athletics. (He ended his athletic career by breaking a shoulder.) Probably his Wechsler before he began drinking would show a modified pattern similar to that found now.

His highest subtest scores, on Vocabulary and Information, suggest current and permanent impairment. He is undoubtedly not functioning as well now as he has in the past.

That some degree of gradual permanent impairment plays a part is suggested by a variety of material. For example, he was given the Shipley-Institute of Living Test at age 37. Extreme results with this brief test are usually not misleading with a subject of patient's intelligence. He did not miss an item on the high-ceilinged vocabulary test and worked alertly and quickly. However, he could handle only eight of the abstraction items, yielding a Conceptual Quotient of 68. Even making some allowance for his customary panic and irritability in the face of difficulties, some permanent loss is suggested. This impression is confirmed by the more subjective interpretation of the Goldstein-

Scheerer Object Sorting Test. Over-generalization, concrete thinking, and mild perseveration appear in a variable pattern.

The fact that the two Wechslers suggest no loss between the ages of 34 and 37 is, of course, interesting. His relative temporary disorganization at the time of the two tests may obscure a gradual trend. However, he may have maintained his general level of adjustment fairly well over these three years. In any case, his downhill course is slow and at different periods may manifest itself in different areas. Actually, his Rorschach at age 37 is firmer and more assured, with fewer disconcerting lapses than appear in the one at age 34.

In summary, his intellectual functioning was always uneven, reflecting his lifelong unbalanced development and personality. Temporary inefficiency undoubtedly played a part at the time of both tests, but some degree of gradual permanent loss must also be assumed. He has always maintained intellectual adequacy with more success than general and social adequacy.

Rorschach

The Rorschach was given at age 34 and again at age 37. When he took the Rorschach at age 34, he had regained some of his superficial control and assurance, but he was still recuperating, mildly tremulous, and easily thrown off by minor frustrations. He was trying to appear competent. In the clinical material, we have seen a man who will go to great lengths to maintain a shell of adequacy and self-sufficiency in a setting where he is essentially very dependent and inadequate. He will cling to his parents and do well in college and law school. He will cling to a fatherly employer for nine years, doing less well but periodically carrying off the role of "a keen and able worker." And he will cling to his second wife for at least seven years, painfully incompetent but at least able to believe that Lili is socially inferior and even more immature than he. When his shell of adequacy is questioned, or when the supporting person threatens rejection, he goes into a panic of angry anxiety and complete demanding helplessness. The Rorschach is that of a man who has long maintained a fiction of adequacy, which has never been vigorous or sufficient, with underlying weaknesses that are now aggravated or brought out by current inefficiency.

RORSCHACH AT AGE 34

I

19"

1. Something like a pelvis—view from bottom toward top.

1. (W.) General contour, from bottom up. The holes should not be there.

2. Two animals with backs to each other—wolf nature.

2. (W. He manages to fit in the whole blot, F —.) Grotesque. Snout out of proportion. (Side wings are snouts.)

3. A mask for a face. Ends for over the ears. Large slits: mouth, chin.

3. (W.)

96"

II

32"

1. Might be the backside of a very fat woman. Black dress, red slippers, red waist, red petticoat.

1. (W.) Hole in the back—wouldn't be there. What's it look like to you? On her toes.

2. Two dancers, ballet dancers, touching their left and right foot. Part of the foreground here. Leaning away from each other.

2. (W.) Spinning around.

117"

III

5"

1. Look like two men, at a cock fight, each holding a cock. Fighting, animals versus men. (Context not clear.)

1. (W.)

2. Red doesn't mean anything to me. A little animal, a dog with a long tail—heads turned to the back. Central red doesn't mean anything.

2. (Upper red.)

95"

IV

11"   1. Could be a—fur rug.   1. Something like a bear rug,
         Something in the na-   except for the head. (Uses
         ture of a steer—horns,   shading.)
         eyes. Stretched out
         flat.
59"

V

3"   1. A bat—wings spread.   1. A bat going away from you—
                                     or could be stretched on the
29"   wall—dead.

VI

22"   1. Aerial view of a high-   1. (W.)
         way. In the center.
         And on either side—
         trees of lighter color.
         Black to the right of
         the trees indicates
         swamp land. Lighter
         gray to the left, etc.
         indicates elevation.
         Therefore, a highway
         surrounded on both
         sides by hills.
113"

VII

16"   1. Huh! Indicates two   1. (W.)
         women, I believe, in
         masquerade — with
         their backs to each
         other — masquerade
         Spanish style — lacy,
         with mantillas.
71"

VIII

20"   1. A frog-like animal on   1. (Frog-like?) Web feet—four
         a lily pad, pond lily,   of them. (?) Stone or green
         gazing at its own re-   stuff that forms seaweed—
         flection in the water.   colors are unnatural. Connota-
                                     tion not from color, but form.
53"   (W.)

IX

22"   1. The pink: roughly an   1. (All of bottom pink.)
         elderly man, with

white or gray hair—
abundant. Mustache,
cigarette. Pointing a
cane with his left
hand.

82"

X

40" 1. Stamen of a plant,
with long pink flower
—in the nature of a
hollyhock—no, a hya-
cinth.

1. (W, centering chiefly around
the two pink D's.)

2. Same, different color.

2. (D, area usually seen as
green worms and rabbit
head.) This might be a sling-
106"   shot, or a portable chair.

A partial scoring summary of this Rorschach may be compared with
a summary of the Rorschach given three years later.

TABLE 2. RORSCHACH SUMMARY AT AGES 34 AND 37

	AGE 34	AGE 37
R	15	20
M	5	5
FM	2	2
Fm	0	1
Fk	0	1
FK	1	0
F	4	5
Fc	1	2
FC	3	5
CF	1	1
W	12	13
D	3	6
Dd	0	1
P	2	6
H	5	5
Hd	0	1
A	4	5
Ad	0	2
A Obj.	1	1
Obj.	0	3
Sex or At.	1	0
Pl.	3	1
N	1	1
Mask	1	1

The Rorschach at age 37 is similar to the one given three years earlier. The later Rorschach does not suggest that the patient is becoming rapidly more disorganized and less efficient over these three years. In fact, it is the firmer, more confident protocol of the two. The increase in R on the second Rorschach, in P and D, and the slightly improved handling of certain responses are the chief differences. Patient dropped the "pelvis" response on Card I, the "fat woman" response on Card II, and improved the Card VIII "frog on a lily pad." He was less helpless on the last two cards and gave seven responses instead of three, accounting for most of the increase in details and in R. No new responses were as poor as those he eliminated or improved.

An adequate discussion of the Rorschach at age 34 would be too lengthy, but a sampling of considerations may be briefly mentioned. These comments will refer chiefly to his intellectual striving and defenses, handling of affect, and dependency or inadequacy.

His attempt to handle every card as a whole might be considered first. This attempt is consistent throughout the Rorschach at age 34, even though three D responses are scored. Two of the D responses (on III and X) merely account for something he has left out of a preceding W response; the third D (on IX) reflects his inability to handle the card as a W. This tendency to give whole responses is associated with his intellectual defenses and with the high value he puts on abstract intelligence. Here is his characteristic way of attempting to handle all situations. At least some of his concepts in sizing up the overall situation show ingenuity and reflect his superior intellectual endowment. However, the record is shot through with flaws in details of execution and elaboration. Any one of these flaws might be passed over, especially in the record of a less intelligent man; but in his case the piling up of inadequacies is striking.

His striving to give whole responses must be considered in evaluating "color shock" and other shock. When he delays a long time before responding to a card, his difficulty may be either the problem of arriving at a W solution or the more traditional form-color problem. Furthermore, the "suppression of affect" (color shock) is additionally complicated by his special need to deny basic drives (sex, dependency, etc.). We might speak loosely of whole shock, color shock, and sex shock. These labels are paralleled by his inability to abandon intellectual defenses, his inability to handle affect, and his inability to accept basic drives. Actually, the picture here is always consistent: he cannot abandon intellectual defenses, and they are inadequate to handle affect and drives.

The delay on Card II and then the progressively longer delays on the last three colored cards reflect his difficulties with affect and with social interactions. Yet, if he could relinquish his striving for W's, he might be more successful. His comments and details of elaboration point up the impasse. He shows helpless dissatisfaction and annoyance with his first response to Card II when he turns on the examiner and asks: "What's it look like to you?" Both his inability to abandon overall solutions (W) and his difficulty with affect (color) are reflected in his Card III comments: "Red doesn't mean anything to me. . . . Central red doesn't mean anything." He has failed to account for the whole card, and the most troublesome areas are red.

For a subject of his conceptual level, the animal and reflection on Card VIII is not a response that suggests strained ingenuity or overreaching. Yet he falls down badly in details of elaboration. The "froglike animal" and the inappropriate "lily pad" are definitely poor for this man. Here affect and "color shock" must be emphasized since he should easily be able to handle this response, and since his irritable denial of color in the inquiry pinpoints the difficulty.

The "red shock" on Cards II and III and the shading shock on VI are probably associated with his denial of, or inadequacy in dealing with, basic drives. He is an extreme and unsuccessful "emotional suppressor." In the Rorschach, his shell of adequacy or control is represented in the M:FM ratio and the FC:CF ratio, where FM and CF are relatively low. The control attempt leads too frequently to poor form, loose relationships, and disturbed content. The backside of a woman with a hole in her back, the two men each holding a cock, the frog on a lily pad, and the flower that may be a hollyhock or a hyacinth suggest part of the picture. He does not give frank sex responses or oral responses. That is, the picture is not one of blatant and overt inadequacy and dependence. There is a general overlay of denial and of strong intellectual defenses, which are consistently unsuccessful and result in conflict, anxiety, and failure. In the Rorschach, the overlay of inadequate control is more readily apparent than the underlying dependency.

The pervasive distrustful, paranoid, hostile feeling tone of the Rorschach should be noted. The human-movement responses could also be discussed at length in terms of the revealing but complex insights related to his attitudes toward self, parents, and others in his environment. However, as a simple summary, the denial and inability to handle affect and basic drives, the persistent reliance on abstract and intellectual defenses, the resulting conflict and anxiety, and the underlying dependence and ineffectual development might be stressed.

Other Tests

Figure Drawings of a man and woman were obtained at ages 34, 35, and 37 and are in general similar at each age. The drawings at age 37 are shakily executed, hostile-looking productions. Patient describes the male figure as: "Forty-five years of age, likes to scare people and dislikes noise because it irritates him." The female appears to be a stern-faced, cold individual, with piercing eyes. The breast area is specifically indicated, but by a broken line that looks like part of the dress pattern rather than anything underneath. She is described as: "About forty years of age, likes to teach school, and dislikes children. She appears to be very grim. Because she's a teacher she appears to be frowning and displeased at something and there's not much you can do about it." His resentment and conviction that dependency needs are always frustrated are suggested. He did give two "oral" responses in a Rorschach at age 35, not one of the two previously discussed. The handling of these is interesting: in one, he sees "two bears nibbling, or licking, salt"; and in the other, he sees "prominent breast areas" on two men, which "might be a flower" in the buttonholes of their jackets. In spite of other considerations, it seems characteristic that oral needs are satisfied with salt, and breasts are translated into ornamental flowers.

His Sentence Completions (Rotter) at age 35 suggest his discouragement, bitterness, remoteness from people, and feelings of inadequacy. As examples:

I failed everything.
I wish I could erase the past six months.
People are overabundant.
A mother is the female of the family.

I need help and some degree of tranquillity.
Sometimes there is a breaking point.

The Patient in Earlier Years

The family history is essentially negative for mental illness and alcoholism, and for cancer, epilepsy, tuberculosis, and diabetes. Father's ancestry was English and mother's English and German. The maternal grandmother was considered mildly eccentric, apparently somewhat rigid, suspicious, and difficult in her relations with neighbors. A paternal uncle left home in his early twenties, was "wild" and drank, but later married and settled down. In the latest contacts, patient has referred to his 76-year-old father as showing some signs of "senility." However, the father at ages 73 and 75, as described by social workers, seems to have been alert and relatively well preserved.

Patient was raised as an only child. A sister died at birth some two years before he was born. Although his father was 20 and his mother 22 when they married, and although they both wanted children, patient was not born until sixteen years after they married. Mother was well during pregnancy. Birth and early maturation were normal, and patient was breast fed and weaned easily. He had no serious illnesses as a child. Parents and relatives idolized patient, but he was strictly disciplined and never "spoiled." He was considered a sweet child and his mother kept him in "white" until he started school. Before school age he was not allowed to play outside with other children for fear he would get dirty.

In reporting that patient was never "spoiled," father stresses that the parents were strict about his training, in regard to such matters as coming in at the proper time in the evening. As another example, patient wanted a bicycle but was never given one since father feared he might hurt himself. The home was a "good Christian one" where alcohol and cigarettes were taboo. Father opposed cigarette smoking vigorously and denied patient cigarettes until he was 21 years of age. He did allow patient a pipe at 16, which he himself gave his son. Father's opposition to alcohol was equally stringent.

Father was a self-made man who owned the largest store in the tiny rural community, and at various times served in respected positions such as postmaster and justice of the peace. The family were staunch Methodists, always took an active part in the church, and centered most of their social activities around it. An entirely clear picture of father's own early home life cannot be reconstructed. He left school to work at the age of 13 but feels that this was customary in the rural community at the time. When he was 20, he married a local girl. However, about this time he enjoyed a brief career and some prominence as a major-league baseball player. He was still in his middle twenties when he returned to the same rural area where he was born and raised. He has spent the rest of his life in the village some twelve miles from his boyhood home.

Patient's mother is some two years older than father. She had a grade-school education, growing up in the country and staying at home until her marriage. She is an "easy" woman who often shielded patient from the father but also insisted on careful training. She encouraged him to bring playmates into their home and let them have complete freedom in their play. The third floor was turned over to him and his playmates, where they boxed, had a phonograph, and used all sorts of amusement equipment. He brought the youngsters in the neighborhood for meals and the mother liked this. She often said she preferred to know where her son and his friends were rather than have them play outdoors. Mother was as religious as her husband, sang in the church choir, and played the organ.

Patient's father followed a policy similar to the mother's, controlling his activities and attitudes as much as possible by a combination of strict supervision and bribing companionship. Father says he made a pal of the patient, played tennis and golf with him, taught him these games initially, took him to baseball games in the city, and to big shows there. Patient was always close to his father and still expresses a strong, disturbing attachment to him. Father taught Sunday School and always took patient with him. As a result, patient early began to teach Sunday School and continued to do so while in college. Patient belonged to the Boy Scouts and similar groups.

Patient finished grade school in the upper third of his class. Father typically promised him money for getting A's and B's and a whipping if he got C's. In high school patient was a good student, took part in many activities, played in the orchestra, sang in church and school clubs, played basketball, tennis, and some football. He managed the football team for the last three years of high school. A shoulder fracture in his junior year ended his active participation in high-school sports and curtailed his athletic activities in college.

Patient attended a small college near his home, continued to do well academically, and participated in various activities. Sports were limited chiefly to tennis because of his shoulder. He was president of his fraternity. In studies he was an honor student, majoring in history and German and receiving a scholarship to attend college in Germany.

However, he did not go to Germany, but instead decided to marry his childhood sweetheart. In one passing statement, father has referred to this as a "forced marriage." All patient's references to his first wife indicate a long-time attachment to her as someone "irreplaceable," for whom he still longs and whom he still resents because she finally divorced him.

This marriage did not result in any greater independence. In fact, whether he managed to have the marriage forced on him or not, the result was that he did not leave home and go to Germany. His father set the young couple up in an apartment so that patient could continue his studies, for two years of law at the same college, followed by two years at a university in the nearest city. In reality, he continued his protected status and became more dependent on his parents than ever. A son, the only child by his first wife, was born ten months after marriage.

Drinking was not allowed on the campus or in the fraternities at patient's undergraduate college, but it was customary for some students to go to a night club nearby for a few drinks. One of his teachers told his father that patient had taken part in some drinking. Father was "heartbroken," talked to his son, and told him of his grief. Patient tried to explain that it was not a serious matter. The only unusual element in the situation seems to have been father's extreme but characteristic reaction.

After his marriage, in the freedom of the apartment provided by his parents, patient began to drink more. He and his wife gave cocktail parties, and from the first it was apparent that patient could not drink much without being overly affected.

Although his first wife did not divorce him for ten years, the marriage began to fall apart after one year. Patient says that his wife's father died in his arms at about this time, and that he was more affected than she. She soon found that his drinking and his helpless dependence on his parents were real problems. The parents were interfering and controlling.

Patient's first wife is described by his father as a fine girl. After finishing her education she taught school and gradually took over her own financial support as patient's inadequacies became more apparent. By the time patient entered the Army at age 30, his parents were caring for his son and his wife had given the marriage up as hopeless. The divorce became final just before he left the Army. Yet she promised to remarry patient on several occasions if he would stop drinking; she went out with him regularly when he returned from service, and stopped doing so only when his second marriage became a probability. Father feels that patient and his first wife were still in love years after the second marriage.

After finishing law school at 25, patient could not face the prospect of establishing himself in his own practice. However, he was soon taken into the office of an older lawyer. He earned only $38 in the first three months and felt that his wife did not give him the encouragement she should have, since she thought he should earn more. His partner always kept a bottle in his desk, and patient was welcome to help himself at any time. Apparently patient initially accepted a work situation where his capacity for independence would be minimally tested, and where his chances of much success were equally limited. He began to drink more than ever when success did not come immediately. Yet, in spite of all the difficulties he created and in spite of his drinking and defeatist dependency, he managed to build up a fairly adequate practice and continued in this partnership for four years, at which time he was drafted.

A year earlier he had been eligible for a commission in the Army where his legal training would be an asset but felt he could not assume the responsibility involved. Soon after he was drafted, he was sent overseas and participated in the first North African landing. Two men on either side of him were killed and he suffered minor shrapnel wounds and a "conversion reaction." He also had dysentery. He was returned shortly to this country, hospitalized for three more months, and then given a medical discharge. His Army service lasted seventeen months.

He then went to work in the agency where he stayed for the next nine years. Two years after his first wife divorced him, he told her that, if she did not remarry him, he would marry his secretary. His first wife refused, solely because he continued to drink. He then married his present wife, fourteen months before the interviews at the age of 34. Her childish impulsiveness, emotionalism, and readily expressed anger and affection seem to contrast with the personality of his first wife. They now have two daughters and the marriage continues.

ADDENDUM

In a hospital staff conference when the man was 37, four points were emphasized: his dependency, his feelings of inadequacy, his arrested or unbalanced "psychosexual" capacity to relate to people, and an element called "masked schizophrenia." As an adult, he might most readily see himself alone, betrayed, and retaliatory. He blames others and the world. It is less easy for him to admit his helplessness, guilt, and hostility. He drinks or otherwise destroys himself as a way of striking back at all those insensitive people who have deserted or turned against him.

His parents coöperated to arrest the development of any capacity for independence in the patient. Their campaign to achieve this end lasted from his birth until at least his twenty-fifth year and actually continues still. His first wife, his son, and his financial support were taken over by his parents until he finished law school; and he was kept geographically as close to home as possible. None too clearly, his first wife seems to have looked on his parents' possessiveness and his alcoholism as a single problem. His mother did not let him play with others before he started school, and then turned over the third floor of their home in order to continue her surveillance. His father exhausted his financial resources continuing this same policy, through the law-school years and down to the present time. The psychology of the parents would make an interesting study in itself. In patient's case, major damage may have been done in early infancy. However, the parents' campaign continued through many years, and patient's social incompetence became glaring at the age when he was finally called upon to show some independence.

That he was born with some compliancy to fit in with his parents' program may be true, but he was not necessarily born to develop serious personality difficulties. His adequacy in school and his dubious adequacy in a specific job need not be considered surprising. These were successes under surveillance, successes in areas where his capacities were allowed to develop.

His choice of alcohol as a method of retaliation and self-debasement is understandable. For both himself and his parents, drinking is an activity loaded with emotional meaning. When he looks for a "negative identity," for the role his parents would least like to have him play, his choice of the part of a drunkard is most effective, possibly more so than his suicidal, head-first dive through a window.

Jack Rabbit: A Study in
Character Disturbance

BY HAROLD LINDNER

The case of J. O. was referred to me in the aftermath of a rather serious prison riot, while I was employed as a clinical psychologist in a mid-Atlantic state prison.

When I first met J. O. he appeared surly, aggressive, and openly hostile. There was an appealing quality about him, perhaps the result of an attitude combining the rejection of any help from others and a seeking for such assistance. He complained that he was being made the butt of institutional prejudice because of his part in the recent prison riot. He insisted that the authorities refused to give him "a break" because they considered him one of the ringleaders of the fracas, and that as a result he could not be assigned to a proper work detail. Instead of working he languished in his cell most days—being called out of it only for those work details that required close supervision and heavy manual labor.

He said that he wanted help, but he doubted whether anyone would or could help him. A buddy of his had recommended that he seek help from the psychologist, and after much confusion and deliberation he had decided to make an appointment at the clinic. J. O. made it very clear to the writer, even at this preliminary interview, that he didn't really expect any aid from the professional staff but that he felt sufficiently desperate to try anything.

Following this interview psychological study was arranged for, social service information obtained, and a psychiatric study requested.

Medical Findings and Appearance

Medical findings were negative for any significant disorder. He had been a full-term baby whose birth was marked by his mother's death immediately after delivery and following a prolonged period of labor. Delivery was at home by a local physician assisted by a midwife and two female members of the father's family. Because of his mother's death the child was given to his paternal grandmother's care. He was breast fed by a paternal aunt until he was about 9 months old, when a bottle was substituted and thereafter continued until his second year, at which time he was completely and easily weaned.

In appearance he was handsome, tall (6′ ½″) and broad of shoulders. He weighed 183 pounds. He had wavy blond hair, blue eyes, and a clear, light skin.

Family History

During the second decade of the nineteenth century, the O. family settled in the farmlands section of a mid-Atlantic state. Nothing much is known of their beginnings in this country. They tilled the soil, married and interacted with other Slavic members of their rural community, gave little thought to education or travel, and seemed content to remain within their locality. Acculturation was slow because of inbreeding with fellow Slavic neighbors, but they gradually modified some of their folkways in favor of those of their adopted community.

The first significant entry in the institutional files on the O. family's history concerns the marriage of J. O.'s parents. From this we learned that his parents were married against the wishes of their respective families and only after much interference and threat of disinheritance. Following the marriage, however, the newlyweds lived with the O. family, and J. O.'s father continued to work on the family holdings as before.

The new Mrs. O. was taken into the family but only with reluctance. Because she was of Scotch-Irish ancestry and totally unacquainted with Slavic folkways, she was treated with contempt. Whether Mrs. O. was mindful of their disrespect for her, we have no way of knowing. She served her husband, kept to herself in the farmhouse, and before her early death at age 28 bore 7 children, 2 girls and 5 boys, of whom J. O. was the youngest.

Mr. O. continued his living arrangements as before his wife's death (there is nothing in the records to indicate that this event caused him to change his routine or interests). As before, he lived and worked with his own family. The children were relegated to the care of the female members of the household, while he remained as cold and distant from the children as always.

Personal History

From the moment of his birth and his mother's death, in February of 1928, J. O. was given to his paternal grandmother's care. In effect he became her child. He learned to call her "Mama" and also to refer to the other family members—including his father—by their Christian names.

During his first five years of life he grew strong under the influence of farm life. His aging grandmother neglected everyone but J. O., whom she showered with affection. His father, in resuming his habitual solitary and non-communicative state after his wife's death, largely ignored J. O. during this time.

After his grandmother died, J. O., then a child of 5, was taken from the protective care of the women and given to his father. Henceforth, he was forced to go to the fields each day to learn to be a farmer. J. O. worked hard under the supervision of his father, who not only told him what to do but beat him sorely for minor, childish mistakes and infractions. J. O. doesn't remember talking to his father during all this time. They would work side by side, but there was no communication. Even at his age he was made to shovel dung, care for livestock, milk, and carry water.

As a result of this treatment the boy developed a considerable hatred for his father. Prior to this, J. O. had hardly known his father. Now it seemed that the latter was taking out all his frustrations and defeats on him. Spitefully, J. O. would deviate from the work rules. He hid behind buildings and learned to lie about his feelings and his work. When caught—and he usually was—retribution was swift and severe.

After approximately nine months of such continual punishment J. O. began to think of running away. One day (according to the social service notes) while J. O. was tending his chores he accidentally overturned a charcoal lamp and set fire to a portion of the barn. This time his father's anger knew no bounds and enraged he beat the child unmercifully. Crying, afraid, hating and being hated, the boy ran away from the farm, not to return for many years.

Since it was not possible for a 6-year-old boy to go very far without being apprehended, he was found a few days later in a nearby town and returned to his home. Evidently his impassioned pleas brought him unexpected aid from his grandfather, and he succeeded in obtaining immediate foster-home placement.

Institutional History

J. O. was given to the foster care of an elderly couple whose farm was located at the opposite end of the state. The people were God-fearing, moral, and hard-working. They showed little personal interest in their charge and other than giving him room and board, keeping him at work, in school and church, they had few contacts with him. His own version of the two years of foster-home placement is at some variance with the official records and suggests that these people were capricious and dictatorial in their demands. Failure to accede to their wishes was rewarded by physical punishment and enforced Bible study for long periods of time.

J. O. finally escaped from his foster home but tasted freedom only briefly. He was now 8 years old and when picked up by a railroad policeman for riding a freight train through a southwestern state was sent to the state's training school for young boys.

The school's routine was based on Victorian ideas of discipline, religious training, and the unstated notion that each boy was a future Dillinger for whom there was no real salvation. Therefore, according to this logic, the best program was to inflict physical punishment so that, at least while in the school, a minimum of difficulty would be had from him. It was in this punitive pedagogical environment that J. O. spent the next four years.

On his arrival at the school he received a lecture from the principal, a lay minister. He was cautioned that the only way to get along was to obey the counselors, rarely talk, work hard, pray, and report anything untoward he might see in the behavior of others. Following this indoctrination he was then introduced to his "cottage parents."

His first day in the school was spent in washing himself because the cottage mother hold him he "stank," and dishes became his first chore. The first night was spent in crying. He was frightened by the other

children's gory tales about institutional life. Also, he was forced to
expose himself to the other boys in the dark by match-light to "prove"
to them that he was a "man."

The second day was occupied by the various intake procedures:
medical, psychiatric, social, and the first of a number of paper-and-
pencil psychological tests and measurements. By evening he was completely overawed by the whole thing and tried to escape into the
protective comfort of sleep—but the cottage boys had different ideas
about how he should spend the night. After lights-out he was assaulted
by a burly youth, stripped of his clothes, and, amidst whispers and
hushed guffaws, marched to a bed upon which he was forced to squat.
The other boys gathered around him. One lad, the leader, commenced
to "teach him the ropes." He was advised that unless he voluntarily
gave his body and soul to their whims, they would take them from
him. After some display of physical force, he was compelled to commit
fellatio on some of them. Then, with renewed threats of what could
happen to him if he should "squeal," he was sent off to bed.

J. O. spent four impressionable years of his life in this place. Probably because he was fortunate in possessing a strong physique, the
others stopped picking on him after a few months. Soon he acquired
the reputation of being an "OK guy." Records indicate a number of
skirmishes with the school's counselors, a few rough fights with other
boys, innumerable imprisonments in "meditation cells," a corresponding development of hate, and a "wise-guyish" attitude and wholesale
disrespect for all authority. He rapidly became an institutional gang-
leader. By the time he was 10, school authorities considered him incorrigible. The records also suggest that he acquired the reputation
among the boys as one to be feared for his physical strength. They were
in awe of him and tendered him respectful envy for his continual
forays against the counselors, the teachers, and, so it seemed, any male
adult who happened to get in his way. Much of his time was spent in
the cottage reserved for "hardened criminal types," where he was the
gang-leader. Evidently he was successful in intimidating many of the
personnel and was soon relatively free to do as he pleased within
the confines of the school grounds.

When he was 12 years old, J. O. organized a classroom riot, as a
result of which his days of relative freedom were temporarily brought
to an end. He was restricted to the meditation cell block for six weeks.

His clinical folder contains notations by guards and professional personnel suggesting that he was unable to control his hostility during the entire six-week period. He engaged in a number of rages during which he literally destroyed the cell by tearing his mattress, pulling plumbing out of the wall and flooding the cubicle, and brutally fighting those guards who tried to restrain him. He was sent to the psychiatrist, who diagnosed the condition as a "temporary hysterical panic state" and recommended he be released from punishment. Accordingly, he was returned to the general school population. Not long afterwards, he managed to break away from his work detail and escape from the school.

According to J. O.'s version of his history, as related to a social worker, once he had made his escape from the training school he stole some money and clothing, bought a gun, and hopped a freight train for his home. He went to his father's house, where he stayed for almost one year, until he could no longer bear the quiet hostility that surrounded him. When he got home his father received him coldly, made a few inquiries about past events, warned him about the behavior expected from him if he was to remain in the house, and suggested that he get right to work. The youth took up where he had left off, working with his father side by side, in silence. He told the social worker who had interviewed him that his family and neighbors were unsympathetic and hostile. He claimed that he made a few unsuccessful attempts at attending local dances and said that he even tried to join a sports club. However, the social ostracism was so complete that no parent would permit his son to be seen with J. O., and none would allow his daughter to dance with him. So rebuked, J. O. retired to the farm, and between heavy work and heavy fantasy he spent almost one year, until the night when he again took up his travels.

This time he left his home with the admitted intention of avenging his family's and his neighbors' rebuffs. His attitude now was one of disdain for social conformity: in essence, he discarded any desire he might have previously had to adapt to social requisites.

J. O.'s first stop was in a nearby city, where he soon contacted people whom he had heard about during his training school days. They befriended him and started him on the road to crime: larceny, armed robbery, mugging, and even one excursion into rape. It was on the mugging charge that he was picked up by the police. When the authorities noted his training-school escape record there was no chance for probation, and he was sentenced to the state reformatory. He spent the next three years there, being released when he was 17 years old.

Before we discuss the reformatory situation it might prove worth while to examine briefly the type of life J. O. followed during his few months of freedom. As noted above, he left home and went to a large city where he contacted other lawbreakers and criminals. They taught him to place a premium on "knowing the right guys," to be a "good Joe," and always to carry protective "hardware." Among other characteristics, his language underwent quite a change at this time: it came to consist almost entirely of hostile innuendoes, street slang, "jive" talk, many expressions of the importance of loyalty toward buddies, and a whole lexicon of aggressive phrases toward authority.

J. O. had his first heterosexual experience during this time. It was most unsuccessful. He had been an inveterate masturbator since childhood and, as shown in our discussion of his training-school days, had had a number of homosexual experiences. In regard to the latter, he expressed nothing but contempt, and insisted, when relating his history to the writer, that these were of two varieties. One type of homosexual experience was the kind he was compelled to engage in through the bullying demands of older boys who had inflicted their sadistic designs on his defenselessness; in these he was passively resistant. The second type was in those situations where he acted the role of the bully and made younger boys commit fellatio on him so that he could "prove" to the other training-school inmates that he was their leader. This type of experience was done for prestige purposes and, he claims, filled him with revulsion, never satisfying sexual tensions. Masturbation, however, was a satisfying practice and his onanistic fantasies were almost entirely concerned with heterosexual experiences with older women. During this time of his life he took up with a local prostitute and had a number of sexual relations with her, none of which were satisfying.

The indoctrination at the reformatory was much less painful than had been the one tendered him at the training school. Now he had a reputation as a "con" and knew all the important people. In short order he learned the routine of the place and managed to get detailed to convenient living quarters and an easy work detail. These three years he admittedly spent in training for a life of crime. He worked hard to perfect his already superb physique. He cultivated all the "worth-while cons" and made the proper political friends, so that on his release he knew exactly whom to contact. He became a voracious reader of detective stories, books on criminology, lewd magazines, and even a number of better fiction stories and novels. He was clever and knew how to absorb from his readings, later using them intelligently to impress others with his vocabulary and knowledge of a great variety of things.

On the surface, then, his reformatory years were relatively quiet. However, official records indicate that he was considered by the institution's personnel to be an "incorrigible psychopath . . . not to be trusted . . . a potential escapee . . . wiseguy and bully . . . troublemaker, clever and scheming. . . ."

From the reformatory J. O. went back to his city haunts. Here he apparently picked up where he had left off three years before. In this way, then, he spent more than a year, until one night during his 19th year he was apprehended for armed robbery and sentenced to the state prison.

J. O. was received by the prison authorities in routine fashion. Because they noted his escape record they were justly wary about security and restricted him to inside duties. Institutional records include numerous incidents of misbehavior and disrespect for regulations. He was given various punishments for insubordination and for fighting with other inmates.

After he had been imprisoned for almost three years, he became an active participant in an institution riot. From the newspaper and official accounts of this melee it was a major one (the writer was not employed at this institution at the time of the riot). Prisoners overran the entire prison and took a number of the guards as hostages. There was much blind running about the prison interior, shouting, cursing, singing, dancing, gibing, destroying, cutting, and breaking. J. O. engaged in all this along with most of the other inmates. Homosexualism was rampant: youths were seduced, fights broke out among inmates, clothes were torn off less-favored convicts, the chapel was almost destroyed, the dispensary was raided and drugs were stolen . . . and, perhaps of most singular significance, J. O., with other inmates, stood on tiers above the guards (who were massed in the outer center-hall) and, while the men laughed, cursed, and chided, they urinated on them.

Eventually the riot was curbed. Those involved in it were severely punished and additional court sentences were added to their existing ones. Order was again restored to the prison community. J. O.'s ringleader role in the riot made him appear even more hazardous to the authorities, who now further restricted his activities. Parole became impossible for him. The court added more time to his sentence. The prison authorities considered him too dangerous to be allowed any latitude, and they made certain that he was always under close surveillance.

It was at this time and under these conditions that J. O. came to the attention of the writer.

Psychiatric Findings

Because J. O. was seen on a number of different occasions by a variety of psychiatrists, it is beyond our means here to attempt complete psychiatric reporting. Instead we will confine ourselves to a résumé. Psychiatric opinion was uniformly consistent on the diagnosis of "psychopathic personality (character disturbance)." He was considered to be an "inadequate personality" who aggressively strove for power to compensate for feelings of weakness and impotence. No hallucinatory or delusional phenomena were noted. No ideas of reference. Sensorium was clear. Insight lacking. Judgment uncritical and affected by the hedonistic, pleasure-principle strivings. Affect was appropriate. He was never considered to be psychotic. It was noted that his hostility and aggression were reaction formations for the basic insecurity felt in interpersonal relationships. And, finally, it was felt that his criminal behavior was a displacement of hostility toward his father and thus a perpetual argument with all forms of authority. Unfortunately, for our purposes here, he was never studied by a dynamically oriented psychiatrist and so the psychiatric viewpoint on dynamics is not available.

Psychological Findings

Psychometric testing (Wechsler-Bellevue) yielded an I.Q. of 116 (bright normal intelligence) with a discrepancy between the Verbal I.Q. (101) and the Performance I.Q. (129) of 28 points in favor of the latter. Such results are often found in those who suffer from character disturbances and who act out rather than internalize their conflicts. The qualitative test analysis tends to substantiate the diagnostic impression, in that he showed an excellent fund of general knowledge and a good vocabulary, but his other verbal subtests indicated less ability in the respective sampled areas. Comprehension, while adequate, was substantially limited by the antisocial quality of the answers he offered (e.g., "Hell, I wouldn't bother looking at it . . . none of my business if a jerk lost his letter on the street . . . oh, I'd throw it in the mailbox if one was on my way.") and thus revealed a deficit in critical judgment. His Arithmetic score was rather poor, and this, in conjunction with the relatively poor Similarities subscore, in which a rather high degree of concreteness was noted, is further evidence that the patient reacts quickly and impulsively and does not use his capacities to work through his problems rationally.

The performance subscale was a simple matter for J. O. and quantitative scores were quite good. Qualitatively, however, there was noticeable a low tolerance for frustration and very little capacity to learn from previous experiences. On the Picture Arrangement subtest he showed how anxious interpersonal relations can be for him and on those picture sequences dealing with sexual relationships his distortions were pathognomonic for sexual disturbances (e.g., "that's a dummy . . . hey, now she looks like a bitch . . . wow! he's feeling her up . . .").

On the Bender Gestalt he immediately chose to use nine separate pieces of paper, one for each gestalt. He rapidly progressed through the test, completing it in less than four minutes. There was turning of the paper to the horizontal plane. He spread out to cover almost the entire page for each drawing. Gestalts were all accurate. No difficulties were shown with angulation; no reversals made. A strong, heavy penciling was used on all gestalts: on number 8 he had some difficulty with side angles because he originally made the horizontal lines too long. After a couple of erasures he managed to satisfy himself, and the end result was a grossly over-enlarged, heavily penciled figure, with much smudging and erasing indicative of unconscious conflicts about power, masculinity, and authority. The clinical evaluation of this test suggested that he was aggressive and power-motivated to a degree which would interfere with any attempts he might make to relate to others in any but a coldly distant and dogmatic way. He showed no capacity for warmth in interpersonal relationships and revealed a need to impress others with his power and drive. From this test one might justifiably assume that his aggressive antagonism toward authority was a defense mechanism behind which he protected feelings of inadequacy and lack of masculinity.

On the Rorschach test the patient showed good contact with reality and exhibited creative imagination. His defensive attitude toward testing was illustrated by aggressive comments (e.g., "Who the hell drew these things?" "Gee, I'm sorry, sir, these are too fantastic to make heads or tails out of, I don't know, Doc"). He returned most cards with a mixture of hostility and obsequiousness indicative of his anxiety (e.g., threw them on the table only to pick them up again and carefully rearrange them in proper numerical order while verbalizing apologies for the contemptuous way he had tossed the cards).

Before we attempt to interpret the Rorschach findings, perhaps a verbatim reporting of some of the more interesting responses might help clarify the dynamic picture: [1]

   I. Looks like one of those army hats . . . eagle emblems. That's a person . . . I don't know for sure . . . might be a man or a woman . . . the butt is wide like a bitch but the legs and the strong hands they're too strong and muscular . . . I guess she's a woman . . . sorta reaching high with her hips spread like wide as if she's carrying a baby . . you know like pregnant.

  II. They look like 2 bears like they're fighting and bloody all over themselves . . . that looks like their legs have been cut-off or chopped up . . . Boy they sure must have had it in for each other. Is that a "private" there . . . no looks more like a wire-cutter.

 III. One of those guys is a Black Sambo and the other looks like his bitch . . . they're dressed up for a ball . . . if they were real they'd sure have a hot time tonight . . . who drew these crazy things . . . must have been a fiend, Doc.

 IV. This looks like a cloud like after a thunderstorm. That looks like a Frankenstein monster . . . a big black ape or a gorilla with big feet and fuzzy hair all over him . . . doesn't look like he has any

---

[1] In the original presentation of the Rorschach test the patient rejected Cards VII and IX. Following his free associations to Card X, Card VII and then Card IX were resubmitted to him in a casual manner without any suggestion that this was unorthodox procedure. The responses recorded here for Cards VII and IX were obtained from this second offering. Following this, the test inquiry was obtained. The responses recorded here represent only those more significant percepts. The patient actually gave 22 responses to the test.

head like as if it's been cut off and all that's up there where his head should be is a bunch of pussy-hair. God-damn!

V. Looks like an old stump of a tree . . . dead wood like rotted away.

VI. That's a bitch's butt there with . . . what are those little things in there? . . . it's her privates all right. Looks like a turtle with his head beneath the shell . . . like he's creeping along and wants to look out but he doesn't dare because he's in unfriendly country and if he does they'll get him.

VII. That looks like a map like from an airplane looking down on it . . . with the water and the coastline and the water cutting into the coast and washing it away and those high mountains up there . . . like as if you look at some land from a plane.

VIII. This looks like a mountain with the sun reflecting on it and snow on some places and the sun is like a fire on it.
A woman's corset there . . . with those strings tying it.
That's a family tree . . . the color of the crest and those buffaloes on the sides . . . it means that they will fight to protect their rights . . . the buffalo is a strong animal and if anyone tries to get in its way it'll tear him apart. Like in King Arthur's days.

IX. Oh yes . . . like an atom bomb blowing up the whole damned place. Wow!
I can't find any other explanation of this . . . I can say it just looks like spilled paint . . . just a mess of paint.

X. Just a whole bunch of insects . . . maybe hopping around . . . like in nature, you know, some eating some and some grabbing the smaller ones . . . that's life . . . survival of the fittest.

The patient's power drive was vividly revealed in his perceptions of crests and emblems. He underscored the defensive violence in those strivings through the inclusion of details for the continuation of insignia of power. The impulsive, infantile affect in the protocol showed how labile were those feelings and had reference to an instability of contact with his environment.

This protocol suggested the theme that his self-concept was one of inadequacy, doubt of his own masculinity and virility. He relied on aggression and impulsivity as compensatory mechanisms of defense. On Card II he expressed the aggressive fantasies and marked hostility so often found in antagonistic, sadistic psychopaths. The percepts "ape" and "buffalo" suggested that his hostility was directed toward the male figure (father), who represented the threatening, frustrating image.

The degree of dysphoric content, however, the vista response to Card VII, and the "corset" on Card VIII all belied his central problem of concern with the castrating father figure. Instead, these latter established the foci of infection in his frustrated dependency needs. Basically, this was a disturbance rooted in a longing for maternal care and the overwhelming unhappiness caused by the mother's absence.

In a very real sense the patient felt so anxious about his masculine role that heterosexual experiences were too threatening and too laden with castration anxieties. That he ran from heterosexual experiences into homosexual ones was, therefore, not surprising. His (psychic) sexual impotence was defined by the incestuous needs.

The Rorschach was pathognomonic for a severe character disturbance in an individual whose self-concept was so inadequate that he had been unable to define a masculine role in life. He was latently homosexual. He was an aggressive, acting-out, hostile person, with an underdeveloped superego. He conceived of his battle against authority as one against the castrating paternal image. The Rorschach yielded a deeper insight into his motivations and suggested that the basic need was for dependency. His was a life of search for the satisfaction of a frustrated maternal dependency.

Clinical Summary

As noted in the social history, J. O.'s mother died in childbirth and he was given over to the protective care of his paternal grandmother. Also, from the time of his birth his father either ignored him or, after the grandmother's death, when the boy was taken into the fields to work, treated him cruelly.

Toward the boy, then, the father exhibited behavior that can only be labeled as vindictive. He treated J. O. as the one who killed his wife —and by so doing had robbed J. O. of his status as the only person in the family who had defied the parents and kept in their house a living reminder of this defiance of their authority.

Pathological interest was also shown the boy by the grandmother. To her, as to his father, J. O. represented the mother's killer; but here, appreciation was shown for this. To the grandmother J. O. represented a treasured image, someone on whom she could shower tenderness. He was the one who had served her by removing the living reminder of her son's infidelity.

A long-forgotten incident, revivified during a treatment hour, offered some substantiation of these inferences. It involved one of the infrequent conversations J. O. had had with his father and occurred at the time of his grandmother's death.

We were alone in Mama's bedroom. She was laid out on the bed. Deathly still. I was afraid to go near her. My father lifted me up to see her face. I cried. He slapped me. Don't cry he said. Look at her and go from here a man. You're no longer a baby. She's gone. You come with me to the fields now. You killed 2 women. Enough. Now you work.

It was in this climate of fear and hate that J. O. and his father formed their relationship. This unhappy experience with his father— so different from the overindulgent relationship with the grandmother —was probably the turning point in the boy's life. It was this that made him *hate*. The daily routine of working side by side with his father, comparing his own childish inadequacies with the strength and mastery of the father's manual skills, made its mark on the child. He not only hated his father for the physical and mental torture the man inflicted on him but also admired and envied the power and strength. This uncomfortable comparison between his own limitations and his father's abilities nurtured the seeds of his inadequacy feelings and made him long all the more for the protection of his grandmother's affection.

Unable to resolve his dependency needs, J. O. strove to compete with the father. Because this was impossible, he felt more inadequate and grew to hate him. Then, since the dangers inherent in aggressing against this powerful figure—who had already shown cruelty to him— required him to suppress his hostility, he took to subterfuge and petty aggression. It is not surprising, then, that he eventually escaped from this uncomfortable situation in which his inadequacies were so prominent and which carried with it the threat of castration.

From this home situation, J. O. was placed in an equally distasteful foster-parent situation. The difference between the two situations was more of degree than of kind. From the father's pathological cruelty he was transferred to an even more difficult situation in which he met with the uncompromising morality of his foster parents.

Thus all his experiences with parent figures were traumatic: first, the over-protection of the grandmother; next, the pathological vindictiveness of his father; and finally, the dictatorship of the foster parents. Each parental figure treated the boy with rigid insistence on obedience to his demands. None offered any personal independence. The people, then, from whom J. O. should have obtained concepts of socialization processes used him instead as the object of their own needs. Under such circumstances it was impossible for him to learn how to socialize, how to relate well with his environment, how to have a warm regard for the rights and feelings of others. Instead he developed a hiatus of such feelings (the so-called "superego lacunae"), and in place of warmth and relatedness his mentors actually taught him how to hate and how to inflict punishment on weaker persons than he. Thus, power became his leitmotif.

The days J. O. spent in the training school supplied him with further proof of the need for power and mastery. His cottage parents proved to be not too different from his previous parent surrogates. Experiences with fellow inmates emphasized the need for strength and the penalties of weakness. He soon learned that the only way to avoid being made the recipient of everyone's aggression was to become more pugnacious and brutal than they. He learned his lesson and reaped rewards of psychopathic behavior in the achievement of prestige, status, and much personal comfort—things that hadn't been his since his grandmother's death.

As a mere teen-ager, then, J. O. had lived more intensively than many persons. He had been the butt of rejection, immorality, deceit, and physical brutality. There is no indication of his ever having been the recipient of interested love, attention, security, or affection—other than the brief encounter with his grandmother in his earliest years. Thus we may now look at J. O. as an aggressive, hostile, consciously antisocial youth who seemed to be committed to unrelenting warfare against all authority. He preferred fighting to coöperating; he chose scheming rather than playing fairly. He needed to appease his power drive by engaging in more and more rebellious and reckless behavior, by trying to achieve prestige from criminal activity, by "proving" to everyone that he was "a man." Our data pointed all this out and suggested that such behavior could only have been an overcompensation for unconscious inadequacy feelings and a reaction formation to defend against an infantile self-concept.

In further substantiation of these clinical inferences it should be noted that J. O. suffered from premature ejaculation. The subject's nickname ("Jackie") was given to him by the prostitute with whom he had lived during those brief periods between incarcerations. She chided him on his "jack-rabbit" habits and coined the nickname "Jackie" for all to know. Instead of being angered by this derisive label, "Jackie" seemed to enjoy her perverse humor and adopted the name as though he felt the need to exhibit his psychic sexual impotence.

ADDENDUM

Although J. O. was 22 years old at the time these studies were conducted, his psychological growth was sorely lacking in comparable development. He was a child from almost every standard except the chronological.

Socially, he lacked those most elementary attributes of the socialization processes which serve to attune one to his environment. He was uncoöperative, surly, dogmatic, haughty, and uncontrollable. He showed no compassion toward his fellow beings and had no feelings of family rootedness.

Psychologically, his self-concept was one of severe inadequacy and contained doubts of his own masculinity. He felt rejected and unloved —showed no sense of belongingness—and, as such, was quite literally *alone*.

From the dynamics of the case, we noted that his earliest days were replete with overindulgence and affection. Thus from birth till about 5 years he showed comfortable development, and it is perhaps worth a conjecture to note that with all the trauma that followed him after these earliest years he never did break with realistic thinking. What course his psychic imbalance might have taken had he not had such indulgence in these primary years can, of course, only be guessed. It may be hypothesized that the strength to withstand the travail, with ego intact, can better be understood because he did at least receive an overly protective beginning.

When, at 5, the dependency on the grandmother was broken by her death, and in its stead he was subjected to the father's hostility and rejection, his dependency needs, which heretofore had been amply nurtured, were no longer nourished and were doomed to remain unsatisfied. It was the paternal image, then, toward whom the hate and rebelliousness were directed as the archenemy of his needs for dependency satisfaction. It was also the paternal image who, by his example of strength, skill, and masculinity, impressed J. O. with a sense of inadequacy, weakness, and femininity.

J. O.'s self-concept, then, representing his childishly conceived comparison between his father's masculinity and his own inadequacy, was laid down at a time when his libido was in a pregenital stage. The psychosexual fixation was at a phallic level of infantile sexuality.

May we not conclude, therefore, that his rebellion against all authority was symptomatic of a classical oedipal conflict, unresolved and in turmoil? He was fighting father—but not merely to defeat father *per se;* rather, the victory over father was for the love and affection of the mother image—for a revivification of that satisfying dependency status in which he spent his earliest years.

CHAPTER FIFTEEN

A Narcissistic Character

BY MARTIN MAYMAN

Introduction

Many of the case studies collected in this book illustrate a variety of well-defined syndromes for which generally accepted labels are available. The case I present here does not fit conveniently under any of the usual diagnostic tags. "Character disorder," "psychotic character," and "psychopathic personality with pathologic emotionality" have all been applied to Mr. W's illness at one time or another. Despite this nosological ambiguity, the disorder itself is a clearly defined one, familiar to every practicing clinician. In patients with this form of personality malformation, the distinction between psychosis and rationality sometimes becomes rather nebulous. Here is a patient who is not estranged from the world of social intercourse, as are so many schizophrenics, but whose judgment and impulse control are often so poor as to suggest a disturbance of near-psychotic degree.

The Initial Contact

Jack W. was 24 years old when he came to the hospital for evaluation and treatment shortly after his honorable discharge from the Army. The decision to come had been his, although it had been recommended by Army psychiatrists. He was a muscular, well-developed man of medium height, who gave as his reason for coming to a psychiatrist the fact that he had never been able to make friends or get along with his parents because of his aggressive behavior. He felt that his personality traits would prevent him from making a success of his life if they were not corrected.

He seemed tense, ill-at-ease, and exaggeratedly self-conscious, but he tried to mask his anxiety behind a loud, flip, sneering, and disdainful manner. He accepted interviews and examinations, but only on his own terms. The description of his interview with one of the senior psychiatrists is quite characteristic:

The patient entered my office with a friendly grin, threw his leather jacket on my couch and himself in the analytic chair, draped his feet over the arm of the chair and then asked me if I minded his behavior. He talked for almost the entire hour, ignoring my questions, or answering them in a rather ironical way, or answering them by another question. When he talked about his interviews with psychiatrists in the Army he stammered much more and laughed them off noisily. His pressure of speech hardly permits an exploration of his condition.

He is an ambitious, self-centered young man who says he is "widely read," knows something about everything and is able to keep up with anybody. But he says these things in a way which seems to ask, "Am I really very bad—How bad am I?" He complains about the Army psychiatrists because they wanted him to help himself and if he could do that he wouldn't need a psychiatrist, but then he admits that he doesn't know what psychotherapy really means and that he knows he is very difficult to handle. He tells me with a pseudo-gay grin that he isn't interested in anybody, that he never had real friends, that his sexual experiences have been limited to only a few adventures with prostitutes. He boasts about lying. When asked what his plans are he states that he wants to be wealthy and raise a family, but then admits that he cannot study or concentrate on anything unless he likes the subject very much, and he doubts whether in his present condition he will really be able to achieve much.

He seems very impulsive and he can not tolerate his anxiety which he tries to hide from himself as well as from others by noisy behavior and a display of relaxed self-confidence.

Mr. W. quickly succeeded in making himself disliked by both patients and staff by being sarcastic, taunting, demanding, and complaining. His air of casual disdain for others notwithstanding, he seemed to be painfully self-conscious. He was extremely jealous of other patients and pathologically alert to any evidence to support his conviction that he was being treated unfairly.

He seemed completely unable to keep from presenting himself in the worst possible light. When he succeeded in provoking nursing personnel, he would say he was delighted, but later would be found crying in his room.

One sample of his sarcasm and insistence, but also deep fear of rebuff, is this mockingly formal note he wrote to his doctor some months after admission.

Dear Doktor ———:

Would you please to be getting me, at morning conference, the optional choice of going in town Saturday *or* Sunday. I do not believe an explanation is due, except to say "I have no control over the elements, and my physical condition is not static."

Your Most Humble and Non-Obedient Servant,

JACK W.

Another such note, addressed to "Dr. P. & anyone who wants to read this," suggests how much depression and self-hate underlie his bitter provocativeness.

Dear Sir in charge of my mental, physical, and spiritual well-being:

This humble and obedient person wants from you, and the rest of this fine noble institution only "T.L.C." (tender loving care). The amount of "A" (aggression) that I possess is in the process of being re-channeled all the way back to my tender?, sweet?, and ever-loving? parents. Plus the producer (some 24 yrs ago) of that damn defective rubber.

It would make this unworthy, frustrated, easily rejected, meal ticket of four employees and half the psychiatric research in the U.S., very happy to be able to set foot on any part of the cow pasture until 2000 hours.

If my slightest whim is denied me I will torture myself by looking at this picture of "Lena the Hyena."

I wish to see you tomorrow. Anytime will do; just so long as it is 1030 hours.

. . . for I need company in Hell.

P.S. Throw your hat in the door first.

Attached to this letter was a newspaper cartoon of Lena the Hyena, and this note:

Dr. P. ———:

I am fully pissed off & confused—I have no desire to make any decisions—nor do I care to follow any made for me. I just want to go into a dormant stage and love myself to death. . . .

It was apparent that Mr. W. was quite sick, but it was not yet clear why he was compelled to behave as he did, and how he came to be the kind of person he was. Only on the basis of some such understanding could we hope to help him, so we attempted to get a detailed picture of his life. The following data are taken from the case abstract which was written two weeks after his arrival.

Historical Data

The patient was the chief informant, even though his parents did come to the hospital to be interviewed. His father added practically nothing to the history except that he thought his son "needed to be socialized." His mother gave only scanty answers to the infancy questionnaire.

The patient is an only child, born when his mother was 34 and his father 44 years old. The father said they had wanted a child but the pregnancy was not planned.

The patient's father, a successful, bad-tempered, 68-year-old retired jeweler, was the youngest of nine children. Born of poor immigrant parents, he had a grammar school education and is a "self-made man." There was little companionship between him and the patient, and he had frequently slapped his son's face. The patient in turn had defiantly tried to provoke his father's wrath. The father was stingy about small amounts of money for recreation and clothes, but generous when large sums are necessary for purposes such as the patient's hospitalization.

The patient's mother, a 58-year-old, meticulous housekeeper, wanted a girl when the patient was born and has "spoiled and spanked me at the same time." The patient said, "My mother's prime obsession is a house where everything must be ready for an inspection at any time." She nagged her son constantly, forced food upon him and bombarded him with countless admonishings to drive carefully, keep himself warm, wear his rubbers, *ad infinitum*. The patient considered her a neurotic hypochondriac. He reported that she never gave him any privacy. For example, she used to walk into the bathroom without knocking when he was there. She subjected him to many physical demonstrations of affection which he abhorred and she expected such demonstrations from him. The patient held her chiefly responsible for his personality problems.

In early childhood he had several operations complicated by infections. He attended kindergarten from 5 to 6 years of age and entered public school at 6. His earliest recollections went back to this age and all of them were unpleasant. All the memories were of painful incidents of being punished, ridiculed, or deprived. He said he was frequently tied to a tree with a clothesline and forbidden to try to break loose. Urinating in bed and dirtying his pants were disgraceful. His rabbit had to be shot, and his dog would not permit him to come near her puppies. "Even at that early age I remembered doing most everything by myself and it is during that time that I think my trouble began, logically centered around my home life." His play consisted of taking things apart. According to the parents, he was independent and spoiled, had crying temper tantrums when frustrated, and behaved better when his mother was not around. Both parents were extremely inconsistent in their discipline, on the one hand being indulgent or making unfulfilled threats, and on the other hand sending him off to military school for a year because he "needed the discipline."

At school and in summer camps he was always the butt of jokes and pranks. At 11 years of age he blinked his eyes excessively. When he was 12 years old he got a job in a store, but found out later that his father had paid the manager to hire him. The patient could recall feeling deeply chagrined at this discovery.

When he was 13, he had a marked growth of hair on his face but his mother would not permit him to shave and insisted that he use barber's clippers to remove it. Also at 13 he began masturbation which he has continued up to the present. His father told him that this habit would make him impotent, destroy his manhood, and ruin his physical health. He has worried for fear that it would result in sterility. Although he had dates with many girls he never had a steady girl friend. Five or six times he had intercourse with "sporting girls," but whenever he gets girls of any other type into a compromising situation, his "chivalrous impulses" prevent him from taking advantage of the situation. Several times he had homosexual relationships with men who approached him. The last occurred when he was 17 years old. When he masturbated he had phantasies of being attacked by a woman. This motif was also present in his dreams.

In the spring of 1939 he quarreled with his family about joining the Army. His father would have consented but was afraid his wife would divorce him if he did. The patient quit school and talked himself into many jobs but lost all of them because of personal relations. In the fall of 1939, at 18, he entered the Air Corps over his mother's objections. He became a proficient radio technician but he made no friends and "tried to work angles to get out of work." Consequently, he was often punished with KP duty and once drank a mixture of liquid soap and vinegar to make himself sick in order to avoid it.

In 1944, he was shot down over Holland and spent seven months as a prisoner of war. He suffered there from malnutrition, enteritis, tonsillitis, and pediculosis corporis.

Following his liberation and return to this country, he was granted a 75-day furlough. "During the seven months imprisonment I could think of nothing but home, but one moment after I got there, the three of us were embroiled in a bitter argument. Why? I stopped down town to buy a pair of shoes instead of coming right to the house. My mother was so nervous that her skin had broken out in a rash. A couple of weeks later father was laid up with a foot ailment. Home life was a round of arguments. I became jumpy, stayed away from home as much as possible, and took up with women much older than myself."

On his return to the Base, he found life increasingly monotonous and boring. He had no appetite; his stomach was continuously upset; he vomited, had headaches and some diarrhea. He was "apathetic and hostile at the same time." He went into town daily and got half-drunk in order to be able to eat, and he headed an agitation committee in order to get conditions improved at the Base for the ex-prisoners of war. While he was feeling his worst he played around with a razor blade, scratching the surface skin of his wrists. He says that he had no intention of really cutting his wrists and after a few minutes threw the razor blade away.

After three weeks he requested a physical examination in the hope of being sent to a convalescent hospital. However, he was hospitalized instead in a neuropsychiatric ward and given pentothal interviews. After one of these interviews he was "feeling high" and called another patient an S.O.B. "in a friendly way." The other patient slapped him in the face several times. He didn't respond at all but, a few minutes later, went to his room and had a two-hour "crying jag." This was the fifth or sixth such "crying jag" in his life and he said he was not able to control himself. He knew something was wrong but couldn't put his finger on it, and believed that it must go back to childhood. Two doctors told him about present clinic and he decided to go there as soon as he received his discharge, which was pending.

The extent of Mr. W's illness was probably not fully appreciated by us until after we had come to know him intimately from day-to-day contacts with him over a period of several months, during which time we could see how severely warped his adaptive patterns were in virtually every area of his life.

He seemed hungry for any small favors which might show that he was loved and accepted, yet he could not let people get close to him without deliberately trying to provoke them into rejecting him. He was rude to everyone, but particularly so to those whom he liked or needed. He called nurses by their first names or by nicknames such as "Stinky." He addressed the doctors with a brash familiarity, using their last names only and not their title.

He made many unnecessary demands, particularly about food. For months, he found fault with every meal and repeatedly told the nurses to record on his chart that he had eaten poorly. Actually, he ate voraciously, usually reordering at least once. He was often preoccupied with physical complaints, too, which he exaggerated and used as an attention-seeking device. His demands were met whenever possible and special attention was given to preparing his food, especially when he was upset.

Hostile, demanding, and self-destructive tendencies appeared in other forms, as well. He told his therapist about the "kleptomaniac" tendencies which beset him on his trips to town, but confessed this only after he felt he had successfully mastered these impulses.

He admitted to the therapist that he sometimes found sexual excitement by stimulating the genitalia of dogs and cats. With women, he often used sexual activity as a form of hostile teasing, especially if he could convince himself that they had antagonized him in some way. He would subtly get into their good graces, stimulate them sexually, and then leave them unsatisfied. This pattern of behavior was not unlike a pattern of behavior he attributed to his mother. Allegedly, she used to win his confidence about many intimate personal matters, then expose his tender points to her friends. He concluded from this that "friends can hurt you more than anybody else," that "anyone is likely to hurt you," and so he was "going to get the first crack in." At the time these confidences were emerging in treatment, he was experiencing repeated accidents and suffered a variety of physical injuries.

Psychological Test Findings

Psychological testing is a somewhat arbitrary procedure which brings into sharp relief important coping devices and weaknesses of the personality. Testing helps point up not only the major features of an individual's "ego structure," but also enables the psychologist to make inferences about the dynamic nucleus of the patient's conflicts which are sometimes revealed in fragments of fantasy which slip into the responses.

In Mr. W.'s case, the tests were helpful in bringing into sharper focus the nature and severity of his illness.

In the testing situation he was derogatory, supercilious, and glib. He tried to create the impression that he was master of the situation and in no way threatened or challenged by the test questions. When he didn't know an answer, he often made wild guesses with the air of someone who knows the answer very well and finds this test to be child's play.

The poignancy of this pathetic defensiveness was matched by the sense of isolation in a strange, inhuman, and hostile world which pervaded the microcosm-world he projected into the Rorschach ink-blots. The people he saw there were, almost without exception, alien, distant, ridiculous, or fantastic figures: Card I—"A witch," "also two people dancing; look like Russian women, Polish women," "A goblin"; Card III—"Two gremlins," "Two people pulling something apart—half people, half animal. The people seem to be nude"; Card V—"Devil's tail"; Card VI—"Two fantastic children at play . . . child, or else it could be a sheep"; Card IX—"Court jester," "A man playing the violin or holding the baby. Looks like the man is nude"; Card X—"A man in a robe who is jumping off—diving." In the 55-response protocol, the patient could find only one good FC response, underscoring his lack of capacity for warm responsiveness to other human beings.

There was a mass of evidence to suggest that Mr. W.'s relationships, rather than being based on a mutual give-and-take, were modeled largely upon oral-clinging, oral-chewing, and oral-devouring activities. On the Rorschach test, 11 percent of his responses were projected fragments of oral-aggressive associations or fantasies: Card III—"A dental plate"; Card IV—"A shark"; Card V—"A bone with some meat left on it"; Card VI—"A cat swallowing a bird," "Claws and pincers"; Card X—"A creature has another creature in its clutches." On the TAT, the story to Card 6MF (2nd ed.), was about a dinosaur which devours a party of people; and on Card 17M, the patient suggested, as one interpretation for the picture, that the girl might have forgotten to burn the wolfbane, is attacked by vampire bats, and subsequently becomes a vampire herself. To complete the picture, Mr. W. had association disturbances on almost all the oral words of the Word Association Test.

From this marked "oral fixation," we would infer that Mr. W.'s aggressions would tend to be expressed in spitting out of invectives, making "biting remarks," or "chewing people out." He would measure another person's love in terms of the amount of nutriment the person could supply. And in his relationships he would tend to engulf, or else be engulfed by, the other person. This is the most primitive kind of relationship one can have, and the prominence of these oral tendencies in Mr. W.'s record indicated the depth of his infantile fixation.

In a person whose relationships with others are as tenuous and warped as this man's, we would expect to find considerable confusion in the ego-identity, or ego-synthesis. There was some test evidence to bear out this expectation, particularly with respect to sexual-role confusion. As often occurs in such cases, the patient's TAT stories and Rorschach responses expressed a contempt for women and disgust for their bodies, while he seemed to yearn for a tender affectionate attachment to an older man.

Perhaps the most significant test finding concerned the degree of "ego weakness" in this case. The evidence indicated a grossly deficient ego structure which could easily give way to impulsive outbursts or psychotic lapses of reality testing. There was even some suggestion that the patient may already have had a psychotic episode some time before admission to the hospital, from which he had made a somewhat tenuous recovery. Many peculiar responses and peculiar distortions in word usage in the tests suggested that Mr. W. tended to slip from orderly rational thought into the more inappropriate confused or contaminated thinking which characterizes the psychotic state. For example, he said "protrudence" when he meant "protuberance," "wares" when he meant "silverware," "organic senses" for "sense organs." He said seclude means "to preconclude." He said a marriage license is to "standardize marriage," and later in the test that "chattel" referred to a mortgage or lien such as in "chattel marriage laws." Such garbling of words and ideas has been found often to be the residual scar of a healed over psychotic episode. When such evidences of ego weakness are associated with signs of pent-up precariously controlled aggression, such as were found in Mr. W.'s tests, then there is reason to anticipate the occurrence of intense, diffusely directed aggressive outbursts when the already brittle ego controls reach a breaking point.

316 MARTIN MAYMAN

Psychodynamic Configuration and Contingent Treatment Program

Probably the most conspicuous feature of this young man's personality was his self-absorption or "narcissism." He seemed so completely immersed in himself and his own needs as to preclude the possibility of any significant investment of interest in any other human being.

This patient, like so many similar patients, loved and ministered to himself precisely because he had come to feel that there was no one else to do this for him. The narcissistic self-absorption fills an inner void which exists when one has failed to acquire a conviction of love-ableness, belongingness, and personal worth. Mr. W. seems to have failed very early to find the ego-bolstering, self-actualizing relationships with others, especially his parents, which make for a basic sense of well-being and personal worth. Instead of a sense of kinship with fellow human beings, he seems to have developed a sense of lonely isolation and unloveableness and the accompanying chronic expectation of impending disappointment or desertion.

Feeling starved for love from a very early age, he grew up in a state of chronic frustration and anger. The inconsistent discipline exerted by his parents made it difficult for him to learn to discipline himself, so he gave vent, in both direct and indirect ways, to his rage. But this behavior only tended to provoke still more rejection and so served to prove to him that he was justified in expecting only disappointment of his wish to be loved.

Eventually he adopted substitute behavior patterns for what should have been positive relationships with parents and friends. He became caustic and provocative, as if to say, "No matter what I do, you will not love me, so I may as well be as obnoxious as I can. That way, you will *have* to pay attention to me." The insatiable quality of his need for attention may be gauged by the enormous "oral" preoccupation on his psychological tests on the one hand, and by the profusion of his irritating ways on the other hand: talkativeness, complaintiveness, sarcasm, stammering, braggadocio. But he had become totally unable to ask for love in any manner other than his peculiarly inverse approach.

All these maneuvers really brought him little more than a reinforced sense of desolation seen most clearly on those occasions when he withdrew to his room and broke into tears. He may have gotten some relief from guilt feelings when he provoked the wrath of others. Perhaps also he got some revenge against his parents and the world through his behavior, but this can only have provoked more feelings of guilt and un-worthiness which led in turn to more self-defeating behavior.

Through it all, Mr. W. sought to hide his hurt. So often, he seemed to say by his attitude, "All this means nothing to me, so I have nothing to lose," and he proceeded to behave accordingly. Over his deep nar-cissistic wound—the deep-rooted conviction that he was unloved and unloveable—Mr. W. added more and more defensive layers to an al-ready ugly and obnoxious scab.

Chronically simmering rage in this lonely, love-hungry man finally threatened to come to a dangerous boil. We may presume that he was dimly aware that his ever-mounting tension might culminate in a psychotic break.

The initial diagnosis given for this condition was "character dis-order, psychopathic personality," but this was changed at the staff conference to "psychotic character"—a term reflecting more accu-rately the precarious balance and deeply malignant distortions in this patient's personality. The treatment recommendation was for contin-ued hospitalization and special psychotherapy. It was anticipated that treatment would be a turbulent process, and that the steady, control-ling environment of the hospital would be a necessary condition for treatment.

The immediate objective of the treatment program was to establish Mr. W. in a friendly and consistent setting. There, with the help of a psychotherapist, it was hoped that he would find more wholesome out-lets for his intense, pent-up rage, and would grow secure enough to permit himself to find closer, warmer, more mutual and more endur-ing ties with people. According to the psychotherapy supervisor, "The key to this type of person is to find a therapist who can really like him despite all of his obnoxiousness. Then the obnoxiousness will abate, and in the atmosphere of security the patient will be able to talk about his early disillusionment and thwartings. He will find that he can, for once, be himself without being punished or disliked."

Yet acceptance of him did not mean giving him license to "act out" in aggressive or self-destructive ways. In coming to the hospital, he implicitly asked for controls. Usually, in such cases, the psychothera-pist must be both accepting and controlling, and must be constantly alert to protect the patient when feelings of rage or fear well up in the patient and threaten to overwhelm him. Patients with such a severe "character disorder"—i.e., with this form of ego weakness—are much like young children who are similarly vulnerable to tides of feeling which may well up and overthrow rationality and controls.

Course of the Illness

Mr. W. was hospitalized at a private psychiatric hospital for a period of thirteen months. He seemed to improve steadily, with only minor set-backs, for eleven months. The attitude which the staff tried to maintain with him was one of active friendliness, with praise for achievements and indulgence of his requests. His aggressive, rude behavior was to be accepted without annoyance or retaliation by all the personnel. Gradually he became able to accept their friendliness and give some in return. His tension and hostility were channeled as much as possible into vigorous activities. When tension would build up, he often asked to have extra time at the punching bag or in some active sport.

He reacted surprisingly well when his first therapist left the staff. This could have stirred up rather intense feelings of rage. Instead, his transfer to the new therapist was smooth and uneventful. He quickly became greatly attached to his new therapist, and his behavior in the hospital continued to improve. He was less demanding, and frequently reported with pride how he controlled his hostile feelings toward others.

He began to use his good behavior to win the support and approval of his doctors. In the fall he was considered well enough to attend the nearby college while continuing to live at the hospital. He was quite pleased over how well he did there, and was elated one day when he got a perfect grade in a quarterly examination.

Two days later the first serious relapse occurred. He returned to the hospital mildly drunk and extremely combative. He was moved to the closed ward. Three days later he was still combative, tearful, and flooded with self-destructive thoughts and impulses. Within a week, this disturbance subsided, but a month later, he began again to grow disturbed. This time he himself asked to be moved to the closed ward. Within a few days, special precautions were necessary. He was depressed, agitated, destructive, and suicidal. Continuous narcosis treatment was instituted for a five-day period. Under this treatment, he was confused most of the time and abreacted some traumatic prisoner-of-war experiences. Following this the disturbance again subsided but only for little more than a week, when he again lost control and had to be transferred to another hospital where there were better facilities for looking after such acutely disturbed patients.

There are several factors which may have caused this relapse. Mr. W.'s rapid progress to semi-outpatient status and his initial successes at school may have been more of a strain on his integrative capacities than had been supposed, especially since his therapy at that time was dealing with the particularly painful subject of his excessive self-love and his intense need for approval and love from others. He was also faced with the homosexual threat posed by an increasingly close relationship with his therapist.

Perhaps most important of all was the fact that his therapist at this time began to make plans to leave. The patient did not know anything about this, but there may have been a subtle change in the therapist's attitude which unconsciously warned this extremely sensitive young man that another major disappointment was imminent. Or perhaps it was only that the therapist was going to be away for a week and so Mr. W. would be alone at Christmas time. The therapist's final note before the patient's transfer is particularly revealing:

This patient has not been seen in therapy interviews since December 19, the day I left on my vacation. In the past week the patient has been extremely upset and quite destructive. He was never physically aggressive toward me although he tried to provoke a fight with me. In his interviews during this disturbed period he has often played a record of "The Whiffen Poof Song" in which the "poor little lamb" portrayed how he felt. He called it his theme song. He said that he would break that record last, and if that record ever got broken then I'd better start running. This was said after I pointed out to him that like the "lamb" he felt very young and very dependent and very frightened. In one of the interviews this past week, after a most upsetting day, he started for me as I came into the room as though he were going to fight. As he reached me, I held my arms out and he collapsed and wept on my shoulder. I carried him over to the bed and helped him to lie down. He talked quietly and shyly like a very little boy with a sort of sweet tenderness. The day I left I brought him a Christmas present, because he had told me that he had never had a Christmas present given him that he had not asked for. The year before, the Clinic had sent him a box of candy for Christmas and then charged it to his bill as he discovered later. This so enraged him while he was talking about it that it had obviously been a severe trauma. I brought him a can of Briggs tobacco which carries the slogan, "When a fellow needs a friend." He thanked me, said that it was of special value to him, that he appreciated my giving it to him and would keep it. He wanted me to tell his hospital doctor that he didn't want the can of tobacco removed and I left word with the hospital that if at all possible it should not be taken out of the room. He was obviously upset by the fact that I was going to leave for a week and would not be with him on Christmas. I told him I would think about him and wanted him to have as good a Christmas as possible.

The crisis reached its peak two weeks after the first episode. The day after the therapist's departure, Mr. W. became increasingly agitated and on December 26 he was transferred.

On admission there he was loud, abusive, obscene, and markedly suspicious. His pressure of speech was so marked that it was impossible to interrupt him. He seemed very fearful, and attacked another patient who approached him to ask for a cigarette. He told an aide he was afraid because he did not know what was about to happen, and that he might have another "episode of hallucinations," probably referring to the abreaction of some war experiences while under sedation at the hospital from which he had come.

Mr. W.'s agitation subsided quickly and he was transferred to an open ward three weeks later.

This break was the last such eruption so far as we know. Mr. W.'s recovery was resumed at this second hospital where he remained for six more months. His doctor there was a forceful, warm, down-to-earth man who was direct and yet protective, a kind of good-natured big brother who talked with Mr. W. only about concrete events and not about deeper motives, feelings, and defenses.

In June, six months after his admission to the second hospital, the patient was given a ninety-day furlough to visit his uncle. He stayed with the uncle for about a month and then, at the uncle's expense, took a trip which took him to Mexico, the Southwest United States, and back to his starting point. The patient reported that his stay with his uncle had been pleasant and that they had had nice talks. On the trip he had had many heterosexual experiences, met many different people and "I enjoyed them all and did not antagonize any of them.

I did not seem to reject them as much as I would have six months ago." He had a pleasant stay with his parents. He felt that they were trying to understand him and that he, on his part, could understand both his mother and father much better and was better able to tolerate them.

Mr. W. was discharged from the hospital, but continued to see his doctor twice a week for a short period after discharge. He then returned to college with the intention of obtaining a B.A. degree. He roomed at one of the college dormitories, and seemed to be doing well, except for the return of some nail-biting and stammering which he attributed to the insecurity he felt in this new situation.

Follow-Up Data

Our information about Mr. W.'s subsequent adjustment is scant. He did obtain his B.A. degree four years later and went on to graduate school. Two years after treatment, he got married, and a year later had a child.

Development of a Neurotic Fear
of Contamination

BY GERALD R. PASCAL and
CARL N. SIPPRELLE

Introduction

The case presented in this chapter illustrates several fairly well-established principles used in clinical psychology. As one reads the case material he will note the subtle influences which had been brought to bear on the patient, resulting in his acquiring enduring habits and attitudes about the self, mother, father, contemporaries, etc. Neither the patient nor his parents were aware of this learning, but the patient had learned these "emotional" habits just as surely as he had learned to walk and talk. It would seem that the patient was well fed, well cared for, and undoubtedly loved; yet a persistent accumulation of pernicious influences inevitably led to a set of habits which, by the principle of generalization, only needed the "correct" stimulus situation to be evoked in later life.

We also see in this patient the development of defense mechanisms, ways of reacting which were calculated to obviate the effects of the habits and attitudes of which he was unaware. For instance, emotional habits such as "fear of females" and "feelings of inadequacy as a male" resulted in defensive habits, "avoidance of intimate relations with females" and "intellectual superiority," respectively.

The reader will note that as the patient's adult life situation approximates more and more closely the situation which obtained during his childhood, he tends to respond in a manner similar to that of his child-hood. The more this latter condition prevailed, the more tendency for the patient to keep adding defenses, some of which we label "symp-toms." The reader will also note the development of symbols and sym-bolic behavior as a defense against unacceptable emotional habits.

The principles of behavior developed in the psychological laboratory are the same principles governing behavior in real life. So-called "emo-tional habits" follow the same rules of acquisition and extinction as other, simpler habits studied in the laboratory. Thus, for the habits in question, we would, using the principle of generalization, predict that the more the patient's environment approached that of the original learning situation, the more he would tend to react in a similar man-ner. For the patient described here, the stimulus situation obtaining after his marriage was similar to a previous one, and his response to his wife was predictable. Principles derived from the laboratory science of psychology were used not only to "understand," diagnose, and pre-dict the patient's behavior but also to treat the patient.

In presenting this case, it is planned to briefly describe the patient and the difficulties causing him to seek psychological help. Next, the patient's history, emphasizing the stimuli and the resultant learning basic to his neurosis, will be presented. Then the projective tests will be related to the patient's personality structure and neurosis as it is seen developing historically from childhood. Finally, the case will be formulated to present a picture of the personality structure, its devel-opment, continuation, and possible restructuring through therapy.

Initial Complaints

The patient was a physical scientist with a Ph.D. He was about average in size, neat and well dressed, friendly and at ease. He was married, had one child, and was employed in a responsible position in keeping with his training. On the job he had been functioning effi-ciently despite phobic symptoms and intense anxiety. However, when he sought treatment his symptoms were beginning to be severe enough to make his work extremely difficult and at times impossible. The phobia included a fear that he would become contaminated bacterio-logically in some insidious way. He felt there would be no way of knowing of his condition until it progressed to a point where his death would be inevitable. At times the fear involved a possibility that his son, aged 10, would also become contaminated. Anxiety related to his fears was severe and persistent, causing him to compulsively defend himself by precautions around food and objects he might come in contact with, and by chronic worrying. He would worry about such things as whether he had paid his car insurance, locked the door, or turned out the lights. At times he was forced to return many miles to his place of employment to make sure that he had put his work away properly or locked the door. He continuously sought medical assurance that he was not contaminated and became very anxious about such things as little blemishes or pimples on his person. He would wash his hands so frequently that they became red and chapped. To smoke a cigarette which had been dropped on the floor, or to take a drink when the ice cubes had been placed in it by someone's bare hand, was completely beyond him and he marveled at anyone who could do this. The patient likened his anxiety to a brush pile requiring all his time to avoid any possible sparks from the environment which might light it. When he was not compulsively taking defensive measures, he would worry for fear the brush pile would be ignited despite him. In his own words: When he was not afraid, he was afraid he would be afraid.

The patient knew his fears were neurotic in nature. However, he also knew that his precautions and constant checking were necessary to avoid anxiety and that if he attempted to ignore the "brush pile" long hours of anxiety were inevitable. Thus, it was clear from the beginning that he was suffering from a quite circumscribed phobia, which permitted him some control over anxieties otherwise uncontrollable by his present repertoire of defensive behavior.

The patient's symbol for the phobia was at times a "brush pile." At other times he described it as the feeling he got in imagining a "fur-lined tea cup." In the next section his life will be presented historically to show how the difficulties basic to the phobia were learned and combined symbolically as a fear of contamination.

It all started about 35 years ago. At that time the family was living in a large city where father was profitably operating his own manufacturing business. The family was Jewish and lived in an area not quite up to their socioeconomic level in an attempt to maintain their identity as Jews. Although father was what might be described as a dynamic, stern, hustling kind of man, it was apparently the mother who, in large measure, was dominant, particularly in matters pertaining to the home and family.

The family consisted of mother, father, and two older siblings—a brother fifteen years older and a sister eight years older. Before presenting a chronological account, the family will be described briefly to clarify their effects on the growing boy.

Family Relationships

Mother. As is usually the case, she was the significant person in his early life. Yet the patient was able to remember very little about her, describing his thoughts of her as being like a picture, remote and unreal. She had a marked tendency to hypochondriasis, constantly dramatizing her anxieties via somatic complaints. These physical complaints were presented with considerable histrionics and made a lasting impression on the boy. Another reflection of mother's domineering ways was the patient's statement that she literally had a "cat-o'-nine-tails" to use in disciplining her children. She attempted to use him as a source of vicarious satisfaction for her status needs by insisting on topnotch achievement scholastically and in other ways. Achievement was expected but not rewarded. She took his successes as signs of her own superiority but used his failures as evidences of his own inadequacy. The closest he could come to love from her was to avoid her displeasure. In talking about his mother the patient expressed fear of her, hostility toward her, and a strong desire for approval.

Father. Small, bustling, stern, he was certainly far from sensitive to the needs of a growing boy. He was not actually the strong figure he worked so hard to be. In their particular culture, the father is customarily an autocrat, ruling the family with a firm hand. In this family mother apparently had usurped that role. He turned almost completely to business, an area where this humiliating condition was reversed. Business, business trips, and the country club kept him away from the family for much of the time. When home his sternness and tendency to take out his frustration by criticizing his son offered little chance for a good identification with father and instilled a deep feeling of inadequacy in the boy.

Brother. With fifteen years separating the two brothers, they had little in common. Brother, like father, could take his frustrations out on the junior member of the family. At the same time, he was older and could do things to please mother. As the first-born, he seemed to achieve in mother's affections a place so firm that the patient could not displace him.

Sister. Eight years older than the patient, she, too, was remote enough in age to offer little support. She tended to treat her little brother as a doll, sometimes playing with him, sometimes doing things for him, and at times joining with her playmates to tease him unmercifully. He had more warmth and affection for her than for any other member of the family, despite her manipulation of him. Probably the manipulation, when it met her needs, was pleasant, such as the occasions when she would take him outdoors to play or to the movies.

Chronological Development

Home to this patient was customarily an apartment in a crowded big city. The neighborhood was Jewish and usually the family lived close to relatives. He described their home as comfortable but gloomy and somber.

Early childhood was marked by repeated abandonment. A succession of nursemaids were employed to care for the child, and each, in turn, became mother to him. However, each in turn left. With father away most of the time and mother represented by a substitute, the feeling of insecurity was reinforced as each nursemaid came to be needed and then disappeared, to be replaced by another.

He thought of his childhood home as a gloomy, dark, cavernous place where he was not allowed to play because it would disturb mother. Forced as a child to go to the homes of his playmates, he perceived their homes as friendly, cheerful places. Home was also a place of rejection. He repeatedly told of his parents promising to take him to a Sunday matinee after they had a nap. They would then go to sleep for the afternoon while he waited impatiently, afraid to awaken them, and horribly frustrated by the growing knowledge that this was to be another example of being let down.

The family lived in a rough neighborhood where a boy must, at times, fight and defend his right to play in the street. Here our patient fell down terribly. He was unable to compete. He was unable to be comfortable and secure with his peers. There was some initial attempt to find friends and playmates; but when the family moved to another neighborhood when he was about 8 years old, he gave up and became an isolate. From then on, sand-lot baseball, traveling with a gang, and all the skills so important in the socialization of a growing boy were denied him. Here began the development and reinforcement of feelings which later were to emerge as "inadequacy as a man."

An example of his frustration at this time centered around having a bicycle, an absolute necessity in his neighborhood. Although he was old enough to have one, a cousin of his, living nearby, was not. As the cousin wept at the thought of not having one, the patient's parents decided that he would continue to ride his tricycle to avoid hurting the cousin's feelings. This, and similar episodes, taught him to feel that mother was more concerned with the feelings of others than with him.

Mother was a hypochondriac given to worrying about her health and dramatizing herself with illness when under stress. From her he learned to avoid dirt and disease through scrupulous cleanliness. This behavior was reinforced by a severe attack of typhoid fever in about the first grade of school. He was extremely ill and all his hair fell out. When he returned to school, behind in his class work and baldheaded, he was particularly vulnerable to the ridicule of his classmates. He lost school time just when his classmates were learning to read. He remembered the first years of school as a time when he was forced to make a difficult adjustment outside of the family, under the handicap of being teased as a "baldy" and being unable to read like the others.

He studied hard, caught up to his class, and from then on embarked on a course of intellectual compensation. Even this was not wholly successful. While it earned a certain amount of respect from mother and teacher, it also made him more remote from boys and girls his age. They regarded him with mixed feelings composed of "sour grapes" and downright hostility at his tendency to be the first one in the room to raise his hand to answer a question.

Summers the family would go to the seashore. Here the other boys and girls spent their afternoons sunning themselves on a raft in the water. The patient lacked the confidence to swim out, finally gave up and talked himself into thinking he preferred fishing. Thus, he spent his afternoons with a group of old men on a breakwater fishing. Although he felt isolated and alone, he also felt proud in being accepted by adults and continued to enjoy fishing the rest of his life.

He was also exposed to the sometimes grim business of summer camp in early childhood. Sister had gone to camp and enjoyed it; a cousin was attending camp. So to the camp he had to go, despite his complete resistance to the idea. He summarized his feelings about camp by recalling that he was always the last one when sides were chosen for competitive games. He could never amass enough points in handicrafts or sports to come close to one of the awards the summer camps used to motivate their campers. He struck out, sank, and had his knots come untied through two summers of thorough and complete misery.

Another problem which contributed to his feelings of inadequacy was that the descent of his testicles was retarded. At a time when other boys were proud of their genitals and completely at ease in the gymnasium and shower room, he was continually fearful that his apparent deficiency would be discovered. Although the missing testicles later made a belated appearance and he learned that such things happen, the humiliation and shame stayed with him. To be baldheaded or testicleless, even temporarily, is no joke to a growing boy who is striving to be just as much like the others as he can.

Gradually his feelings of inadequacy as a man, athletically, physically, and sexually, became compensated for by intellectual achievement. He had the ability to excel in school and used it to gain some measure of acceptance with mother and teachers. To him physical adequacy, popularity, and all the things he couldn't get became signs of intellectual inadequacy and were ridiculed. As one might expect, he was unable to succeed in heterosexual endeavors. Because of his rejecting and domineering mother and teasing sister, and because he felt inadequate and incomplete as a man, girls were just too formidable. Although he wanted and tried periodically to attain comfortable relationships with girls, he increasingly fell back on ridicule of them and a hostile, intellectualizing, scorning approach to the feminine sex.

When he finished high school, he was academically well prepared to attend a noted technological school. However, because of his extreme youth, he was advised to wait another year. He attended a college in his home city for one year and then went on to the university of his choice, where he quickly and easily acquired a B.A. and an M.A. degree. He perceived college as offering him a new chance in life and resolved to make the best of it. He changed his name to a version which was much more "American" sounding and did not reveal his Jewish origin. He had dates, learned to drink and to dance, and acquired the social graces expected of a college student. However, his personality was by then well fixed in some ways. Although he could manage to come out of his shell and drop a lot of his supercilious, intellectualizing scorn of things social, it did not come easily to him. By then his fear and hostility toward females, fear of sexuality, inadequacy as a man, and expectations of rejection were firmly fixed. These attitudes, in conflict with his intense and well-fought battle to be like other people, gave rise to considerable anxiety.

His attitudes toward sexual contacts at this time reveal the incipient phobia. In fantasy and in practice, his behavior was defensive. He could enjoy the company of girls, became outwardly comfortable around them, and even had some success in his relationships with them. However, he could not, in fact or fantasy, go beyond the stage of petting. Sex to him had to stop short of sexual intercourse. If he stopped there, he was safe.

His first compulsive hand washing followed an occasion in which he had manipulated the genitals of a girl he picked up in a motion-picture theater. He became terribly anxious, feared he had contracted syphilis on his hands, and repeatedly washed them with very hot water and soap. This behavior alleviated his anxiety. In time he became aware that hand washing, for some unknown reason, would reduce or even prevent anxiety. He resorted to it whenever he became anxious until his hands were chapped and sore. From here the hand washing defense gradually evolved into a need for scrupulous cleanliness in all ways, and he began to anxiously avoid all possible forms of contamination. The leftovers on his plate, the dirt on his shoes, and the fishy smell in his fishing creel (an interesting symbol in itself) all became dangerous and to be avoided as a defense against anxiety.

After he received his M.A. degree he attended another large university where he earned a Ph.D. The competition there was intense. He became discouraged and wanted to quit but was urged to continue by his adviser and a girl friend whom he was later to marry.

He felt that Jews were discriminated against in science and that they could compete on equal terms only if employed in the mercantile field. This belief seems to indicate an attempt at identification with father. As a boy, father had been scornful of his son, had little to do with him, and showed partiality to the sister. Father took the sister on business trips with him, leaving the boy with his mother for long periods of time. Yet the boy spent all his free time at the father's factory in an effort to learn the business and to see more of father. His academic success did not impress the father or mother. He became severely depressed while finishing graduate school because by now he felt committed to a course which he did not want. He cheated in his doctoral prelims and used this as further evidence for his inadequacy and guilt.

After getting his degree he married the girl he met in graduate school. She was attractive, stable and intelligent, and non-Jewish. Marrying her was at least partially in defiance of his parents and their background. By now his phobia was well developed and sufficiently disguised so that he was able to have what appeared to be a very comfortable and satisfying marital sexual adjustment with no fears of the female genitals. However, the hand washing became more compulsive and he spent more and more time anxiously avoiding any possible source of contamination both at work and at home. Gradually his defenses, which initially began as care to avoid contamination, became generalized until he became careful as an end in itself. Compulsive perfection in all ways had a defensive value. Thus a scratch on the fender of his car could cause unbearable anxiety. Every detail of everything he said or did or owned had to be perfect.

His superior intellectual ability and meticulous attention to detail paid off professionally, so that he was rapidly advanced to positions of greater and greater responsibility. The higher he climbed professionally the more inadequate he felt. This intensified his need for defenses, and the lurking brush pile became more and more ominous and ever present. The slightest mistake could mobilize anxiety and set off a flurry of compulsive meticulousness, hand washing, checking and rechecking of work, and other activities of like nature. He gradually rose to an administrative position requiring increased delegation of responsibility. He found it almost impossible to trust anyone. He was unable to accept anything without checking it himself.

When he applied for therapy his compulsive meticulousness and worry about contamination had become so severe that he believed people were beginning to be aware of how severely handicapped he was.

RORSCHACH SUMMARY

R = 75

W = 8	M = (—1)(+4)	H = 3	Ay = 1	F% = 65
DW = 1	FM = (—3)(+4)	Hd = 4	Hh = 2	F +% = 71
D = 57	CF = (+1)	A = 22	Sci = 2	H% = 9
DdD = 1	FC = (—6)(+6)	Ad = 8	Nα = 1	A% = 40
DdDs = 1	FY = (—1)(+6)	Ls = 3	Cl = 1	S = 2
Dd = 7	FT = (+3)	Pr = 3	Cq = 1	P = 11
Ap = (W)D:Dd	FV = (—1)	Imp = 3	Mu = 1	W/M = 9/5
Seq. = Irreg.		Fi = 1	Bt = 2	EB = 5/7
Col. Index = 50%		An = 9	Sx = 1	Tot T = 45'
		Geo = 3	Fd = 1	T/R = 36"
		Art = 1		T/FstR = 7"

331

Projective Tests

The diagnostic interview, the essence of which has been previously given under history, was followed by the projectives. In this case the patient was given the Rorschach, Thematic Apperception Test, and Draw-A-Person tests.

Rorschach. On the Rorschach 75 responses were given, making it too lengthy to include in this presentation. However, the Rorschach summary sheet is presented to permit the reader some overall picture of the test.

TIME QUANTUM

	T/FstR	Tot. T		T/FstR	Tot. T
I	3"	180"	VI	5"	300"
II	7"	225"	VII	15"	225"
III	4"	180"	VIII	13"	285"
IV	4"	195"	IX	7"	525"
V	4"	105"	X	4"	480"

Perhaps the first impression one gains in examining the psychogram is that although this man is a patient, with a felt need for help, his psychogram does not give an impression of too ominous a picture in terms of psychological deficit and inadequate functioning. In scanning the record we note that the 9W are not in accord with the total R of 75 and his undoubted intellectual ability. He is having trouble intellectually in dealing with stimuli from the environment in the adaptive way expected in a man of his talent. The M/C ratio indicates a nearly ambiequal personality with a nice balance between inner and outer living and a 50 percent color index to emotional stimuli. FM equal to 7, and greater than M, is mirroring a tendency to childish thinking and unfinished psychological business. The preponderance of FC over CF in a personality of this potential richness, as revealed by 21 kinds of content, seems to mirror a certain amount of overcaution in the face of emotional stimuli. Again, FY, FT, and FV balance nicely against the chromatic determinants, indicating a fair balance between inner living and outer action. F% and F+% are within normal limits, although they show some tendency to constriction in the face of emotional stimuli and a tendency to be somewhat on the unconventional side. A low H% seems to reflect a certain touchiness or oversensitivity to people, who are a threat and to be avoided. Examination of the time scores gives an impression of a rather freely functioning but careful man who was upset by the female figures of Card VII and by the sudden impact of color on Cards II and VIII.

All in all, the psychogram is not readily identified as a neurotic one. Anyone who has tested very many "normal" people has seen worse ones. One could interpret this as an indication that the phobic defense, up until the time when stresses became too great, was reasonably adequate in permitting this man to function in his environment. He has not accumulated extreme psychological scars of the nature of faulty perception, narrowed range of interests, or deviant balance between spontaneity and constriction. Touchiness with people, immaturity of thinking, and a lowered ability to integrate stimuli from the environment are the chief indications that all is not well in a man who at first inspection would seem to be functioning quite adequately.

Analysis of the content of the responses indicates a fearful attitude to a world seen as biting and dangerous. There was preoccupation with anatomy responses of a dysphoric type, usually including intestines, stomachs, and other visceral organs. These seem to be reflecting his continued preoccupation and defensiveness against bacteriological infection. The Rorschach bears out the expected hostility to and fear of females and anxiety and inadequacy relative to male figures. Also notable is a tendency to perceptions indicating a feminine orientation to the world such as clothing, flowers, and making the M responses females. No really bizarre responses were given, although a few were somewhat on the personalized side.

The Rorschach, then, presents a picture of a man of superior intellectual ability but with some impairment in functioning due to heightened sensitivity to emotional stimuli. He is fearful of the world and concerned with his own physiological welfare. Females are feared and hated and he feels inadequate as a male figure, showing many evidences of a feminine orientation. Reality testing ability is adequate, his defenses of intellectualizing and avoidance are not overly crippling, and he is best described as having problems of neurotic intensity.

Draw-A-Person. The Draw-A-Person Test was administered with instructions simply to draw a person. When this was done the subject

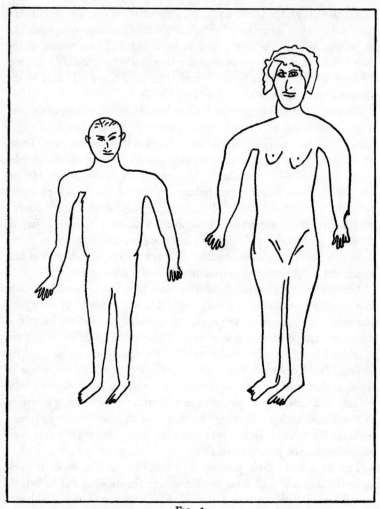

FIG. 1

This is a smug man, self-confident   This is a cheerful, energetic, and
and arrogant.   thoughtful woman.

was requested to draw a person of the opposite sex. The drawings were
done on separate pieces of typing paper and were fairly large, the male
one being about six inches in height. The male figure was drawn first.
The drawings have been reproduced side by side to expedite comparisons between them.

One is immediately struck by the fact that this man perceives females as larger and more powerful than males. The female seems to have small, ungiving breasts and a rather large and threatening vagina. Both drawings consist principally of an encapsulated body, separated from the environment by a solid and continuous line. This could be representing the patient's fear of his environment as a threatening and potentially poisoning place which must be partitioned off or excluded from the inner person. If that interpretation is reasonable we might really go further and note that in both drawings the only break in the circumscribing line is in the genital area. This fits the patient's perception of the genitals as the breach in his defensive wall through which he was being contaminated.

His comment on the male: "This is a smug man, self-confident and arrogant" reflects the role that he had tried to play in life through achievement and a sort of hostile aloofness in behavior. The comment on the female: "This is a cheerful, energetic and thoughtful woman" is flattering but superficial. It is in contradiction to his feelings about females as seen in the history and Rorschach and points up the disparity between his conscious and unconscious perception of them.

Thematic Apperception Test. The Thematic Apperception Test added little beyond confirmation of the inferences already made. His compensatory aspirations for success and achievement as a cover for inadequacy as a man were evident. Sex was handled gingerly and suspiciously as though the stories were reflecting his unconscious feelings of danger in that area. The stories were sometimes given in a formal, easygoing burlesque of real life to deny his anxieties.

His story to Card 17BM, a picture of a man climbing or descending a rope, reflects his underlying feelings:

This is a gymnasium meet and this is a boy who is trying a rope climb. If he can win the rope climb his class can win the meet. The boy is lame, he can't compete in other sports, and so he has never been able to be a source of enthusiasm for his classmates. He has never felt the admiration showered on basketball players, football players and swimmers. But today, if he can win the last event his class will win the meet, and then, he will share in the lime-light with the boys who succeed at other sports, and so he is climbing just as fast as he can. But yet, he doesn't win; disappointed and dejected, he leaves, and no one stops him. No one pats him on the back. No one wishes him well, and so he goes his solitary way, limping through life, misshapen, feeling unwanted and unloved.

In this story one can easily detect the terrific longing for adequacy and the acceptance he feels it will bring, and one can see his perception of himself as an inadequate, crippled, unaccepted person. He states an important lack in his life when he claims to have never felt the admiration which he feels has been showered on more successful people.

Case Formulation

In this section we have the task of attempting to integrate our data in a manner which will make "understandable" the patient's behavior. To do this we need a systematic frame of reference based on known principles of human behavior, principles which when applied to the individual case make the patient's present behavior a logical prediction from a series of known events.

We will make two broad assumptions which will involve us in the consideration of two classes of variables. On the one hand, we will assume that the human organism, like other organisms in a cultural medium, needs to maintain a satisfactory state of equilibrium in the culture within which it lives in order to survive. It needs to react "satisfactorily" with the environment in order to maintain its integrity. From this basic physiological fact, the need to maintain the integrity of the organism, a whole host of psychological needs basic to our culture can be derived: the need to be safe from physical attack, to be secure, to be loved, to belong to a group, to obtain prestige, etc. (2, 3, 4). In addition to these needs, there are needs particular to specific subcultures. When the organism is deprived of satisfaction for any such need, there is a tendency for it to be responsive to stimuli in the environment which may lead to the satisfaction of the deprived need to the exclusion of other stimuli in the environment. Such a tendency to be over-reactive to stimuli connected with the deprived need and unresponsive to other stimuli in the environment may lead to deviant behavior. Thus a student overly anxious to belong to a particular fraternity in order to satisfy status needs may behave in a manner considered deviant by his peers who are considering him for inclusion in their group.

The other broad assumption we will make is that in the course of a life history the human organism acquires a set of habits and attitudes; that is, it acquires experiences with particular stimulus situations which make predictable its responses to similar stimulus situations in the future. This latter assumption involves us in the principles of human learning. The subject is complicated, and in its complexities not easily separated from our first assumption, but for our purpose here we shall treat this assumption as separate from the first. Broadly, there are two classes of habits (which we shall call "emotional habits and attitudes"), those that are maladaptive and make for increased deprivation and increased deviant behavior, and those that tend to defend the individual from the effects of the first set of habits. For instance, a child learns to grasp brightly colored objects. He encounters a brightly colored hot radiator and is burned by it. He acquires a habit of fear or anxiety which "defends" him from the deviant behavior he would display if he went on grasping brightly colored hot radiators.

We have postulated, then, two classes of variables: (1) deprivation of needs, which we shall call *stress,* and (2) habits, which we will divide into two categories—those which are "maladaptive" and those which are defensive in that they tend to protect the individual from the effects of the maladaptive habits. We can formulate this position somewhat as follows (3, 4):

$$\text{Deviant behavior} = f \frac{(\text{stresses} \times \text{"maladaptive" habits})}{\text{defensive habits}}$$

Our patient was a deprived organism. He did not feel loved by his parents; he felt no security at home; he did not feel belongingness as a male; he had no sense of membership in the Jewish religion. He learned fear and hostility from his mother and fear of his father (although this habit was less intense). He learned a feeling of inadequacy as a person and as a male. He learned a lot of other associated habits too numerous to mention here—for instance, fear of the female genitalia. He learned to avoid his mother's wrath by scrupulous cleanliness, a reaction which was later manifested in fear of other females. He was rewarded for intellectual superiority by being able to belong to a group of other intellectuals and, in fact, made an adjustment of sorts by thus satisfying belongingness and prestige needs in this manner. But to belong to this group he had to make contact with females. He had a need to feel himself a man, to "belong" to a group of men. And it is in this first contact with adult females that we see the beginning of phobia. The reaction of scrupulous cleanliness was an old one and evoked by the principle of stimulus generalization on contact with adult females. Society pressured him still more. He married. Now he was in close relationship to a large, demanding, female figure. He became meticulous and clean, to the point where it interfered with his efficiency on his job and he had to ask for help.

We should bear in mind that the patient was intellectually superior. He had attained a position of prestige in his profession. In addition to the habits cited above, he acquired many habits which were efficiently satisfying many of his needs. The patient was, therefore, able to keep his anxiety in check by a phobic defense over a considerable period of time. It was only after the patient was promoted to a position of authority where he had to delegate responsibility, to trust and depend on other men, that stress mounted to the point where his defenses were no longer adequate.

Treatment

The patient's case was presented in staff conference, where it was decided that he was a proper candidate for intensive treatment. The patient accepted the recommendations of the staff and treatment was begun.

Initially, the patient eagerly attended his interviews with the psychologist. As treatment progressed, however, he became increasingly hostile to his therapist, being sarcastic, demonstrating his intellectual superiority by questioning the scientific status of psychological treatment, etc. He behaved in therapy in a predictable manner. On his first contact with this essentially social situation with his therapist, he reacted with his first line of defense, so to speak; that is, he intellectualized. He had expected treatment to be intellectual chitchat, as the jargon goes. This behavior was non-rewarded in that the therapist did not respond. The "second line of defense" was sarcasm, demonstration of intellectual superiority. Neither was this behavior rewarded! The "third line of defense" was withdrawal, escape. The patient left therapy. He did not, however, stay away long, for in the course of the several interviews leading to his temporary withdrawal he had learned that his therapist was permissive, accepting, understanding. The patient was a deprived organism, sensitive to minimal cues along the lines in which he was deprived. The patient was insecure. He did not feel at ease with any male figure, particularly with a prestige figure which might represent father. He had previously, as a child, learned from his frequent change of nursemaids and from his father that to get close to someone and become dependent upon him made him vulnerable to painful rejection. He had been hostile and sarcastic with his therapist, but the therapist was consistently accepting and understanding. Although the patient was unaware of it, some of his needs were being met in the therapeutic relationship. He asked to come back and was accepted.

From that point on he progressed with great rapidity. The patient reacted to the therapist in a manner similar to his reaction to other, similar figures in the past. These repeated reactions to the therapist were not rewarded. The reader can look upon these as extinction trials and can, if he is interested, look up the factors affecting rate of extinction, e.g., strength of the habit, etc. (1). At the same time the patient was being otherwise conditioned. He was learning that the therapist could be depended upon, that the therapist was always accepting and permissive, that the therapist was non-threatening and non-rejecting, that he could be secure with the therapist. By this process the patient was brought to a state of spontaneity wherein most of the myriad stimulus situations to which maladaptive responses (habits) had been attached could be vicariously relived and extinguished.

During this time the patient was dependent upon the therapist. His needs for security, acceptance, and belongingness were satisfied. He no longer needed his defenses. His reactions to environmental stimuli became more efficient. These were rewarded by the therapist. In this manner new habits incompatible with the old habits were reinforced and established. As the patient began to react more efficiently (with decreasing psychological deficit) to the environment, he was increasingly able to satisfy his needs in it and became correspondingly less dependent upon the therapist. Therapy was brought to a close by the patient. Free of his maladaptive habits and his inefficient defenses, he had learned more efficient, more socially acceptable ways of satisfying his needs.

That, in essence, was the process of psychological treatment with this patient. Space does not permit us to describe the complexities of the process, nor can we expound here on the implied ramifications of this all-too-brief presentation. If the reader will look back to the formulation he will see that the process consisted of a manipulation of the independent variables to effect a decrement in deviant behavior. Con-

340   GERALD R. PASCAL AND CARL N. SIPPRELLE

trary to much popular opinion, the process of psychological treatment is not esoteric and intuitive; it is systematic and theoretically predictable.

ADDENDUM

A case of a phobia has been presented. The patient, a Ph.D. in his thirties, was suffering from an increasing fear of bacteriological contamination. His compulsive defenses had become so extensive they were markedly impairing his efficiency. The phobia consisted of a symbolic avoidance reaction designed to keep the patient safe from the perceived dangers of masculine behavior. Data from the history and projective tests were combined into a theoretical formulation which has proved useful as a working hypothesis in the diagnosis and treatment of the patient.

REFERENCES

1. McGeoch, J. A., and Irion, A. L. *The psychology of human learning.* New York: Longmans, Green & Co., 1952.
2. Maslow, A. H. A theory of human motivation. *Psychol. Rev.,* 1943, *50,* 370–396.
3. Pascal, G. R. Psychological deficit as a functional stress and constitution. *J. Pers.,* 1951, *20,* 2.
4. Pascal, G. R. The psychoneuroses. In Pennington, L. A. and Berg, I. A., *Introduction to clinical psychology.* New York: Ronald Press, 2nd ed., 1954.

Neurodermatitis: A Psychosomatic Disease[1]

BY IVAN N. MENSH

Introduction

Symptoms of psychosomatic disorder have been reported in all systems of the human organism. In many cases individuals suffering from such symptoms have been treated by general practitioners, various medical specialists, representatives of other professional specialties, or not at all, so that incidence of psychosomatic illness is difficult to establish. In neurodermatitis this situation prevails as well, so that much of what is understood about this condition stems from cases observed in clinical practice. One such case is presented in this chapter, without claim that it is typical or representative, but with the details of psychiatric and psychologic diagnostic and therapeutic efforts designed to understand and relieve the patient of his distressing symptom.

Stokes and Pillsbury (16) had by 1930 accumulated nearly 300 references on "The Effect on the Skin of Emotional and Nervous States"; and in 1940 Stokes and Beerman (15) summarized the literature on psychological factors in skin diseases. More recently, over a hundred articles were listed by Dunbar (3) in her chapter on the skin. Within the past few years, H. S. Klein (7) briefly reviewed a number

[1] Grateful acknowledgment is made to Dr. Wanda M. Lamb, Assistant in Charge of House Staff in Psychiatry, Washington University Hospitals, for her coöperation in this study; and to Dr. Donald B. Rindsley, Washington University School of Medicine, for making available his data on a follow-up study of the patient described here.

of studies of psychogenic factors in dermatitis among a half-hundred references in United States, British, and European journals. He summarized in five areas the dynamic factors involved: *"The erogenous role of the skin . . . exhibitionism . . . hatred, fear and guilt* towards the parent . . . *secondary gain* of the illness . . . *type of skin lesion and the personality of the patient* . . . [and] *intolerable situations."* There is then a considerable body of literature on psychosomatic disease of the skin—"the skin as an organ of expression" (10)— but unfortunately few experimental studies with controls to afford more than an anecdotal understanding of this significant area.

Theories attempting to define the etiology of skin disorders in psychosomatic illness include among others Alexander's theory of specificity (certain psychosomatic disorders are characterized by specific psychodynamic constellations, 1); the Cornell group's emphasis on adverse life situations (e.g., Graham, Wolf, and Wolff, 4, 18, 19); Dunbar's organismal theory of organism-environment equilibrium (3); Saslow et al.'s formulation of comprehensive medicine with schema of environmental life stress, state of the individual at time of stress, physiological changes and mechanisms reflected in various signs and symptoms, and further responses as a function of drive state (5); and Selye's development of concepts of stress, the General-Adaptation-Syndrome, and diseases of adaptation (13). Against this background of case reports and of theory is presented the following study of neurodermatitis.

Admission Note

This is the first hospital admission of this 32-year-old white married male, with chief complaint of a skin allergy. Patient says that he has had a skin rash since the time he developed a "neck rash." This rash occurred off and on during his childhood. When Ray was in grade and high school it was never severe or incapacitating. He states that it made him somewhat self-conscious when he was in school, but mainly when he was around strangers. His skin condition was not severe until about seven years ago, when he obtained a job with a defense plant where he was in contact with some kind of oil. He went to a dermatologist at this time, who recommended wet packs over the entire body, every hour on the hour for eight weeks, and the patient's wife applied them for him. He got along fairly well after this until he got a job with an aluminum and steel company and the rash became worse again. He again consulted various dermatologists and was treated with "everything in the book." About three and a half years ago the rash became so severe that he decided to get out of any kind of work that might have allergic factors, and he and his wife became business agents. However, the rash has apparently become progressively more severe, with changes involving thickening and cracking of the skin until now the patient can be outside only about an hour at a time because of the drying of his skin. He anoints his skin almost constantly during the day with non-allergic creams and for the past six months the patient's wife has had to do most of the work at their office. During this time he also has been seen by various dermatologists, some of whom have told the patient he had "a neurodermatitis with his emotions playing a big part in it." He also states that he has been seen by chiropractors because he was "grasping for any straw that would help him." The patient states that whenever he is under an emotional tension, especially under the stress of talking to business associates whom he doesn't like, his skin begins to itch more and he is much more uncomfortable.

The patient was born in the midwest United States of German stock, one of two children. He has a brother who apparently is also allergic and has a mild skin rash and hay fever. His mother and father are both living and well, 57 and 59 years old, respectively. Ray graduated from high school at the age of 16 and went to work in his father's real-estate office but didn't like this because he was not receiving a regular salary. He then held various jobs, such as filling-station attendant and working in a factory, and at the age of 19 started to teach dancing. At this time the patient met his present wife, who was also a dancing instructor. They decided to team up as ballroom dancers, and traveled around the country as a professional dance team for the next ten years. During this time Ray had very little trouble with his skin allergy and states that they enjoyed their work and did very well. The patient's wife states that they decided not to get married as long as they were traveling around because they didn't want to have any children who would be subjected to the kind of life they were living. However, about seven and a half years ago they decided to settle down and have a family, and so were married. They have two children, ages 6 and 3.

With the exception of an appendectomy in 1934 the medical history, except for the present illness, is noncontributory. At times when the patient's skin rash is worse he apparently has a generalized lymphadenopathy, sometimes including swelling of the feet, and a rather profuse, oily skin secretion. The patient is a well-developed, well-nourished, but rather small, jittery man who appears to be his stated age of 32 years. He has a generalized dermatitis with thickening of the skin, especially over his face. He speaks rapidly and answers all questions at great length. He was extremely tense at first and then became noticeably calmer. Although he doesn't seem remarkably depressed he states that he considers his hospitalization his last chance, because "If you can't cure me, nobody can." There is no evidence of memory impairment, delusional thinking, or hallucinations. He was coöperative, but was upset when the nurses took away all of his personal belongings on admission. After this was explained to him he accepted it as part of the routine.

The impression is that the patient has chronic dermatitis with chronic skin changes. There apparently are multiple etiological factors, some of which at least seem to have a psychogenic basis.

Psychological Examinations

General observations. Ray told of skin disturbances since he was an infant and said that he was "allergic to almost everything." He was rejected for military service because of this dermatitis and within the past year has had severe attacks accompanied by insomnia which he attributes to financial worries. He said that when he was dancing the "violent exercise in a few minutes got rid of a lot of poison" so that he suffered little from the skin condition. He looked much older than his years and talked almost constantly, so that it was necessary to interrupt him in order to present him with test stimuli. In responding to the projective stimuli he remarked very dramatically that he had absolutely no hate—"It is not a part of my make-up." Also, when presented with some of the pictures of the TAT series, he said that he "itched all over" and disliked the projective tests much more than the well-structured situations. He was quite insistent that the former disturbed him so that his itching became much worse, and that "I just don't hate anything at all; that is something I keep out of my make-up." Although the symptoms seem quite severe, he did say that he has gotten rid of a lot of worries since his stay in the hospital, even though this has been only a few days. Now he has gone to the extreme and feels that he doesn't have any worries.

Personality evaluation. The Full Scale Wechsler-Bellevue I.Q. is 130, with Verbal and Performance I.Q.'s approximately of the same order. The following is a summary of subtest scores:

SUBTEST	WEIGHTED SCORE
Information	15
Comprehension	15
Digit Span	14
Arithmetic	17
Similarities	11
Vocabulary	13
Picture Arrangement	14
Picture Completion	13
Block Design	14
Object Assembly	11
Digit Symbol	12
Verbal I.Q.	130
Performance I.Q.	124
Total I.Q.	130

This is a superior intelligence in a mentally alert, methodical, rapidly reacting individual who is, however, uncritical. There is superior vocabulary and verbal facility, fund of information, comprehension, memory, social intelligence, visual-motor response, and new learning. He sacrifices accuracy for speed in analyzing his experiences, and the quality of his abstract ability is below the general level of performance but still above average. There is no evidence of bizarre or distorted thinking, but his responses reflect an egotism observed also in other test situations.

Ray was much more ill at ease in the projective situations, asking a number of questions about the procedures and demonstrating his discomfort in other ways. The rapid flow of words was singularly interrupted and inhibited as he was exposed to the various projective stimuli of the Rorschach test (2), Thematic Apperception Test (6), Rosenzweig Picture-Frustration Study (8), and Rotter Sentence Completion Test (9). The personality pattern shows an individual in whom rationalization is a principal defense. Typically he was overcontrolled and stereotyped in his responses, permitting only conventional expressions. He is uncritical and generalizes too quickly and easily from his experiences. There is "normal" fantasy activity but little emotional expression. In only a single instance did he allow himself to report an emotional expression, and this was carefully controlled. He is aware of the emotional quality of stimulus situations in which he operates, has the capacity for social relationships and is responsive to emotional stimulation, but lacks the ability to adequately integrate the emotions into his experiences. Neurotic behavior is characteristic, with a narrow, stereotyped range of interests. He is defensive and rigid in his reactions, and the anxiety which is present appears related to his sexual problems. Although the patient is of superior intellect he was unable to produce more than fifteen responses to the Rorschach cards, only about half the number expected from individuals in the average range of intelligence and much less than would be predicted from an otherwise very verbal individual. His responses were as follows:

I

5″	1. Could be a bug, the two little pincers near the center.	D F+ A	
	2. Or almost a bat if not for the four spots (describes blot characteristics). Dark and light spots, shades of ink.	W F+ A	P
	3. Wings on the side. Symmetrical except in spots.	D F+ Ad	
2′ 11″			

II

13″	4. Now, color on this one. Who knows what it is? Two characters dancing together. Red and black ink shaded together. Imagination of somebody who drew the thing.	W M+ H	P
1′ 26″			

III

14″	5. Red and black ink again. Could be a pretty butterfly (the general shape, symmetrical wings, and I like pink).	D FC+ A	P
	6. Head of a chick.	D F+ Ad	
	7. Or an ant. Symmetrical, different shades again.	D F− Ad	
	8. Cartoon of a movies—ants or animals doing a dance like in a Walt Disney cartoon.	D M+ A	P
1′ 46″			

IV

10"   9. Looks like breast of a chicken al-
        ready fried, maybe because I'm
        hungry. Symmetrical like the rest
        of them.   W F—   Ad(Fd)
1' 19"

V

7"   10. Without the wings here (outside
        edges, D10), looks like a butter-
        fly. Symmetrical again, shading,
        perfect details.   D F+   A   P
1' 19"

VI

8"   I don't know what that possibly
        could look like.

21" 11. The top looks like head of a cat-
        erpillar with antennae. Symmet-
        rical, four-five shades. I don't
        know anything else it might look
        like.   D F+   Ad
1' 2"

VII

13" 12. The top looks like clouds.   D FY+ Cl
     13. Or caricature of someone. The
        reason for the clouds is the light-
        ness and darkness.   D F+   Hd   P
1' 17"

VIII

9"   Getting technicolor now, one-
        two-three-four-five shades, color.   C descript.
39" 14. Looks like drawings of cliff dwell-
        ers, of ancient animal. Symmetri-
        cal again, same careful details.   D F+   A   P
1' 34"

IX

62"   More colors, one-two-three-four-
        five colors of various pastel
        shades with it. Pastel shades are
        nice.
1' 8"   C descript.

X

| 2″ | | Has more colors than we had before, one-two-three-four-five-six-seven. | C descript. |

| 62″ | 15. | Looks like shoreline of California; partial, not a complete map of it. Symmetrical, pretty fine details on some of it. | D F+ Ge |

1′ 48″

Total time: 14′ 48″

Poor integration of emotional response, denial of affect and personal meaning, and repeated efforts to withdraw from emotion-producing situations all appear against a background of tension and anxiety which indicates how ineffective these several defenses are in the personality response pattern of this patient. The high level of anxiety, occasional depressive moods, and superior intelligence suggest the possibility of suicidal ideas; but there is not now apparent the severe conflicts and depression which would round out the clinical signs of suicidal risk.

RORSCHACH SUMMARY

	R	15	T	14′	48″				
W	3			M	2	H	1	F + %	80
D	12			C	0	Hd	1	A%	73
Dd	0			CF	0	A	6	S	0
	15			FC	1	Ad	5	P	6
				FY	1	Cl	1	T/R	60″
				F +	9	Ge	1	T/R	13″
				F −	2		15		
					15				

Z: 12.5
Ap: W D (Dd)
Seq: Regular
Exper. Bal.: 2/.05

In the projective tests, Ray affirmed how much he wanted to find out the source of his neurodermatitis so he could rid himself of the discomfort of his symptoms, yet he was unable to bring himself to discuss difficulties in his adjustments. Further, he could not reject outright the test stimuli, and so his resistances appeared in a lack of productivity and with such comments as "You could put down a lot of things" (in beginning the Sentence Completion Series), "You have enough pictures for an hour!" (to the TAT); but finally he was able to state in reference to the TAT series, "This I don't like!" His responses to the Sentence Completion stimuli illustrate the superficiality, denial, and conventionality which also characterized his responses to the Rorschach test. The following are his responses to the Rotter Sentence Completion Series (9):

1. I like . . . the thrill of living, every day a new adventure, every day something new; life is good.[2]
2. The happiest time . . . was my courtship days, after I met wife.
3. I want to know . . . the why's and wherefore's of lots of things in this world of today.
4. Back . . . when I was half of a dance team, we used to travel constantly, but it was always good to come home.
5. I regret . . . that I have to leave now.
6. At bedtime . . . If I am real tired, I like to contemplate on going to sleep and the enjoyment of arising fresh in the morning.
7. Overseas . . . is someplace I would like to visit sometime.
8. The best . . . is none too good.
9. What annoys me . . . more than any other kind, are these Sunday drivers.
10. People . . . are all very interesting. There is always a story somewhere.
11. A mother . . . and a father is a kid's best pal.
12. I feel . . . great.
13. My greatest fear . . . is something that I have never given much thought.
14. Combat . . . back in football days was very exhilarating.
15. I can't . . . is a word I threw out of my vocabulary.
16. My stomach . . . must be of cast iron, because of some of the rich foods that I eat.
17. When I was a child . . . I had lots of fun.
18. My nerves . . . and the whole nervous system I would like to know more about, because I like to at the least, know something about everything.
19. Other people . . . always interest me.
20. I suffer . . . from excema or allergy.
21. I failed . . . because of inability.
22. The most dangerous . . . is the wrong way.
23. My mind . . . is made up.
24. The future . . . is glorious to those who will work at it.

[2] Errors in spelling, punctuation, and grammar are preserved from the responses as given by the patient, e.g., items 6, 20, and 26.

25. I need . . . that item.
26. A wife . . . is a mans best pal.
27. I am best . . . at that particular work.
28. Sometimes . . . it will not work.
29. What pains me . . . is his lack of good behavior.
30. This hospital . . . seems to be one of the best, if not the best.
31. I hate . . . (after urging by examiner, patient responded: "I just don't hate anything at all. That's something I keep out of my make-up.")
32. I am very . . . sorry that it had to happen that way.
33. The only trouble . . . is there are not enough hours in the day.
34. I wish . . . that I could be rid of this excema.
35. My father . . . is a grand fellow.
36. I secretly . . . know that it is true.
37. I . . . hope they win the pennant.
38. The Army . . . of the U.S. seems to be in great shape.
39. My greatest worry . . . I have no worries at present. I got rid of a lot of worries since I've been here. I haven't any.
40. Most girls . . . are fine people.

Of the 40 Sentence Completion items only to item 21 did Ray express a negative quality, and on item 31 it was only after much urging by examiner that patient completed the sentence.

Ray's caution and his attempts to prevent discussion of personal material tell of tension, anxieties, and resistances, but in a general way and without reference to specific social situations. Although still not free in his responses to the TAT, he reveals in his stories the disturbed social relationships, built over earlier behavior, goal expectations, and conflicts, which provoke tension and anxieties. The attempt to reject Card VI of the Rorschach series seems related to the vagueness in response to Card 13MF of the TAT (VI and 13 MF, the "sex cards" of the respective series). Ray "talks around" the sexual theme but cannot express freely the content and so deals with it in abstractions. After 13 MF the patient seeks relief by reporting a series of themes which are philosophical and so displaced that he need not relate them to his personal world, denying personal meaning and talking in such terms as "the world . . . civilization . . . science. . . ." A third of his themes reveal internalized emotional stress (6), and about the same number suggest a "Pollyanna" attitude, illustrating patient's concern that "everything will be all right" as stresses mount. His TAT stories are given here:

(First session)

1. Music. It has always helped me in my life. In the past it helped me over rough spots, such as teaching harmonica. This helped me earn my way through school. It has always helped me appreciate better music and will undoubtedly in the future.

2. The farmer boy tilling the soil and his girl friend that teaches, waiting for him. He is happy with his past life, simple and wholesome though it was. And his present efforts will reap him rich rewards of material benefits in the future.

3BM. This picture reminds me of a person in the slum area of some city, that has had a rough time and doesn't quite know how to cope with the situation at present, or what to do in the future.

4. What does this girl want? She doesn't really know. In the past she didn't hold him back as she is doing at present. He wants to do things for now and the future but can he, without some push instead of pull.

5. Mothers are always trying to find ways of making you more comfortable, than when you were a child and will continue to do so throughout eternity.

6BM. He must have done something in the past to get such a forlorn look on his mother's face and a face that asks forgiveness for his past and present misdeeds.

7BM. This young gentleman is very sorry about something in his past, and his father is trying to console him with the fact that it is past history and that the future holds far better things. His father will also help him if he can with his problem.

9BM. These men are taking a siesta after having worked hard all morning in the fields. They will soon have to get up and start pitching with no more time for rest until quitting time when they will go into town with a few of the boys to have a good time.

10. Is it some father and mother holding on to each other thinking of the past which had been a bit rocky at times, and wondering how it would be in the future or they could be thinking of their son at war somewhere, that has had some close calls and will have some future ones.

(Patient scratched frequently during this series and reported emphatically: "You have enough pictures for an hour! . . . This I don't like!")

(Second session)

11. It seems that in the far distant past in this world, life was one eternal struggle. If you didn't have eyes in the back of your head, you didn't exist today to tell the tale or have tomorrow to look forward to. Life was rugged and only the most fit survived. Man with his superior intelligence was able to survive and progress to the present day, while other living things of those long ago eras have become extinct.

13MF. The past love of these two people has ceased to exist in its past form of something sacred, and the man is already remorseful at what he is about to do, knowing that his and her future will be blotted, not only between themselves, but also by society in general. The girl has not given any thought about the situation as yet but will undoubtedly feel the same way as the man.

14. To look up at the stars and commune with oneself once in a while about your past deeds, good or bad, and about the past of the world; and about your present problems when solitude is sometimes necessary to straighten out your daily problems, when maybe a prayer or two is needed for strength to carry on with tomorrow, next week and next year, is sometimes needed by everyone in the fast pace today.

15. Death is something that no one can avoid. It is to be expected at sometime in the future and should not be looked forward to but should not be dreaded, but accepted as the general rule of this world. Death has been apparent in this world for its entire past, and present.

16. This picture of the future of the world is just a small idea of what can be expected. The world will be a better place to work and play in, than our small imagination can encompass. That is, if history does not repeat itself and civilization does not destroy itself or nearly so. But even if it does civilization will again push itself up and back with larger strides.

17BM. Climbing a rope is something everyone should try. When you start out at the bottom it is fast and easy, half way up you slow down and near the top it requires superhuman effort to reach for that last handhold, but after you have acquired it the fast descent down the rope is joyous because you have done a job well done.

19. A winter storm can be beautiful if you have the right surroundings. If you have been traveling in the storm and you see a cheery lighted window it will look like heaven, and the contemplation

of a nice warm, log fire will spur your efforts to get to that warm-looking window and get inside and relax with a hot liquid and a warm meal and good conversation with friends.

20. Never having been to London and experienced its dense fog I can imagine what it is like from what I have read. Even with all of today's wonders it is no easier to get around town than it was 100 years ago and unless science can make a discovery in the future of how to penetrate fog it will not be any easier then than now.

Finally, it is also of diagnostic significance that Ray's responses to the Rosenzweig P-F Study reveal direct expressions of feelings which patient did not permit himself in the other tests. His initial response was, "Put down what you think, or what you'd say?" When told to write down "the very first reply" he went to the task and demonstrated a level of extrapunitiveness (52 percent of his responses; normative mean is 45 percent) which was inconsistent with his overt statements about his work and other social relationships. The intropunitive percentage of 19 is more than 1 S.D. below the normative mean of 28, suggesting the infrequency with which patient directs aggressive feelings against himself when frustrated. The consistently discrepant (from normative data for males) distributions of responses along the obstacle-dominant, ego-defensive, and need-persistive dimensions yield further data of value in understanding the stresses to which the patient is susceptible. Much of his energy goes into ego-defensive behavior with uncritical attention to the characteristics of the frustrations which block his goal satisfactions. The patient's ability to express hostility against others in his social environment, under the stress of frustration, does appear but it is important to note that there is much variation in his reactions to frustrating situations. Thus there is only one period (items 9–13) during the P-F when more than two successive extra-punitive responses appear, and in this instance three of the five responses involve ego-defensive behavior. When Ray's responses otherwise were successively extrapunitive (items 6–7, 23–24), these again were brought into play in ego-defensive behavior, and in each pairing one of the responses conformed to normal adult male behavior, thus generally socially acceptable. The conformity and conventionality are shown clearly in the above-average incidence of GCR (Group Conformity Ratio) of 75 percent, more than 0.5 S.D. above the norm mean value. The Rosenzweig profiles are shown below.

ROSENZWEIG PICTURE-FRUSTRATION PROFILES

	O-D	E-D	N-P	TOTAL	%	NORMS M	NORMS S.D.
E	1.5	10.0	1.0	12.5	52	45	13.3
I	1.0	1.0	2.5	4.5	19	28	8.3
M	1.0	5.0	1.0	7.0	9	27	9.5
Total	3.5	16.0	4.5	24.0	100		
%	14	67	19	100			
NORMS M	20	53	27		GCR 75%	NORMS M	NORMS S.D.
S.D.	7.8	11.3	10.3				
Time: 20 min.						68	11.1

In spite of Ray's reports of depression because of his skin disease, and his insistence on repressing emotional feeling and expression, e.g., "I hate no one," the P-F response data indicate that characteristically patient does not turn his aggressiveness inward, and though he is generally over-conventional he can directly indicate his strong feelings against others when he has been frustrated in social situations. These data are important in view of patient's statement to the hospital admitting officer that he had contemplated suicide because of inability to obtain symptomatic relief. The Rorschach data also suggested that neither depression nor conflict was severe enough at this time to warrant suicidal precautions. Further, patient was able to recall to examiner several occasions when he had felt very strongly hostile toward business clients. He expressed these feelings very indirectly by indicating his intellectual superiority in maneuvering the situations to achieve his goals at the clients' expense. Since his neurodermatitis persisted, two assumptions follow: (1) the occasional relief by discharge of tension in the latter achievements was not sufficiently frequent; and (2) the skin changes arising from continued symptoms were irreversible, a phenomenon found in many types of psychosomatic illness (11).

Summary. The patient is egotistical, employing rationalization as a principal defense, and his behavior is generally characterized by uncritical and rapid reactions. Although responsive to emotional stimulation, and with the potential for emotional relationships, he now has little emotional contact and lacks the ability to adequately integrate the emotions he experiences. Although he disclaims any hate or hostility toward others, projective responses show that he has many ego defenses and often turns hostility toward his environment. This strong evidence of hostility is quite inconsistent with his statement that he has no hate for anyone, that hate is not a part of his personality make-up. He was extremely uncomfortable in the projective test situations and said that his itching became much worse during this stimulation. In general, the test data at this time do not suggest a suicidal risk. Over-control and other repressive behavior are typical, with indirect methods for expressing strong emotional feelings and a striving for intellectual achievement in social interactions.

Psychiatric Grand Rounds

The points for discussion were multiple in this case; they included the etiological and therapeutic factors involved in a case of chronic neurodermatitis with the expected prognosis and the relationship between these factors and the general emotional make-up of the individual. The following represents a brief summary of the comments made about this case:

Allergist. The physician stated that follow-up studies with transfer tests showed that by restricting certain foods one often obtained a decreased sensitivity (as shown with the tests of patient under discussion), but these findings were not consistent in cases of neurodermatitis. He mentioned that the skin of these patients was naturally susceptible to infection and that occupations in which the patient comes in contact with dirt and grease of course added to the risk of infection, and it was noted that this patient had acute exacerbations of his dermatitis at times when he had had contact with such materials. He pointed out further that all of these patients seem to improve with hospitalization, probably for several reasons, one of which seemed to be merely changing the environment in addition to removal from contacts. He said, further, that he had never seen one of these patients cured, believed this patient was not an exception, and indicated for him a poor prognosis.

Supervising psychiatrist. The psychiatrist explained that one of the important reasons for hospitalizing this patient, in addition to the fact that his illness was actually disabling at the time of admission, was the opportunity for an overall, generalized work-up of the case. He mentioned this patient's liability to stress situations as one of the more important points to be investigated. In this respect, it was stress itself which was the important thing and not a specific type of stress; in other words, he thought that one was just as likely to see a flare-up of dermatitis of this sort when the patient became emotionally keyed up from happiness as from sadness and so forth.

Resident psychiatrist. It was his opinion that there were probably specific stress situations which caused an exacerbation of the dermatitis, and that these situations probably followed certain patterns associated with the patient's childhood experiences—in this case it seemed to be hostility toward the patient's father, which was never expressed overtly. He mentioned that in most patients of this sort the relationship with men seemed to be an important factor in that it represented competition from a powerful male figure and was, therefore, a powerful threat to the patient. He believed, also, that this patient demonstrated the tremendous anxiety about the durability of the sex act which patients with neurodermatitis frequently showed. He stated that they often showed a tendency for exhibitionism and that when they had an opportunity to act things out they usually felt better. In other words, they were utilizing an accepted form of aggressiveness. He mentioned that there were unusually strong heterosexual tendencies in these patients and pointed to several indications of this in our patient. He then brought up the question of what might be expected from psychotherapy, said that usually the defenses of these patients were so fixed that they were extremely hard to evaluate, and pointed out the similarity of patients of this sort to asthmatics who seem to improve but always have difficulty in working out their problems.

Staff psychiatrist. This psychiatrist pointed out that as far as permanent results in patients of this sort were concerned, follow-up studies revealed that one's attitude for the future could only be pessimistic.

Resident psychiatrist II. He feels that it is relatively easy to either provoke or relieve attacks in these individuals, as has been shown by producing various stress situations and then discontinuing them. He felt that this patient was a very energetic person whose needs had to be met by his mother and who was constantly restricted by his father, and that he harbored resentment against his father. He felt that resentment toward his father's restriction, which had been carried throughout his life, was related to the patient's need for "getting around people"—in other words, getting what he wanted—and believed that until this more or less lifelong pattern could be pointed out to him in such a way that he could understand it psychotherapy would really not accomplish very much.

Staff psychiatrist. The psychiatrist felt that the fact that this patient chooses occupations enabling him to meet goals which are predetermined dooms him to stress situations which produce an exacerbation of the dermatitis. Because of this very complicated picture he believed good psychotherapeutic results would be quite difficult to obtain.

Discharge Note

This 32-year-old married male entered hospital for the first time in September and was discharged in October with chief complaint of skin allergy.

Physical examination. Revealed skin changes as above described. Inguinal, axillary, and epitrochlear lymphadenopathy. Scattered expiratory wheezes in the chest. Moderate distension of the abdomen.

Impression. Neurodermatitis with chronic skin changes, which condition was obviously agitated by various psychogenic factors, especially stress situations. Lymphadenopathy. Questionable bronchial asthma.

Laboratory data.[3] Red blood corpuscles 4.63 with 14.8 grams hemoglobin. White blood corpuscles 10,250 with 22% eosinophiles. Urinalysis essentially negative. Blood Kahn negative. Stool examination negative. Nonprotein nitrogen 16 mg.%. Fasting blood sugar 84 mg.%. Blood calcium 9.1 mg.%. Blood phosphorus 4.4 mg.%. Plasma chlorides 362 mg.%. Blood cholesterol 225 mg.%. Total protein 7.2 mg.% with 4.6 mg.% albumin and 2.6 mg.% globulin. Thymol turbidity 2.2 units. Cephalin floculation negative. Three basal metabolic

[3] Normal values (**14**):

Rbc	4.5–6.0	NPN	25–40	Cholest.	110–300
Hb.	14–18	Gluc.	80–120	Total prot.	6.3–8.0
Wbc	5,000–10,000	CA.	9–11	Albu.	3.5–5.5
Eos.	1–3%	Phos.	3–4.5	Glob.	1.5–3.4
Chlor.	350–390				
Thymol	0–5				
CC Floc	0–1 +				

rates showed values of plus 40, 16, and plus 15, respectively. Values of repeat complete blood chemistries were essentially the same except for 12% eosinophiles. Electroencephalogram showed a fast dysrhythmia with perhaps a paroxysmal tendency. X-ray examination of the chest was negative. Electrocardiogram within normal limits. Allergy skin testing revealed that the patient was especially allergic to ragweed pollen, house dust, and cat epidermis and showed slight sensitivity to certain foods.

Course in hospital. The patient was under the care of a dermatologist while in the hospital. He was seen almost daily in psychotherapy (fifteen sessions during the four-week hospitalization) and there was definite subjective and clinical improvement, with a rather marked subsidence of the dermatitis. The patient became much more relaxed and better able to accept hospital routine, could sleep without sedation, something he had not been able to do for several years, and showed no evidence of depression at the time of discharge.

Follow-Up Study After Four Years

Patient, in his late thirties, was seen in connection with a study of the vasomotor reactivity of individuals with disseminated neurodermatitis, from which he has suffered for many years. The subject is a stocky, highly kinetic, voluble man whose skin bears the signs of a chronic dermatosis. The entire body was not examined, but the skin of the face, antecubital spaces, and neck appeared dry and somewhat thickened, and bore increased pigmentation and dermal markings of moderate degree. The rubor of the vermilion border of the lips appeared somewhat increased, and there were a few spots in the above skin areas which were excoriated, indicative of recent unhealed or partially healed scratching.

The subject has apparently received no specific dermatologic therapy since last being seen in psychotherapy, although to ease occasional to frequent itching he employs local soothing balms. He stated that his skin became and has remained markedly improved following psychotherapy, and that it itches in connection with tension-producing or otherwise emotionally disturbing life situations. He states that he is "adjusted" to the relative permanence of his dermatosis, and that, in his opinion, were it not for psychotherapy he might very well have committed suicide. His general health is otherwise excellent.

The subject's cold pressor test response is as follows:

Basal blood pressure: 140/70
Maximum blood pressure during immersion of the right hand
    in ice water at 4 degrees C.:   162/104
Time to return to basal B.P.:   13 minutes

The basal blood pressure would be considered by some to be border-line hypertensive, although this is a disputed point among clinicians. The patient's systolic rise of 22 millimeters and diastolic rise of 34 millimeters are considered abnormally high, and his recovery time of 13 minutes is a markedly elevated value over the control average. He is thus a marked hyperreactor to the cold pressor stimulus.

Finally, patient at follow-up told of a recent incident in his business contacts. He had been discussing a contract with a client, felt comfortable and satisfied that his dermatitis no longer was incapacitating, and then observed that his client was scratching uncomfortably!

ADDENDUM

There is an extensive literature reporting on skin disorders in psychosomatic illness, and a number of theories exist which attempt to define the etiology of these conditions. The present study describes an individual with neurodermatitis and reviews the efforts to understand and to relieve his symptom. One of the clinical problems was patient's mention of suicidal ideas, always a disturbing report to those professionally responsible for a patient's care. The original psychological examination did not reveal the threat of suicide verbalized in the past by patient, and four years later it was still mentioned but no overt attempt had occurred. This is consistent with the findings of Schmidt et al. (12), who studied 109 suicidal attempts. In none of these was a physical symptom, no matter how distressing, reported as precipitating an attempt at suicide, although about 20 percent of the sample had major physical symptoms.

In the case under discussion, patient had some understanding of the psychological stress situations which exacerbated his dermatitis but had been unable to modify his behavior before psychotherapy. This suggests the classical picture of the ineffectiveness of verbal insight, without change of behavior at other than a verbal level, to serve in relieving tensions and anxiety. Patient was unable directly to express strong emotional feelings; rather his behavior seemed to characterize his skin as "an organ of expression." Why this organ was selected as target remains theoretical and part of the larger and unknown question of organ selection in illness. Finally, four years later, patient still was a hyperreactor to at least the physical stimulus of cold and continued to demonstrate this reactivity in other areas by a neurodermatitis which he related to tension-producing life situations, behavior bearing out the predictions made at close of psychotherapy four years before—this in spite of a more favorable attitude toward his disease reported in terms of his conviction that his dermatitis no longer was incapacitating, and which led him to observe that one of his clients was scratching uncomfortably!

REFERENCES

1. Alexander, F., French, T. M., et al. *Studies in psychosomatic medicine.* New York: Ronald Press, 1948.
2. Beck, S. J. *Rorschach's test. I. Basic processes.* New York: Grune & Stratton, 2nd ed., 1949.
3. Dunbar, F. *Emotions and bodily changes.* New York: Columbia University Press, 3rd ed., 1946.
4. Graham, D. T. The pathogenesis of hives: experimental study of life situations, emotions, and cutaneous vascular reactions. *Proc. Assn. Res. nerv. & ment. Dis.,* 1950, *29,* 987–1009.
5. Guze, S. B., Matarazzo, J. D., and Saslow, G. A formulation of principles of comprehensive medicine with special reference to learning theory. *J. clin. Psychol.,* 1953, *9,* 127–136.
6. Klebanoff, S. G., Plenk, A. M., and Mensh, I. N. TAT Analysis. In Watson, R. I. *The clinical method in psychology.* New York: Harper & Brothers, 1951, pp. 478–481.
7. Klein, H. S. Psychogenic factors in dermatitis and their treatment by group therapy. *Brit. J. med. Psychol.,* 1949, *22,* 32–52.
8. Rosenzweig, S. Revised norms for the adult form of the Rosenzweig Picture-Frustration Study. *J. Pers.,* 1950, *18,* 344–346.
9. Rotter, J. B., and Willerman, B. The incomplete sentences test. *J. consult. Psychol.,* 1947, *11,* 43–48.
10. Sack, W. T. Die Haut als Ausdrucksorgan. *Arch. f. Dermat. u. Syph.,* 1926, *151,* 200–206.
11. Saslow, G. On the concept of comprehensive medicine. *Bull. Menn. Clinic,* 1952, *16,* 57–65.

12. Schmidt, E. H., O'Neal, P., and Robins, E. Immediate management of attempted suicide. *J.A.M.A.,* (in press).

13. Selye, H. *The physiology and pathology of exposure to stress.* Montreal: Acta, 1950.

14. Smith, Kline and French Laboratories. *Normal laboratory values.* Philadelphia: Smith, Kline and French, 1952.

15. Stokes, J. H., and Beerman, H. Psychosomatic correlations in allergic conditions. *Psychosom. Med.,* 1940, *2,* 438–458.

16. Stokes, J. H., and Pillsbury, D. M. The effect on the skin of emotional and nervous states. *Arch. Dermat. & Syph.,* 1930, *22,* 803–810, 962–993; 1935, *31,* 47–499.

17. Wechsler, D. *The measurement of adult intelligence.* Baltimore: Williams & Wilkins, 3rd ed., 1948.

18. Wolf, S. Experimental research into psychosomatic phenomena in medicine. *Science,* 1948, *107,* 637–639.

19. Wolff, H. G. Life stress and bodily disease. In Weider, A. *Contributions toward medical psychology.* Vol. I. New York: Ronald Press, 1953, pp. 315–367.

Index

Volume I

Revised December, 1966

harper ✦ torchbooks

HUMANITIES AND SOCIAL SCIENCES

American Studies: General

† The New American Nation Series, edited by Henry Steele Commager and Richard B. Morris.
‡ American Perspectives series, edited by Bernard Wishy and William E. Leuchtenburg.
* The Rise of Modern Europe series, edited by William L. Langer.
¶ Researches in the Social, Cultural, and Behavioral Sciences, edited by Benjamin Nelson.
§ The Library of Religion and Culture, edited by Benjamin Nelson.
Σ Harper Modern Science Series, edited by James R. Newman.
º Not for sale in Canada.
△ Not for sale in the U. K.

1

FRANCIS J. GRUND: Aristocracy in America: *Social Class in the Formative Years of the New Nation* TB/1001

ALEXANDER HAMILTON: The Reports of Alexander Hamilton. ‡ *Edited by Jacob E. Cooke* TB/3060

THOMAS JEFFERSON: Notes on the State of Virginia. ‡ *Edited by Thomas P. Abernethy* TB/3052

JAMES MADISON: The Forging of American Federalism: *Selected Writings of James Madison. Edited by Saul K. Padover* TB/1226

BERNARD MAYO: Myths and Men: *Patrick Henry, George Washington, Thomas Jefferson* TB/1108

JOHN C. MILLER: Alexander Hamilton and the Growth of the New Nation TB/3057

RICHARD B. MORRIS, Ed.: The Era of the American Revolution TB/1180

R. B. NYE: The Cultural Life of the New Nation: 1776-1801. † *Illus.* TB/3026

FRANCIS S. PHILBRICK: The Rise of the West, 1754-1830. † *Illus.* TB/3067

TIMOTHY L. SMITH: Revivalism and Social Reform: *American Protestantism on the Eve of the Civil War* TB/1229

FRANK THISTLETHWAITE: America and the Atlantic Community: *Anglo-American Aspects, 1790-1850* TB/1107

ALBION W. TOURGÉE: A Fool's Errand. ‡ *Ed. by George Fredrickson* TB/3074

A. F. TYLER: Freedom's Ferment: *Phases of American Social History from the Revolution to the Outbreak of the Civil War. 31 illus.* TB/1074

GLYNDON G. VAN DEUSEN: The Jacksonian Era: 1828-1848. † *Illus.* TB/3028

LOUIS B. WRIGHT: Culture on the Moving Frontier TB/1053

American Studies: The Civil War to 1900

THOMAS C. COCHRAN & WILLIAM MILLER: The Age of Enterprise: *A Social History of Industrial America* TB/1054

W. A. DUNNING: Essays on the Civil War and Reconstruction. *Introduction by David Donald* TB/1181

W. A. DUNNING: Reconstruction, Political and Economic: 1865-1877 TB/1073

HAROLD U. FAULKNER: Politics, Reform and Expansion: 1890-1900. † *Illus.* TB/3020

HELEN HUNT JACKSON: A Century of Dishonor: *The Early Crusade for Indian Reform.* ‡ *Edited by Andrew F. Rolle* TB/3063

ALBERT D. KIRWAN: Revolt of the Rednecks: *Mississippi Politics, 1876-1925* TB/1199

ROBERT GREEN MC CLOSKEY: American Conservatism in the Age of Enterprise: 1865-1910 TB/1137

ARTHUR MANN: Yankee Reformers in the Urban Age: *Social Reform in Boston, 1880-1900* TB/1247

WHITELAW REID: After the War: *A Tour of the Southern States, 1865-1866.* ‡ *Edited by C. Vann Woodward* TB/3066

CHARLES H. SHINN: Mining Camps: *A Study in American Frontier Government.* ‡ *Edited by Rodman W. Paul* TB/3062

VERNON LANE WHARTON: The Negro in Mississippi: 1865-1890 TB/1178

American Studies: 1900 to the Present

RAY STANNARD BAKER: Following the Color Line: *American Negro Citizenship in Progressive Era.* ‡ *Illus. Edited by Dewey W. Grantham, Jr.* TB/3053

RANDOLPH S. BOURNE: War and the Intellectuals: *Collected Essays, 1915-1919.* ‡ *Edited by Carl Resek* TB/3043

A. RUSSELL BUCHANAN: The United States and World War II. † *Illus.*   Vol. I TB/3044;   Vol. II TB/3045

ABRAHAM CAHAN: The Rise of David Levinsky: *a documentary novel of social mobility in early twentieth century America. Intro. by John Higham* TB/1028

THOMAS C. COCHRAN: The American Business System: *A Historical Perspective, 1900-1955* TB/1080

FOSTER RHEA DULLES: America's Rise to World Power: 1898-1954. † *Illus.* TB/3021

JOHN D. HICKS: Republican Ascendancy: 1921-1933. † *Illus.* TB/3041

SIDNEY HOOK: Reason, Social Myths, and Democracy TB/1237

ROBERT HUNTER: Poverty: *Social Conscience in the Progressive Era.* ‡ *Edited by Peter d'A. Jones* TB/3065

WILLIAM L. LANGER & S. EVERETT GLEASON: The Challenge to Isolation: *The World Crisis of 1937-1940 and American Foreign Policy*
    Vol. I TB/3054;   Vol. II TB/3055

WILLIAM E. LEUCHTENBURG: Franklin D. Roosevelt and the New Deal: 1932-1940. † *Illus.* TB/3025

ARTHUR S. LINK: Woodrow Wilson and the Progressive Era: 1910-1917. † *Illus.* TB/3023

GEORGE E. MOWRY: The Era of Theodore Roosevelt and the Birth of Modern America: 1900-1912. † *Illus.* TB/3022

RUSSEL B. NYE: Midwestern Progressive Politics: *A Historical Study of Its Origins and Development, 1870-1958* TB/1202

WILLIAM PRESTON, JR.: Aliens and Dissenters: *Federal Suppression of Radicals, 1903-1933* TB/1287

WALTER RAUSCHENBUSCH: Christianity and the Social Crisis. ‡ *Edited by Robert D. Cross* TB/3059

JACOB RIIS: The Making of an American. ‡ *Edited by Roy Lubove* TB/3070

PHILIP SELZNICK: TVA and the Grass Roots: *A Study in the Sociology of Formal Organization* TB/1230

IDA M. TARBELL: The History of the Standard Oil Company: *Briefer Version.* ‡ *Edited by David M. Chalmers* TB/3071

GEORGE B. TINDALL, Ed.: A Populist Reader ‡ TB/3069

TWELVE SOUTHERNERS: I'll Take My Stand: *The South and the Agrarian Tradition. Intro. by Louis D. Rubin, Jr., Biographical Essays by Virginia Rock* TB/1072

WALTER E. WEYL: The New Democracy: *An Essay on Certain Political Tendencies in the United States.* ‡ *Edited by Charles B. Forcey* TB/3042

Anthropology

JACQUES BARZUN: Race: *A Study in Superstition. Revised Edition* TB/1172

JOSEPH B. CASAGRANDE, Ed.: In the Company of Man: *Twenty Portraits of Anthropological Informants. Illus.* TB/3047

W. E. LE GROS CLARK: The Antecedents of Man: *Intro. to Evolution of the Primates.* ° △ *Illus.* TB/559

CORA DU BOIS: The People of Alor. *New Preface by the author. Illus.*   Vol. I TB/1042;   Vol. II TB/1043

RAYMOND FIRTH, Ed.: Man and Culture: *An Evaluation of the Work of Bronislaw Malinowski* ¶ ° △ TB/1133

DAVID LANDY: Tropical Childhood: *Cultural Transmission and Learning in a Puerto Rican Village* ¶ TB/1235

L. S. B. LEAKEY: Adam's Ancestors: *The Evolution of Man and His Culture.* △ *Illus.* TB/1019

ROBERT H. LOWIE: Primitive Society. *Introduction by Fred Eggan* TB/1056

EDWARD BURNETT TYLOR: The Origins of Culture. *Part I of "Primitive Culture." § Intro. by Paul Radin* TB/33

EDWARD BURNETT TYLOR: Religion in Primitive Culture. *Part II of "Primitive Culture." § Intro. by Paul Radin* TB/34

W. LLOYD WARNER: A Black Civilization: *A Study of an Australian Tribe.* ¶ *Illus.* TB/3056

Art and Art History

WALTER LOWRIE: Art in the Early Church. *Revised Edition. 452 illus.* TB/124

EMILE MÂLE: The Gothic Image: *Religious Art in France of the Thirteenth Century.* § △ *190 illus.* TB/44

W. O. HASSALL, Ed.: Medieval England: *As Viewed by Contemporaries* △ TB/1205

DENYS HAY: Europe: The Emergence of an Idea TB/1275

DENYS HAY: The Medieval Centuries ○ △ TB/1192

J. M. HUSSEY: The Byzantine World △ TB/1057

ROBERT LATOUCHE: The Birth of Western Economy: *Economic Aspects of the Dark Ages.* ○ △ *Intro. by Philip Grierson* TB/1290

FERDINAND LOT: The End of the Ancient World and the Beginnings of the Middle Ages. *Introduction by Glanville Downey* TB/1044

G. MOLLAT: The Popes at Avignon: 1305-1378 △ TB/308

CHARLES PETIT-DUTAILLIS: The Feudal Monarchy in France and England: *From the Tenth to the Thirteenth Century* ○ △ TB/1165

HENRI PIRENNE: Early Democracies in the Low Countries: *Urban Society and Political Conflict in the Middle Ages and the Renaissance. Introduction by John H. Mundy* TB/1110

STEVEN RUNCIMAN: A History of the Crusades. △
Volume I: *The First Crusade and the Foundation of the Kingdom of Jerusalem. Illus.* TB/1143
Volume II: *The Kingdom of Jerusalem and the Frankish East, 1100-1187. Illus.* TB/1243

FERDINAND SCHEVILL: Siena: *The History of a Medieval Commune. Intro. by William M. Bowsky* TB/1164

SULPICIUS SEVERUS et al.: The Western Fathers: *Being the Lives of Martin of Tours, Ambrose, Augustine of Hippo, Honoratus of Arles and Germanus of Auxerre.* △ *Edited and trans. by F. O. Hoare* TB/309

HENRY OSBORN TAYLOR: The Classical Heritage of the Middle Ages. *Foreword and Biblio. by Kenneth M. Setton* TB/1117

F. VAN DER MEER: Augustine The Bishop: *Church and Society at the Dawn of the Middle Ages* △ TB/304

J. M. WALLACE-HADRILL: The Barbarian West: *The Early Middle Ages, A.D. 400-1000* △ TB/1061

History: Renaissance & Reformation

JACOB BURCKHARDT: The Civilization of the Renaissance in Italy. △ *Intro. by Benjamin Nelson & Charles Trinkaus. Illus.* Vol. I TB/40; Vol. II TB/41

JOHN CALVIN & JACOPO SADOLETO: A Reformation Debate. *Edited by John C. Olin* TB/1239

ERNST CASSIRER: The Individual and the Cosmos in Renaissance Philosophy. △ *Translated with an Introduction by Mario Domandi* TB/1097

FEDERICO CHABOD: Machiavelli and the Renaissance △ TB/1193

EDWARD P. CHEYNEY: The Dawn of a New Era, 1250-1453. * *Illus.* TB/3002

G. CONSTANT: The Reformation in England: *The English Schism, Henry VIII, 1509-1547* △ TB/314

R. TREVOR DAVIES: The Golden Century of Spain, 1501-1621 ○ △ TB/1194

G. R. ELTON: Reformation Europe, 1517-1559 ○ △ TB/1270

DESIDERIUS ERASMUS: Christian Humanism and the Reformation: *Selected Writings. Edited and translated by John C. Olin* TB/1166

WALLACE K. FERGUSON et al.: Facets of the Renaissance TB/1098

WALLACE K. FERGUSON et al.: The Renaissance: *Six Essays. Illus.* TB/1084

JOHN NEVILLE FIGGIS: The Divine Right of Kings. *Introduction by G. R. Elton* TB/1191

JOHN NEVILLE FIGGIS: Political Thought from Gerson to Grotius: 1414-1625: *Seven Studies. Introduction by Garrett Mattingly* TB/1032

MYRON P. GILMORE: The World of Humanism, 1453-1517. * *Illus.* TB/3003

FRANCESCO GUICCIARDINI: Maxims and Reflections of a Renaissance Statesman (Ricordi). *Trans. by Mario Domandi. Intro. by Nicolai Rubinstein* TB/1160

J. H. HEXTER: More's Utopia: *The Biography of an Idea. New Epilogue by the Author* TB/1195

HAJO HOLBORN: Ulrich von Hutten and the German Reformation TB/1238

JOHAN HUIZINGA: Erasmus and the Age of Reformation. △ *Illus.* TB/19

JOEL HURSTFIELD, Ed.: The Reformation Crisis △ TB/1267

ULRICH VON HUTTEN et al.: On the Eve of the Reformation: "Letters of Obscure Men." *Introduction by Hajo Holborn* TB/1124

PAUL O. KRISTELLER: Renaissance Thought: *The Classic, Scholastic, and Humanist Strains* TB/1048

PAUL O. KRISTELLER: Renaissance Thought II: *Papers on Humanism and the Arts* TB/1163

NICCOLÒ MACHIAVELLI: History of Florence and of the Affairs of Italy: *from the earliest times to the death of Lorenzo the Magnificent. Introduction by Felix Gilbert* △ TB/1027

ALFRED VON MARTIN: Sociology of the Renaissance. *Introduction by Wallace K. Ferguson* TB/1099

GARRETT MATTINGLY et al.: Renaissance Profiles. △ *Edited by J. H. Plumb* TB/1162

MILLARD MEISS: Painting in Florence and Siena after the Black Death: *The Arts, Religion and Society in the Mid-Fourteenth Century.* △ *169 illus.* TB/1148

J. E. NEALE: The Age of Catherine de Medici ○ △ TB/1085

ERWIN PANOFSKY: Studies in Iconology: *Humanistic Themes in the Art of the Renaissance.* △ *180 illustrations* TB/1077

J. H. PARRY: The Establishment of the European Hegemony: 1415-1715: *Trade and Exploration in the Age of the Renaissance* △ TB/1045

J. H. PLUMB: The Italian Renaissance: *A Concise Survey of Its History and Culture* △ TB/1161

A. F. POLLARD: Henry VIII. ○ △ *Introduction by A. G. Dickens* TB/1249

A. F. POLLARD: Wolsey. ○ △ *Introduction by A. G. Dickens* TB/1248

CECIL ROTH: The Jews in the Renaissance. *Illus.* TB/834

A. L. ROWSE: The Expansion of Elizabethan England. ○ △ *Illus.* TB/1220

GORDON RUPP: Luther's Progress to the Diet of Worms ○ △ TB/120

FERDINAND SCHEVILL: The Medici. *Illus.* TB/1010

FERDINAND SCHEVILL: Medieval and Renaissance Florence. *Illus.* Volume I: *Medieval Florence* TB/1090
Volume II: *The Coming of Humanism and the Age of the Medici* TB/1091

G. M. TREVELYAN: England in the Age of Wycliffe, 1368-1520 ○ △ TB/1112

VESPASIANO: Renaissance Princes, Popes, and Prelates: *The Vespasiano Memoirs: Lives of Illustrious Men of the XVth Century. Intro. by Myron P. Gilmore* TB/1111

History: Modern European

FREDERICK B. ARTZ: Reaction and Revolution, 1815-1832. * *Illus.* TB/3034

MAX BELOFF: The Age of Absolutism, 1660-1815 △ TB/1062

ROBERT C. BINKLEY: Realism and Nationalism, 1852-1871. * *Illus.* TB/3038

ASA BRIGGS: The Making of Modern England, 1784-1867: *The Age of Improvement* ○ △ TB/1203

CRANE BRINTON: A Decade of Revolution, 1789-1799. * *Illus.* TB/3018

D. W. BROGAN: The Development of Modern France. ○ △
Volume I: *From the Fall of the Empire to the Dreyfus Affair* TB/1184
Volume II: *The Shadow of War, World War I, Between the Two Wars. New Introduction by the Author* TB/1185

J. BRONOWSKI & BRUCE MAZLISH: The Western Intellectual Tradition: *From Leonardo to Hegel* △ TB/3001

GEOFFREY BRUUN: Europe and the French Imperium, 1799-1814. * *Illus.* TB/3033

ALAN BULLOCK: Hitler, A Study in Tyranny. ○ △ *Illus.* TB/1123

Intellectual History & History of Ideas

6

8

Christianity: General

Christianity: Origins & Early Development

Christianity: The Middle Ages and The Reformation

Christianity: The Protestant Tradition

9

LUDWIG VON BERTALANFFY: Problems of Life: *An Evaluation of Modern Biological and Scientific Thought* △
TB/521
HAROLD F. BLUM: Time's Arrow and Evolution   TB/555
JOHN TYLER BONNER: The Ideas of Biology. Σ △ *Illus.*
TB/570
A. J. CAIN: Animal Species and their Evolution. △ *Illus.*
TB/519
WALTER B. CANNON: Bodily Changes in Pain, Hunger, Fear and Rage. *Illus.*   TB/562
W. E. LE GROS CLARK: The Antecedents of Man: *An Introduction to Evolution of the Primates.* ○ △ *Illus.* TB/559
W. H. DOWDESWELL: Animal Ecology. △ *Illus.*   TB/543
W. H. DOWDESWELL: The Mechanism of Evolution. △ *Illus.*
TB/527
R. W. GERARD: Unresting Cells. *Illus.*   TB/541
DAVID LACK: Darwin's Finches. △ *Illus.*   TB/544
ADOLF PORTMANN: Animals as Social Beings. ○ △ *Illus.*
TB/572
O. W. RICHARDS: The Social Insects. △ *Illus.*   TB/542
P. M. SHEPPARD: Natural Selection and Heredity. △ *Illus.*
TB/528
EDMUND W. SINNOTT: Cell and Psyche: *The Biology of Purpose*   TB/546
C. H. WADDINGTON: How Animals Develop. △ *Illus.*
TB/553
C. H. WADDINGTON: The Nature of Life: *The Main Problems and Trends in Modern Biology* △   TB/580

Chemistry

J. R. PARTINGTON: A Short History of Chemistry. △ *Illus.*
TB/522

Communication Theory

J. R. PIERCE: Symbols, Signals and Noise: *The Nature and Process of Communication* △   TB/574

Geography

R. E. COKER: This Great and Wide Sea: *An Introduction to Oceanography and Marine Biology. Illus.*   TB/551
F. K. HARE: The Restless Atmosphere △   TB/560

History of Science

MARIE BOAS: The Scientific Renaissance, 1450-1630 ○ △
TB/583
W. DAMPIER, Ed.: Readings in the Literature of Science. *Illus.*   TB/512
A. HUNTER DUPREE: Science in the Federal Government: *A History of Policies and Activities to 1940* △ TB/573
ALEXANDRE KOYRÉ: From the Closed World to the Infinite Universe: *Copernicus, Kepler, Galileo, Newton, etc.* △
TB/31
A. G. VAN MELSEN: From Atomos to Atom: *A History of the Concept Atom*   TB/517
O. NEUGEBAUER: The Exact Sciences in Antiquity △ TB/552
HANS THIRRING: Energy for Man: *From Windmills to Nuclear Power* △   TB/556
STEPHEN TOULMIN & JUNE GOODFIELD: The Architecture of Matter: *Physics, Chemistry & Physiology of Matter, Both Animate & Inanimate, As it Evolved Since the Beginning of Science* ○ △   TB/584
STEPHEN TOULMIN & JUNE GOODFIELD: The Discovery of Time ○ △   TB/585
LANCELOT LAW WHYTE: Essay on Atomism: *From Democritus to 1960* △   TB/565

Mathematics

E. W. BETH: The Foundations of Mathematics: *A Study in the Philosophy of Science* △   TB/581
H. DAVENPORT: The Higher Arithmetic: *An Introduction to the Theory of Numbers* △   TB/526
H. G. FORDER: Geometry: *An Introduction* △   TB/548
S. KÖRNER: The Philosophy of Mathematics: *An Introduction* △   TB/547
D. E. LITTLEWOOD: Skeleton Key of Mathematics: *A Simple Account of Complex Algebraic Problems* △
TB/525
GEORGE E. OWEN: Fundamentals of Scientific Mathematics   TB/569
WILLARD VAN ORMAN QUINE: Mathematical Logic TB/558
O. G. SUTTON: Mathematics in Action. ○ △ *Foreword by James R. Newman. Illus.*   TB/518
FREDERICK WAISMANN: Introduction to Mathematical Thinking. *Foreword by Karl Menger*   TB/511

Philosophy of Science

R. B. BRAITHWAITE: Scientific Explanation   TB/515
J. BRONOWSKI: Science and Human Values. △ *Revised and Enlarged Edition*   TB/505
ALBERT EINSTEIN et al.: Albert Einstein: Philosopher-Scientist. Edited by Paul A. Schilpp   Vol. I   TB/502
Vol. II   TB/503
WERNER HEISENBERG: Physics and Philosophy: *The Revolution in Modern Science* △   TB/549
JOHN MAYNARD KEYNES: A Treatise on Probability. ○ △ *Introduction by N. R. Hanson*   TB/557
KARL R. POPPER: Logic of Scientific Discovery △ TB/576
STEPHEN TOULMIN: Foresight and Understanding: *An Enquiry into the Aims of Science.* △ *Foreword by Jacques Barzun*   TB/564
STEPHEN TOULMIN: The Philosophy of Science: *An Introduction* △   TB/513
G. J. WHITROW: The Natural Philosophy of Time ○ △
TB/563

Physics and Cosmology

JOHN E. ALLEN: Aerodynamics: *A Space Age Survey* △
TB/582
STEPHEN TOULMIN & JUNE GOODFIELD: The Fabric of the Heavens: *The Development of Astronomy and Dynamics.* △ *Illus.*   TB/579
DAVID BOHM: Causality and Chance in Modern Physics. △ *Foreword by Louis de Broglie*   TB/536
P. W. BRIDGMAN: Nature of Thermodynamics   TB/537
P. W. BRIDGMAN: A Sophisticate's Primer of Relativity △
TB/575
A. C. CROMBIE, Ed.: Turning Point in Physics   TB/535
C. V. DURELL: Readable Relativity. △ *Foreword by Freeman J. Dyson*   TB/530
ARTHUR EDDINGTON: Space, Time and Gravitation: *An Outline of the General Relativity Theory* △   TB/510
GEORGE GAMOW: Biography of Physics Σ △   TB/567
MAX JAMMER: Concepts of Force: *A Study in the Foundation of Dynamics*   TB/550
MAX JAMMER: Concepts of Mass *in Classical and Modern Physics*   TB/571
MAX JAMMER: Concepts of Space : *The History of Theories of Space in Physics. Foreword by Albert Einstein*   TB/533
G. J. WHITROW: The Structure and Evolution of the Universe: *An Introduction to Cosmology.* △ *Illus.*   TB/504